# Conversations

# *Conversations*

A Companion Book to Idaho Public Television's
*Proceeding On Through a Beautiful Country*
*A History of Idaho*

## Susan M. Stacy
Editor

**IDAHO EDUCATIONAL**
**PUBLIC BROADCASTING FOUNDATION**

Idaho Educational Public Broadcasting Foundation, Boise 83725
Copyright © 1990 by Idaho Educational Public Broadcasting Foundation
All rights reserved.
Printed in the United States of America

Conversations
Stacy, Susan M.

Designed and Illustrated by
Kathleen A. Higgins

Cover photo by Stan Sinclair

Library of Congress Catalog Card Number
90-083688
Softcover Edition
ISBN 1-56221-015-7
Hardcover Edition
ISBN 1-56221-014-9

*The Idaho Constitutional Convention was quite literally the honeymoon for the north and south parts of the state. It was the period in our history when there was the most harmony and the most good will. And that is what the Centennial ought to be about.*

– Dennis Colson –
University of Idaho

# *Contents*

**Contributions:** From Idaho to the Nation

# Introduction

Several years ago I asked my great aunt Nettie Gray, a retired Arkansas school teacher then approaching one hundred years of age, if I could interview her about her life and history. She resisted the use of a tape recorder and asserted that she and her life were hardly the stuff of "history." Then she told me about "old George," a household slave who did not want to leave her family after the Civil War; how she had survived the great influenza epidemic at the end of World War I; and about how she drove an automobile from her home in Arkansas to Washington, D. C., in the early 1920s without benefit of maps—and nearly without roads. Still, she did not see herself as "historical."

Aunt Nettie's reactions were not unlike those of many Idahoans when asked about their pasts. Although they participated in the remarkable changes that have built Idaho, they do not always see how something as everyday as their own lives could be considered something as elevated as "history."

Ninety percent of Idaho's one hundred years as a state have passed in the twentieth century, a fact that has two fascinating corollaries. One is that the history of Idaho as a state is firmly lodged in the history of twentieth century events, ideas, and people. The other is that a very large percentage of the people who have made Idaho what it is today are still living and are able to explain their decisions, choices, and feelings.

In ten more years the twentieth century will have the aura now surrounding the nineteenth as a time of long ago. The environmental movement, the application of technology to resource industries, the evolution of a new order in the use of water, the accommodation of new ethnic groups into society, the preservation (and loss) of species diversity, the urbanization of the state, the transfer of political control to new interest groups, the rise of materialism and reactions to it, changes in land use values: these are only a few of the themes that today are "conversations," and tomorrow will be "history."

The Idahoans who talk in this book about these and other themes were originally in front of the video cameras of Idaho Public Television. They were generously cooperating with the producers of Idaho Public Television's Centennial project, "Proceeding On Through a Beautiful Country, A History of Idaho," a thirteen-part series of one-hour televison programs aired during Idaho's Centennial of Statehood in 1990. Some were asked to tell about their experiences doing what they do everyday—raise cattle, carry out campaigns to save the wilderness, make quilts, teach skiing, publish a magazine, or dozens of other occupations. Others were asked to explain something because they are experts—archaeologists, geologists, or hide tanners. Some were asked to share their remembrances of some of the historical giants of the state.

At the beginning of the television project in the fall of 1987, no one imagined that there would be a book based on all of these interviews. However, by December of 1989, as the editing of the thirteen television shows progressed, it became clear that each program could include only a few minutes of any one person's story. The balance of the interviews seemed too compelling not to preserve in an accessible form for the public.

I proposed to edit the interviews for a book that would stand as a companion book to the television series. Idahoans and others would be able to read what was on the minds of Idahoans at the turn of its first century. The director of Idaho Public Television, Jerold Garber, enthusiastically approved the idea, and we were off.

We transcribed each of the interviews verbatim. Their length ranged from less than twenty minutes to nearly three hours, and resulted in thousands of pages of material. Editing commenced, which is to say that decision-making commenced. Five main principles were employed to help resolve the many decisions involved in converting the spoken to the written word.

The first was to translate the conventions of oral speech—hand and facial gestures and repetition—to the conventions of written text: commas, dashes, periods, paragraphs, standardized grammar. The participants were willingly sharing information and stories, so this type of translation seemed consistent with their intentions. Idiosyncracies of a subject's speech and diction were sometimes lost, but not without careful thought to maintaining the integrity of each interview.

Second, we asked the participants to read the "first edit" draft of their interview for its faithfulness to their intent. Most responded; they corrected transcription and typing errors, added essential explanations, and occasionally deleted material.

Third, the arrangement of material within each interview sought to present the logical order of the speaker's thoughts, whether they were expressed in that order originally or not. Cutting and pasting is an anticipated procedure with video, so there was a certain amount of "let's do that over," and "could we go back to," and "what about before that?" in the video. If a speaker's story included his or her own introduction somewhere in the interview, it was moved so that each person could introduce themselves.

The fourth principle pertained to the arrangement of the interviews in the book. It was based on the idea that everyone's story is part of a recognizeable thread or theme of Idaho history. Each chapter suggests a way for the reader to perceive such a thread. This made for hard choices because many of the stories are complex enough to fit logically as part of three or four different threads. However, many threads make up a cloth, in life and in Idaho history. The reader is invited to discover ways that one person's conversation reaches across the borders of a chapter to shade or enhance, support or contradict that of another. (And to forgive the editor for allowing certain detours for no better reason than that they seemed too interesting to leave out.)

The final editing principle was to be as spare as possible with voices other than those of the participants. The journalists who conducted the interviews did not intend that their own images would be part of the television programs. They asked open-ended questions, often invited people to talk without interruption, and anticipated using only selected portions of the interviews. Removing the questions seemed to be a logical approach for the book, also.

All of the participants could have had a lengthy introduction presenting vital statistics and comprehensive lists of achievements. But the "spare" principle was to use the introductions mainly to provide just enough background to help a reader make sense of the events or issues mentioned by the participant in the context of that chapter's theme.

At press time for this book, the production of the television programs was still under way. Because of various constraints in preparing those programs, some of the conversations in this book may not appear in the television series.

Those who might wish to listen to the original interviews may do so by visiting the Idaho Historical Society Oral History Center in Boise, which has accepted the audio tapes and transcripts into their collection.

# Acknowledgements

*Conversations* would not have been possible without the consent of the 129 people who agreed to be interviewed for the television history series, and then consented again when they were presented with the idea for this book. In addition to helping edit their own sections, many supplied photographs and illustrations.

The interviews were conducted between April 1988 and April 1990 by most of the people involved in the production of the television history series: Royce Williams, scriptwriter; Barbara Pulling, executive producer; Jeff Tucker, chief videographer and editor; Peter W. Morrill, videographer and coordinating producer; and Joan Cartan, associate producer. Dr. John Milton of the University of South Dakota permitted use of his 1967 interview of Vardis Fisher. Other interviewers, dates, and locations are identified in the Appendix.

The book project began with the expeditious conversion of the interviews from video to audio tape by Jennifer Crowe. Helen Fletcher of Alpha Secretarial in Boise transcribed the interviews and did an outstanding job in an unbelievably short period of time. Sally Eames efficiently managed lists, mailing labels, and the dispatching of mail.

Since I was asked to produce the manuscript on a Macintosh, a computer system new for me, I asked for and received generous assistance from Allen Parks of Idaho Public TV, the helpful folks at the Simplot-Micron Technology Center and Bill Mech, both of Boise State University. Gail Richardson and Bob Pyle allowed invasions of their computer domains for special needs. A warm thanks to Dave Blankenship for his occasional before-breakfast and other odd-hours computer help.

I am pleased to thank several people who read chapters and kindly offered suggestions and corrected mistakes: Dr. Patricia Ourada and Dr. Monte Wilson of Boise State University; Mary Anne Davis and Glenda King of the Idaho Archaeologist's Office; Frank Carroll of the U.S. Forest Service; and Virginia Ricketts of the Twin Falls Historical Society.

Amy Stahl edited the manuscript, and many of the Idaho Public TV staff took their leisure time to proofread successive drafts of chapters: Dianne Crowe, Lynn Allen, Barbara Pulling, Joan Cartan, Kelly Belveal, Gail Richardson, and Gayle Valentine. A special personal thanks to Margie Stoy-Smith for lending books and for giving me an opportunity to participate in the history series project.

Kathleen Higgins designed and illustrated the book and cheerfully adjusted to the normal evolution of ideas that such an effort involves. Gila Ford and Elizabeth Jacox at the Idaho Historical Society helped with photographs, although "helped" is a weak word to describe their outstanding contribution to the television series in general and this project also. Chuck Scheer and Glenn Oakley of Boise State University also assisted with photographs. My thanks to them and all the many other people all over the state of Idaho for assistance provided during both projects.

Photos not otherwise attributed were made with a video printer provided by Visual Technology of Salt Lake City. This machine transfers images electronically from frames of video to photographic paper in just a few seconds.

It is a pleasure to acknowledge the support and help that Lynn Allen, the station manager of KAID Television in Boise and project manager for the book, provided at every stage of production. Her enthusiasm for the project, skillful editing, and thoughtful management made for a very rewarding experience. I owe her very warm thanks.

Finally I thank my husband Ralph McAdams for his encouraging support of a mate who was mostly "camping out" at home during the production of the project.

# Dawning

## PREHISTORIC PEOPLE

*Although many of us mistakenly learned that Lewis and Clark found an empty wilderness when they crossed the West, the mountains and deserts of Idaho had been home to people for thousands of years. Every part of Idaho—mountains, river valleys, deserts—provided the necessities of family and community life. There was probably no part of Idaho in which people did not live or travel. Ingenious men and women managed to use the plants, animals, and minerals around them for food, shelter, clothing, weapons, and diversion.*

*Pioneer settlers were well aware that others had occupied the land before them. It was said that hardly a pioneer shack or cabin existed that did not have an old stone mortar to prop open the door in the summer. For thousands of years before those pioneers arrived, people had used such stones for a grinding surface and left them behind rather than carry such heavy objects on their journeys.*

*The archaeological frontier is still a new one in Idaho. Archaeologists visited the state as early as the 1920s, when an occasional find stimulated someone from the eastern museums to head west and collect artifacts. But systematic archaeological surveys of the places where people had lived, hunted, fished, and gathered together did not begin until the 1950s.*

*Archaeologists have examined in detail relatively few of the sites identified in such surveys. There are still scores of questions that remain to be answered about how people came to Idaho, from what direction they came, and how their lives changed over time.*

*Finding the answers to such questions requires the careful collecting, cataloguing, and correlating of data on a site-by-site basis. Insight about Idaho's first human inhabitants may come from visiting archaeologists at work in the field and from watching experts recreate the manufacturing procedures that people used to make the tools and implements of daily living. Flintknappers, archaeologists, tanners, and Indian people who still retain the knowledge and lore of their ancestors have all spent time thinking and imagining what life was like for the first Idahoans.*

# Return To Wilson Butte

*Dr. Alan Bryan, now at the University of Alberta, was one of the archaeologists in Idaho during the 1950s doing one of those early surveys. He encouraged Dr. Ruth Gruhn, who was then a doctoral candidate, to excavate Wilson Butte Cave, which turned out to be a particularly fortuitous choice. The contents of the cave revealed for the first time in Idaho in a chronological and radiocarbon-dated sequence that people had occupied the cave intermittently for over twelve thousand years—and possibly longer. In the oldest layer, she found two pieces of bone that may have been used by human beings. Gruhn and Bryan returned together to the cave in 1988 to seek answers to lingering questions about how long it had been since the earliest occupants of the old cave had been there.*

ALAN: I was hired in 1957 to do a cave survey in southern Idaho. My partner was a geologist, Don Peterson, who knew of Wayne Parron, a local schoolteacher in Dietrich. We introduced ourselves, and Wayne showed me this cave that he was then digging. He agreed, with some persuasion, not to do any more digging. He understood the reasons for saving it for professional excavation. I knew Ruth Gruhn at Harvard University, a fellow student. The following year, she needed a Ph.D. dissertation topic, so I showed her several of the caves that I had located the previous summer. She chose Wilson Butte Cave, and excavated there in 1959 and 1960. We were married in Pocatello in 1961, and spent our honeymoon in the Centennials and Birch Creek Valley.

*Conveyor belt carries excavated sands from interior of Wilson Butte Cave*

RUTH: In 1959, I found two artifacts of bone, possibly modified by man. Then there were three stone artifacts. All these came out of the lower part of sand deposits for which we got a radiocarbon date of 14,500 years ago.

So this site is important because it's quite old. People might have been here as early as 14,500 years ago. Right now this is the earliest archaeological site known in the Intermountain West. It is several thousand years earlier than most people had perceived man had come into this country.

ALAN: A couple of years ago, John Lytle, the Bureau of Land Management archaeologist in Shoshone, approached Ruth at a conference. He said there might be a possibility that there was an undisturbed deposit underneath. We discussed it. We said we would need conveyor belts and adequate lighting to work in the back. He said he would see what he could do. He came up with everything, so we volunteered our time, brought down Ian Franck, a student; and Sue Mathes from Ketchum volunteered her time.

We have been at the cave now for five weeks, and have demonstrated that there are undisturbed deposits. The lower meter in the rear of the cave has not been disturbed. This is where we hope to find the confirmation of the original date of 14,500 years ago.

*Ruth Gruhn*

*Alan Bryan*

RUTH: We have only that single radiocarbon date from 1959. We would like to get more material in order to confirm that date and get more artifacts from that early period. Bone is a fair material to date by the radiocarbon method, but it would be preferable to get charcoal. It would also be preferable to have more artifacts than just a mere handful. So our objective is to clear off all the disturbed deposits, get down to the early level, and try to find more artifacts and material that can be dated. Perhaps we will find the remains of an old fire, which is going to be scattered. If we can collect that material, we can get a radiocarbon date on it. Because of the advance in radiocarbon technology, just a few grams of it would be sufficient.

The upper layers of the cave are completely gone, completely destroyed by the collectors that dug here after the excavations closed in 1960. The only record we have now is the record that I got in those earlier excavations.

The area of interest to us now is undisturbed coarse sand. We have found a fair number of artifacts in it this season. The gray sand below it might correlate with the early dated level that we had in the previous season. The artifacts from that early level are quite sparse indeed. So far we have not found an artifact in the basal gray sand.

Just above the bedrock there is a layer of yellow-brown clay, laid down by water, which has a great deal of disintegrated lava rock in it. We have never found undisputed cultural material in that clay. Apparently it was laid down there soon after the lava blister opened and deposits could wash in from outside.

However, the yellow clay and all of the deposits in the cave have yielded animal bones, particularly of small mammals like ground squirrels and pocket gophers and some of the smaller carnivores and mice and voles.

These animals have particular environmental requirements. Studying the changes in frequency of particular types of these animals gives us a picture of climatic and environmental change that has occurred in this area since the time the clay was deposited. A radiocarbon date on bone from the yellow clay indicates that it is about 15,000 years old. In the subsequent deposits we can see a trend from cooler and more moist climatic conditions to the kind of sagebrush semi-desert environment that is more characteristic of modern times.

So these animal bones from the undisturbed levels are being processed and will be identified. We will have that record. It's not simply the artifacts, and even the charcoal for dating that we're after here, but also more information about what the environment was like and how the environment has changed over time. That in turn gives us an indication of what kind of conditions prehistoric people faced when they were living here at various times.

When the climate was cooler and more moist, there may have been a forest on the butte. We have found some kinds of forest animals—a blue grouse for example, and a marten, which is a forest animal. The presence of certain types of pocket gophers and ground squirrels also suggests that kind of environment. We have also found bones of extinct horse and camel. If people were here at that time they may have been responsible for bringing these bones into the cave.

Many, if not most, archaeologists still believe that man was no earlier into North America than about twelve thousand years ago. A route down the coast is one feasible passage by which people traveled from the Bering land bridge. The idea was originally put forth more than ten years ago by an archaeologist named Knut Fladmark, of Simon Fraser University in British Columbia. Fladmark found that it is quite feasible that people with very simple watercraft and a relatively simple technology could have come down the coast.

One can think of these people coming down into the northwestern part of the United States, into California, down the coast to Mexico and South America. They could have used resources like fish, shellfish, sea mammals and birds. Some of these early people could have moved up the Columbia, the first gap through glaciated mountains.

There are now several sites in South America that date substantially earlier than any in North America. This would suggest that people arrived in South America before the interior part of North America was populated.

The more conventional idea for the route from Asia is that people came through the interior of Alaska and down the east side of the Rockies through the "ice free corridor," where the mountain ice sheet and the continental ice sheet came apart as the glaciers melted. Then they could have gone into the northern part of the Great Plains and into the interior by that route.

The opening and closing of the corridor is not very securely dated. The evidence suggests that it had been opened at the end of the ice age after about fifteen thousand years ago. But another question is what conditions were like even with the ice parted. All that ice was melting at a great rate; there were lakes and marshes in all directions. It was still pretty cold, what we would consider a pretty miserable and difficult environment. On the coast at the same time, the environment would have been much more favorable for people, with a richer biomass and the resources one can find in a coastal zone.

People would have needed more sophisticated technology, I think, to follow the interior route, coming through the interior of Alaska and down through the Yukon. You would be under Arctic conditions, which does require fairly sophisticated technology; whereas in the coastal zone the technology needed to adapt and survive would be relatively simple.

We don't have any early dated sites that are actually in the ice-free corridor. There is no explanation for the early South American sites. So the coastal theory is an alternative that really deserves some serious thought to explain those early dates from South America.

## Finding Clovis Points

*Because much of Idaho is sparsely settled, it is still possible to stumble over something interesting and previously undiscovered. William D. Simon, a farmer from Fairfield found a cache of spearpoints that someone had lost or hidden there 11,000 years ago.*

*William D. Simon*

We were filling up a ditch and using a bulldozer and a carryall one evening. In the morning I looked and there were about six of these artifacts lying there. We began to look for them, and soon we had everybody looking for them. We pulled a Graham homeplow with a tractor on through the dirt. We kept doing that—back and forth—while my family watched and picked them up. Some of our neighbors found some, and gave them back to us. We have thirty-four of them.

We took them to the museum at Boise and a man looked at them and said, "My gosh." He phoned Dr. Earl Swanson in Pocatello. "You can't imagine what these guys have got," he said. Dr. Swanson asked me to bring them up there. After I did he had copies made of them and took four of the points to conferences in Russia and Paris. We had a letter from him about it. He said the people there were amazed at the workmanship on them. They were trying to compare them with something in Siberia because they figured that people came by the land bridge eleven thousand years ago.

I think they are so beautiful because they've never been used. Then they were buried about eighteen inches under the ground so they didn't get the sun on them or anything. They are just like they were when they were made. I asked Dr. Swanson about the eighteen inches under the ground, since you would think after eleven thousand years they would be deeper. He said that the world doesn't change in the thousands of years—it changes in the millions of years.

I think the people living here were just as bright as people who live here now. With the type of work they did and the way they lived, they had to be smart or they couldn't have survived.

We get all kinds of people coming to look at the points, mostly college students. One time there was a Christian minister here looking at the points. I said to him, "These are eleven thousand years old. That's before Adam and Eve." He said, "Oh. I have to think that over."

## Making A Clovis Point

*Clovis is the name of a small town in New Mexico. It was where archaeologists first found and named the style of flaked stone points like the ones in William Simon's field. This particular point style has been found throughout the North American continent. Some of them have actually been found next to the bones of extinct elephants. By using the kind of logic and deduction used at Wilson Butte and other sites, archaeologists have developed a theory about this point style and the people who used it.*

**Clovis point**

*Clovis points were used by people from 12,000 to 10,000 years ago, when elephants roamed all over North America. Since Clovis points have not been found in Siberia, they are thought to be a North American innovation. The people who used them probably lived a somewhat*

*nomadic existence, following big game and using cooperative hunting and capture techniques. Meat, organs, hide, bones, sinew, tusks—most likely each part of the animal—supplied some item of clothing, shelter, food, or tools.*

*The people who made Clovis points lived and traveled in Idaho, as the Simon cache indicated. Another of the fluted points turned up on the banks of the Portneuf River next to a baby elephant tooth. Others have been found at the Crystal Springs Fish Hatchery near Buhl, at Sailor Creek near Glenns Ferry, and other places in south Idaho.*

*Kimberly, Idaho, was the home of Don E. Crabtree, who revolutionized the study of stone tools all over the world. Until Crabtree developed a new way of analyzing points, archaeologists simply classified them by their shape and presumed function.*

---

# FLINTKNAPPING GLOSSARY

**ANTLER BILLET:** A tool used for percussion flaking. It is usually the section of antler that adjoins the head of the animal. Billet length and diameter depend upon the size of the stone being knapped.

**BASE:** The part of the point that attaches to the foreshaft or spear.

**CHANNEL FLAKE:** The center flake removed to form a channel in each face of the point.

**CORE:** A piece of stone from which predetermined flakes are removed, modified, and used as tools.

**FACE:** The flat portion of the point, in contrast to the edge or the base.

**FLAKE:** A piece of stone that has been removed from a larger piece. Flintknapping in general is the process by which flakes are removed from a stone until what remains is the weapon or tool ready to use.

**FORESHAFT:** A part of a thrusting weapon (or spear) to which the stone point is attached, and which is in turn attached to the spear. The point and the foreshaft would enter the body cavity of the animal being hunted, and the spear would fall free to be used again.

**PERCUSSION METHOD:** A method of removing a flake by striking the edge with a hammerstone or antler billet.

**PLATFORM:** Preparation of the stone edges or faces by beveling and abrading them, so that blows made by the hammerstone or billet to remove the flakes will not break the stone in unexpected or undesirable ways.

**PREFORM:** A point that is partly made, but not complete.

**PRESSURE METHOD:** A method of removing a flake using steady pressure against the edge (rather than a blow.) The pressure is applied with an antler tine or section of bone.

**PRESSURE TOOL:** A tool usually made from an antler tine or a cut-out section of bone from a large mammal.

7

*He studied the actual manufacture of the item, looking at the flake scars, the features of the margins, and other attributes of the tool. He tried to duplicate the methods used centuries before. Crabtree became a world renowned authority and teacher in stone age flintknapping. One of his associates, Gene Titmus, talked out loud one day as he sat making a Clovis point. He used a special glossary of words to describe what he was doing.*

Once you have seen a Clovis point, you probably will never confuse it with any other style. Most are three to four inches long, thin, and have a characteristic groove or channel two-thirds of the way up the center of each face. The channel probably served to help affix the point to the shaft of a spear.

The prehistoric people went to the quarry site to get stones to prepare cores. They would take flakes off the cores that could be made into tools. In this part of Idaho aboriginal people used obsidians or ignimbrites, which are easily obtained. There are many quarries in the hills south of Twin Falls, near Boise at Timber Butte, and near Idaho Falls at Big Southern Butte. They also used agates and chalcedonies and other material from the Salmon River area. Then there are quite a few sources of cryptocrystalline and microcrystalline stone.

After they removed flakes from the cores, we know that they heat-treated the stone in almost all cases. They would take the flakes and probably put them under the camp fire. It is quite a sophisticated system to heat-treat stone. They probably had it down to a real science—how to put it under the camp fires, how hot to get the fires, how fast to heat it up and let it cool so it did not destroy the stone.

Using a kiln today, we can probably do all this in a twenty-four hour period, but it may have taken them two to three days to get the same process done under the camp fires or special fires for heat treatment. Heat treatment usually makes the stone much easier to work. It also changes the surface texture of most stone so that it becomes more shiny and gives it a sharper cutting edge.

Reducing this large heat-treated flake down is done by what we call percussion flaking. It means to strike the stone on its edge either with a hammerstone or an antler billet.

I would say that probably all of the Clovis people could do this, but it was probably like any society—some people were better at it than other people, so there could have been some sort of a trade between people. Maybe someone made dart shafts much better than the rest, so for his dart shafts, he traded for the finished

**Gene Titmus uses hammerstone to remove flakes from core.**

*Flake is ready for shaping into a point.*

*Titmus grinds the platform to prepare for hammerstone.*

*Antler tine is tool for pressure method, which removes small flakes.*

*Titmus fits point and foreshaft into main shaft.*

Clovis point. But I'm sure they all had the knowledge of how to do this, just with various degrees of skill.

You have to remove some small flakes to create a platform. The platform has to be strong enough not to collapse when you hit it with the hammerstone. The first objective is to thin the large flake down close to the size of the finished point. As you reduce it down, you have to be more refined with the percussion technique. As you thin it, it will become narrower. After that you prepare to remove the channel flakes.

It took me about a year to a year and a half to learn how to do the many different facets of flintknapping. At that point I felt fairly comfortable that I had enough knowledge to tackle just about anything.

Ultimately the point will be set into the foreshaft with pitch and then wrapped with sinew to bind it there. The base of the point has to be V-shaped with flat surfaces so it will fit like a wedge into the foreshaft. All sections of the foreshaft have to withstand the pressure evenly at all points when the weapon is in use. All portions of the wood that surround the stone help withstand all the forces. By the way, no one has ever found a foreshaft. They may not have even had foreshafts, they may have only had thrusting spears.

I am grinding the platform to strengthen it to withstand the force of the blow of the hammerstone used to remove the flake. I grind the point end too because it will be supported against the rock anvil when I remove the channel flake. Resting the tip against the anvil helps insure that the channel flake will not come off incorrectly or cut the point in half.

Once the channel flake is successfully made, there is more

finishing to do on the base. I need to straighten it out where the channel flakes were removed, and resharpen the tip because it was ground to stand the force of removing the channel flakes.

There, now that was a pretty formidable weapon!

# A Cold Day At Owl Cave

*Susanne Miller is an archaeologist at the Idaho Museum of Natural History at Pocatello. She has spent several seasons at Owl Cave, one of three caves known collectively as the Wasden Site in Bonneville County. She revisited the site once more and focused her attention on the events of one dramatic winter day about eight thousand years ago.*

One of the interesting things about archaeology and the study of prehistory is that it's a lot like a detective story. Quite a bit can be said from the evidence that has been found at Owl Cave. It tells us about the cultural and natural history of the area, the way in which the people lived, the tools that they used, and the animals that they ate. One of the most important things that happened here was a major bison kill about eight thousand years ago.

The people in this area were hunting a large form of bison, now extinct, an ancestor of the modern bison. What we envision is that they took advantage of a large collapsed depression in the lava. It is essentially a hidden ground level trap. We think that perhaps the bison were feeding to the east and north of it below Cattle Butte and were somehow gotten on the move. Once they started to run they were brought to the lip of the cave, and the people drove the animals in.

We know from studying the bones that the kill took place in late winter. The collapsed depression was probably camouflaged by a deep snow bank, and the buffalo couldn't see it. They ended up in the depression, which at that time was probably considerably deeper than it is now. We estimate that over a fairly short period of time the people killed at least 350 animals minimum. They butchered and processed the bones down in the protection of the cave.

The spear points that we found with the bison are a part of the story that tells us approximately when all this took place. It is a style of spear point that is found throughout the

***Susanne Miller***

central and western part of the United States and is known to date about 8,000 years ago.

The way in which the Indians obtained food is a major concern of ours, as it certainly was of theirs. Bison jumps like this one have shown us one way in which Indian people would work together and obtain a large amount of food at one time. There is a lot of evidence from the western part of the Great Plains that, both before and after they had the horse, people used communal efforts to drive bison off of cliffs, into arroyos or rivers. They took advantage of the natural terrain to get the bison moving.

The bones of the animals tell us quite a bit about what happened. We found their skulls and all the bones of their bodies here. This tells us that when this kill was made, it was made right here on the spot. The animals were not killed elsewhere and parts of their skeleton and their flesh brought into the site.

Another thing that the bones tell us by their size is that many were fairly young

## THE OWLS OF OWL CAVE

One of the things that we have learned from at this site is due to the behavior of owls. Owls roost and nest and feed their young here. When they hunt they break up the bodies of their prey and swallow them almost whole. They are not able to digest the hair, fur, feathers, and bones. The owl retains this material in its lower throat region, and later passes it up as a pellet.

We know that owls have roosted here for approximately the last eleven thousand years. Each season they pass these pellets onto the ground. The little bones contained in them survive. As we excavate we carefully recover the bones of these animals and identify what they were. The small bones of mammals, birds, reptiles, amphibians and fish at Owl Cave serve as indicators of past climates and environments.

*Hunters stampeded bison into hidden depression in lava field*

animals. Some are bones of unborn bison, which tells us that the kill probably took place in the late winter or early spring.

Some of the spear points we found were broken at the base. We can imagine that when the bison went into the pit, most of them were probably not killed, but were cushioned by the snow. They had to be killed so the people could process the flesh for food. Some of these spear points were apparently used to kill the bison. We also suspect that people just grabbed a handy rock and used that as well. You can imagine what it was like down here with the many injured animals milling around.

Other indirect evidence for the way in which the animals were killed comes from the marks on the bones. A number of the skulls are broken, but there are very few actual cut marks on the limb bones themselves. The people probably took advantage of the abundant supply of meat rather than using the animal completely, as they normally do. They probably butchered the animals lightly, removed the best cuts of meat, and didn't break up the bones extensively for their marrow. The butchering marks show how the animal was cut and the way tendons were retrieved for sewing or hafting.

The skulls show very distinctive breakage marks along the forehead. People would open the skull and take out the brains, which were used later to tan the hides. There is something special about the chemistry of the brain and the changes that take place as soon as the animal dies that are important to the tanning process.

## Using Animal Brains To Tan Hides

*The eight thousand year-old practice of tanning hides with the brain tissue of the animal still survives in Idaho. Dave Bethke, brain-tans hides at the workshop near his American Falls home. His customers include Indians who value the softer, more comfortable, easier-to-work qualities of brain-tanned leather. He works on a large flat table in a workroom away from the house, often accompanied by his cats.*

To start with, we get us a hide to work on. The hide has been soaked for three or four days in water. We are going to put this up flesh-side-out and take some of the flesh and membrane off of it. If we don't take it off it's going to spoil or start smelling pretty bad after awhile. None of the brains would penetrate that hard surface. It is relatively easy to get it off, and the younger the deer, the easier it is. I used to use just a draw knife on it but I devised a tool for my own use and it seems to work a lot better. I watched Native Americans use a draw knife on it, but this probably resembles some of the scrapers that they used in the old times. The only bad thing about it, it gets plugged up once in a while.

I like to leave the tails on the hides, so you can see where the middle is. I tell the Indians that leaving that tail on as long as I can is my superstition that brings me good luck. It is kind of interesting to listen to some of their superstitions and folklore, too. Once in a while you come up with a hard hide, and you wonder why it got that way. You ask them why, and they say, "Maybe the dog touched it," or "Maybe you drank too much water while you were working it."

I guess I don't know how in the heck they ever got all that hair off in the old days without a good steel blade. They must have used an awful lot of scrapers in order to do it. This epidermis has to come off if you are going to have brain-tanned

*Dehydrated deer brains.*

*Bethke rubs the reconstructed brains over deer hide.*

*Dave Bethke prepares to work hide over metal scraper.*

*Workshop cat wants better look at scraping work.*

buckskin the way the Bannock and Shoshone make it. These fresh hides I'm getting now are just excellent, because it comes off a whole lot easier.

After we've gotten all the flesh and the hair off of that hide, it is just a clean deer hide. I can either make rawhide out of it or we can make buckskin out of it. If we want rawhide, we just stretch it out, let it dry, and cut up whatever you want to use. But we are going to make buckskin, brain-tanned buckskin.

We lay it out nice and flat and get us some brains now to put on it. These brains have been cooked and dehydrated. What I like to do is just put them in a sock and put them in hot water so they reconstitute themselves. It makes this fine paste as we put them on the hide. This is the hard part.

This looks like cracklings from boiled-down lard. And smells like it. Usually the cats and dogs get about half of it before I get done.

Now I just work it in. I try to stretch the skin and break down some of the fibers in it. It seems to make the brains penetrate a lot easier than putting it right on a fresh hide. After I put the brains on, I hang it up for half an hour or an hour.

I've never been able to find out from anybody just what the brain does, or if there is a chemical that you could use rather than brains. But the brain-tanned looks better. They say it will breathe when you wear it. It is not a heck of a lot hotter than a good pair of Levis in the summertime when you wear them. And they are easier to work with later; they are fluffed up and thicker for some reason.

I sell a lot of my hides to Indian ladies and guys. If they are going to use them for sewing, the first thing they do is test it to see if they can put a needle through it.

Each hide has its own personality.

Some of the old bucks have got gouge holes in them. Maybe you see a bullet hole that's healed over from previous years. I wish they could tell their stories. Well, we've got this brained up good enough. Now we're going to just roll it up, and let it mellow out and let it penetrate.

Well here we have our hide again after an hour or so. As you can see it shrinks down a little bit. We will work it to make it big again. We pull it over a stake to soften it up. Once you start this process you should stay with it continually till you get it all done and dried out. If you stop before you get all the moisture out, it'll get hard just like a pair of wet leather gloves. A lot of people use the back of a chair to do this nowadays. In the old days they used a stone to scrape across it. I use this iron post I cemented into the floor. It has a kind of curve, like the prehistoric scrapers you find out in the desert sometimes. It works real dandy, but after a while it starts wearing. I take a file and square the corners up a little bit once in a while and give it a little more traction. It makes the skin drag a little bit better.

To prepare the hide for the smoker, we plug up any bullet holes in the hide with tape to prevent losing the smoke. I've got some dried juniper that are chipped up real fine. Rotted pine gives a darker color; I use that sometimes. I'll put a piece of tin over it so we don't have any flare-up. I burnt up two hides one time, and they were both one hundred dollar hides.

Smoking gives a coating to the skin. It keeps it from getting stiff when it gets wet. It also covers a lot of smudges and mistakes. How much time it takes depends on the weather. I smoked one in twenty minutes one time. That was just the prettiest smoke job you could ask for. Sometimes it takes an hour.

There. That's what the finished hide looks like. It is ready for sewing.

## Village Life In Hells Canyon

*With the disappearance of the elephants and other large animals that roamed Idaho during the ice age, and the warming of the climate, people had to learn a new economy if they were to remain and survive in Idaho. They discovered that they could make an annual circuit to specific resource-rich places, and find all that they needed to live rather comfortably. They learned the travel habits of animals, and the growth properties of plants. Archaeologists refer to this economy as the seasonal or annual round.*

*The annual round, and the more predictable and settled life that it allowed, is evident in the sites that archaeologists have recorded in Idaho—hunting blinds, gathering sites, fishing weirs (in-stream traps for fish), bison jumps, quarries, and villages. Dr. Frank Leonhardy, of the University of Idaho, and a group of his students and volunteers examined one of the village sites in Hells Canyon a few miles below Hells Canyon Dam.*

To hear the word "village," you should not think of an English village with a lot of neat houses made of field stone and thatched roofs with a road going through.

An Indian village is a social group of people who live together and are related. They depend on one another and they live in a certain place. But the place isn't fixed in the European sense. The village is a bunch of houses and a bunch of families. One year the houses are down the river aways, and the next year up aways.

A village in Hells Canyon is very small, with twelve people on the low end, and thirty on the high end—one, two, three families. It is a social and economic unit of people who were hunters and gatherers. They were responsible for keeping themselves alive. They are the people who do the fishing for themselves, who do the root collecting for themselves, who do the hunting for themselves. The village was the basic economic unit. This is the group that gets the food.

These villages date, as best we can tell now, between 3,500 and 4,000 years ago. About 5,000 years ago, people were not living like this. Before that the pattern was of small mobile groups. Then something changed. We call the new pattern the "winter village," which is typical of the Nez Perce people. About 2,000 years ago at the village we are investigating this summer, there would have been three or four houses.

Envision coming here early in the morning. You would see smoke come out of the center of the house. All sorts of activities would be going on: food preparation, cooking, making tools, taking care of the kids, taking care of grandma—all of the things that any family does. Some people were doing things inside the house, and others were outside here and there. Probably it was a pretty busy place. They were the same activities we have today, but done in a different arrangement in time and in space, and without a special room inside for everything that we do now.

Perhaps the occupants here were a group of men who called themselves brothers. The brothers are a group of males who grew up hunting and fishing together since they were children. They learned the country and where everything is. They married women who probably grew up calling each other older sister and younger sister. Again they might be siblings, cousins, or friends. Grandma and grandpa, if they were still alive, would be here, maybe two grandpas and grandmas. Then there would be children, maybe even grandchildren. So the family could be three or four generations deep. The older people sit back and take care of the grandchildren. They can't climb out of these canyons very well anymore. They sit back and tell stories, practice religion, and take care of the kids.

*Frank Leonhardy*

Men do the fishing and the hunting, and make tools. In the Nez Perce world, plants are women's things. Women collect and process the plants. They make clothing and the processing tools.

People from age fifteen or so to their mid-forties were the most economically productive, able to collect the roots, go hunting, get berries, and catch fish. As one ages, you get more status, you get a little arthritic, you get a little tired. You sort of smooth into semi-retirement. You get to sit around and take care of the grandkids and tell everybody how it was done in the good old days.

We have excavated one of the circular pits, the site of a big house, about three feet into the ground. It is about twenty feet in diameter, and has a framework of poles over the top. Over that there are mats, and over the mats, dirt. It would have been a very warm and comfortable enclosed structure. Near the center hearth would be a big flat rock, which we call a hopper mortar base. They would use a bottomless basket for the top of it. They used a long stone tool called a pestle to pound up the dried roots and dried meat before making soup. There might be some fist-sized cobbles for breaking animal bones. They used the bone to get the grease out of it—very, very good foodstuff.

Around the circumference, people had their mats and beds. Their robes hung from the rafters, as did baskets full of dried roots and dried fish. So all of life's activities go on around this house, perhaps in a concentric progression: fire in the center, prepare the food around the fire, do other work around that, then sleep further away, and store things near the outer edge.

Once made, the house had just one circular room with no corners. Even now Indian people don't want corners. We Europeans, who like square deals and like to get straight to the point, like our world angular and with straight lines. We don't fit into an Indian world. And they don't fit into ours in that sense either. Indian life was good when you went around a circle.

The critical time of the year in the villages would be February and March. If you ran out of stored food, you might get pretty hungry for a little while until those first roots came out, and you could get the new food. The big religious thanksgivings, with ceremonies and festivals, for Indian people, were in the spring when the first roots and the first salmon came. People today still have root feasts to welcome those first roots.

In the summer, there would be racks to dry meat on, shades for cooking, food preparation, sewing, and making bows and arrows and spears. Probably there were lots of sticks stuck in the ground to hold something or other.

People had their pleasures. Good food, good stories, wonderful jokes, lots of games and gambling. The stick-game was a great pleasure. There was singing, playing the drum. There were fun songs, dance songs, stick-game songs, love songs, and religious songs. Always there was the feast.

They had their hazards, too. Before they had horses, falling and breaking a leg would have been a serious problem, when the only way to get somewhere was to walk. They had the ordinary hazards of staying alive—illness, accidents, avoiding rattlesnakes, avoiding breaking an arm. Interestingly enough, after the advent of the horse, lots of people had broken legs because they would fall off the horse and break a leg! Maybe somebody starved once and then everybody remembered it and never quit talking about it. These people may have gone hungry once in a while, but I doubt that starvation was very frequent. There are, of course, catastrophes that happened. Occasionally there would be someone who wanted to take what you had—your food or women. All in all, however, I have a notion that essentially these were pacific people, peaceful. I think they got along well.

One of the things that characterizes Indian culture in northern Idaho and Washington is the winter spirit dance. After people got the food stored, they would relax without a lot of economic concerns. They would turn to religious concerns in their free time. For the winter spirit dance, a piece of ground is made holy, made sacred and clean. A special lodge is built. The village sponsors a winter spirit dance, and people come from all over. For several days they practice the religion of the guardian spirits, the weyekin.

The religious specialists, the shamans, would practice their craft and get in contests with one another. It was a time that united people. Relatives would be there. Concerns with the spirit world created social solidarity. It tied people together with the environment they lived in, too.

For many Indian people, not just the Nez Perce, the sweat house is pretty special. It was for getting spiritually and physically clean. It served a social function. In the old days, there would be two of them in a small village, one for men and one for women. If you were to come to this village a thousand years ago, you would go to the sweat house to visit the "Old Man," the Creator. It was a very complex thing to simultaneously bathe, practice religion, and meet with the spirit world. People were together on neutral ground regardless of any other considerations. Visitors always came to the sweat house first. You were introduced into the village that way.

So the village is a social and economic center. It is not really proper to think of it as only a winter village, but "the village." People lived here all year round. But at different times of the year, when different resources were available, people would go to collect roots and come back, go to fish and come back, go to hunt and come back. The village was never abandoned, so the name "winter village" is a misnomer. It was a dynamic place.

There are a number of explanations as to why people began living in villages, none of them altogether satisfactory. I like to assume that people like to be together in groups because we are social animals. We like to be around others of our kind, whether we're related to them or not.

But the economic question is: How can a whole lot of people stay together in one place for a long time? As hunters and gatherers, their resources are scattered in time and in space. That is, they must go to the food at different times of the year, and to different places.

The first explanation is that improved technology for catching and preserving salmon permitted them to gather in one place. Salmon were very important in the prehistoric diet. So if somebody invented a technique of getting two or three times more salmon than they could a year previous, people could preserve them. With food on hand, the group could stay together longer.

Another explanation is that one of the resources that they depended on intensified—became much more abundant. It would have to be something concentrated in some area, and able to be preserved and stored. In European culture, it was wheat. For the Indian people it could have been salmon or roots. Salmon are abundant, predictable and concentrated (most of the time.) If you can catch, preserve, and store them, then you have food to live on.

But it may not have been salmon, but roots. There are a number of roots in the lomatium family, the biscuit root, that are very abundant in Hells Canyon. Anthropologists Alan Marshall, who teaches at Lewis-Clark State College, and Ken Ames of Portland State, came to the idea that it was the root crops that let people stay together in one place in large numbers. They are abundant and predictable, with all the other good attributes. Moreover, they are available in the early spring, which, for hunters and gatherers around here, was always the hard part of the year.

Archaeologists are still talking about these ideas. Whatever caused it, there was a transformation of the way people lived here around 3,000 or 4,000 years ago. The sites are larger, there are more houses, there are more people living in one place for longer periods of time.

This type of village life was spread across Idaho from the tip of the Panhandle down the Snake to the Wyoming border. The sizes of villages varied. There were little ones here, big ones there. Regardless of the environment, the mountains, the Snake River Plain, down in canyons, up in the high valleys, the village pattern was common throughout Idaho. I don't know of a place where it did not occur, except maybe in the most extreme south. Even there, I would bet that it was there at different times.

The village pattern ended because the people were put on reservations. It is as simple as that. They lost the economic base that supported their village life. They lost access to the root grounds, the hunting grounds; access to fishing was greatly reduced. No matter what the treaties may have said, the root grounds became farm land and the roots disappeared. It is not coincidence, I suspect, that for Indians, the ceremonial importance of roots and fish and game have increased. It is still economically important to some people, but mostly the ritual is important. There simply are not enough of the native resources here to support the native life way any more. Now people work in factories and on fire crews, and become lawyers and doctors.

## Women's Work

*With winter the most difficult time in the annual round, people relied on the plant foods that they had gathered and preserved for storage the previous summer and fall. This entire sector of the food economy was managed, organized, and carried out by women. It was their skills that meant the successful and comfortable survival of the group through the months when relying on the hunt would have been relying on chance.*

*Indian women and their ancestors had a pharmacological knowledge of the plants around them. Women's botanical vocabularies were large; they could name each part of a plant, and knew the different properties of plant parts according to the time of the year. They knew nutritional, medicinal, and*

*Judy Trejo with rye grass*

*Horsetails*

*Pulling apart horsetails at the joint*

*Milkweed*

*practical uses of plants. Judy Trejo is a Paiute Indian from McDermitt, Nevada, who teaches elementary school in Schurz, Nevada. She went for a walk in the Owyhee desert country on a hot summer day to identify some of the plants that Indians used to use, and even still use, for the various needs of everyday life.*

## Horsetails

Mothers used horsetails to make up a game to entertain their children. It wasn't necessarily entertaining, for the sake of entertaining. Our women did the majority of the fishing, and the children often went with the women. As children do, they have a tendency to become very noisy. So they were cautioned, "If you're noisy you're going to scare away the fish." So to keep them occupied the women—grandmother, mother, aunt—would take a handful of horsetails and take them apart. They have a joint, and fit together like a puzzle. They took apart several of these and mixed them all up, and gave them to the children. They offered them a little treat if they put them together. It kept them occupied for quite a while.

Besides being fun for children to play with, horsetail was used as a diuretic. Many times people had kidney ailments, bladder ailments. As everybody well knows, your body needs to get rid of this poison. Horsetails were boiled to make a tea. When they drank it, it gave the urge to urinate. This is the equivalent of the water pill.

## Rye Hay

Desert people often had problems with irritated eyes because of wind, dust, and other irritants. We didn't know very much about allergies back in those days. A lot of irritation was caused by small water blisters under the top eyelid that scratched your eye and caused it to itch and burn. There were certain people who had the ability to cure this ailment. They would scrape the eyelid, and rye hay is what they used. Some rye hay is a dark green, very strong, almost razor-blade sharp.

The blade was broken into pieces. The person with the problem would lay his head in this person's lap. They turned over your eyelid and very gently scraped these water blisters off. After this was done your eyes were rinsed in a tea made from the root of the wild primrose. Then you were asked to go and stand, let a breeze blow into your eye and it felt very, very soothing.

Another way this plant was used was when the women went fishing. Many times there would be a lady in the group who was expecting a baby. She was not allowed to gaze upon the fish that were rising to the top of the water unless she first made a belt out of rye hay. It didn't matter how she got it around her waist, but it had to go completely around her tummy. The reason was that if the fish could see her, and see the shape of her stomach, they would say, "Oh, she is too full already! She doesn't need us for food." And they would all sink to the bottom, and that would be the last they would see of that particular bunch of fish.

## Milkweed

See the milk dripping from the milkweed? This was used for new mothers who had difficulties with milk coming in when it should. This sticky stuff was applied directly to the breast. It had a drawing effect, and pulled the milk in as it should. If it didn't work the first time, then they took lava rock, heated it, and applied the heat to the breast along with more of the sap.

Certain times of the year, when the pods were very, very young, they were edible. They were very valuable as a green in your diet.

One of the more important things about this plant is that the pods were gathered and saved and put away when ladies were going to have babies. They gathered pods long before the babies were born, and other people gathered for the new mothers, too. The silk in the pod was used as a diaper liner. It was a disposable diaper, so Pampers didn't really have the first disposable diapers.

## Wild Primrose

The wild primrose is one of our most valuable plants. It is important because the seed pod is a valuable source of vitamin C. It is very sweet and you can eat the red part surrounding the seeds.

They are pretty to look at, but the most important thing about them are the roots. You dig up roots from the young plants, and dry them. They are very easy to preserve. You make a tea from it. This tea has been responsible for saving the lives of many infants, children and adults. It lowers fevers, stops dysentery and settles upset stomachs. It was important in preventing dehydration. I don't know if people still use it.

Where there are primroses, you can see grandparent plants. They do not work anymore, but still like to be with the young, just like people. They still have roots, and are still responsible for the healthy plants next to them, so they are not worthless plants. They may look dead, but are not. There are many plants that have their grandparents nearby because they enjoy being with the young.

## Sweet Sage

This plant is one of our sacred plants. I am going to start by giving an offering to this plant. We call it sweet sage, but other people may call it other things. It is a very aromatic plant. If you have a cold, you break it off and boil it. Make sure you leave the root so it will grow again next year. We just lay it out to dry in a bunch; don't put it in an airtight container or it will mildew. We strip it, and after it is dry, we wad it up into as tight a ball as possible and light it.

When we pray we bless ourselves with the smoke that comes from this plant. We take it throughout every room in our house and give thanks for all of our blessings. We ask that whatever imperfections and impurities we have will be removed. You are familiar with incense. This is pretty much the same thing, only it is very powerful. Other tribes do not have access to this, so we trade it for sweet grass, which we don't have. When we travel, we smudge with it.

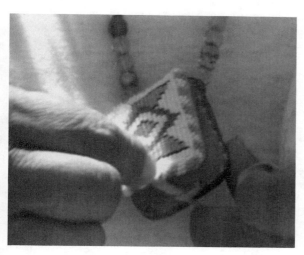

We also carry it on us. People say that your mind is one of the strongest things you possess. If people have bad feelings toward you, they can often cause you illness. So we carry this on us. Men wear it inside their hats sometimes; women put theirs in their jewelry.

*Judy Trejo's medicine bag*

## Sagebrush

Sagebrush was given to the Great Basin people as a gift from our Creator. At one time long ago our people promised they would use plants only for food and medicine. They also promised to leave enough for seed or to root. They promised not to destroy. They also promised that they would leave an offering every time they picked or dug a root. They would leave a gift, which could be bits and pieces of cloth or buckskin, a pretty rock, or a shell they were fortunate to have. Later on when glass beads came along, they left a bead in the hole to give thanks.

In turn the Creator gave our people sagebrush. He also gave them a promise that in their most dire need this brush would shelter them. People had a way of making brush shelters, even in winter. When it becomes soaked from snow or rain, you can make a fire and it will burn for you.

Crush the leaf of the sagebrush, and you will find it is very aromatic. You can boil it if you have a cold and drink the tea. If you have a headache, the tea is good for that. It also makes an excellent hair rinse when you want nice clean hair.

If you have a way of getting the very narrow inner bark center, you can chew it until it builds moisture and turns into rubber. You have chewing gum. If you are susceptible to severe nose bleeds, you pack the leaves in your nose and it will stop the nose bleed. There is no medicinal value in gauze. If you have to go to a doctor they pack your nose with gauze. I would prefer something that has medicine in it, like the sagebrush.

Early in the spring, we find sagebrush gall. They are very puffy and shiny. They are very sweet and kind of pithy. When you open them, you see that the gall is a home for bugs. There is a bug egg in the center of every gall. When they are still green and sweet, it is very simple to open it, take off that piece with the bug in it, and eat the rest. It looks like cotton candy.

## Yarrow

This plant is called yarrow. From far away it looks like one big white flower, but when you get up close to it, you see that it is made of clusters of individual little flowers. It is valued because of its ability to cure pain. You boil the stem and leaves. We usually leave the flowers for seed. Any part of it is very good to cure a toothache. You just take the leaves and stuff a cavity, or chew it for sore gums. Boil it for a gargle when you have a sore throat. If you have a sprain in your ankle or hurt your hand and there is swelling, you boil the whole plant and soak the hand in it or apply hot packs made from the tea of this whole plant. It was used as a topical. It gets rid of pain on your outer body, instead of your inner body. There are no chemical changes in your body when you use this for pain. Incidentally, the more bitter the plant, the more powerful it is as a pain reliever.

## Willow

Here we have willow. People gathered willow before the buds came out. They split the stems three ways and took off the bark. They used pieces to make cradle boards, to carry babies. Willow was for the base and the hood. They also made baskets. Many of the Idaho tribes were known for the hats they wove with very intricate patterns.

This is a cool plant. It has a lot of moisture in it regardless of the hot weather. When you peel the bark, it's cool in your hands, and very absorbent.

When you harvest these, you split it three ways. Take one part under your teeth, and split the other part in two with your hands. Then remove the core. Start weaving.

Willow is good when you are out fishing for trout. You gather a bunch of these with the leaves, make a bed of them, and put them in the water to keep your fish fresh until you get them home.

Naturally, willows were used for discipline when you were naughty. At one time I thought my mom gathered willows only to make me behave with. You know, they rather sting.

# A Hunting Site

*Just as it is today, fall was a good season for hunting two thousand years ago. When a hunting party left the village, the group walked to a favorite spot and camped along a stream. Their camp-fire rings have remained in place just where they were built, sometimes covered over with those of more contemporary campers, along with discarded tools and flakes.*

*When he was eight years old, archaeologist Lee Sappington, of the University of*

*Idaho, found his first arrowhead and determined to make a career of finding more. On this occasion he was two miles up the Lochsa River in north central Idaho. He and his team were asked to excavate the site by the Idaho State Transportation Department prior to road improvement work along U.S. Highway 12. In addition to projectile points, this excavation revealed other stone tools, charcoal, and camp fires.*

This hunting camp dates to about twenty-five hundred years ago, and fits within what we consider the ethnographic pattern. This means that for the past four and a half thousand to five thousand years ago, people followed a similar life style. In the winter, scattered groups of people all congregated in a main village. There are forty or fifty of those winter villages known up and down the Clearwater River.

The villages were all situated at the lower elevations next to the major rivers, where streams came in. People spent about half the year there. They were near salmon that would come in the spring. Their stored resources were concentrated there.

This spot would have been an important stop-over or base camp for people working out of the village. It would have been a small satellite camp. Our team wants to find out about the lifestyle of the people who once lived here. We want to know why they were here, and how their lifestyle changed in comparison to the lifestyle of people in historic times.

A feature is an activity area, not just a single artifact. It is a cluster of things that are related. A typical feature here is a cluster of burned rocks from the old camp fire, the charcoal, and the tools someone made and used around that fire. These things seem to be associated with processing animal bones as part of a larger hunting camp.

*Lee Sappington*

Basically this place is still a good camping spot. There is a cabin on the site built in historic times, demonstrating that this place had many attractive assets. There is access to travel routes, firewood, water, shelter against the hill, fish in the creek. And the deer and elk are still here today, too. All those things were attractive to the first miners and homesteaders in this area. It was a good sign that there would be a prehistoric site underneath.

Someone brought a large rock up from the river to serve as a work surface—the equivalent of a table top, workbench, or an anvil. Maybe they were processing bones, taking apart some animals for their meat. They brought up other rocks and took flakes from them to make an expedient knife, a quick tool, something to disarticulate joints or scrape some of the hair off a hide. They would use it for one task and then discard it.

A cluster of artifacts is basically a little time capsule. If we're lucky, we'll find some charcoal and get radiocarbon dates. Let's look at this fireplace. The rocks were heated basically like the heating element in our ovens now. Underneath we can see where the soil has been burnt. Here is some more charcoal—and a hammerstone. They probably used this to drive off flakes to create other tools. Here is a burned bone from the animals they processed, part of a lower leg from a deer or elk. Here is a spear or arrow point that has been broken from use; it has been burnt a little bit.

We can only find out so much because of the problem of preservation. People had mat lodges or skin tepees, but those things don't preserve. All we have are stone and bone. But that gives us clues about their technology and where they got the resources to make their tools.

This site seems to be a hunting camp. It has probably been occupied off and on for several thousand years, although not every day, not every week. This site would be most attractive here in the fall. The deer and elk come down from the mountains around here and concentrate in canyons like this one, where they are easiest to hunt. The chinook and the steelhead spawn in the creek over here and come back again in the fall. The berries become ripe in the late summer. Even today there are blackberries and thimbleberries here.

There are several other hearths around this site, built the same way as this older one. The charcoal in one of them was radiocarbon dated at 310 years ago—about 1640 A.D. The persistent use of the same type of features suggests that people were still using the same types of technology to hunt elk.

We found preforms here too—opal, chert, and jasper. These were shaped roughly, probably before they ever got to this camp. They had them ready to turn into a knife or projectile point or whatever the situation called for. Sometimes we find them partially worked or broken. When you look at how some of them broke,

*Lochsa excavation site*

you can see by the way the stone fractured that there was a defect in it that didn't show up until near the end when they were making the notches.

Tools like this perforator or drill probably traveled with them, at least as a core. At this site, we find a lot of the small pressure flakes by the thousands. But we don't find the larger flakes from the manufacture of tools. So they probably retouched some of their tools, made things as they needed and discarded them here.

The most exotic type stone we found here is obsidian. The obsidian in this point came from hundreds of miles away. It could have come from Montana or northeastern Oregon, but I think it probably came from Timber Butte, near Emmett. It is a favorite stone because it works so well. It's easy to flake.

## Making An Arrow

*The shapes and styles of stone weapon points changed to accommodate different kinds of targets. Thrusting spears for wounding large herd animals gave way to atlatls (a tool for throwing a spear) and then, in the last few thousand years, to bows and arrows that could bring down smaller game from farther distances. One of the practical features of a bow and arrow was that a hunter did not have to be standing up, as he did to throw a spear. One could crouch behind a blind or other hiding place, and surprise the animal, or even shoot while lying down.*

*Making these weapons is another art that is not entirely lost. Jim Woods, director of the Herrett Museum at the College of Southern Idaho in Twin Falls, is a student of prehistoric flintknapping, and often teaches others the old methods.*

**Jim Woods prepares sinew for attaching arrow point to shaft.**

The first step in manufacturing an arrow is straightening the shaft material itself. In the central part of the Snake River in southern Idaho, phragmities, or common reed, seems to have been a favorite material. It is a natural cane grass that grows quite crooked. The first step is to cut, store, and dry if for a short time.

To straighten out the shaft you take a small grooved stone, which some people incorrectly refer to as shaft sanders. They are very dense and smooth and can hold a great deal of heat. You place it next to a fire, heat it, and then put it on a nearby stone. You start with the worst of the kinks—put that kink right on top of the stone and leave it there for a few moments. The heat transfers into the reed and starts to loosen the fibers enough to straighten out that particular kink. You let the shaft cool, then move down to the segment where the next biggest kink is. Within about five or ten minutes, a person can take a crooked shaft and straighten it so it is very functional.

Now you just cut it the length you want with a sharp flake or an arrowmaker's knife. You hold the cane and rotate it over the sharp spot on the knife blade several times to start a slight groove and then snap it. You try to cut the shaft just ahead of one of the segments because that's a very strong part of the shaft. Cutting it there prevents it from splitting.

Once cut to length, you reinforce the ends with sinew, both the point end and the knock end. After that, you attach the fletching (feathers) and haft the point onto the shaft.

I am using dried sinew from an elk leg. You have to pound on it with a hammerstone to break the fibers down. Be careful to use a smooth stone; otherwise you could cut through the fiber. The inside of a tendon is stringy, fibrous, white, and very tough. From just one piece of tendon you end up with many yards of good, usable material. You peel it off in various thicknesses, depending on what you're manufacturing. For sewing you would peel it very fine and thin for thread.

But for arrowmaking you need a little bit larger bundle. Now you put it in your mouth and soak it for three to five minutes. Let it soak up moisture and start to loosen. It has absolutely no taste whatsoever, but it gets very sticky because of the natural glue in the hide. You can stretch it, a quality the arrowmaker really likes, because you can wrap it tightly around the shaft. When it dries it will shrink, and the wrap is very snug and tight. You can see how useful this would be for a lot of other purposes like attaching knife blades to handles.

The same sinew is used on the backside of the archer's bow too. This added tremendous strength, and the bow could be flexed without breaking. It takes about five minutes in the sun for this sinew to dry. If you want to seal it and make it waterproof you melt a little pitch or resin and paint it over the top of the sinew and then it will be weatherproof for years to come.

*Straightening the arrow over grooved stone.*

*Shaft sander is used to smooth the shaft.*

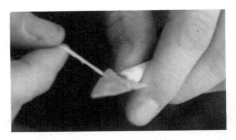

*Woods wraps sinew around notches in point.*

*The finished arrow*

Woods sands the shaft between two pieces of welded tuff, a kind of volcanic rock, to smooth it and make the circumference even all along the shaft. He attached duck feathers, using more moistened sinew. Here the archer has to determine how far from the knock to affix the feathers and how much to trim it with an obsidian flake. The art is in crafting the arrow so that it will have just the right spin in flight to fly true to its target. Since Woods is using a hollow cane for the arrow, he has to make a solid foreshaft to which he could attach the point. Then he inserts the foreshaft into the arrow.

I have selected wild rose, which was a favorite material in this area. I cut it to the approximate length and used an obsidian biface to cut a groove into it and match the shape and cross section of the arrow point itself. These were generally not attached very deeply. Just a little more than a quarter of an inch is sufficient. You attached these with sinew, often with the help of pine tree pitch. You would already have a supply on hand of pitch and ash mixed together rolled into cigar shapes to form a little pitch stick. It was hard when it was cool, but when you melt it over a fire, the end of it gets soft, becoming very gummy and gooey. It makes a very strong cement. You drip a slight amount into the groove of the foreshaft, stick the point into the groove, and let it cool for a moment. At the same time you are moistening the sinew.

A couple of wraps around the shaft keeps it from splitting. Then you wrap it up and around one notch in the point and then the other. Then around the foreshaft to strengthen the end. The arrow shaft takes most of its abuse at this juncture. It tends, upon impact, to force the arrow point into the shaft and so the archer needs to prevent it from splitting. You use liberal amounts of sinew for that. As it dries, the sinew shrinks, and the cross pattern pulls the point tightly down into the groove of that shaft. Within ten or fifteen minutes, it will be very firm.

You just slip the foreshaft into the phragmities to form a very tight friction fit. And now we have a complete arrow of the style that was used along this Blue Lakes section of the Snake River.

## Rock Art

*Stone weapons and tools are the most well-preserved artifacts of the lives our predecessors led in Idaho. The less preservable parts of their material culture, such as items made of plant materials, do not remain. Even less accessible are the intangible elements of their lives—child-rearing practices, jokes and humor, religious beliefs, personality types, songs, interpersonal relationships, explanations of the universe.*

*Still, we would like to know those things about them. They wrote us no letters and left us no diaries, but they did commit to cave walls and rocks images that are now known as "rock art." These mysterious images are the most vivid evidence of the intangible life of the mind and spirit common to all human beings. Understanding the meaning and purpose of "rock art" is part of the archaeological frontier in Idaho.*

*Dr. Max Pavesic, professor of archaeology at Boise State University, went to Wees Bar on the Snake River, one of the hundreds of places where Idaho Indians pecked or painted designs onto rocks. The rock art at Wees Bar is found on large boulders deposited in the canyon during the Bonneville Flood.*

There are two types of rock art common in the western United States. The first are pictographs, which are painted images. The paint is made by mixing dry pigments made from hematite or other materials. People mixed the pigment with water or grease or blood, and commonly applied it with a brush. Or there was a method of blowing it on with a lot of water. Simple finger painting would work, too.

The second kind, petroglyphs, are completely different. This is an art form where the rock surface is carved by abrasion or incision or cutting. At Wees Bar, they used a pecking method, where you take one rock as a tool and smash it at a point on the rock time and time again until the design is exposed. This exposes the unweathered surface underneath. That is what gives the color contrast.

Wees Bar petroglyphs are an example of what is known as the Great Basin abstract style. There are two sub-styles: rectilinear and curvilinear. Most sites in southern Idaho have a combination of the two styles. The design elements of this style are found in the dry desert West from the Sierra foothills in California, across the Great Basin and east to the Wasatch Front. It is common south of the Snake River in Idaho.

The two styles are defined partly by technique of manufacture and also on the superimposition of figures. In a curvilinear design you will notice connected dots or circles. A rectilinear design such as connected triangles is also very typical of Great Basin rock art.

One of the ways we verify that this is rock art (contrasted with one individual's personal graffiti) is that the design elements are continuous. From site to site, we can see the continuous use of certain patterns, which shows that they are part of a cultural tradition. It wasn't just one person coming out here and manufacturing this on their own. Somebody had some shared beliefs, ideas, and values when they were creating these designs.

What the images mean is one of the great mysteries of rock art studies. We think this material is quite old, based on the patina. We have also compared it with design elements found on portable objects that have been recovered from stratified archaeological deposits that had been

**Max Pavesic**

radiocarbon dated. Much of the art in the western United States was produced between about 2000 B.C. and 600 A.D. After that, people quit using these designs, and other ones took their place.

What they mean is anyone's guess. It is not a writing system, not a notational system. The symbols do not represent words. We have a tendency in our culture to look at things and say, "I have to be able to read this." But this is not what these symbols mean. The symbols have some kind of value or symbolic belief behind them.

We know from historic times that a lot of rock art is individualized. A shaman or someone was seeking supernatural power. The ideas are unique to the individual. Even so, he or she was working in an artistic tradition. The Indian religion among the Shoshone or Paiute or Nez Perce people can be a very individualized experience. So the actual meaning of the art dies with the creator. Sometimes we can say when it was done or who did it, or that it was done around an initiation or puberty ceremony.

Many of the design elements in the Great Basin are associated with game trails—deer, mountain sheep, and antelope—or spring sites in the desert. I think it is a sophisticated medium, because it is abstract. There is meaning behind that abstraction. It is not naturalistic at all.

The archaeological profession has only become concerned about rock art in the last fifteen years or so. It was something that was always left to the amateur archaeologists throughout the United States. The profession felt that there really wasn't much we could do to interpret it. But we have changed our view of what archaeology is about in the last twenty years. We used to be concerned only with the technological or economical accomplishments of people. Now we have evolved to a point where we study the social and political organization of people, too. Today we look at questions of meaning and value, religion and symbol in ancient societies. It is just as critical to understand the total cultural picture of western North American groups as it is a great civilization like Egypt or the Mayas.

*Petroglyphs*

So we have succeeded in dating rock art and determining its distribution. We have defined which archaeological culture they belonged to in the past. We are only now beginning to interpret meanings. There have been some breakthroughs lately, but not in the particular abstract style that we find here at Wees Bar.

We have no idea what these triangles stand for. On some rocks you can see a series of meanders or snakes. There is a famous one known as

Map Rock on the north side of the Snake River. Local people believe that the meander on the rock is an actual outline of the Snake River from Hells Canyon all the way upstream to Yellowstone Park. However, the design appears throughout the West. I think these meander lines are part of a compositional element to divide the panel, or outline it in relation to the natural configurations of the rock.

There are only six or eight hunting and gathering and collecting societies left in the world today. They are found in very marginal environments, like the Kalahari Desert in Southern Africa or up on the northwest corner of Hudson Bay, where you find the Caribou Eskimo. One of the reasons they have survived so long is because even our technology has made only limited intrusions into that environment.

The people we find there survive at a level of culture which is the primary level of existence for most of human society. That is, over 99 percent of human evolution had cultures that were living off of natural food—hunting, gathering, collecting, and fishing. These survivors, even in these difficult environments, probably put fewer work hours in a week than we do. Among the Kalahari, the men put in about a three and a half-day workweek, and the women put in about a five-day week. The men sit around in their spare time and talk about their great hunting exploits and how the group depends on their abilities as a hunter.

But we have also found out that if the group depended on these great hunters, they would starve. The individuals that often keep the group alive are the women and children through their daily collecting of tubers, roots, and other vegetable products. These people are balanced with their environment. They do not over-exploit it. They move on a seasonal basis and only exploit foods that are fully ripened. You have to make sure that the foods are ready to exploit, because if you process them while they're green, they will rot during storage.

So the people in these societies had time for art and religion. For any society the activity of religion, philosophy, or mythology is a form of social cohesion. It reinforces who you are, why you live the way you do, what kind of decisions you make in life, and why you live in the environment that you do. It is just part of being human.

*Curvilinear petroglyph sub-style*

*Rectilinear petroglyph sub-style*

# Indians

## OUR FEET IN TWO WORLDS

*The contact and clash between EuroAmerican cultures and the ancient Indian and African cultures of Australia, Africa, Asia, and the Americas has been one of the great stories of world history for the last few hundred years. Idaho Indians and their EuroAmerican neighbors are a part of this grand global event. Many Indians living in Idaho today were born in and spent their early childhoods around a tipi. Many had parents who did not speak English.*

*Idaho Indians have faced conditions overwhelmingly favoring their demise as a people: catastrophic epidemics, loss of their economic base, discrimination, suppression of religious freedom and native languages, invasion by an alien population with access to superior energy sources, United States Indian policy, racism, and despair. They have survived it all. They adapted to extremely rapid changes, which in many other parts of the world completely destroyed aboriginal cultures. Idaho Indian people are today alive with the pulse of change and the prospect of ever more successful adaptations.*

*Indian people of Idaho are intently conscious of this process of adaptation and of the fact that they must often make difficult choices. Each person has a unique story about managing the demanding experience of deep and lifelong association in two completely different cultures. Indian politics and polemics reflect the wide range of experience and outlook accumulated by the members of the group. At one time Indian adaptation to change was a necessity merely to survive. Today, Idaho Indians have more choices and more opportunity to determine for themselves the course of their own future.*

*The following conversations highlight a few of the problems and events of initial contact with EuroAmericans and then tell of the particular experiences of several men and women of twentieth century Idaho.*

# The Creation Of The People

*Allen Slickpoo is a Nez Perce who lives in Kamiah. He is a storyteller, has been a member of the Tribal Council, and has written a book about the history of the Nez Perce people. Their history begins, as do all histories of people, with their creation and an explanation of how they came to live where they are today.*

Well, all the animals were in human form at one time. When the great monster began to swallow up people, Coyote became lonely. One of the surviving animals told him the monster was swallowing up all the people. Coyote immediately planned how he could be swallowed so he could free all the beings that were within the monster's stomach. So he tied himself with rawhide rope to three mountains—the one on Cottonwood Butte, one on Seven Devils, and one on Pilot Knob. He made five knives. He challenged the monster and allowed himself to be swallowed.

When he first got inside the monster, the first being he ran into was Bear. Coyote said to him, "Who are you? Who should be scared of you if you let the monster swallow you?" Coyote kicked him in the nose and made his nose flat. Thus he created Grizzly Bear.

*Allen Slickpoo*

Coyote went on and there was Snake, all coiled up. Coyote said, "Who are you? Trying to be fierce and you let the monster swallow you?" So Coyote stomped down on his head and made his head flat. He became rattlesnake, with a flat head.

Then finally he got inside the stomach. He began to cut on the heart. He kept cutting away with the five knives. As he worked on the arteries and veins, the knives broke one by one. With the last knife, he cut the last part, and the heart dropped. He told all the beings to go quickly out the back exit. They all exited out the back instead of out of the mouth. All the beings got out except for one little guy. As he was almost out, the monster died and the exit closed. His tail was caught. Coyote and all the animals went to help pull him out. They pulled and they pulled and finally got him out. And all the hair came off his tail. To this day that little guy is known as the Muskrat.

Coyote cut up the monster into pieces and threw him in different directions. Where they landed, people grew up. He threw some over toward Montana to the Blackfeet country. "These people will be tall and war-like." He threw some down to southern Idaho. "These people will be war-like, fierce and mean." Some he threw over to the Columbia River. "These people will be small people, but they will be real good fishermen." Then he threw some up to the north in the Coeur d'Alene country and said, "These people will be good gamblers."

After he had done that, Coyote noticed that there was still no one around. One of the animals asked, "Why don't you create people here?" So Coyote went, taking the blood and sprinkling it around the area. "These people will be the Nee Me Poo. They will be intelligent, the real people, the Nez Perces." And the heart of the monster is still in Kamiah.

## Contact

*The Coeur d'Alene Indians first met EuroAmericans with the arrival of missionary priests in 1841. Ernest Stensgar, chairman of the Coeur d'Alene Tribe, told the story as the tribe gathered at Cataldo Mission for the annual festival celebrating their heritage.*

*Ernest Stensgar*

The Coeur d'Alene people were spread out on all the major waterways from the Silver Valley down to the south end of Coeur d'Alene Lake. We were along the Palouse River, up into the head waters of the St. Joe drainage, the Clearwater drainage. The Spokane River at Spokane Falls was common ground for the Spokane Indians, the Kalispel, and the Coeur d'Alenes. Probably the Okanogan and Palouse Indians came up and shared in the salmon and camas and berry grounds. Many of the customs and language of these people were the same.

A medicine man had a vision and foretold the coming of the missionaries. They would bring us powerful medicine that would bring healing and peace to the tribe. I learned very beautiful stories from my parents about medicine men and spiritualism. They told me about the vision quest and sweat houses. Powerful men worked by using herbs and fasting for days. They would foretell sickness and good fortune through these visions.

That is what happened to Circling Raven. He probably went on a vision quest up on a mountain. It came to him that the Blackrobes were coming. He passed away and the Blackrobes did come. They came to us from the Flatheads. They found out that the tribe was ready to accept them because of the fortune-telling of Circling Raven.

People in those days prayed for a hunt, for good health. They prayed for their families, much as we pray when we go to church. They prayed for a good summer and that not too many people would die during the winter. To have a vision that white men were coming probably was rather extraordinary.

When Father DeSmet first came, he Christianized a lady by the name of

Siu-wheem. She is instrumental in the story. Siu-wheem was said to have been the first to learn the teaching and doctrine of the Catholic faith and to really accept it. The priests trusted her enough to teach the catechism and songs and prayers. It was said that she always had a lot of children around her and brought the faith to them. She was also a leader inside the church.

You can imagine that these white visitors were an encroachment on the medicine man. Here he was, the doctor in the village. Now who are these people? These intruders come. They are not of our clan or even of our people. They cannot even speak our language; yet they come here to be the new healers and the new doctors. It must have been pretty hard to accept, if you put yourself back in that time.

The story of Circling Raven is a legend. But I like to think that stories or fairy tales happened once in a while. Maybe it did happen. There is certainly no doubt that the Coeur d'Alene people accepted the white visitors more readily than any other tribe. Faith was so strong, the church was built. People came from all over—Indians and white men both. They looked at the mission as a beacon whenever they passed through the territory. The place was very instrumental throughout history ever since.

When white settlers first came after initial contact with the missionaries, the head man and the chiefs sat around wondering how to deal with these people that were invading. They talked about maybe escorting them if they wanted to pass through our territory. Others said, "No, let us stop them at the borders." Another idea was to let them through, but take their weapons and give them back after they passed through. One idea was to sort of treat them like tourists. "If they want to look around, fine. We will take them to look around, but they can only stay a few days and move on."

So there was a lot of powwow about these intruders. They could never understand how a person could just appear and claim a piece of land and say it was theirs when everybody had enjoyed that land all throughout their history. If there was a good camas field everybody shared in it. If there was good fishing, everybody shared in it. The same with hunting and camping spots. The herds ran all over, too. So how could somebody come and claim this land?

## The Seasonal Round Gives Way

*The missionaries and the Indians only had a short time to work together before road builders and miners arrived on the scene. With the discovery of gold, the swarm of miners quickly ended the possibility of isolation or tranquility. The boom and bust of mining soon gave way to agriculture and permanent settlement. The lands and resources that had supported Indian economies in Idaho became the basis of the EuroAmerican economy, and Indian lands diminished into reservations of smaller and smaller proportions.*

*The Lemhi Shoshone had a reservation in the Lemhi Valley from 1875 to 1907. Against their will, the 474 Lemhis were forced to join the other Shoshone people at Fort Hall. Emma Dann is the granddaughter of one of those who came to Fort Hall.*

I am a Shoshone Bannock Indian, living on the Fort Hall Indian Reservation in the United States, situated in North America. My father comes from the Lemhi Shoshone. He has a Bannock/Cheyenne mother. Her mother was kidnapped from her tribe and gave birth to my grandmother.

My mother is from the Tukudeka Lemhi tribe, the Sheepeater Tribe. Her mother lived in the caves in the Rocky Mountains when the white man first came out this way. And they viewed everything from their situation.

In 1907 they were force-marched to Fort Hall. They spent overnight at Howe. One of my grandmothers was in labor and she died there, birthing her son. There is still a very bad feeling about being force-marched.

One of the first ones that we know of in our line was placed on allotted land at the northern end of the reservation. It felt like a poor place to live. I went to see it. At the time, it was all sage and rabbit brush. But now it is good for producing potatoes and grain or sweet peas. I think a lot about how they lived. They moved by foot and horse and had dogs to pack their travois. I do like their life.

When the new year frosts set in, they would have whitefish. Whitefish is succulent and fat at that time because they have done their year's growth. After the yellow willow buds, the steelheads come up. That is when they would go up to the Salmon River. When the yellow willow turns yellow in the late summer, then the bigger sockeye salmon are up, and that's our time to fish. They come and spawn. When they go back out to the ocean my people wandered down the river and down to the root area.

They came off the mountaintops and went westward to the Camas Prairie. Before they got that far, they would meet the Anadromous tribe in the Salmon River area. They made nets of thistle. They would catch fish and then start going downstream again. That would be their first meeting of the year.

*Emma Dann*

Courtesy of Emma Dann

They would dehydrate roots and fruits for winter storage and put them in caches up and down the valleys or across the mountains. That was done so we would be noticed as being poor and without food. People did not know at that time that my people had caches. After the fruits were dehydrated, then they would go up into the mountains, over the summits, and into the meat world.

On the way they

would have fresh peppermint tea, sage tea, bitterbrush tea, roseroot tea, many kinds of teas, even mountain tea. Today I use imported coffee in the morning, and then some kind of tea at noon or peppermint tea at night to soothe my throat throughout the night. Or sage, or sweet sage, or cedar or some kind of tea that is natural. So that is one way I live now, like our ancestors did.

I would miss coffee, if I lived entirely the way my ancestors did. I've learned to drink coffee and chocolate. Many things that are imported are good, Chinese and Japanese teas, black and green and different kinds you mix together. But still, roseroot tea is about the best.

In the spring, there would be rockchucks and squirrels, ground squirrels for meat. People had to be strong to walk, for they walked in great strides. When we were children, our grandmother took care of us. We would run along behind her, and she would stop and wait for us. She was a nomadic person who had traveled many, many miles into the buffalo country, into Yellowstone country. They walked, with dogs to pack their things.

## Treaties

*The United States began its relationship with Indians by regarding the Indians as owners of the land. Since they were independent nations, the government negotiated treaties in order to acquire land and the rights to use it. Until the last twenty or thirty years, Indian people were often not in a position to enforce the terms of the treaties.*

*One of the provisions of many treaties affecting Idaho Indians was that they could continue to hunt and fish in their "usual and accustomed places" on off-reservation lands owned by the United States. As treaty-maker Isaac Stevens, the governor of the Washington Territory, said in 1855, "The Indian will be allowed to take fish...at the usual fishing places and this promise will be kept by the Americans as long as the sun shines, as long as the mountains stand, and as long as the rivers run." In 1969, after several Northwestern Indian tribes went to court in Oregon to defend their right to this promise, Federal District Court Judge Robert Belloni affirmed treaty fishing rights. Later, Northwestern tribes intervened in a case against Washington State in 1979. The decisions favoring Indian treaty rights were reinforced by Judge George Boldt of the Ninth Circuit Court of Appeals in 1974, and eventually by the U. S. Supreme Court in 1979.*

*In 1970, one year after the Oregon decision, Shoshone-Bannock Indians in Idaho were in court challenging the right of the Idaho State Fish and Game Department to prohibit their fishing on unoccupied lands of the United States in one of their accustomed places.*

*Keith Tinno, a Shoshone-Bannock from Fort Hall, recalls his role in the Yankee Fork fishing trip that ended up in court. Allen Slickpoo discusses some of the problems with the treaties.*

KEITH TINNO: It began when the Fish and Game Department closed our fishing area, so we couldn't fish. I was up fishing on the Yankee Fork, just below Six Mile.

When we had court in Challis, we were found guilty of fishing in closed areas. There was an appeal before Judge Arnold T. Beebe in Blackfoot. There was a linguist (Dr. Sven Liljeblad) who testified that when the treaty was made there was one word that meant both hunting and fishing. Our elders testified that their fathers and mothers often fished in that area years before, and their fathers before that. Judge Beebe ruled in favor of the tribe.

It was written in the treaty that we had the right to hunt and fish on unoccupied land in the United States. When the state closed the area, it was not really thinking of treaty rights, but of the lower number of fish coming up and the problem of the number getting lower.

ALLEN SLICKPOO: The Belloni decision is very important to the Nez Perce people. It supports the rights that we have asserted from the time that the treaties were made in 1855. The language of that treaty was not written out by the Indian himself but by the government's representative. Sometimes the interpreter did not understand Nez Perce very well, either. In interpreting treaties, the courts have gone by what the Indians understood they were negotiating, not by the precise language of the treaty.

*Keith Tinno*

The interpretation of the treaty has caused a lot of antagonism among some non-Indian people who are misinformed and do a lot of hollering. I have yet to see anyone go broke or bankrupt because of my tribe's treaty. Some people want more than what they already have. Sometimes Indians gave more than what they had. The treaty is the supreme law of the land according to the Constitution of the United States and also according to the State of Idaho Constitution.

## Alcoholism

*Wholesale changes in the social, religious, economic, and political structure of Indian societies, in the midst of U. S. policies that led to dependency rather than self-sufficiency, have forced Indians to pay a heavy price. Velma Bahe, on the Tribal Council of the Kootenai Indians, talks of how alcoholism led to the destruction of many of her people.*

Alcoholism was really heavy back in the fifties and sixties. We lost a lot of people. They would get to about age forty-five and we would lose them to cirrhosis and all the disease that alcohol brings. When younger people died from that, their elders ended up in nursing homes. The nursing homes weren't the kind of life they were used to, and they all died one after another.

Back in those days the children were removed from the homes because of alcoholism. The parents began to wise up after that because they realized that their relationships were dwindling. They searched for learning about alcoholism. The children that were gone came back. They were more aware of what alcohol does. I believe we have overcome that problem. Today we're down to about thirty percent that are still heavy into alcohol. The number has dropped.

I was one of the children that was taken away, put into boarding schools all my life. I was sent to St. Joseph's children's home in Lapwai from grades one to seven. I went there not knowing a word of English. That was really hard. I was there with one of my brothers and one sister. We corresponded because we didn't know what English was. I finally picked up the language.

From grade eight I came here to Bonners Ferry, graduated, and was able to have my grandmother watch me, which filled her with pride. I stayed here for freshman year, then went off to Chilloco Indian School in Oklahoma.

Being in an Indian school, you realize you're not the only one with the same problem. You learn that the same thing

*Velma Bahe*

happened to others around you—alcoholism, children being taken away. The Bureau of Indian Affairs was hoping to dissolve tribes that way, so that you wouldn't want to come back to the reservation. So being educated to be aware of what was happening, you go home and help your people to keep growing.

I feel I have helped. This is the first time I have ever been honored by being a tribal chairperson. I've always been on the tribal council. I have been in this position for eighteen months and have eighteen more months to go. Things are just booming, and it makes me have pride for my people.

The others on the council are all pretty young, in their thirties. We've all been through the same kind of experience. Before the Kootenai War we were all scattered in different homes or boarding schools. There was only one house on the reservation, our chief's, who at the time was very old. He told us that if all of us were run off the reservation, then the white people would have accomplished what they were trying to do. So he begged us to come back to the reservation. But the houses were all destroyed, and there was no way we could come back here. Our chairwoman said, "We have to declare war."

# The Kootenai War Of 1974

*In the 1930s the Kootenais lived in tipis near Bonners Ferry. Their allotment lands had been dissipated by BIA mismanagement. A local physician managed to persuade the government to build eighteen houses. They had running water, but no bathing facilities. Those were provided in a community center. Nothing had changed by the 1970s, although the Indian rights movement was underway in many parts of the country. Amy Trice, then the chairwoman of the Kootenai, determined to do something about it.*

It was to try to get housing for the Tribe. My people needed employment, housing, roads. It was so depressing out here. There were only two or three houses left. The kids were on their own. They had no future. They were lost. People lived in anything, anyplace. We had a man who died, living in a place with the water pipes frozen and holes in the roof. At the time we didn't know he had Alzheimer's disease. It was snowing and he died of exposure. It was so sad; no one seemed to care. But they didn't know what to do. We tried to get help from the local people here, but "A good Indian is a dead Indian" was their motto. I think they believe differently now. But that was the kind of feeling some of the people had.

With all this in mind, I tried my best to talk with the Bureau of Indian Affairs to get housing for my people. The answer was always, "Well, your tribe is too small. We can't help you." They said we had to have three hundred enrolled in the tribe. Our tribe had about sixty-five enrolled. Of those, thirty were children.

We were small, but when you are small, you don't have anything to work with. No matter what we did to get employment and housing, it was like going against a brick wall. That was the role of the Bureau of Indian Affairs—to stay down here to keep themselves employed. It is a sad thing.

I got together with other tribal members. One thing led to another. They said, "Well, no matter what we do, we will be right back where we started. We are too small." So we discussed how we could let the public know about our cause. We were so oppressed nobody even saw us. When you hear "Bonners Ferry," nobody knows where it is.

I had the opinions of my parents and other

*Amy Trice*

elders, none of whom are with us anymore. I told them that we needed to get the news media out here to see if we could stir something up. Not to the effect of a full-scale blood and gut war, but a war with the mind, with the pen. Everything went into place. The tribal members said, "We'll send letters out to speak our cause. We'll even send a letter out to the president." Which we did.

We had a meeting downtown, where the office was. The people came in. I told them the steps that I would like them to take. I needed their opinions and input. The majority of the people said, "Yes, this is the only way we can be heard." I told them that it was going to be dangerous and hairy and scary. I didn't guarantee anything because we would just play this by ear. Hopefully there would be no bloodshed. But there could be.

Not all my people wanted to participate. I told them, "It is your discretion. Take your families and leave." I didn't want to force them. But I had made a commitment. This is the only thing I could do to help my people. There were a few that left. I know a couple that hitchhiked out of here. I sent my girls to Tacoma so that they wouldn't be hurt. I sent my mother to Montana—my dad wouldn't budge—to get away because it was going to be dangerous.

I think I slept, if I did sleep, about three hours at a time during that whole two weeks straight. We didn't know for sure what was going to happen. There was a little old lady, very frail. She must have weighed a hundred pounds. I told her, "I will understand if you leave." She just burned my ears right off. She told me, "When I light a fire, I stay until it is burnt to the fine ash." That told me that she wasn't about to leave, bless her heart. She stayed with me.

*The Kootenai War consisted of a Declaration of War on September 20, 1974, against the United States of America and the placement of a toll-collecting booth on the state highway. Youths carrying signs asked for ten cents or whatever a traveler wished to donate for the Kootenai cause.*

We told the media. Everything just worked beautifully. Mark St. John, from KREM, I think it was, was very good at that. I think there was a group from Boise TV as well. They just kind of talked for us, and that was the best thing that could have happened. We were on nationwide.

Then it just kind of got out of hand. The state police were hilarious. They came in with their sawed off shotguns. There were thirty-five state patrol cars. A Sandpoint newspaper reporter was out at three o'clock in the morning surveying, so to speak. He said there were patrol cars coming in. So we said, "What for?" He said they were going to the hospital. This was supposed to be a secret and we weren't supposed to know this.

But we already knew. They were brought to the hospital basement to be hidden there, which to me is the worst place. You have patients up there who could have a heart attack from the excitement. The scariest part was when I left the office. The sheriff's office is across the street from where our office was then. A state policeman got on his knees and aimed a shotgun right at me at close range. What if I had stuck my hands in my pocket?

Fortunately I had some body guards with me and I knew how the state police worked. I had seen pictures where they had done the same thing at Wounded Knee. A medicine man who had been at Wounded Knee had told me that things could get rough. So he sent some of his boys down here to be my personal bodyguards. I wasn't here to make trouble, I didn't want any bloodshed. I just wanted to be recognized, to have everybody hear my needs. We just wanted housing and some federal funds to pay my people to work.

It was so comical at times. We heard some noises across the street one night and couldn't figure out what was going on. The sheriff's office was nailing a light to shine on our front door. I said, "That's silly." So the little old lady said she was

*Declaration Of War*

going to undo her braids and dance around out in the front just to give them a good show. We were just silly. The boys did some drumming and singing. Word got out we were on the war path. I mean the silly things you see in the western shows—John Wayne-type things. They thought we were getting ready to attack! All we had was just a fly swatter. That was the strongest thing we had. The only real tragedy we had was that the newspaper kid from Sandpoint was thrown from his motorcycle. He went around the corner too quick and tumbled over. His helmet went rolling down what we called the militarized zone. One half was the sheriff's side, the other was our side.

All we wanted was just to be seen and heard. The Affiliated Tribes had a meeting in Spokane later that week. They had one whole day designated for the Kootenai to present our case, to explain why we wanted to be recognized. They made arrangements with the then Commissioner of Indian Affairs, Morris Thomson, to come down and negotiate.

We do have houses now. This particular building came from the Economic

Development Agency. Al Aimes was very instrumental in helping us get this building. The highway going out toward town is one of the grants that we got. The first batch of thirteen houses were beautifully built and nice. We have a home now, and twelve and a half acres on which the houses and the center are located. It's not a gift. Some people think, "Those Indians have everything free, they get monthly checks." We don't get monthly checks. We pay for our homes. We paid for these. We borrow and we work just like anyone else. If given the chance we pay our debts back.

I think I would do it again—a little differently, now. As I look back in my scrapbook, I swear I must have been in an altered state. Where did I get that strength to continue? Cameras came clear up to my face on the third day that I hadn't slept. I could hear the camera people saying, "She hasn't shown any signs of being tired, after so many days." I thought, "Good grief, is that all they're looking for, to see my tired lines?" Speaking for my people, and they are looking for tired lines.

You put your whole life into the Great Spirit, do the things that he is telling you to do. You kind of hypnotize yourself. Each day before I start my work I make offerings to the Great Spirit, to my Eagle Feather, to the Good Lord. I need all of those before I set out. When I retire I do the same thing. If I'm troubled I tell him, "You make the tired go away. Put it in my dreams what should be done tomorrow. Because I'm only human and I can't do all this." There are times I make decisions that way.

During the war, I didn't have time to sleep because everything was important. "Therefore I put everything that I have into you," I would pray. "You speak for me, because I can no longer do it." And it does. It does work.

If I didn't have God to believe in, I wouldn't be here. I'd probably be an alcoholic. I would have been dead a long time ago. That is what happened to the majority of my people. There is nobody else that I can look to, to do these things. So I feel that when my job is done, then I will rest. I figure there is a reason I'm still here. I guess it's to preach to my children, my grandchildren. If nobody else will hear, they will still listen to me. If and when I get somebody else to follow in my footsteps, then God will come down and say, "You have done a good job; it is time to go home." That's the way I look at it.

## Creation Of Capital

*In their drive to forge a new set of cultural relationships and a new basis for economic life, Idaho Indians seek ways to generate their own capital: capital that they can use freely to finance health, education, and opportunity for their people to grow. Raymond Abraham, chief of the Kootenai Indians since he was eighteen years old, discussed his goals.*

We are going into our second year of operation of the Kootenai River Inn. That was an economic development project the tribe started back in 1974. It was part of a ten-year comprehensive plan. We needed some way to bring revenue to the tribe. We took a survey, and people wanted to develop some type of motel resort.

The Council hired consultants to explore the potential of developing a motel in this area. The area on which the inn sits was an island at one time and had been filled in. We approached the owner and negotiated a purchase price. We had a feasibility study and market analysis prepared by a Seattle consultant. They concluded that a motel could profit in this area.

With that, we researched what funding could help us develop this motel. The Bureau of Indian Affairs guaranteed a loan from the local bank. We submitted a proposal to the United States Department of Housing and Urban Development for a grant to purchase the site from the landowner.

Once that was accomplished, the Tribal Council sat down and discussed management. The Bureau of Indian Affairs was leery of the project because other tribes had developed motels in the past and some of them failed. From my years of being the chief of the tribe and going to conferences, I learned that businesses tend to fail because tribes want to manage and operate their own businesses before they have the expertise to make it survive.

So we approached several different management firms of large successful motel businesses. One was the Coeur d'Alene Resort. We talked with Duane Hagadone and Jerry Jaeger of Hagadone Hospitality. They accepted a proposal to manage our facility. They also offered to build it as a turnkey facility. They had architects and their own construction company.

I believe it was in June of 1986 that construction started. The Department of Housing and Urban Development gave us a HUD Urban Action grant. These help communities and Indian tribes to develop projects where there is a depressed market.

Then we talked about hiring tribal members at the inn. It is hard to suddenly change a way of life for people. We couldn't just take our people and place them in here, because some of our people like to work at logging or some other type of activity. So, rather than making it a stipulation that the management had to have a certain number of Indian people working here, we wanted them to train interested tribal memb. 's to work here. It wasn't locking management in to people whose interest might not be in the motel field.

When the motel opened up in December of 1986, eight Kootenais were

*Raymond Abraham*

43

hired into different positions. That was before the gift shop opened up. We had to get additional funding to develop the gift shop. One of those eight is still there today. She started out in housekeeping. About three months ago, she was promoted to be manager of housekeeping, when the previous one retired. So that is one person that has managed to get a promotion into a managerial position in the facility. There are four Indian people working in the Eagle Springs Gift Shop.

I've always believed that the businesses I engage myself in developing are not really for people of my generation because a lot of us are employed. But we have children who are entering high school. Now they have something they can look forward to. Maybe their interest someday will be to manage. Now they have something to go to college for. They could learn the skills of actually managing the facility.

## The Rescue Of Tradition

*Many Idaho Indians, like Indians all over North America, are concerned about the collective loss of memory of their traditions, designs, ceremonies, stories, and language. Unlike immigrants to the New World, American Indians cannot return to an "old country" to hear their ancestral language or visit old shrines. The roots of their culture exist only with them. Once a language or traditional craft is forgotten, it is gone forever.*

*People in every tribe are engaged in a variety of projects to restore and perpetuate their cultural heritage. Allen Slickpoo, Nez Perce, explains his motivation; Dixie Cooper, Kootenai, was a participant in a program designed to instruct younger people in crafts no longer widely practiced, and learned how her grandparents made canoes; and Lawrence Aripa, a Coeur d'Alene artist and tribal council member, carries out a deliberate agenda of instruction and example.*

ALLEN SLICKPOO: My generation is interested to show as much authenticity as possible to the younger people who are coming up. We want to show them how and why things were done. Some of our culture is becoming too commercial. We used to dance because we enjoyed practicing our culture. It meant something in our heart. Now we find that dancers at powwows get prizes for dancing—one thousand or two thousand dollars for first place. That attracts a lot of dancers, not to practice the culture, but to dance for the dollar sign.

The old drumming songs honored a warrior who had scored in battle or taken many horses. They would honor a chief or drive away evil spirits. There were many different kinds of songs. Today the songs are changing. Now what counts is being louder and beating the drum harder. I guess it is like the problem some people have with rock 'n' roll in white culture. It isn't like the old Glenn Miller music. Today, many people won't come to play the drum because they enjoy it, but they have to be paid so many dollars to come.

DIXIE COOPER: When I was a little girl, my grandmother used to make canoes. I spent time with her every summer and used to help her. To me it was just passing time, but I didn't know this is what people used. I picked up on how to do it, then I lost the memory of it for lots of years. When they asked for volunteers to do this, no one did. I kept thinking, "Oh ask me." Finally they came and asked if I would like to be the apprentice. I said, "Sure." I jumped at it because I wanted to start one from the beginning and do it all the way through.

I don't think I really lost my heritage. It's just something that you possess. But to learn something like this, that you already knew something about, makes me feel really excited. My kids and I want to put a canoe together. Because my kids are very young, I thought it would be neat to teach them how to make one.

*Dixie Cooper*

I've always been intrigued by the way my ancestors used to travel on horseback and live in tipis. I've always thought that was an era I would have loved to have lived. To build a canoe makes me feel like I could have related to them.

When we first started, we had to find the material. The lady that taught me how to make it is from Canada. We went up there and found the maple and the cedar root. She showed me that if you just look down in the creeks you can see maple roots. That's where we gathered these. They have to stay wet to be flexible enough to tie them.

The outside part is the white pine. It's turned inside out so it will go faster and more quietly through the water. The hard part was getting the bark. The first I found was too thick and not wet enough. I had to go back out and find one that was more wet.

Now we whittle down some cedar to see if I still have the touch! The thing that I had most problems with was the knots. There are certain ways to tie the knots. I would start to wrap it and tie, but she would tell me, "You are tying it wrong."

We seal the wood with bull pine pitch to keep it from leaking. Any time it leaked, they just made some pitch soft and stuck it on there and it was ready to go.

LAWRENCE ARIPA: In my art, I try to fix some of the historical events or stories that I have heard from grandparents or other elders. I also talk to school groups and anybody that will listen to me. I tell the little ones Coyote stories. For children in higher grades I have different stories. Sometimes I talk about Indian foods. For high school and college students, I talk about tribal government or current events.

I also dance, I like to dance. I make my own dance outfits. I go to powwows. Those are the ways I try to keep the culture going and express myself at the same time. I use oils, acrylics and watercolors, and I do sculptures. I designed the Centennial coin.

## Walking In Two Worlds

*Many Idaho Indians refer to their accommodation to cultural change as an experience of walking in two worlds. While they identify strongly with the cultural ways and values of their ancestors, their lives are impacted by Christianity, television, higher education, military service, and economic ties to the world outside the reservation. To be in command of one's life often means being able to manage living in two different cultural environments simultaneously.*

LAWRENCE ARIPA, Coeur d'Alene: Many tribes will not use the owl for any artistic designs. They have their own beliefs about the owl. It may be a symbol for death or bad luck. Each tribe has its own interpretation. Since we were Christianized, we don't go by that too much anymore. But some superstitions stayed with us. Whenever my grandmother heard an owl, she thought it was some sort of message coming through. If the owl seemed to try and talk, rather than hoot, she knew that it was bringing a message of death. She never liked the owl. Strangely enough it was usually true—and scary. I remember two or three

*Lawrence Aripa*

times when my grandmother would tell my grandfather somebody was going to pass away because she heard the owl trying to talk.

I go with my feelings about hanging on to those sorts of things. I believe that I can feel whether something is right or wrong. I go by that. Some things I do believe in, and some things I throw aside. I think I try very hard at recognizing the changes in contemporary society.

I'm on the Tribal Council. There are many things that come to the Council that are different from the ways I was taught. I have to sit and think about it for awhile. I have to think about whether something new is going to be good for the tribe. Because of the tremendous changes that keep coming, some things that would not have been good ten or fifteen years ago would be good now. I have to decide on those things. There are a lot of things that I was taught as a youngster that people see from different angles now.

EMMA DANN, Shoshone: Well, you have to have money to get into and through the white world. You have to be linguistically educated to talk and speak to them. When my grandmother took care of us, she spoke the trade language. Instead of saying "grandmother" she would say "guymama." She was our guymama when she was speaking with a white person or person from another language.

When my uncle was sick, I got Indian-educated. I would go and sit with him. He taught me days of the week, months of the year, counting up to ten. Then I was put in a boarding school. Most of the education I have comes from the boarding schools. My aunt took me to Fort Hall. She took me to the matron and the matron asked her, "What is her name?" She said, "I think it's May." And out the door she went. She left me there like that. So I spent those days in the boarding school at Fort Hall.

Life there was regimented. I missed my parents and my grandmother, and other people whom I knew at home. You had to line up in the morning for roll call. An officer marched you to breakfast. We got ready for school and we went to school. We went to classes, recess, then lunch—marching over to the dining room, getting seated at tables, and then back to school.

We were not allowed to speak our language, which I knew. It was ingrown in me when I was small and stayed with me. We said things to each other in our language which the matron or some of our peers wouldn't understand. When I came back from Chimawa Indian School out in Oregon, I still retained my Indian language after six years. The Indian women here said, "You are still one of us. You are not like the other children who have lost their language and do not speak it anymore. We like you. We can ask you to say anything for us, anywhere." So they were nice to me; I liked their way of telling me so. They were good to me.

One of my daughters was going to Idaho State University. She said, "Mama, come and help us. We want to be in an international program to represent the United States. We want to show that Indians are here in the United States, and going to school here." So I said I would go, and we did an international night program for Idaho State University. My nephew said we should go to Europe, where there was a festival of minority groups in Nancy, France. We went as the Idaho State University dance troupe and went through eleven countries.

When you put your talent out for the Creator, you are able to dance anywhere. You start out with a prayer dance, and you can do it anywhere on Mother Earth.

Mother Earth gives us the food. We make tracks on her, but she regrows the grass. It keeps on growing and generation after generation it goes on and on. The circle of the year is the same for us today as it was for our ancestors. We grow in it like our ancestors did. I still go out and dig roots for my own use. They gathered seeds, roasted and pounded them to make into meal. But today we need money, too, for survival. We have more crops growing in the fields where we used to gather sunflower seeds.

I think of how strong my ancestors were that they survived generation after generation. We could live the same way today, except mechanized things have come to be. The Creator wants mechanized things for this country—it is here that we have to grow. It is up to every individual being. You have five senses in your one brain that the Creator wants you to use.

In my life, famous people have helped me along the road. When I was trained to speak English to the rich tourists who came to Sun Valley, the Union Pacific railroad provided me with two more years of education to be fluent. I met William Harriman and William P. Rogers, ambassador to Russia. Now and then I was asked to go to Hollywood to be in the pictures, but I turned that down. I wanted to be back here where I was born.

At that time my father told me no matter how far I went, I would come home. When I come in on the airplane, I know that the Big Butte and the Twin Buttes are our ground. When I came back from Europe I liked the clear water, sagebrush, and pine trees. We didn't have to plant them, they just regenerated. It was a happy feeling to come home.

RAYMOND ABRAHAM, Kootenai: I became chief when I was eighteen. It's been so long ago. I didn't understand English until I entered the third grade. My grandfather was a chief during that time. I used to watch the way he would carry on in trying to run his people the right way. There was another elderly gentleman who was chief before me. He was already old, and got ill after only being chief a year. He passed away. Then I was asked to run for the position of the chief. I said yes, because I'm very fluent in my native tongue and I still practice the culture.

I hold on to a lot of what my grandparents taught me and told me of what their lifestyles were. I used to listen to them talk at Council meetings when I was about five or six years old. I still remember what they used to say. They used to try and convince the younger generation that they should develop something for the children further on down the line. It was very difficult because during that time alcoholism within the tribe was terrible. You would have to have actually lived here during my time to know how terrible the alcoholism problem was. Watching alcoholism and growing up in an alcohol-oriented family helped me to see the importance of having something for your children when they grow up.

So I remember what the elders told me and I remember the way I grew up. That's what keeps me pushing to try different projects that will help my people along.

I try to encourage parents to teach the children the culture of the Kootenai. Your own culture is the most important. I try to keep the culture alive as the chief. It can get very frustrating, because to this day we still have a problem with alcoholism. Hopefully that will decline once programs are helping people. I believe in education, that you have to educate children from the time they are born as to what the culture is about. Then they will understand that it is a hard world.

But it is difficult. I hate to say it, but even today the language is dying out. A lot of the kids in their early teens on down no longer know it. The parents don't always encourage their children to learn it. Some parents only teach their kids a few words. Ninety percent of the language spoken in my home is Kootenai. My children understand their religious culture because I've exposed them to it. They understand it. I have cassette tapes where I've sung a lot of songs for them to listen to. They hear me and my mother speak. My two children talk to each other in the language because they're so used to it and they know it. But if the parents don't talk it, the children won't.

EMMALINE GEORGE, Shoshone-Bannock, Fort Hall: I went to school on a bus. I was fortunate, because my brothers and sisters had to walk five miles to school. There were more cultural activities when I was growing up. We had traditional ceremonials and religious dances. Indian people were still part of their culture in the fifties. I could see and understand the importance and the meaning of the Sun Dance and Native American Church ceremonials and the work of the traditional healers. Although education was always stressed to us, Indian culture was too. Having the two was always a little difficult for me. I enjoyed school and learning English.

You had to pay for your lunches. My parents weren't able to pay for my lunch, so I had to go to my grandmother's. She lived within walking distance of the school. I spent a lot of time with her. She would ask me what I was learning, and I'd tell her. She would ask me how to say various English words. And she would try, but English was very difficult for her to learn. I can understand why, because education is easier at a young age. My grandmother was trilingual. She spoke Flathead, her Shoshone language, and Kootenai.

My life was different from my parents'. I had the opportunity to learn English at home, because my brothers and my sister had already gone to school. My mother had attended a boarding school near here. My father went to a government boarding school at Tendoy in the Lemhi Valley. When they moved the Lemhis here between the years 1907 and 1909, they sent him directly to Chemawa. After that he came to this reservation. His education was vocational training. The government tried to teach them all how to be farmers and till their lands.

I used to ask how it was to live among white people. The superintendent's wife was my teacher. She asked me if I would consider going away to live at a home in Boise. I was not too sure. I felt a loyalty and didn't want to leave home, but at the same time I did. My father gave his approval. He said, "In your lifetime there are going to be a lot of things that you're going to experience. If this is what you choose, you have my blessing." My mother was not too sure. I really didn't go with her encouragement; she preferred that I stay.

When I did move to Boise, I lived with a wonderful couple who had no children of their own. So this little reservation Indian girl went to a great big city. I was terrified. I had an experience that I'll never forget, prejudice. Being a dark person in a school wasn't too bad. The kids accepted me without really involving me. When I had been at Fort Hall, I had a lot of friends and had been something of a leader. At Boise, I was not able to do that. I felt like I was alone. I had to struggle to keep myself occupied. I did like being away from the reservation. I was in a nice home, attended the summer Y-Teen activities, and had other experiences I would not have had on the reservation. My foster mother had friends who were very well-to-do people, the elite of Boise, I guess. I recall going to beautiful homes. I never would have known they existed.

*Emmaline George*

On the reservation we had a large extended family. But in Boise it was just my foster parents and some cousins. I felt a kind of partiality or loyalty to my big family, so I had trouble calling the Boise family by relative names. I enjoyed it while I was there, but that enjoyment was something that I could never, never share, even after I came home. As a matter of fact, I never did share that at all until just in the past few years, when it has gotten easier for me to talk about it.

It is hard to have two families. My parents brought me up to respect them. I knew that they were my mother and my father. I also called aunts and uncles "mom and dad." Then all of a sudden here I was, calling Anglo people my parents. They wanted to adopt me. I think that was when I felt fear. I was really close to my foster parents, but there was fear of something that I didn't know. I decided that I'd better make other plans.

I still did not want to return to the reservation. So I talked with the superintendent and wrote him a letter asking him to talk to my father. I went to a boarding school at Chilloco, Oklahoma. Again I experienced cultural shock. I went from an all non-Indian school to an all-Indian school. When you've been living among white people, you find they live a different way. Time was very important to non-Indians. My foster parents were both working people, so time was always a factor with them.

Now all of a sudden, I had never seen so many Indian students. I wondered if I would be accepted. And I was not really accepted. Maybe it was the clothes that I had or the way I carried myself or something.

The students asked me where I came from. I explained. I felt they wanted to ask more questions, but not with true understanding. I was not easily accepted. I did the next best thing, and made friends with the matrons since I always got along better with older people. Of course that wasn't the right thing to do, because those friendships brought certain advantages. It was difficult for me. But after a while they started accepting me. There were some students there from Fort Hall. I felt really good with them. After three years I returned to Fort Hall due to my mother's illness. I went back to school, but never did really complete high school. I started taking care of my elders. I completed the GED program at Fort Hall and took advantage of other programs. They were minimal but good.

I got married. On the reservation here, you don't have a choice of employment. My husband worked at the Gay Mines. That put us in an income bracket in which I never could get educational grants. But pursuing an education was always in my mind. My non-Indian family had planned for a college education for me, but I had given up those plans to return to the reservation. I've always felt a sense of guilt about that, that I owed myself something better. It was very difficult because I didn't have those advantages here on the reservation that I would have otherwise.

I think living with a non-Indian family changed my politics. Time was so important. Everything they did was planned. They planned the whole year. We Indian people didn't plan activities like non-Indians do. It's not that we didn't have a concern. We didn't plan in-depth. Their planning was very different.

VELMA BAHE, Kootenai: Once I saw a newspaper ad about bounties on Indian males and females. It hurt to know there were feelings like that right here in Bonners Ferry. When I was growing up I didn't feel that we had those problems. Seeing that on paper showed me there were feelings out there that I was unaware of. Some felt that if they could get rid of all of us, it would be a white community.

One time I watched my grandmother, who was about seventy-six at the time, being shot with a BB gun. I was with my mother, walking on the street. I heard kids yelling, "You squaws, get out of here." It was frightening. But back in those days we were teen-agers too, and that was part of teen-age life. You just yelled back again. We survived.

CAP HUGUES, Shoshone-Bannock, Blackfoot: I'm the human resource representative at FMC Corporation. The job involves everything from affirmative action to labor relations, hiring, firing, safety to training. You name it, it falls under HR.

I was born right here on the Sho-Ban Reservation. As a child, I remember my father having to work ten to twelve hours a day just to make ends meet. Because of my parents' divorce when I was seven years old, my brother, sister, and I spent most of our earlier years in Indian boarding schools, which were more like reform schools than they were educational institutions. They were holding-pens until you were old enough to be out on your own. I visited one not too long ago, and you know what? They still are.

In those schools we were not allowed to speak our native language. Even our own family members discouraged it, because during those years it just wasn't the thing to do. In the schools we were required to be especially obedient, have short hair, and march in formation to all of our classes. Only the very basics of education were taught, normally by ill-trained, and in some cases, sociopathic teachers. My father remarried when I was in the eighth grade and I left there. After entering a white public school, I found that I was so far behind my white classmates, socially and academically, that it took me until I was well into high school to catch up.

When I graduated from high school, I went to work as a laborer in a local phosphate mine here on the reservation. It was working at that job which helped me make my first real decision on what to do with my life. The guys that I worked with, other tribal members, were much older than myself, but were making the same amount of money. Unlike me, however, they were struggling to support families, pay mortgages, car payments, and provide the bare essentials for their families. For some, the struggle was too hard. Those who couldn't conform to the employer's needs ended up getting fired, usually for absenteeism, trouble with the law, drinking, or some similar reason. I didn't have to be a rocket scientist to figure out that was exactly where I, too, was headed unless I did something else with my life.

About that time a fellow in a blue uniform came by and said, "Follow me. Join the Air Force and see the world." He certainly had a willing follower in me. It was the Air Force that provided me with the opportunity to finally get a meaningful education. They put me through college and made good on their promise to show me the rest of the world. They sent me to twenty-eight different countries during the twenty years I stayed in the Air Force. Visiting all those other countries gave me an appreciation of other cultures, religions, and beliefs. After more than twenty years in the Air Force, I decided to come home. Armed with a college degree, a lot of management experience, and the additional education of being a world traveler, I would come back to my own reservation and put some of that knowledge to use for my tribe.

I was hired by FMC because of my qualifications for the job. My specialty is human resources, which is essentially what my degree is in. I suppose there will always be those who think I am a "token" here, being the first Indian in FMC's management structure. Being the first at anything, I suppose, is cause for a lot of skepticism by many different groups. People

*Cap Hugues*

seem to watch and wait for you to stumble.

For the most part, I've usually found that most people initially see me as an Indian, or just someone different than they are. But once they get to know me, they get past that. Thereafter, they either like or dislike me for what I am as a person. Which, of course, is the way it should be.

I like to think that things are going to be better for the next generation of our people. I think every parent wants to make the world better for their children than it was for them. But if it is to be better, we can't make the same mistakes that prior generations have made. By that I mean values change with each generation. If we try to impose our moral values on our children, we handicap them. For example, these days I see many Indian parents making their children wear long braids, because that is the parents' value of wanting to return to a time which they think was better. They teach the "traditional" ways of our people, rather than teaching them the social skills that they will need to succeed in the real world.

I'm not saying that what they are doing is necessarily wrong, but we also need to teach our children how the rest of the world lives and allow our children to "fit" into that culture at whatever level they are capable of achieving. We should teach our children how to keep one foot in each world, because if they choose to leave the reservation and enter the mainstream of American life, and most do, they will certainly be better prepared. The one lesson we seem unable to learn is that not being prepared for that event is the main reason for the myriad of social ills that we now suffer from on most reservations.

However, I am optimistic about the future. We are politically, socially, and economically coming of age, like an awakening giant. We have tremendous potential for all types of development on our reservation. We are becoming more and more aware of those. If we use them prudently, we can rightfully earn our place in this world—rather than have it handed to us. We have many natural resources and are in a growing part of the country. With enlightened leadership we will continue to be a part of this country's growth.

I know that is not a very "traditional" way of thinking, probably because I am not a traditional Indian. And there is nothing wrong with wanting to be a traditional Indian—whatever that is. I just don't think we can have it both ways. I have a hard time with those who dress like the white man, watch the white man's television, drive the white man's car, enjoy all the advantages that the white man has brought to our lives, and then turn around and blame the white man for everything that is wrong instead of accepting the responsibility for their own destiny.

ERNEST STENSGAR, Coeur d'Alene: Our Council pretty soon will be all college educated. They are able to speak, they are able to converse, they are able to fight in the halls of the legislature. Just like anybody else, we lobby issues of taxation. It seems like our sovereignty is infringed every time we turn around. It is a constant struggle.

We use the pageant at Cataldo to put ourselves in the limelight and tell a little bit of our story. We can use the Centennial year to let people know who we are. We are Catholics who go to church just like any other Catholics. It is the same doctrine and faith. We go to the same schools with other people. Just because we're brown and have a tradition and history doesn't make us that much different.

We would like people to realize that we are people. Our self-esteem is high. Our young people are not ashamed to say, "I am an Indian and I'll walk anywhere I want to." We're making a statement in Idaho that we are here. We go to Chamber of Commerce meetings and attend all kinds of functions just to make a statement.

We're jumping into politics. We don't really want to get involved in it, but we're finding that we have to. Now we get out and shake hands with the governor. We go meet the attorney general and state legislators and find out who they are. We encourage our people to get out and vote. For the most part, I think people know that we are around now and making a statement. They see us in the news and we are not always in traditional outfits.

# Settlement

## IDEAL AND OTHERWISE

A large number of towns in Idaho were deliberately founded by people who had visions of what an ideal community ought to be like. Some of the visions were inspired by religious values, such as those of the Church of Jesus Christ of Latter Day Saints (also known as the Mormon Church) and the Church of the Brethren. Other inspirations were more secular in origin, such as the ones acted upon by William Smythe at New Plymouth and the Potlatch Lumber Company at Potlatch.

The Mormons established their communities based on the ideal that homes and towns should emulate Gardens of Eden on earth. Their design and spacial arrangements, with people living in villages rather than spread out on isolated farms, was a deliberate choice intended to foster the best in mutual aid, personal development, and communication.

The Church of the Brethren settled communities in the Palouse River valley in the 1870s and in the Snake River Plain in the 1890s, hoping to create a spiritual oasis where members could be separate from a society they felt was too materialistic and too removed from the practice of pure Christianity. However, the membership of the churches was too small to sustain the kind of isolation that they had desired.

William E. Smythe was a midwestern newspaper editor and the chairman of the first National Irrigation Congress in 1895. A severe drought in the midwest in the 1890s had impressed upon him the benefits of irrigation. He felt that western communities based on irrigated agriculture held the answer for "transforming society" to a much improved condition. He decided to develop a colony to prove it, and organized a search committee to inspect and buy land, plat it, plant trees, and establish community standards for temperance. Filled with a spirit of optimism, the committee found land in Idaho and chose to name it after the first settlement at Plymouth.

When the Weyerhaeuser timber interests located a site for their state-of-the-art mill in 1905, they needed to provide housing for employees. They founded a town which incorporated not just the practical goal of employee housing, but also ideals for behavior, conduct, medical care, and other community needs.

While religious motivation and the surging optimism of the early twentieth century account for many Idaho settlements, the seasonal nature of the agricultural and logging industries required more labor than was available in the settled community. Idaho, and the rest of the country, sought laborers from anyplace in the world they would come—China, Mexico, Japan, Spain.

Great numbers of people labored to build railroads, irrigation canals, flumes, and roads in Idaho. The huge harvests that followed required laborers to weed, thin, hoe, and pick by hand. Most of those laborers never intended to stay. But the trains *and trucks that carried people off after the work season invariably left a few behind.*

*Minority people who could be defined or identified by religion, race, or some other convenient feature often took the blame for economic ills brought about by national economic depressions. Their ideals for personal and community progress and settlement were often thwarted or repulsed. Still, they persevered and continue to settle Idaho, grubbing out their place on new social and political frontiers. Whatever their initial difficulties with learning a new language, poverty or discrimination, people of many ethnic backgrounds have assimilated into the wider culture of "Americanized" Idaho.*

*Thomas E. Ricks was one of Idaho's greatest town and community builders, an activity he did not take up until he was fifty-two. He had already helped to settle Mormon communities at Farmington and Logan in Utah, and had been a sheriff, colonel, farmer, and builder of canals, bridges, and roads. He thought the Rexburg area was so promising that people would come eagerly from the Salt Lake Valley once they found out about its abundant possibilities. His granddaughter Marjorie Ricks Romrell and great-grandson Dean R. Grover recall family stories of the man and his work.*

DEAN R. GROVER: Thomas Ricks was my great-grandfather. He was a robust individual, comparatively short by today's stature. I suppose average height in his day was 5'8." He had a solid, square build. He was a go-getter type of individual, always involved in everything, and always getting things done. He never let any grass grow under his feet; he was always out completing one project and starting several others.

Ricks wasn't just called to lead, he led. When he was young, he got shot by Indians after the Indians had stolen some horses. Thomas E. and two other fellows, all about seventeen years of age, automatically jumped on their horses and took out after the Indians to get the horses back. In the process, the Indians shot him. He carried three of those buckshots in his back until he died. They were in too deep to remove.

His companions had thought him dead and left him. His father went back to get him. They put him on a litter and took him back to camp. They were half way across the plains before he could get up and get around. The church annals say that no one thought he had a chance to live.

He went out from Salt Lake Valley six different times to help wagon trains and handcart companies get across the plains. Then he was called to go down to help settle

*Dean R. Grover*

Las Vegas mission, which was in New Mexico Territory. He went down there for a year and a half. Then they discovered it was in Nevada. They abandoned it mainly because of the trouble they were having with the Indians. He was a pioneer type, going out on forays all the time, helping where it was needed.

In 1845, Thomas E. went to England on a mission for his church. Because of the harassment over polygamy and the pursuit of the marshals, Thomas E. established various houses for his wives and didn't have them all in one place. Thomas E. left two of his wives down in Logan when he came here, including my grandmother Tabitha. Another didn't come up here until 1893, which was eleven years after Thomas E. established Rexburg. It was hard to pin polygamy on them because they were only living with one wife. Nobody could testify to anything else.

*Courtesy of Dean R. Grover*

**Thomas E. Ricks**

His assignment was to establish the town of Rexburg and settle the upper Snake River Valley, which extended to the Wyoming and Canadian borders, to the Snake River on the south, and Roberts on the west. Whatever it took to do that was all well and good. That was part of the program as far as he was concerned.

He was fifty-two when he came up here, and was here for nineteen years before he died. It was an unusual accomplishment in that respect. He got asked to do those kinds of things because he could be depended upon. Brigham Young was the engineer of the whole program, and he used all the people who were willing to follow his directions.

Financially, Thomas E. was about at the end of the road when he returned from the mission. He went several times down to Logan to dispose of some of his property to get money to further the progress of Rexburg and the surrounding communities.

When they first came to Rexburg, he established the first store, the first grist mill, the first lumber mill, and a ferry over the river west of Rexburg that went to Roberts. He was in the middle of most any enterprise. He didn't hang on to all of those things; he usually passed them along so that other people moved into them. Most people didn't have any ready cash, but he had enough wealth to start things and get them going.

He didn't have time to sit down very long. Thomas E. had to organize and keep track of the wards and the stake. He was the stake leader. There were nineteen or twenty wards. He went around to visit them and hold conferences at the various places. People said that he was one of those kind of men who, if it was time to start a meeting, would start that meeting on time, even if only one person was there. He was so well known for that people tried to get the best of him.

Up in Teton Basin one time, he was a minute late to a meeting. His brother started the meeting without him, starting with a prayer and a song. Thomas E. just acted like nothing had happened, asking someone to pray and had another opening song. They kidded him about that for a long time. It was just part of his nature and pride, that he was going to run things the way it was supposed to be. That's the way he operated.

He accumulated his first money when he worked for the railroad. He engineered the railroad to Butte, Montana. He would hire relatives and friends. His wife's nephew William Hendricks and he were partners. They ran the company that laid the track and roadbed from Utah to Butte, Montana. He was also a farmer, and had a few thousand acres of land.

Thomas E. should be remembered for his integrity. He gave his all to establish the town. He was the instigator of Ricks College. He went out and bought the benches and chairs when they first started. When some people suggested that only children recommended by the bishop could go to school, Thomas E. said everybody should have an education. Being upstanding in the church should not have anything to do with it.

*Marjorie Ricks Romrell*

MARJORIE RICKS ROMRELL: I can tell you a lot of things that my grandmother, Ellen Marie Yallop, told about my grandfather Thomas E. Ricks. I guess he was very progressive, an industrious and energetic man. The wives lived in a circle over at Rexburg at one time. He had a child in each home who was appointed to polish his boots each night. Whenever you saw grandfather's boot sitting there, then the child was to polish his boots. I said to my mother, "If I had been alive then, I would have put the boots on the other doorstep so the other kid would have to do it." She said, "Oh, no, you wouldn't, not with President Thomas E. Ricks you wouldn't." She always called him President Thomas E. Ricks, my mother did.

I can remember my father telling me that Thomas E. approached him when he was nineteen years old. He said, "Your mother is your responsibility now. You need to house her, feed her, and clothe her because I have so many responsibilities and places I need to be. So you take over." I'm sure my father kept the promise that he made to Thomas E., and took care of his mother the rest of his life.

I think of Thomas E. as a great big stalwart, strong, muscular man. I always thought he was good looking. He was a devout man and stood for what he lived. I can vouch that my father and his brothers were those kind of people. I've always had a great respect and love for Thomas E. Ricks and my grandmother Ellen M. Yallop Ricks. I'm sure she had lots of trials and tests, because her life was not normal compared to our way of life now. But she had the necessities, and my father Alfred Ricks, Sr., made provisions through different avenues to see that people were taken care of; he was very mindful of people's needs. He was that disposition of a man I'm sure, because of the things that were done and accomplished.

*One of the earliest residents at the New Plymouth colony is Armoral Tuttle, a woman who also pioneered the public library in the town.*

New Plymouth was all plotted on paper before it was ever known where the town was to be. It originated as a reclamation project by a group that met at the Sherman House in Chicago. They made the plan and started a corporation. It was to be a place that would be especially good for fruit raising, with good soil and plenty of water for irrigation.

They sent a group out to find a place. I was very much surprised there were a couple of women on the committee that was sent out to find a site. I think there were seven on the committee, and several were women.

They toured the Northwest country here and found this place in the Payette Valley was very well suited. This was all sagebrush here, but they said that where good sage brush grew, there was good soil. Then the job was coming out and making the streets and all. It all had to be done with horses and scrapers. My husband's father helped to grade the streets in 1893. That was just two years before the city was started.

It was set up as a corporation. Each person who bought a twenty-acre farm was given a share in the town and a one-acre lot, if they would build a residence on it. That was a nice idea on paper, and nice for the people who first came here. But they found that "gentlemen farming"—living in town and working the farm—just didn't work. You had to irrigate, be on duty at the farm every day, and at all times of the day.

Many of the very first ones who came to New Plymouth did not last. They were rather well-educated people who must have had a feeling of adventure, too. I'm sure they felt they could make money. A project like that was always built up as a moneymaker. Some of them were not able to take the hard work of an irrigated farm. Getting started, with all that land clearing, was very difficult work.

Many of them were from around the Cleveland and Chicago area. I don't think that they had to work as hard farming there as they did out here. Grubbing that land was really a terrible chore in itself. But some of them stayed. Their descendants are still here.

Some moved outside to the farms, and a few stayed in town. It wasn't easy to do that. They built houses out on their farm properties later. The house that I lived in over forty years and where all three of our children were born, was one of the original ones. It had almost always been the property of a woman. It was a boardinghouse when

*Armoral Tuttle*

we moved into it and had a serving window between the kitchen and the dining room.

I can't remember that there was any great hassle about the temperance rule as long as I can remember growing up here. It was written in the original city charter that the deed to property would be forfeited if liquor were sold on the premises. Forty years later it was changed. The founders did not think it was necessary to have liquor. That was the only religious aspect to New Plymouth, if you can call that the religious side of it. The rule was broken probably, but never openly at least. I can't remember that we even thought much about it at all. Now there is a liquor store, but still no liquor by the drink. I think we've always been just a little bit on the temperate side here. We haven't had too much trouble with anything like that.

My dad came here for a job. We had left our home, an orchard farm that we had in Prosser, Washington. Prices were so bad and the times were so bad, he just could not make a living. He got a job on a cattle ranch near here. He worked there for several years and then rented a farm of his own east of town. I was married in that house.

My husband was a blacksmith. His father was more or less a blacksmith, and they had a little shop on their farm about three or four miles from town. He came out here in 1893 before the town was started. My husband spent two years in the Army during the first World War. He went through the horseshoeing school in the Army and never got overseas. Just before he was to go, a disease got started among the horses, and they had to be quarantined. Somebody had to take care of them, so the horseshoers all had to stay. When he came out he was a graduate horseshoer. His diploma reads "extra good plus," a pretty good recommendation.

When I came here in 1917, the place was solid orchards, almost over the whole valley. Then it changed very radically. There got to be too many rules and regulations being set on the orchards. Late spring frosts would ruin the crop, and the valley would be nothing. People went into dairying and row crops. The type of machinery changed entirely and the blacksmith shop surely had to change. We needed a larger place then, because the equipment was larger and of a different type. There was much more mechanical stuff than before. Horseshoeing had given out considerably by that time. He still had a horse now and then, but there were more riding horses than anything.

The library here had been started by a group of women that were just interested in reading. They were educated people and they felt the need of the library. They sent to their friends in the East and asked for books. Plus they had books of their own. I don't imagine we had more than a couple of hundred books when it first started in 1915.

I had started substituting when I was still in high school. The woman who was the librarian was ill occasionally or couldn't be there. I was in there every week to get books, so I knew the books as well as she did. She would ask me to substitute for her. After her health broke down she had to quit. So in 1922 they asked me. In the meantime I had got married and was living here in town. I became the librarian. The city paid fifty dollars a year. I got paid that for about twenty-five years. I was very directly connected with the town library for the next sixty years. I was completely and utterly unqualified as a librarian because I had no library training whatsoever. It was just because I loved to read.

Before we turned the library over to the city, we raised enough to purchase a little house and a lot. My father helped remodel it. Then I began getting a tax notice for that little house, because my name was on the deed. I persuaded the city to take it over. They were building a new city hall at the time, so the group of us gave it to the city for the assurance that we would always have a room.

*Joe Cada grew up in Potlatch, worked at The Potlatch Mercantile, the general store, and still lives there today.*

Mr. William Deary, the general manager of Potlatch Lumber Company built the mill and got it going. Then Mr. Allison Laird, his assistant, saw to the townsite department. He dictated the policies for the town itself. In the original days, the

*Joe Cada*

*Courtesy of Joe Cada*

Potlatch Company had an employment office in Spokane that would advertise for people to come to work here. They told of the advantages of low rent. There were three-room houses, four-room houses, and five-room houses. There were modern houses, which meant they had their own bathrooms, and some that weren't modern, which had outhouses. A three-room house would rent for six dollars. A four-room house that wasn't modern would rent for eight, and a five-room house for ten dollars. That's the way it was.

Those big modern houses were more or less up on the hill. They were built for a lot of the company officials that were first here in the early days. They built them according to their specifications. I don't know what those rented for, but they weren't expensive.

The employees of Potlatch Lumber company were taken care of in real good shape. People here didn't have any regrets. There were people of every nationality. There were Italians with their own little settlement. There were Swedes and Chinese. The Japanese had a boarding house in the early days.

Most all the people who worked for the company traded at the Mercantile. They were given credit and could charge anything. The store had everything in it—meat department, grocery department, dry goods department, drug department, men's furnishings, furniture department, and hardware.

Each department of the Mercantile had its own manager and little crew. They would have terrific sales. People would come from miles around to trade here. They would only have them three or four times a year. The first manager was A. McDonald. He was the one that would conduct these sales. People still remember those sales to this day. The store would feed their horses, give the men free haircuts at the barber shop. The store was just packed all the time. There would be a dance at the end of the week.

The hotel was across the street. It was really a nicely operated hotel, too. They had a manager in the hotel and it had its own dining room.

All these places were heated by steam from the lumber company. They had their own power plant down there. They ran the steam to some of the officials' houses, and to the churches, the Mercantile Company and the hotel.

We always paid the bills at the company office. Everybody was billed for their rent. The company took care of all the houses for everyone. If you needed something done on your house, inside or out, they'd put you on a waiting list. When they'd get around to it, they'd come and fix your house.

If you were real independent and wanted to do things for yourself, you wouldn't come to Potlatch. Since the company owned everything in the town, they didn't want any competition with what they had here. There were no beer parlors. They wouldn't allow anything like that in the town. That's how a lot of other little towns got quite a reputation—Onaway, Princeton and Harvard. They catered to single guys who wanted to go to the beer parlors. This was before Prohibition.

The company had their own schools here. Company officials were head of the school board and they hired all the teachers. They had real good teachers, better than other schools in the area around here, including Moscow, where you'd think they'd have the best. But a person would have to come up to a pretty high standard to be a teacher in Potlatch. They had the best principals and superintendents of the school here, too.

The original grade school building is now the Hiawatha Apartments. I went through school here, so I know that they had the best teachers. When I got out of school, I went to work for the Mercantile. I started in the depth of the Depression. Employment at the mill was about at its lowest point. When the sawmill first started, it ran two shifts ten hours a day.

The company had its own union called the Four L's, the Loyal Legion of Loggers and Lumbermen. The union and the company were more or less run hand-in-hand. The company gave them a picnic once a year and things like that. There wasn't the AFL or CIO, as in later years. The Four L's was their own company union.

In the Depression, they had to shut the mill down for two or three years and just ship lumber. My dad was working for twenty-seven and a half cents an hour. He could only work so many hours. They would run the planing mill two days a week or for whatever they had orders for. It was tough times.

Those were the days when people really appreciated the Mercantile. A lot of people charged whatever they wanted. Sometimes the store couldn't collect, so the company had to take it out of paychecks, as they did the rent.

It was a nice place to live even during the hard times. When the Depression gradually got over in 1935, they reopened the mill and things slowly got better as things got better in the whole country. When the war came, everything took off. Then they ran the mill by what the government wanted. They sold all they could ship.

Potlatch was the best small town in the United States when people lived here. Why wouldn't it be? They had the cheapest rent in the United States, I think. They had the biggest store in this whole area to trade in. They could go to their own schools here, right from first grade through high school. There was the highest standard of living for a town of this size anywhere.

The company took care of them if they worked for them at the mill; they had their own doctors. The company charged people a dollar a month for the finest doctors. At one time they had three doctors here. They had their own hospital owned by the company. The company would take a dollar a month out of their check to take care of everything. If you got sick you'd go to the doctor. That was it, a dollar a month.

*Seichi and Chiyeko Hayashida were among the 110,000 Japanese-Americans living on the West Coast who were forced to leave their homes during World War II. The Hayashidas lived near Seattle, were interned in Idaho, decided to remain in the state after the war, and now live in Nampa.*

I am not bitter. I was disillusioned. I guess that would be the word you would use. I never expected to be evacuated. At least not without being charged for something. The Army just came and said, "Within two weeks, pack a suitcase and one duffle bag. Be at this railroad siding at twelve o'clock sharp on a certain day. And get your affairs in order." They didn't tell us how long we'd be gone or when we could expect to get back.

*Chiyeko & Seichi Hayashida*

Some of our neighbors hated to see us leave. The high school principal let the school out to see us off at the railroad siding, which was about four miles from the high school. I understood that he was demoted to bus driver after this incident, after we left. He was a real fine principal and had been principal for years. One day we were all there, and the next day at noon we were gone. No Japanese-Americans left in Bellevue, Washington.

We hoped against hope that it wouldn't come to pass. Being citizens by birth, without being charged for anything, we didn't think that the government or the Army would come and uproot us. I was very disappointed.

Of the Hunt Minidoka Relocation Center, my first impression was that it was better than the one we left, the Tule Lake Center in northern California. I got to Minidoka in November 1943 and spent December, January, February there. I then went out on a permanent leave. Two months later I came after my wife and baby son.

Our son was born in January 1944 at the Minidoka center. We named him Yukio. Yuki in Japanese means snow. The day he was born, it was snowing very hard. That's why we named him that. He was born at the camp hospital. I got him home and he cried all night. So that he wouldn't bother the whole barracks, I had to carry him all night to keep him from crying. Our "apartment" was a room twenty by twenty feet square with no running water. It was just a bare room. It had a pot-bellied stove for heating purposes. We strung some rope and put blankets down between to separate families. There was a central mess hall, latrines, and showers.

I remember lining up for breakfast, lunch and supper. We had to wait in line. Every now and then they would get ice cream. You waited in a line a block long to get it. We sure got tired of lamb and mutton stew. It had curry in it. To this day I can't eat curry. But we never went hungry, we got fed. I say that much.

Life was regimented. Security was tight. You wouldn't dare go near the fence. Very little privacy. There were rows of wash basins where we brushed our teeth every morning.

It was like a city. When all ten thousand people were there at full capacity, it was the third largest city in Idaho. Evacuees in the nursing profession took care of hospital work, those with newspaper experience started a camp newspaper, barbers cut hair. People experienced with restaurants did the cooking. There were some electricians and plumbers and there was a fire department. There were block managers, who would be like the mayor of a small town. There was a landscape artist, who really made the flowers bloom.

The first spring they cleared the sagebrush and grew most of their food. They had plenty of water, being located right next to the North Side Canal. They raised chickens, hogs, cattle, and all kinds of vegetables.

In order to get leave from the camp, you had to say you would help any way you could. Since I was a farmer, and my wife was from a farm family, and that was the only work that was really open at the time, we went out to do farm work. I didn't like the life in camp, being cooped up in a mile square with ten thousand other people. We went out as soon as we could. I spent less time in camps than most of the people.

We did farm work. There was nobody to do the work, so they wanted us to come. Farmers' groups and the sugar factory sent recruiters to provide their own bus and everything. I even watched over German prisoners of war, picked them up in their camp, brought them back in the evening.

It was harder work than we were used to, back-breaking work—thinning beets, weeding onions, picking potatoes by hand. That was before mechanized farm equipment. We were given the credit for saving the beet crop in western Idaho in 1943.

I went back to Bellevue in 1945 to see what was left of my property. Everything was gone. I had left all my stuff with a man who I thought was a friend and had known for a long time, all my adult life. He wasn't there. The man that was there showed me a government bill of sale for all the stuff I left. He showed me an itemized listing of everything I left behind—farm equipment, tools, household goods. I didn't have any money, so I went out to work. I didn't own my land, I was leasing my land. Those that owned their land went back because their farm was still there, although they'd lost a lot of their possessions. Those that had businesses started over again.

But farming out here was better than farming as I knew it there. I was going to farm anyway. There wasn't much I could do with only a high school education. Today I could go back, but I don't feel like going back. Relocating in Idaho from the Minidoka center, I don't regret. I like Idaho. I say Idaho is home now. The last few years have been good to me.

My son's reaction to our experience is that he does not understand that it could have happened. He went through high school and college in Idaho and to the University of Oregon. He has been a math teacher for twenty-two years. When he was fourteen we thought he was old enough to understand if we told him of our experiences, which we did. The first thing he said was, "I can't believe that it ever happened." We explained why, and gave him all the books that related to it, and the reasons that led up to it. He doesn't talk about it, but he knows. Many parents our age have not explained this to their children. I think people of his age don't believe it could happen again. They kind of put it in the back of their minds. I don't think it will happen quite as easy again, especially with Japanese-Americans. The Japanese American Citizens League would fight something like that, no matter what.

The main reason that we were evacuated was because the leaders and public in California had been trying to get the Japanese-Americans out of their area. They wanted the farm land and the businesses. This was a good time to do it, because people were saying that there would be fifth-column activity helping Japan. We all lost what we had. We were only allowed to come to camp with a suitcase, what you could carry by yourself, and a duffle bag for bedding. There has never been one documented case of espionage or any fifth-column activity by any Japanese-American citizen or alien. The FBI has said so, and the Army has said so.

People should not forget these things. That's my biggest concern. I'm past that age where it's going to hurt too much now. But the government put people behind barbed wire, without charging that group of people with any wrongdoing whatsoever. There was never a trial. You were just told, "Because your name is a Japanese name and we are at war with your forefathers' country, we are going to round you up and put you in camp for the duration." I'm sure that they knew they made a mistake after about a year and a half. They didn't have to wait for the war to end before they knew.

I have been asked why we waited so long—forty years—to start redress legislation. The main reason was that the Japanese American Citizens League did not have access to the facts to prove that it should not ever have happened. When the Freedom of Information Act was passed, we were able to go into the archives and get the facts to back our reasons for asking for redress and an apology.

On August 10, 1988, President Reagan signed a bill that would offer an apology and a lump sum payment of $20,000 to each and every individual that was confined to a camp. Nothing has been paid to us because Congress has not appropriated the money.

_Idaho continues to support a population of migrant laborers who stay only part of the year. Alberto Fuentes, a native of Eagle Pass, Texas, is one of them. He_

_supervises other workers, and paused from his responsibilities at a farm field near Weiser to talk about his work._

Q: How long have you been involved in migrant labor?
A: Count the year 1951.
Q: And have you been coming to Idaho since then?
A: To Idaho, ya.
Q: Every year?
A: Every year, ya.
Q: You must be pretty skilled at this work right now?

**Alberto Fuentes**

A: Yes, a lot of time.  A lot of years.

Q: And doing pretty much the same jobs?

A: Yes, same jobs, thining beets and weeding onions.

Q: These are the kind of jobs that have to be done by hand?

A: By hand, yes.

Q: Even thirty years later?

A: Yes.

Q: How come they don't have machines to do that yet?

A: I don't know.  I don't know.  Maybe the machine is no work pretty good. Echemano, he try one machine, it's no good.

Q: Are these people here pretty proud of the work that they do?

A: Ya.

Q: Does it take a while to learn it?

A: Ya.

Q: How long, would you say?

A: Well, too long and pretty good, maybe take about three weeks, four weeks. Every year come new people here, it takes a long time to learn it, you know. What they are doing is pretty hard to me.

Q: Is it hard being a supervisor?

A: Oh ya.

Q: What's the hardest part of that?

A: Ya, well the hard part is all the time watching and keep going.  That's all.

Q: How long have you been a supervisor?

A: Oh, about 1963 to this time.

Q: What do you like best about this job?  Why do you keep coming back here year after year?  Is it the money?

A: Well, over in Texas is pretty hard for me.  Over there make sick.  Coming over here is pretty good.

Q: Are there enough jobs down there?

A: Right now, got plenty jobs.  Have plenty jobs in Texas.  Pay pretty good. Some people coming over here, no have school.  They live close to the border and not talk English and have no job.  Some people just have little English and have pretty good job.  Coming over here, you no have experience in the job. You get the job, you know.

Q: Do you find enough people?

A: Oh, yes.  Is enough people to harvest this year, I think.

Q: Is it hard to find people usually?

A: Sometime hard.  No place to stay, just a labor camp.

Q: And that's not big enough sometimes?

A: Not big enough, ya.

Q: What about the money for this kind of work?  In Idaho is it about the same as anywhere else?

A: I don't think so.  Over here it pay, pay $3.50 right now.  I don't know in other place.

Q: Does that sound low to you?

A: No, is all right.

Q: Is the life here as good as it is in Texas for you in Eagle Pass?

A: Ya.  Ya.

Q: Better than it is in Mexico?

A: Mexico, I don't know.

Q: When was the last time you lived in Mexico?

A: Oh I don't live in Mexico.

Q: Do you ever think about staying here in Idaho, settling here, making this your permanent home?

A: No, I stayed here five years and the doctor say, yes go Texas. Over here is pretty cold for me.

Q: Cool in the summer but too cold in the winter?

A: Ya, I work for Cider Products, five years.

Q: But, some people do think about staying, don't they?

A: Yes, some people, ya.

Q: And do you think that this makes a good place for them to make a home? Can they find work and good places to live if they stay?

A: Maybe.

Q: Do you feel welcome when you come up here in the summers?

A: Oh ya, ya, ya.

Q: And when you go into the towns, are you treated fine?

A: Ya, ya, ya. Fine, pretty good.

Q: Do you notice any discrimination at all?

A: No, no, no. Is live over here, born over here in United States. Is my home.

Q: Is Idaho a little bit different than maybe Texas is?

A: Oh ya, different, ya, lot of difference. Pretty good weather.

Q: Are they not as friendly, there in Texas?

A: No, is same, I think. Over there in Texas is different. Everybody talk Spanish. White and Mexican and Negro talk Spanish. San Antonio, talk spanish, Houston, Dallas everybody talk Spanish. Here is different.

Q: Since 1951 what kind of changes have you seen?

A: Oh, lot of changes. Put a lot of chemicals in the onions, no weeds and just big hoe, you know, lot better that way. For me.

Q: Before it was a short hoe and there were a lot more weeds?

A: Ya, more weeds, ya. Right now, is pretty good.

Q: Do you ever worry about the stuff they put on? The pesticides and all?

A: No, no I don't think so. I don't have a case that way. All the people don't say nothing.

Q: Have the camps changed?

A: Oh ya. Well the camp has changed. In 1951 they have a little one. Right now is pretty good cabins over there to live the people.

Q: And the cabins are fine?

A: Ya, right now is pretty good, ya. They have a school for little kids.

Q: In the summer?

A: Ya, in the summer, pretty good.

*Camilo Lopez is an attorney from Caldwell. He is active in politics and as a spokesman for Hispanic people in southwestern Idaho.*

I first came to Idaho in the early 1950s and saw the signs that said, "No Mexicans or dogs allowed." I remember those days. Many of us do. When we came into towns like Caldwell we could only come in on Saturday afternoons to do our shopping. The farmer would call the local sheriff and say, "Well, I'm sending my Mexicans down. They'll be in to do the shopping. Shepherd them around." The sheriff would say, "Get them out of town by six o'clock, otherwise if they're still here I'll put them in jail and I'll call you, and you can come get them. But you will have to pay a fine." We had to endure that.

People ask me, "Well, Camilo, why don't you go home?" But this is my home, and in Idaho, I feel comfortable. Idaho, being twenty years behind the times, prejudiced, with the hatred and bitterness, is still like an old coat. I wear it, and I feel comfortable. Isn't that tragic? But it's true. This is the environment that I grew up in, and I feel comfortable.

The only consolation we have is that our next generation at the turn of the century will be able to say, "We have arrived and put old dinosaurs like Camilo to rest." Great, then I can retire.

Idaho has got to get its act together and help us. Part of that is recognizing that we are here. We are hard working, productive members of society. We have our problems, bad guys and good guys. We have our proportionate share of everything, just like Anglo-Saxon America. But don't blame us for all your ills.

I returned to Idaho in 1968 from California where I was successful. I had been to the other side of the mountain and had competed with the Anglo and I was successful. When I returned to Idaho, nothing had changed. The Hispanic communities were divided and were fighting each other. It was chaos. No wonder we were having problems. We couldn't get beyond our own petty concerns to look at the bigger picture. White Idaho was moving and we browns of Idaho were not. Through the 1960s and into the 1980s, individuals like myself started getting together, saying, "This has got to stop."

I came to Canyon County in 1978. There was no unity. We had some professionals making it here and there because of the Great Society programs of the 1960s. But not many. The Hispanic community was in chaos. That's when we started organizing. We started bringing people together,

**Camilo Lopez**

saying, "This is it, we will unite. We may have our petty problems, and we can take care of those problems, but when we confront white Idaho, we will confront it united. That's the only way they will listen to us."

And it has worked. The Hispanic community in Idaho has united. It has a sense now that we do matter, that we do count. We have made a little progress, and we will make more. Now the question is, "Will Mr. and Mrs. White Idaho work with us?" Will they say "Those folks are here, they deserve just as much of a chance as I do?" Or will they resent us and fight us? I don't know. In my old age I am starting to mellow, and I think maybe there is light at the end of the tunnel. Maybe there is a glitter of hope for my children in the future as far as Idaho is concerned.

When I ran for the Legislature, I was trying to prove that failure is not bad. Here I am, a short fat Mexican, and a radical liberal Democrat to boot (and who has been called worse names than that) running in conservative Republican white Idaho. I didn't need a sign from God to tell me that I was going to lose. What I was trying to prove to young Hispanics coming up was that there is nothing wrong in playing the game, playing it fair and losing. Somebody, somewhere, ahead of me will make it. I've run for every office that you can imagine. If there was an office for broadcaster, I probably would run for that, too. Did I want it? No. Had I got it, what would I have done? I don't know. It scares me to think about it.

We have seen progress. We've seen a little, here and there. Hispanics are on the school board, on city councils. We are moving. People from the Hispanic community are now willing to face failure. But it is very depressing to read "Lopez loses by a landslide." It hurts me, too. Well, we made the point, and I can get my pats from my community. That was the lesson to the young Hispanic: you don't have to fear failure, failure is good, if done for a purpose.

That was in 1984. The best thing was the pats I got. I ran against a nice prim and proper little lady. I couldn't razzle and dazzle this beautiful lady. They would tar and feather me, send me out of the county on a rail. But I got 10,000 votes in Canyon County. That tells me maybe there is hope. My community voted for me, those who could. But they were only 2,000 votes. Had I only gotten those, then I would have really felt bad. I would have said the run was worthless. But I got my 2,000 Hispanic votes and 8,000 Anglo votes. People were willing to judge me and say, "Hey, Camilo! maybe we should give you a chance." Was I defeated? No, I won. When I run for city council or other offices, I see my margin of votes increasing. I guess if I run long enough, I'll get elected. But I don't want it. Other Hispanic individuals, young men with more to offer than I, are going to get it. That's what I want.

*Tom Zabala is a third-generation Basque who lives and works in Boise as an architect.*

My grandparents emigrated here just after the turn of the century. They came as part of the sheepherding industry. My father was born in Jordan Valley, Oregon. He worked in that area and eventually came to southern Idaho. My mother's parents also came as part of the sheepherding industry. Later they went into the boarding house business. Their boarding house, Capitol Rooms, was at the present site of the 700 Idaho Tower Building.

My grandparents came from the Bilbao region of Spain. I don't know much about their lives there, but suspect that they were involved in agricultural activities.

I think my grandparents would probably be very proud of the fact that we've been able to come to this country and be absorbed into the culture of this country. Speaking as an architect, I think my profession has universal acceptance in any society. There are probably not very many practicing Basque architects within our area or in the Northwest. Unfortunately, my grandparents passed away before I was able to achieve that recognition, but I think they would be very proud of me.

In a sense I had a foot in both cultures. Because my grandparents were here, we had their influence with food and language. My parents, for whatever reasons, chose not to teach us the Basque language. They both speak Basque and Spanish fluently, and they often used that to our disadvantage and to their advantage! They chose to Americanize us, I guess.

*Courtesy of Tom Zabala*

**Tom Zabala**

At this point in my life, I regret that I didn't take the time, or that they didn't take the time, to tell us more about the Basque culture and our heritage. It's embarrassing at times for me now, because there are occasions when I would relish knowing more. My fear is that my son will carry on my name, but not really have the benefit of that knowledge or experience.

The Basque culture is unique and the language is not based on any of the Romance language groups. I hope that my son will see it as unique and investigate it more. I hate to see him lose it; I think it's an essential part of his heritage. What he carries forward will be important for his children and their children.

The Basque history in this area is a very strong one. People are very proud of that heritage. They are doing a lot to reinforce it and to get their children knowledgeable and sympathetic to the importance of knowing where they came from. Whether you're a professional or a blue collar worker, we've all come a long way—conquered language problems, getting people in every walk of life in this community, and being an essential part of the growth of our immediate area, the state of Idaho and the entire Pacific Northwest. We have become politicians, professional people, blue collar workers, just as people from other cultures have.

I am not aware of any circumstances that may have prevented the Basque people from retaining their cultural roots. There has not been the discrimination that one sees with other groups and other cultures. We've really been accepted on our own. We are a hard-working people, a very moral people, a very religious people. Others have accepted us for those values, and we have been able to take our place in Americanized society.

# Religion

## CHRISTIANITY IN IDAHO

### Missionaries To The Indians

*Long before Father Pierre DeSmet met the Coeur d'Alene Indians in 1841, the Jesuit priests had brought Christianity to the native people of South America. The Jesuits' experience there gave them an ideal for which to strive when they decided to establish missions for the Indians of North America. A Jesuit missionary, Father Thomas E. Connolly, S. J., still lives among the Coeur d'Alene Indians in Idaho.*

It was Father DeSmet's idea to model the Indian missions of the West after the "Reductions" of Paraguay. This was a type of missionary effort intended to create a self-sustaining community which would be away from white people, the traders, the settlers, and all those who wanted to use Indians as slaves or to pillage their resources. That effort ultimately failed in Paraguay, because the Indian mission cities were so economically successful for 150 years. There was tremendous jealousy over this totally Indian state in the interior.

But this was Father DeSmet's dream for the Rocky Mountain missions of the West. He tried to develop mission communities that had an economic base, so people would not have to continuously travel. He tried to develop peace with the Blackfeet, so the western tribes wouldn't always have to be fighting them when they went buffalo hunting in Montana. That's why he wanted the missions to be away from the crossroads of the immigrants and settlers.

Still there was always a lot of crossover and cultural exchange. The missionaries learned to speak the Indian languages and to eat Indian foods. They also taught farming, and the Coeur d'Alenes became very successful farmers. There was good farm land at Cataldo before the tailings washed down from the mines. But there wasn't enough land there for everyone, so the missionaries looked for another place to settle.

Cataldo was also on the crossroads of civilization. The Mullan Road was bringing wagon trains through there on the westward journey toward Walla Walla. The discovery of gold in the mountains to the south had prospectors flooding into the area. On several occasions, hundreds of prospectors camped around the Cataldo mission. They had heard a rumor that the fathers had the Indians mining gold in the mountains, and everybody wanted it. So Cataldo became an untenable place.

The mission moved to a spot south of Coeur d'Alene Lake. They named it "DeSmet" after the founder of the Rocky Mountain missions and tried to create an all-Indian society. It was finally made into a "reservation" where they could have their own land, their own tribal government, run it their own way, sustain themselves, and educate their children.

They were very successful, but it was a "communal" system. Reformers in those days thought that Indians would do better by learning the concept of "private property." So in 1909 the government allotted each living Indian 160 acres. On the Coeur d'Alene reservation that took up about one-third of the reservation land. The other two-thirds was then declared surplus and white settlers were invited to come in and take the rest of the lands that the government had promised the Coeur d'Alenes could keep forever.

That made it impossible to sustain an Indian homeland and an Indian government because land ownership was now all checkerboarded between the Indians and the whites. Now there was increasing pressure to be "white." The government demanded that no Indian languages be spoken in the schools. In time, everything "Indian" came to be looked down upon.

During all these times, missionaries were usually good to people and got along well. But they also pushed them and were often insensitive in many ways. Indians had to give up a lot of things they probably shouldn't have had to give up. They could have remained bilingual, as most Europeans are today.

Older spiritual ceremonies relating to the forces of nature also had to be given up. The missionaries had no way of understanding Indian "medicine power"—a kind of psychic power of relating to the forces of nature through the spirits of animals, birds, fish, and natural phenomena. In the old days, many people could go into a kind of trance to become one with an animal spirit and share some of its power.

It was not possible for early missionaries to see this as a good "natural" power. Missionaries tended to think in terms of either "angelic" or "demonic" spirits. "If this isn't formally of Jesus, it must be demonic." So Indians were forced to give up their "medicine" ways and accepted "Catholic" ways instead.

What do I think of Circling Raven?* Well, the real essence of Christianity is that the Creator-God wanted to manifest himself more intimately to his people—so much so, that he became a human being himself in the person of Jesus. The words and the power of Jesus spread throughout the whole world, and they continue to act upon his people everywhere.

It seems to me that if God wants to enrich the lives of his people in this way, he prepares them for it.

The prophets and the Jewish people of the Old Testament were prepared for the coming of the Messiah. They were expecting him. There is no reason to think that God does not do the same thing for every people, on every continent.

From that theological perspective, I think Circling Raven's vision was God's revelation. It prepared the Coeur d'Alene people for deeper enrichment and for refined spiritual teachings that would enhance what they already had from their

*Thomas Connolly , S. J.*

* See conversation with Ernest Stensgar in "Indians"

elders and their medicine men.

Jesus refined some of the teachings of the prophets and the teachers of the Old Testament. This led to some conflict, but also led to a more purified spiritual way. Perhaps Christianity has done the same thing here. Here, too, it has caused some conflict; but here, too, it has led to a refined spirituality. The thrust of Christianity has been to focus everything on the task of universal love and universal forgiveness. The Christian sacraments are a new ceremonial way of obtaining the power of Jesus for this task.

Times have really changed a lot in almost 150 years of Coeur d'Alene mission history. In the early days at DeSmet much of life revolved around the mission. There was a large girls' boarding school and a large boys' boarding school. Everyone went to school here. They had great ball teams for youth and adults, boxing matches, social events, and dramatic presentations. The annual Cataldo pageant about Circling Raven's vision grew out of mission life in the 1930s.

After 1945 automobiles became common. People traveled more, and there was a lot more to do in a much more materialistic world. People have lost much of the spirituality and religion of their grandparents and elders. The times are not as spiritual as they once were.

But I think the real Indian values are still spiritual and non-materialistic—love of family and sharing. Indians are still much more willing to share and loan everything they have to anyone else within their extended families. They often don't think of taking care of themselves and their own needs first if there is a call to share with someone else. Material things aren't as important with them as they are with us. They will sometimes say, "Well, it's just money." If somebody borrows a car and wrecks it, it's not as big a thing for them as it would be for us.

They enjoy the things of the earth, of nature, and having things more natural. If they have a nice home that meets their needs on the inside, they often don't worry so much about whether it needs a new coat of paint. They don't worry about keeping up a lawn and gardens for the sake of appearance. They have warm shelter, food on the table, and room for all their family to come.

My thirteen years at DeSmet have been something like riding a roller coaster, flying along between tremendous highs and tremendous lows. People are very human and spontaneous, often very caring and sharing, and always with a good sense of humor and of survival. There are powerful spiritual times at feast days, and especially when they gather at wakes and funerals.

But there has also been a lot of social and cultural disintegration, a lot of broken families, frustrations, financial problems, and a lot of sickness from hard lives. I've shared a lot of sad times with them, and I'm very touched by it.

It's a good life in many ways because of the depth of what people feel—the depth of their sadness and the depth of their joy. It's an intense and powerful life. I laugh at their stories, stuff myself at their feasts, cry at their wakes, dance at their powwows. I've found it a life of highlights, nothing humdrum!

But you have to be able to shift gears from one culture to another. It's been much easier for me to understand the difficulties of their path of integration by seeing my own difficulty in acculturating to their ways. In order to survive, Indian people have had to adapt to the ways of others. If they move to the city for employment or education, they have to live in a very different world. That is extremely difficult. Many of them choose to come back home. They haven't necessarily failed, but the call of family and what is traditionally the "right" way for them is so strong that they want to come back home and be able to do things in their own "right" way.

That same cross-cultural conflict occurs for somebody like myself, born in a non-Indian world, who comes to live in an Indian community. To maintain my own identity, I have to be able to hear the call of my own roots and be able to do things the "right" way taught me by my own parents. But to live here and adapt successfully, I also have to be able to hear the call of the Indian community's roots, and to do things the "right" way taught by their ancestors.

To shift gears from one culture to another is not easy. But it is a rewarding experience. It's just important to learn how to shift gears comfortably.

## Circuit Riding Preachers

*Eliza and Henry Spalding, Presbyterian missionaries who went to live among the Nez Perce in 1836, were also dismayed by the intrusion of violent and godless miners and the vices they brought with them. Still, gold fever gave way to permanent settlement eventually. But settlement was sparse, and people were too poor in most areas to support a church and its furnishings, much less a permanent pastor to live amongst themselves. Preachers had to ride a "circuit" in order to bring people formal contact with their God. Still sparsely settled, Idaho continues to be regarded by many denominations as missionary territory. Outside of the few larger cities in the state, ministers of the Lord are still riding circuits. One of them is Clifton Morey who rides between Juliaetta and Southwick often accompanied by his wife.*

*Clifton Morey*

The reason we are here in Juliaetta is that these people asked us to come after they lost their previous pastor, an older fellow who retired. They needed somebody to fill their pulpit on Sunday mornings. That is all they really wanted. Because they are a small church they don't have the financial means to support a full-time pastor. So they were looking for somebody who could supply a spiritual meal for them at least on Sunday mornings.

We were at Southwick at the time. They called us down and asked me if I would bring their Sunday morning services. This whole community works this way. The Methodist pastor here serves Kendrick and Cavendish up on the hill. The Lutheran pastor serves the Lutheran church at Cameron and also the one here in town. So there are a number of pastors who do double duty simply because the populations of the churches are not large enough to support full-time ministers.

It's not like riding a horse from place to place now. I've got a little 1986 Toyota. We have put 150,000 miles on that little car. We move up and down the road all right. But it's worth that to me for a ministry. If I have to work the rest of my life in order to support a ministry in a community so the people can come to know the Lord on his terms, then it's worth that to me. I've seen what he can do to change lives. I'm in favor of him doing that in all the lives that he possibly can.

The congregation shows its support in a lot of ways. It's more of an understanding than anything else. You know when somebody appreciates you by the way they talk to you. They tell you periodically that they really appreciate your ministry. I hear things backdoor. I heard backdoor from somebody in the Southwick church that somebody in the Juliaetta church had indicated how much I had helped them spiritually in their lives. That's why I'm in it. When I hear something like that, it means I'm doing my job. They assist financially. They are more than generous.

They know I've got a full-time job down in Lewiston. I work as a consulting civil engineer down in Lewiston for a private consulting firm. We stay busy, my wife and I. We have two kids—they're both gone from us now—so we stay real busy between church and preparation for church. We recently started an exercise program, so that's taken some time out of our day as well.

From time to time, people need to be visited. When you work during the week, you spend a lot of time on weekends catching up on things that need to be done around the house. We just have pretty much a full load on weekends it seems like. They don't need to assist me all that much. They support this ministry in just about any way that you could possibly think of. More than anything else, they are glad that there is somebody here ministering in their church.

There will always be a need for small community churches in Idaho. I'm confident of it. It's a rural state. There are so many tiny towns like Southwick and Juliaetta where there are not a lot of people to support a big thriving church and a full-time pastor.

*Quincy M. Jensen*

## The Mormon Experience

*The religion preached by the Church of Jesus Christ of Latter-day Saints appealed to many people in Europe who heard about it in the decades after prophet Joseph Smith founded the church in 1830. The teaching of the church, as revealed in the Book of Mormon, was that the Garden of Eden had been located in the New World. This continent would be the gathering place at the end of the world when Christ would come to rule the earth for a thousand years.*

*Anyone who converted to the church, therefore, would almost certainly choose to immigrate to the United States. The church was so successful that it had to find some way to help its new members leave Europe and to arrange for their settlement in the New World. From his center at Salt Lake City, Brigham Young organized a colonization and settlement program that filled Utah's Wasatch Valley and then extended into a territory that now covers part of ten Western states.*

*After the settlement of Cache Valley in northern Utah, it was only a short time before the potential of the country north of Bear Lake would be discovered. People poured into the valleys of eastern Idaho, gathered in villages, and practiced their faith. Mormon communities were utopian in nature, in the sense that economic organization, town planning, civic duties, and religious practice were all integrated into a coherent whole.*

*In territorial days Mormons voted in a block, usually for Democratic party candidates. As their proportion of the population of Idaho approached one-third, they held the balance of power between Republicans and Democrats. To deal with this, Republican Fred Dubois led a drive to make his party dominant in Idaho. He capitalized on the national and local repulsion for the Mormon practice of polygamy, practiced mostly by Mormon leaders, in order to bar Mormons from voting. Part of the strategy was to put such polygamist leaders in prison. To this end, Dubois, who was the federal marshal, did his best to round them up, try them, and send them off to prison. One of those imprisoned was David Jensen, the grandfather of Quincy M. Jensen of Idaho Falls.*

Grandfather David grew up in Norway, married Sarina Jensen and had two children, one of whom died in Norway. He joined the Mormon church and immigrated to America, bringing his wife's eighteen-year-old sister Julia. They first went to Lehi, Utah, then Franklin, and finally homesteaded Worm Creek north of Preston.      The story is that Sarina looked for a husband for Julia, but couldn't find anybody suitable. So Julia became the second wife of David. Sarina was sickly, and passed away. This left Julia.

In May 1886 the marshals started having polygamy trials. The modus operandi was to gather in the courtyard of the Blackfoot courthouse in the morning. They called out the names of the ones to be tried in the morning. The rest would come back at one o'clock in the afternoon and hear a further list of names. Finally David was called for the trial. The family account said that three men testified against him. In the official records they have the full name of one, the last name of another, and the third name was never filled in. The family says that he didn't know any of them.

Even though he only had one wife at the time, they made it retroactive and charged him anyway. That might have been why he was only given a six-month sentence and sent to Boise. The ones who were sentenced for longer were sent to Detroit. There were twenty-three others sentenced that day. They had started at ten o'clock in the morning and quit about four, so they must have run them through rather rapidly.

*Courtesy of Quincy Jensen*

*Sarina, Julia, and David Jensen*

David took his son aside and told him to hitch up the team and get started for Preston. He could probably make it to Portneuf or Pocatello by that night. The next night he could get down through Red Rock and then he'd be home sometime on the third day. He gave him instructions about what should be done with the cattle and so on.

David went down the old steps to the bullpen and was kept for the night there with the other polygamists. He went to Boise and worked in the quarry part-time. That's about all we know.

David came back and picked up where he left off. My father was born in August of the next year and then a younger brother was born. Since he had been sentenced for polygamy when he only had one wife, he came back and said, "Well, I've been sentenced for more than one." So he went out and got him another wife.

In the little cabin on Worm Creek that David and Sarina lived in was a big wooden round table. It had four feet that went out from the center column. There was a rug under that, and below the rug was a hole in the floor. It was dug deep enough and big enough so a person could get down in that hole and be there for a while without any severe discomfort while hiding from the marshal.

In the Preston cemetery there are three graves that say "Wife of David Jensen." So that was the story of my grandfather.

I think back to this time and the people who lived that particular part of their religion. I'm glad it's not me to judge; there is another judge who will take care of all that.

It's strange, but in the families who really practiced polygamy, the wives got along well. They looked out for each other. It has been said that a very small percentage of people practiced it and only those who could afford it. But sometimes you hear that the ladies were so poor they only had one good dress and had to take turns wearing it to town. There were other families that were not so fortunate. Some problems were overlooked.

I don't know that very many people talk about polygamy. I don't think they're as interested in it as I am. The only way to accept it is to feel that it was an inspired commandment. But when you start to talk that way, you seem to start defending it, and then you seem to be advocating it. Then you start getting in trouble. So most people just don't discuss it.

*Besides discontinuing polygamy, Mormons also stopped voting in a block. Church leaders after 1890 committed themselves to full participation in the two-party political system and encouraged the same from the general membership.*

*The church did not give up its interest in the economic and social well-being of its members. It invested in the expansion of the railroad from Utah north into Idaho and Montana so that the farmers along the way could transport their crops to markets. The church developed cooperative enterprises and stores in towns. It financed the establishment of factories to make sugar from sugar beets, so that farmers would have a cash crop as a result of their summer labor and also have employment during the winter.*

*When the Depression struck the country, the church had to deal with another form of economic need. Willis H. Yost is the Multi-Region Welfare Services agent for the church in eastern Idaho. His district covers the area from Salmon to Jackson, Wyoming, Firth to Yellowstone. He discussed the system from the Idaho Falls Bishop's Storehouse.*

The church welfare system was established in 1936 right after the Depression because there was so much unemployment. The church felt that people needed to get on with their lives and become employed. There were a lot of needy, so it began by people helping people. The idea was to eliminate the dole. The church wanted to make people self-reliant and increase their self-esteem.

The system is a bit complex, but most intriguing. Most of the products that you see in the bishop's storehouse have the Deseret brand, which means that they were produced, prepared, or canned through a church-owned welfare project. After it comes into the bishop's storehouse, it is dispensed throughout the world on a bishop's order. This is a store where money cannot buy anything.

There are many and varied activities. In Idaho Falls, we produce peas. We can peaches, pears, and apricots, and make stews and soups. In New York, for instance, they make soaps and cleaners and solvents. There are different projects all over the world. San Diego has a large fish and seafood cannery project. Even macaroni and spaghetti are produced. Dried milk. Rolled oats. We have a dairy in Menan, Idaho, that produces all of our dairy products. We don't have the facilities to process the milk, so we hire Challenge Creamery to process the milk and return it to us.

Apples are grown over in the Boise Valley on one of our production projects and then brought over here for canning. The cannery operates strictly under Food and Drug Administration guidelines and they watch us very carefully. People wear aprons and cover their hair. Everything has to be done right, up to code.

When people need help, they go to their bishop. The bishop and the Relief Society president evaluate their needs. If the family needs commodities, they fill out a bishop's order and the order is filled. It is something like a grocery store, only we don't have cash registers.

The Relief Society president usually writes the bishop's order. The Relief Society is the largest women's organization in the world. They do a great deal to teach and train in the areas of being a wife, homemaker, and mother. They have a great sensitivity to the needs of those who are less fortunate. The Relief Society manages to fill those needs. They play a very important role in carrying out the assistance and getting information to where it is needed. It is people looking after people. That's what the Lord intended, I think: "Feed my sheep, take care of each other."

We expect people to work according to their ability. If they can come here to the bishop's storehouse and assist us in stocking shelves and filling orders, they do so. They may come over to the cannery and assist in the cannery operation, or they may volunteer at Deseret Industries or one of the production projects. In the Idaho Falls area, we have several production projects. Taylor View Farm raises all the potatoes for the entire church welfare system. We also raise half of the peas for the entire welfare system.

Many people volunteer who are not receiving assistance. At the cannery, there are probably forty to fifty people. I

*Willis Yost*

would doubt that any one of them are receiving assistance through the welfare system. They just come and volunteer. Right now they are canning applesauce that will end up throughout the world.

I think this is a very important part of church activity, not only to the receiver, but also to the giver. It is important that we share our time and talents to assist those who are in need—socially, emotionally, or materially.

Even though the Depression is long gone, we find that the need seems to be ongoing. Public welfare seems to increase year by year. Unemployment presents a problem. Sometimes people mismanage personal funds. There is an ongoing need to take care of the poor and the needy.

To be self-reliant, to have self-esteem is most important. People cannot feel good about themselves unless they are doing what they can to achieve, to accomplish, and to build themselves up.

Deseret Industries provides work for people who cannot compete on the commercial market. We take them into Deseret Industries and train them to be productive employees on the open market. Other people donate and share their products. We sell them and use the revenue to pay the rent and make it possible for the handicapped and those with other problems to have a job and to be self-reliant.

*Mark Ricks*

Courtesy of Mark Ricks

*Religious experience in Idaho continued to include intolerance of others even after the Manifesto of 1890 eliminated the practice of polygamy from Mormon life. Mormons, once the victims of partisan politics, have managed to restore their presence in partisan politics and other facets of public life. State Senator Mark Ricks of Rexburg discusses his experience.*

My grandfather's name was Joseph, he being the son of Thomas E. Ricks, founder of Rexburg and Ricks College. He established a homestead which my father later purchased. My father also acquired a homestead on the Rexburg Bench and eventually sold it to me.

Less than 3 percent of the church membership was ever involved in polygamy. Some people were violently opposed to that kind of practice. Fred T. Dubois set out to make life miserable for them. But Mormons held together as a community. They worked together, pulled together, supported one another. The settlers who did not belong to the LDS church resented that.

The church looks back on those days with favor, even though there was persecution. It was unfortunate that Mormons were persecuted, but they had been persecuted back in the Midwest prior to coming here. Coming out West, they were prepared.

I'm not embarrassed by my family's history with polygamy. The whole purpose was to raise up a righteous generation. Many of the people who came from those polygamist families found themselves in high ecclesiastical positions in the church. When I served an LDS mission myself, back in 1948 and 1949, there were about a hundred of us assembled in the training group; by far the majority of us were from polygamist families. If it was doctrine today, I would support it. Those are hard questions. I do respond to direction from church leadership when a doctrine is taught.

I still sense some discrimination of the church in Idaho. Yet church members have been widely accepted. There are people in very prominent positions—elected to governor and to leadership in the senate. In many communities they are elected to high positions in community administration.

I don't know all the reasons for discrimination or resentment toward Mormons now. I haven't noticed any in our legislative chambers. Once in a while I feel that media people make remarks they probably ought not to. They single out Mormons, but never Catholics or Presbyterians. I feel that is unfair reporting.

No matter who is elected to a public office, they take their own personal philosophies into the chambers. We can't help but do that regardless of our background. Training is what we've grown up with. LDS people certainly have moral principles they adhere to. I feel that way myself.

When LDS people came West, the majority were Democrats. That was because of discrimination against Mormons back in the Midwest, particularly in Missouri. The governor of Missouri at the time Mormons were expelled from Missouri was a Republican. That created animosity among the people.

Those who were in a leadership capacity in the church actually had to go down the street and designate different ones to become Republicans. "You are a Republican, you are a Democrat; you are a Democrat and you are Republican. This was in order to encourage people to belong to our two-party system.

The ecclesiastical leadership of the church in Salt Lake City has in the past had both Republicans and Democrats. The church as an institution does not try to get involved in partisan politics. They do work through people in office on either side of the political aisle.

As for the future, I think the church will continue to grow and expand. The church's membership is around 30 percent of the total population of the state. The numbers are growing all the time. Still, the church does not try to get involved in the political atmosphere of any given state, unless it's a moral issue. They will take a stand on a moral issue.

There is no doubt that the church has an impact on my personal life. If I were asked today whether I would be happier with a high position in the political world or in the church, there is no question in my mind that I would rather have an ecclesiastical position of leadership than I would a political leadership position.

The reason for that is when you're talking in an ecclesiastical way, you're talking about the salvation and eternal life of individuals. This earth life is just one brief step in our eternal progression. We have a responsibility, of course, to set up our own laws to govern society as we live here upon this earth. We do pass some laws that have eternal impacts, too. For instance, when we punish people for murder, there is a connection with the Lord's laws.

## Women And Church Institutions

*One of the opportunities for women to exercise their managerial and professional talents and ambitions in the past (and present) century was to assume leadership roles in their churches and church-sponsored institutions. The first career woman in Idaho was probably Eliza Spalding, who wanted to be a missionary to the Indians of the American West. In order to do so, she had to marry a missionary, which she ultimately did. The pair acted as a partnership in running the mission at Lapwai.*

*Women in Idaho founded, organized, managed, taught in, and sometimes financed elementary and high schools, hospitals, and nursing schools in the name of their churches. In small communities without churches, women were often the principal fund raisers and organizers of campaigns to erect church buildings, acquire tower bells, pianos and organs, hire pastors, and supply relief for people in need.*

*Grace Jones wanted to be a professional nurse. She enrolled in the Saint Alphonsus nursing school at Boise and went through the three-year course. She recalls Sister Fintan Doyle, who was the director of Saint Alphonsus Hospital from 1896 to 1919 and from 1921 to 1926, a woman whose management skills resulted in regular surpluses and contributed to the growth and expansion of the hospital. Sister Fintan's strong will and presence still dominate Grace Jones' memories of her experience.*

I graduated in 1919. My diploma is seventy years old. I don't know whether they still have diplomas like this that the doctors signed or not. I doubt if they do. The main doctors of the hospital signed their names, and so did Sister Fintan, the director of Saint Alphonsus Hospital.

She was a very buxom, big sister, and stern. She had lots of ability. She made enough money and stored it away in the bank so that when she wasn't able to run the place any longer, the new sister who came to take over had enough money to remodel the hospital completely.

After I had graduated, they took the money that was left by Sister Fintan and built the nurses' home with a swimming pool. All of the girls had private rooms. It was just a beautiful place.

We slept on the third floor in bunk beds, three to a room. We had little crevices for places to hang our clothes. There was one bathroom way down at the end of the hall. If you got down there first, you got a bath; if you didn't, you waited. Sometimes the water was cold when your turn came. It was just a little cubby hole on the third floor. The new part of the hospital was lovely, but we were in the old section. All the nuns slept up there, so if they could sleep there, it was good enough for us nurses.

When I was there, it was terribly strict. Ten o'clock was the limit. If you weren't in at ten o'clock it was just too bad for you. There was a side entrance. Once in a while we were late, out until maybe eleven o'clock, and we'd sneak up those stairs. Every step, the stairs would squeak. Squeak, squeak, squeak. You could hear it clear down on the first floor. So you couldn't go out and come in without being caught.

You could have a special permit to go out occasionally. When that happened, the man would ask for you at the front office. Sister Fintan was always there, at that front office. Her office adjoined the front door, and she had it open most of the time. She'd be in there interrogating whoever was

*Grace Jones*

coming. Where did you meet Miss Monroe? How long have you known her? And where are you going? And what time will you be home? They only came once. They never came a second time. She was a stern old lady, and believe me, they were afraid of her. That's the way we lived for three years.

I was sixteen when I started, but they didn't know that. They thought I was eighteen. I was good-sized and didn't have to show my birth certificate. It was really rough. We did everything from mopping the floors to Lysoling the beds. The nuns said you had to be a good housekeeper if you were going to be a good nurse. So they made nurses out of us. I remember waxing those hall floors. Later they laid a kind of Congolium on the floor, but at one time those were all waxed and polished by a bunch of nurses. There was no outside help. We got six or seven dollars a month. They considered we were learning something and could pay for it.

In those days there weren't any girls there who were from affluent homes. Most of them had to work. They came from good farm families mostly. People that had means, I suppose, wouldn't put up with what we put up with. But we wanted a profession, and in those days to be a professional nurse was very important. Just very important.

Sister Fintan generally tried to keep twenty-five student nurses. When you had been six months or a year in training and had proved that you were good at taking care of people, she would put us on "special." She would charge twenty-five dollars a week for a special nurse. People would hire special nurses because they were okayed by the nuns. The nuns saw to it that they were being taken care of, and the hospital got the money.

They put little cots in the room; we had to sleep with the patient. It was twenty-four hour duty, but we had two hours off in the daytime. That was the way we lived. There were women by the dozens who took the course and wanted to be nurses. They were good ones.

The sisters discouraged having boyfriends. They would ruin our work, and that's what we had come for. If we wanted to be nurses, if we wanted to graduate, we had to tend to business. We could find a boyfriend when we got through nursing. That was the attitude they had. They were very strict with us. Several girls got sent home because they sneaked out at night or had boyfriends. The sisters didn't go for that stuff. They just didn't go for it.

I had a friend who was an Elk. Very nice young man who worked at the Idaho First National Bank. I had known him a long time and I knew his sister. He would ask me to go the Elk dances. He was quite a bit older than I, but he came up to the hospital. After answering a hundred questions from Sister Fintan, she said, "Yes, you can take her but she has to be in at twelve o'clock." If you knew Sister Fintan, you'd know why she managed to keep twenty-five girls in line. She was a firm old lady.

I hadn't been in training but about three months. I'd never seen a baby born, so there was a lot of curiosity on my part. I wanted to know everything that was going on. Sister Marco, she was awfully sweet, said, "Miss Monroe, you want to see something?" I said, "Yes, what is it, sister, what is it, sister?" She said, "Come on." She took me down to the delivery room. It was a darkie lady having a little darkie baby. I got the biggest kick. I had never seen a baby born, you know, never paid any attention to livestock hardly. But here was a baby, the first thing. I was just so amazed. And a black one. That was quite an experience. There was always something along the way to enlighten you and make you think about it all.

*Florence Bowman of Rexburg is a member of the Church of Jesus Christ of Latter-day Saints and has been a stake Relief Society president. She is a music teacher at Ricks College, and has served on a church mission.*

My parents were faithful members of the church. I was christened in the church and baptized a member when I was eight years old. Malad, the little community I grew up in, was predominantly Mormon. Rexburg is about 90 percent Mormon. So most of what I do revolves around the church. Since I teach at Ricks College, which is owned and operated by the church, even my working day is involved with the church.

As far as I'm concerned, women's roles in the church are about what I like them to be. A lot of people think that women don't have a lot to do in the church.

*Courtesy of Florence Bowman*

**Florence Bowman**

But I was a stake Relief Society president for five years. I had jurisdiction over about two thousand women in our stake. There are about six thousand people in a stake. That was quite a responsibility—about as much responsibility as I want. I don't feel restricted as a woman in the church.

Someone once said that if you went to all your Relief Society meetings it would be like a college education. I think that's probably true. We have lessons on raising families, spiritual lessons on the gospel, homemaking meetings, lessons on first aid. Someone came the other night to speak on protection for women. As a single woman (I've been a widow for a number of years), since it is a women's organization, I feel very comfortable there.

I've had some wonderful experiences in music. A lot of that has been church-related. In April, 1988, I went to Salt Lake City and directed a four hundred-voice choir of Ricks College students at the General Conference, a semi-annual meeting of the LDS Church in Salt Lake City. That was a wonderful experience. The years my husband was alive were wonderful ones. He was a musician too, and we did a lot of singing and playing and performing together. My happiest times revolve around our family.

I've been a widow now since 1972. The night that my husband was killed in an accident, it was probably not more than fifteen minutes before my bishop was at our home. He did a lot of the things you have to do at the time of a death—helped with phone calls, arrangements for funeral service, the obituary. My family was also there almost immediately, as soon as they could get there. One lady that I really didn't know very well took all my ironing. I'm not an ironer and I hadn't ironed for months. She took it all home and did it. Another woman I didn't know very well brought in a big ham. There was so much food, I think it was three weeks before I had to cook a meal.

I would never feel that the Lord was ever indebted to me. I've received so many blessings from just being a member of his church. I'm always in debt to him.

The basic doctrines of the church mean a lot to me in my life. For instance, since my husband died, and because we were married and sealed for eternity in an LDS temple, I know that I can be with him again. It gives peace of mind. It makes it a lot easier to go through a trauma like that. It's never easy to lose someone, but it makes it easier knowing that if I live a worthy life, my husband and I will be together again and the children can be with us.

The church has been wonderful in helping me develop the skills of my profession. I'm a musician and so I've had many opportunities to direct choirs and sing and teach. I hope that I've been able to help a little through using my talents.

I think you are probably aware of the missionary program. I served a mission in 1982 in Indiana, and I plan to serve another one leaving July 1990. I did field teaching in Indiana. I met a lot of absolutely wonderful people. It was what we call a "proselytizing mission." We didn't always knock on doors. Sometimes someone would refer a family to us that they thought might be interested in hearing about the church, and we would go and visit with them. That was a wonderful period in my life. I know that's one of the experiences that helps strengthen me to be more faithful in the church.

It is probably the hardest time that a person will ever spend. But it would be very hard for you to find a returned missionary who didn't say they were the best years of their lives. You never live so close to your heavenly father as you do at that time. It's a good feeling. I really loved it.

## Identity And Intolerance

*In the 1920s the Ku Klux Klan sent two men to Idaho to organize the Klan in Idaho. They avoided the southeast and northern portions of the state and concentrated on the southwestern corner. American society after World War I was in rapid transition from the agrarian and isolated country it had once been.*

*Industrialization, migration of blacks from the south, gambling, jazz, emancipated women, unemployment, corruption in Washington, Catholic schools, and many other changes inspired fear and insecurity among native-born Protestants. The Klan looked for scapegoats. In those days, there was a certain local flavor to Klan organizations, and they were willing to select whatever targets were most available. In Idaho, it found targets in blacks, Mexicans, and Catholics.*

*There were also protests to the Ku Klux Klan in Idaho, its methods and its goals. Opponents enacted city ordinances that forbade the wearing of masks or disguises that hid one's facial features. The city council of Twin Falls enacted one of the earliest of these anti-mask laws in 1924. These, and a national decline of the Klan, contributed to the demise of the group in Idaho.*

*In the 1970s and 1980s, rapid changes in American society and in its global relationships prompted new groups to search for someone to blame for the problems of the day. The Church of Jesus Christ, Christian, also known as the Aryan Nations church, is one of them. Its leader, Richard Butler, recognizes immigration, drug problems, alienation of youth, divorce, women's liberation from the home, decline of American educational standards, and the decline of economic abundance in America as contemporary problems. His theory of history and the* Bible *justify, for him, blaming all of society's problems on Jews and non-Jews who are traitors to their Aryan race.*

*As an "identity church," this organization uses biblical references to bolster its doctrine that Jesus "identified" his chosen people for all time on the basis of race. Anyone not of that race is an outsider and cannot inherit the entitlements of the chosen people. Mixing of races by intermarriage or other social interchange is believed to dilute and spoil what God intended to remain "pure." This religious belief translated itself, as religious belief often does, into political and social action. Richard Butler came to northern Idaho in 1970 and started the church in 1973 to preach the gospel of the Aryan Nations.*

The time I was overseas during World War II, I started thinking about the destruction of my race and my people. An Indian set me to thinking about it, actually. Jayrom was an Indian who kept our suits and uniforms pressed and boots shined and so forth. He started talking to me about the Aryan letters and Aryan rule in India, prior to the mongolization of the white race in India. India had long been ruled by the white man. We got on the subject because he was describing to me why the caste system existed.

We were at war with our kindred. Every person who was in the China-Burma-India theater knew that the war was really being fought in Europe. The Japs never gave us any problem. They never were a real fighting force, a problem. Sure, they killed a lot of our people, but it was Germany that was the real fighting force. That was the real force that had to be destroyed, according to our masters. Roosevelt was the Jew running our country at the time.

John Jay, the first chief justice of the United States Supreme Court, declared in 1790 that providence blessed us to give us a new country. Of all the nations, we were all of a common culture, a common language, and for the most part a common faith. He said that this is land for white Aryan people from Denmark, Sweden, England, Ireland, Germany, France. They even had a census of who was here in 1790. In my view, what he was saying was that this was the regathered House of Israel.

As you start a church you don't expect trouble among your own kindred. From white people you don't expect that. We haven't had trouble. It's always been outsiders who have tried to give us a bad time. Never have the people of Hayden Lake, Coeur d'Alene, or Post Falls or any place else ever given us a bad time.

As I've said many times, the phenomenal growth of North Idaho has been due to the fact that the people who have come here have had a genetic reaction to the mongolization in California and Chicago or wherever. They come up here because there are white people here. They can send their children to school with white children. They can go to a supermarket and deal with white people, be in the malls with white people and not fight a mongolized mess.

Oh yes, we came up here because this is the Northwest, the far corner. This is where a lot of Southerners came after the Civil War. This is white man's territory. It has a Nordic climate, it's a Nordic territory.

When the Supreme Court ruled in 1954, Brown vs. Board of Education, that ruling was for that case and that case only. But Jewish people applied it to the entire land. That is when bayonets got turned against our own people. I don't blame the Jews. I say the fault lies with us. We are the ones who have strayed from the law. They are just adversaries. They test us.

When Adam fell, the

*Richard Butler*

whole white race fell. We're now going through a testing period of several thousand years. Nobody can put down the white man when he is truly a white man—white inside as well as outside. There wouldn't be any Jews here if we had listened to Benjamin Franklin, would there? So it isn't their fault that they are here, any more than it is the black man's fault that he is here. Nor is it the fault of the Vietnamese who are here. It is our fault. We dig them out of the swamps and bring them over here or allow it to be done. That's permissiveness. When we are tolerant of evil, we become evil ourselves.

Our membership has gone up and down. We attribute that to the news media. The media, of course, is always in the hands of the Jew. The Jew has a vital interest in suppressing Christianity. It has always been known. Every book the Jew has written has been to suppress or destroy Christianity and the white race. The ones of our race who are treasonous to our race, race traitors, go along with the Jew because the Jew gives them the money.

Laws will not stop drugs. Laws never stopped booze, did they? You can't tell people they can't do something. You can't send policemen or schoolteachers around to tell children to say "no" to drugs. Youth is not going to pay any attention to you. You have to give them something more noble, something of higher value, in place of it. You have to give them a righteous cause in life. Drugs, alcohol, sex—none of this used to exist prior to World War II, did it? This is one of the things that happened when we defeated our race. Indeed, we were defeated. That was a racial genocidal war waged for the destruction of the white race. The side effects were the disorientation of youth, the destruction of their moral values, the destruction of the family, a destruction of who they are, their identity.

Of course, World War II broke up the family of America. Women went to work while the men went overseas. Today we have that little cartoon, "you've come a long way baby." The child is on beer and drugs at home while she is at work. That destroys a society, a nationalistic race. That was the purpose. All these things work together. The war was the excuse, but the main thing was the destruction of the people.

My responsibility is to preach the truth without fear or favor. The responsibility of Judaism is to suppress and deny it. As Jesus said of the Jews in John 8-44, "You are of your father, the devil. The works of your father you will do." That is the core of Christianity. That used to be taught in every church in the land from the pilgrim fathers up to the 1850s. When religion ceases to be the energizing force of a race, then the power, the prosperity, the energy, the mental energy of that race will disappear, both mentally and physically.

When you hear some stupid politician say to blacks and Mexicans and Asians that "we are all one nation under God," it is the most stupid, insane remark ever made. We are not all of one race. They come back at you and say "human" race. What color is the "human" race? You have a black race, yellow race and white race. When you come along and start up the idea of this "human" race, it is insane—a play on words. People have got to learn to understand what words mean.

Why is it we were the finest educated people on the face of the earth in 1940, and today we are thirty-seventh on the educational level? Can you tell me how any nation that had the finest educational system in the world can drop down to thirty-sixth place from 1954 [the year of Brown vs. Board of Education]? It is because the armed forces of our nation were directed against the citizens of the nation. The citizens who had supplied the money and the men for the armed forces had the armed forces turned against the very same citizens. That is why education is down to zero. I don't care what you do, you're never going to bring the educational level of blacks up to that of Asians, much less whites.

I am absolutely certain about the future. We probably have to go through a swamp before we get to the promised land. I'm entirely optimistic because our father in heaven gave us a promise. He said we are going to have victory. I think in the eighth chapter of Daniel, he said: "The saints or the living offspring of the most high God shall take the kingdom, (which is the government) and possess it forever and ever." We were told in the first chapter of Genesis: "You have a mission." It is why Yahweh brought Adam onto the face of this earth, and then gave him Eve. It is why we reproduce. We were to have dominion over the earth. We were to subdue it. If we don't do it, then God was a liar. I don't think he is. I know he is true. I'm optimistic that the war will be over by 2002. It may be over sooner than that, I just think it will be over then.

*The beliefs of Aryan Nations followers and groups associated with them, such as the Order, have led to violent social and political expressions. Communities in North Idaho responded by promoting non-violent responses, among them the creation of several new laws and educating citizens about the grave consequences of scapegoating. Tony Stewart from Coeur d'Alene, a vice president and board member of the Kootenai County Task Force on Human Relations, was one of the leaders.*

Mr. Butler and others have indicated that they came to the Northwest because, of all parts of the United States, it had the most homogeneous population. They saw it as a "white enclave." They took the position that if they came here the people of this area would rally around their philosophy. I think that's why they chose the Northwest.

I think there's something about Idahoans that is perhaps true of all Northwest people. Our people believe in "live and let live." When someone moves into this area, if they do not bother you, do not engage in violence, then people respect their right to live here.

When some of the individuals and groups first moved here, before they became vocal and took certain actions, there was not a lot said. Then the Order emerged from the hate movement and there were crimes committed, for which people were convicted and sent to prison. Here and in neighboring states people engaged in counterfeiting, murder, and bank robberies. When the people around here learned of these activities they moved swiftly to support victims, law enforcement, human rights organizations, and legislation.

Idaho is at the top of the list in the United States with the most comprehensive legislative package against hate crimes. We have a malicious harassment law with criminal and civil penalties, an anti-paramilitary training

*Tony Stewart*

law, a hate crime statistics reporting law, and other such legislation. People rallied at human rights celebrations like Martin Luther King Day. The schools adjusted their curriculum to teach the very young about human rights with programs prior to Martin Luther King Day.

Historians will have a lot to say about those examples and events demonstrating that people said "no" very loud and clear to bigotry and prejudice. I'm not suggesting that our society here in the Northwest is totally free of prejudice and bigotry. Overall it's very clear that individuals are saying "no" to hate groups: "You will not find a haven in the Northwest."

The first mistake that any community can make is to ignore a problem. The issues we ignore are not confined to the human rights issue. There are others: medical issues, rearing children, dealing with sex education, and others. There is a tendency to say that if we ignore the problem it will go away. History has been very definite on this point: by being apathetic or ignoring it, you send the wrong signals and messages. But when you organize and have legislation and policies, you send the opposite messages. I think you have to be vigilant at all times.

There is another movement in this country that illustrates this—the racism of skinheads. All skinheads are not racists, but there are tragic consequences with racist skinheads. Friends in leadership positons in Portland, Oregon, have told me that they ignored the movement of skinheads into Portland for awhile. But it reached such a magnitude that it resulted in murder, for which people have since been convicted. The police department in Portland reported in a fairly short period of time fifty-three crime incidents with skinheads. Portland is now saying that they can never go back and ignore it. They have to deal with the immediate problem and educate themselves so it won't happen again.

Democracy is wonderful, but there is never an assurance that it will always be. We have cycles. The KKK in the United States has gone through cycles. Membership has gone up to as many as five million or six million people, then gone down to ten thousand, but it raises its head again. As minority people come into a community, they want to know that there are organizations that will speak in support of any victim who might exist. As long as there is one victim, there is one too many.

Through the 1980s no people in the Northwest have been more sensitive to the issue of what hate can do than the people of North Idaho. We are a good people, we have something to be proud of, we have responded with dignity and strength. We have never turned to anger or violence, even when bombings took place here. People immediately rallied. That takes special courage and strength.

Sometimes people in the hate movements come from a background where they have been defeated a lot. They may have had a lot of economic crises. Some of them have said they were accepted by hate groups. Some have had a terrible family life, rejected and thrown out at age thirteen or fourteen. They were often frustrated. So it is thought that prejudice grows out of great insecurity. If a person is very insecure, there is a temptation to look for scapegoats. It helps if they can find people "below" them or people they can put into a lower position. That helps restore their own sense of security. Some people even do that subconsciously. That's the best explanation that I've heard.

The bottom line of what hate groups are preaching is that some people are superior to others, that some people have certain basic rights to be the leaders of the country or the world. Sometimes they change their phraseology. Recently, they have been more willing to use terms like "separatism" instead of "white supremacy." I do not make that distinction, it is just their public relations. I think it's still white supremacy.

Historians may classify this group as a fringe political movement, similar to others such as the KKK we have had in our society. I hope historians will say that certain leaders came forth and did certain things to counter it. I believe hate groups will be a small footnote in history—that there was an attempt to move our country away from democracy toward prejudice and bigotry, and that it failed.

## Wilderness And Religion

*Despite their significance in the social, economic and political life of Idaho, organized churches claim only about half of Idaho citizens as members. Large numbers of the original settlers were unchurched; the frontier attracted some of them because they wanted to be free. Then it was another generation before settlers could afford to support churches. Some devoted groups faced obstacles in the practice of their faith, such as Basques being assigned Irish priests who spoke no Basque.*

*Retired Bishop Sylvester Treinen of the Catholic Church arrived in Idaho in 1962, one of the youngest bishops in the world at the time of his appointment. He retired to Arco in 1989, where he serves the small congregations there. Always sensitive to the chronic shortage of priests in the state, he used unorthodox methods to recruit them, including the placement of ads in Catholic newspapers.*

I came to Idaho in 1962. There were about forty-five thousand Catholic people in Idaho. Now there are probably closer to eighty thousand. That indicates that a lot of people are turning to religion. Some of that growth is through baptism of children and in-migration. Most of the Hispanic population is Catholic. A growing number of adults come into the church every year.

We are living now in a more ecumenical age when the various religions are getting along more peacefully. In the early missionary days there was open animosity and competition for the time and effort and energy of Native Americans. I suppose it continued quite a while.

The biggest change was after Vatican Council II, which took place between 1962 and 1965. That was a council of the bishops of the Catholic church. We invited many representatives of other religions from around the world, especially other Christian religions, and they came. They got acquainted with us better, and we got acquainted with them better. From that time on I've seen a continued growth in ecumenism and good feeling. We have stressed the things that we're united on rather than the things that we're divided on.

In the Catholic church, once a bishop is retired, his leadership is curtailed quite a bit. I could have sat in Boise or some other town and spent my time reading and recreating. But I chose to keep active because I am still healthy, fairly healthy

*Sylvester Treinen visits hospital patient*

at least. They needed a priest in Arco and Mackay. I wanted to help the new bishop, Bishop Tod Brown, with the supply of priests and keep my hand in the work of the church, even though this group is very small. I don't speak out on issues as much as I did before because it's not my role. It is the role of Bishop Brown. So rather than risk a conflict of opinions from the bishops of Idaho, I have not been doing that.

This is still retirement. I spend a lot of time praying and studying, reading, a little time watching television, more time fishing. I travel to Idaho Falls, or Boise, other places like Salmon. I don't have the administration of the dioceses, which was the big burden. I enjoyed going to parishes Sunday after Sunday, all around the state. I enjoyed that very much—being with the people, being with the priests, and the religious and the deacons, the children and the young people, in their conventions and so on. But there comes a time when you get older and somebody else with younger ideas should take over those jobs. It happens all over, in the business and political world, too.

Studies made during the past decade or two show that in this part of the country there are a lot of unchurched people, people who do not have a close affiliation with any religion. We find a lot of former Catholics living out here who don't really practice their faith. Ministers of other religions say the same thing. I read a statistic a few years ago that said about 44 percent of the people of Idaho do not have a church. I think it is because people are spread out, a lot of people live out in the woods, out on farms. They have to go a great number of miles to get to church on Sunday. Gradually, they develop their own religion. I think most people in Idaho believe in God. At funeral, wedding, or baptism time, most people get in contact with a church of one name or another. "Hatched, matched, and dispatched," we say. Religion is important to them. I think they pray, I think they believe in God.

They probably pray by themselves. They are very close to nature in the mountains, the rivers, the lakes. It is easy for them to be in contact with a Supreme Being. In a sense they probably go back to the religion of the Native Americans who were here, living in nature, depending upon the land, their neighbors a mile away or farther. They depend upon themselves, they probably read a lot about religious things. The *Bible* probably is still very close to their lives. In these days of radio and television, they get a certain amount of exposure to formal religious practices through those media.

I can understand that way of life very, very well. In areas like Mackay and Arco, we live right in the mountains. I find a lot of people go further into the mountains on weekends to camp, to fish, to hunt.

I think religion does have an influence in our ordinary daily life in Idaho. We have religious observances that almost everybody takes part in—Christmas, Thanksgiving, Easter. At those times, ministers and priests report overflowing crowds. Where do they all come from? Why don't we see them the following Sunday? That says to me that religion is still very alive in most people's lives. They are good people. God is important in their lives. They might not be as involved as a lot of other people are, but in their own way, they keep in contact with the Creator.

*The natural beauty of Idaho has also attracted men and women who are members of religious orders and wish to spend their lives in prayer and contemplation. In eastern Idaho, the Sisters of Marymount settled on their own ranch for that kind of life. Father Peter Bourne and his associate Brother Maurice Mansfield are building a hermitage near Leadore, using discarded or abandoned log buildings. Desiring isolation from the world, they have the problems of the world ever on their minds, despite the ancient tradition they represent.*

During the Crusades, around the 1100s, some Crusaders became disillusioned. They had seen places where Jesus had walked. Most of these men were Europeans, knights and ex-knights. They began retiring from the world and living in caves at Mount Carmel in the holy land near Haifa. There was a long history of hermits living in those caves, so they were taking up where other hermits had left off, in a sense. They lived there until about 1209 when the Patriarch Albert of Avogadro drew up a rule of life for them. It was based on how they were already living in the caves. He brought them together under a common rule. Of all the rules in the western church, it probably is the only one that was composed specifically for hermits. They became known as Carmelites. They built a church in honor of our Lady of Mount Carmel and dedicated themselves to her. She was their liege and lady under the feudal system. A Moslem invasion wiped out most of the community, but some had migrated to Sicily, France, and England.

In Europe they revamped their rules and lived a mendicant way of life, traveling and preaching. From then until the present day, there was always a tension between the contemplative and the active life. Some houses were contemplative, others were active. Since Vatican II, the emphasis in the church has been on social action. Many mendicants went into the active field. When that happened, we decided we wanted to get back to our roots.

We had a clash with our own province. The order was very reluctant to allow the hermit type of expression within their regulations and rules. The Vatican suggested that we get a bishop to foster our way of life. We didn't have Idaho specifically in mind when we set out, but we did have an area in mind—the Northwest, where there was little influence of religious orders. And there was this great call of the wilderness. I wrote to the bishops of Wyoming and Utah. They decided against it. I wrote to Bishop Treinen in Idaho and he was interested.

We were looking for solitude, a place with enough land to set up a group of hermitages that wouldn't be on top of each other. We found this place that has space and a variety of terrain on which to choose sites for hermitages. It had a nice creek through it, which was a nice plus. It is close to the forest so we could get logs for building. We started out by appropriating log cabins. The place has to be beautiful, too, as this place is.

*Peter Bourne*

When you have a place that is solitary, apart, out in the woods, in the forest, away from population, it is quiet. It helps you live a spiritual life, the life that we are attempting to live according to the rule of Saint Albert. It can be a desert place or a high mountain place like ours, which is also semi-arid. You have a chance to slow down, dedicate your time for prayer. You offer up your whole day to God. The only thing you can give to God is your will, your time, whatever he has given to you. You can do it better in a situation like we have here. Ultimately we do this for our own salvation.

There are economic reasons for reusing these old buildings. We can get them for nothing. Most people don't want them, and we have a little sense of history. They are part of the Lemhi Valley and we'd like to preserve some of that. If I had my way, I'd collect a whole lot more. We like living in the log buildings because they hold the heat pretty well. They are sufficient for us. If an earthquake comes, they wouldn't shake apart very easily.

In ten years, we hope that these buildings will be a monastic compound. Visitors could come and use the chapel and wander around a kind of quadrangle made by the main building. Hermitages are for the individual hermits and would be somewhat off limits, as much as we can expect.

It is a contemplative group. It is oriented toward ourselves in a sense; in another sense it is oriented toward the community and to the good of the community, and the worship of God. That's how we look at it. It's not a selfish thing that we're trying to build, because all our apostolate has got to be focused on God's creation, God's people. In this age of activism and social works, I suppose it's different. But it's not different insofar as the church has always had recluses, always had hermits, monastics who lived to themselves, perfecting their own lives for the good of the members. That's how we look at it.

All monastic orders limit their communication with others, only for the benefit of their own self-betterment or the worship of God. If it were just for a selfish reason, it wouldn't sustain a person very long. You really have to love the world enough to be a good hermit, you can't hate it. A person who is looking for an escape won't find it in this way of this life. He couldn't take it.

I'm attracted many times to social action. Bruce Ritter is helping kids, Mother Teresa helps the poor and sick. You have an attraction to these things, but you can't do them all. I think that we are called specifically to do this thing, even though we might be momentarily attracted to other things.

We pray for ourselves to be better people, pray for sinners to be converted, pray for the world that it will run its day-to-day business morally. Our prayers are intercessory prayers to God for upholding goodness in the world. We believe in the efficacy of prayer. As a Christian you have to believe that. The Lord says, "With faith and prayer you can move mountains." We've got to take him, I suppose, at his word.

# Water

## THE ESSENTIAL RESOURCE

*Mormon settlers, pioneers in western irrigation, usually began constructing irrigation works for new settlements the first day they arrived. They regarded water as a resource belonging to the community rather than to private individuals. They also realized that there would be disputes over rights and priorities, so they set up procedures to deal with them.*

*The delegates at the Idaho Constitutional Convention in 1889 contended with parallel issues as they debated what the constitution should say about water. They decided that water was so important to the development of Idaho that private property owners would have the right to condemn land on a neighbor's property in order to bring a ditch or flume across it. The development of the state as a whole demanded this concession to otherwise "sacred" private property rights.*

*Further, the delegates anticipated future water shortages and knew there would be disputes over who would have priority to water when it was in short supply. Northern and southern delegates had somewhat different visions of the role of water in the future of their base industries. There were hours and days of debating the competing claims of "first in time" northern miners and the "little Italian ranchers" who had settled on mining streams "to raise their truck." There was more debate and discussion about southern irrigation development contrasted with mining and timber uses of water. In the end, the delegates defined the beneficial uses of water and ranked priority uses in low-water years as: domestic, agricultural (except in mining districts), and manufacturing.*

*One hundred years later, the same issues still generate debates all across the state. However, the list of beneficial uses now includes "the protection of fish and wildlife habitat, aquatic life, recreation, aesthetic beauty, transportation and navigation values, and water quality." Potential water users now include electricity consumers from all over the West as well as the growing urban populations within Idaho. A series of lawsuits, compromises, and legislation over the use of the water in the Snake River and the priorities of each use led to a current program of adjudicating all the water rights in the Snake River drainage.*

*To Idaho's group of three traditional water-using industries, a fourth has been added, recreation. A "new order" in water is evolving rapidly, not only within Idaho, but within the western United States as well.*

*Scott Reed an attorney from Coeur d'Alene served three terms on the Idaho Water Resource Board, a policy-making board created in 1966 by amendment to the Idaho Constitution to develop plans and policy for the use of Idaho's water. On the board until 1980, Reed was in a position to observe the variation in attitudes toward water in different parts of the state. He was involved in the debate over the designation of part of the St. Joe River as a Wild and Scenic River.*

There is a world of difference between northern and southern Idahoans in their attitudes toward water. The north has a lot of water. We see recreation uses of it, people build houses on it and haul logs on it. We've got lots of it for summer recreation use. In south Idaho, they use the phrase "use it or lose it." Unless you use up every bit of water, then you're going to lose it to California or to the guy downstream. Many a winter and spring we've had so much rain in this part of the country that we want to lose it!

There have been dreams at times about taking water out of north Idaho and moving it to south Idaho. In the sixties there were some ideas of taking the Salmon River water and putting it down to south Idaho. Those ideas never came this far north. In California there have been actual projects to take water out of northern California and move it to southern California, but no real plans to remove it from north Idaho for south Idaho.

Still the north has a very high regard for what our waters are, and for water quality. It's been relatively recent that south Idaho has expressed great interest in water quality. But it's always been a high interest in the north, from the very earliest days of mining. In the 1880s and 1890s people downstream were very concerned about what those mines were doing to their water quality. In south Idaho that was not a concern; their concern was putting water on the land. We can put all the water on the land up here we want and we still can't grow potatoes like they grow down there.

*Scott Reed*

There has not been a lot of friction between north and south Idaho over water, generally speaking. The north just simply ignored it. Under Idaho law, you were always supposed to make an application for the right to divert water. When you wanted a well you were supposed to make an application for a permit. When you wanted to use water out of a lake, you were supposed to get a permit. Nobody did it.

In south Idaho, filing for rights was very important very early on. It wasn't actually until the mid-seventies in the north that people around here finally got the message that they had to have a permit to take water. It never occurred to them before because water was always going to be there. What inspired them in the seventies was that the state of Washington had some kind of adjudication process going on, and ran an ad in the paper. Everybody in Idaho ran to file an application, because they thought there was some kind of panic. Up until then they didn't pay any attention to it. It's still not a competitive problem.

The St. Joe River was designated as a study river at the time that the Wild and Scenic Rivers Act was passed. The reason for the designation was a belief that classification as a Wild and Scenic River might provide protection against some dredge mining operations going on in the upper St. Joe. That general concept was supported by the locals down there and politicians and people in general. That was in the 1960s.

In the early 1970s we went through the process of designating it. As the study proceeded, people saw it as the federal government coming in to take their rights away and interfere with the use of the land. There was a fear that it would create some kind of overwhelming bureaucracy that was going to deprive them of what they had. We ended up with a tremendous confrontation between environmental groups, which felt that designating it as a Wild and Scenic river would protect its scenic values, and the landowners, who thought that it would take their property rights away.

The conflict ended a little like Korea, where we just drew a dividing line between north and south. We drew our line at the boundary of the national forest. Supposedly landowners would not have any possible concern about that part of the river within the national forest boundaries; there are no private property owners up there. But forget about designating the rest of it!

The Wild and Scenic River Act was really intended to stop dam construction. In truth, there were two possible dam sites on the St. Joe, neither of particular significance. We did put language into that act that prohibited dredge mining in the upper area. The effect has been to eliminate that nasty little cancer from digging up those streams. Perhaps of more importance, we used the same language on the Salmon River when the central Idaho wilderness was created. It was a useful precedent.

The St. Joe designation was very much a compromise. I think it was a good compromise. It brought "peace to the valley." We haven't been fighting with each other since then. There are other things to talk about.

In the south Idaho context, you would not call even the south half of the St. Joe a working river, however. A working river is a Snake River, where you take water out, put it on the land, grow crops, and put it back in the river. You build dams. The St. Joe wasn't a working river. Barges went up and down hauling logs, but it was still a playing river. We have playing waters up here, not working waters.

The disputes on the Snake are the same sort of disputes that are happening in the national forest. Different groups have a different value for water. It has been accepted in south Idaho forever that the purpose of water was to put it on land to grow crops. It was incidental that you could run it through turbines to make power. Those are both working purposes.

As we become more urbanized in this state, and as values change, and environmental values become much higher, that old acceptance will end. People now have entirely different sorts of values for that water. They want water to be in place, in the streams and in the rivers themselves. Recreational use conflicts with diversionary use.

I think that we are ready mentally and socially for more development based on water—in both tourism and diversions. Whether we are ready legally is something that remains to be seen. With the controversy over anadromous fishery and its restoration—the Northwest Power Planning Council's efforts to use Bonneville Power money to provide restoration to pre-dam status of the fishery—you have to recognize that the interest in fisheries is very, very strong. It is an economic interest, a recreational interest, a tourist interest. This enormous vital and lively interest is a complete turn-around from thinking that the loss of salmon is just the price of progress, which a lot of people thought only fifteen years ago. To say that the salmon are going to stay, it's going to get better, and we're going to pay to get them back—that is a major, major change.

I think there will be major opposition to the use of water for making energy to divert somewhere else. The Simplot interests talking about this are being seen the same way as the Los Angeles city councilman who wanted to take the water itself out of the Snake River. Many in south Idaho, once exemplified by former U.S. Representative George Hanson, thought it was criminal for water to leave the state of Idaho. I had this vision of a big dam at Lewiston that would flood everything all the way back up to Idaho Falls, and not let any water leave the state. But water is going to leave the state, there isn't any question about that. People downstream have rights.

Idaho appreciates its water tremendously. It's the lifeblood in north Idaho. By lifeblood I don't mean economic lifeblood, though it is certainly that. But this is what people relate to, this is why they're here. They come for lakes, for streams. They feel very strongly that these are an integral part of what they are doing. Whether they spend their time on the water or just looking at it, it's part of the heartthrob of this particular area. That's happening in other parts of the state to some degree now. The same sort of affection is growing. It is not quite to the same degree, but it's there.

We started out, like every other state, with the idea that "beneficial use" was economically beneficial use for power, running timber, farming. Those were the only beneficial uses we had. Then, starting with the Malad Canyon case and later with legislation, we now have established that beneficial uses include fishery, water quality, and recreation. By means of judicial decisions, legislative action, and the state water plan, we have gone about as far forward as any place in the West with an appropriation doctrine. I think we're in good shape by recognizing those values.

A process is in place. We are going to have conflicts between diversionary uses and the tourist uses in certain areas. Tourism is a wonderful thing to happen, but it can become a somewhat scary and unpleasant experience, too. A couple of years ago, we had a couple of deaths on Lake Coeur d'Alene due to boating accidents. If you project the past growth in the number of boats to the future, you get to the point of an unbearable amount of use. From the viewpoint of those who were here before, we'd like to keep it the way it was.

There are tremendous benefits from irrigation, from the crops that are grown, and from the wildlife values that are associated with that. There are some real negatives involved in tourism. So it's not that easy to draw lines at any particular beneficial use.

*Captain Floyd Cardwell, tug boat operator on the St. Joe and Coeur d'Alene Rivers, lives in Harrison.*

I've been working on this river since 1954. I worked on the Columbia when I was a kid for a while. I suppose rafting the logs could be dangerous if a guy wasn't careful. He's got to use his head. Anything could be dangerous. I don't know of anybody who got hurt rafting logs. The insurance people say this is a dangerous job, but very few people get hurt doing it. They stopped towing logs that were not tied together around 1973.

Bundling logs started in the late sixties, but up on the Coeur d'Alene River they didn't start bundling until the mid-seventies. We used to take them from Cataldo Mission, but it was too shallow up there to get a bundle down. There used to be pilings driven all the way down the middle of the river. There used to be a big sawmill down here and this was all storage area for it.

It's more efficient this way. Every year, there are more pleasure boats. It used to be really hazardous because a loose log could roll out of the boom. There was always the danger of somebody hitting one. But it is mainly on account of efficiency. If you took the logs down to storage and they laid there a long time, a lot of them would go to the bottom. This way, they don't.

The last few years, we've gone practically the year-round. We had to break up to eighteen inches of ice trying to get to the logs, but you tear up quite a bit of rigging that way. We usually take a month or six weeks to get the boats in shape for the following year. It all depends on the lumber market and how bad they need the logs.

The Coast Guard used to patrol Coeur d'Alene Lake, but they gave it up. We still have to get a Coast Guard license to operate. There's getting to be so much boat traffic anymore, that I think it would be a good idea if they licensed everybody. That's just my personal opinion.

Thirty years from now, I don't know. It will be the same, because after all, what can you do with a saw log? Either pull it or push it. Nothing lasts forever, but lots of things will stay the same as far as

**Floyd Cardwell and his tug**

this operation goes. They'll have to fight more environmentalists and more pleasure boaters. I shouldn't say "fight" either; everybody's got to have their own nitch.

*J. R. Simplot is the head of a diversified set of industries engaged in potato processing, mining, cattle, real estate, and other ventures. He was an investor in Western Power Corporation, a group which set out to explore the potential in producing and transporting power to markets in the southwestern part of the United States. Many Simplot Company plants generate surplus heat which can be converted to electrical energy and used to operate the plant or sold, an activity known as co-generation. Simplot also supported a proposal by Western Power Corporation, since abandoned, to install a run-of-the-river hydroelectric dam in the North Fork of the Payette River, a project which would have impacted the growing recreational use of the river.*

Well, we're in co-generation. We're going to furnish power to the Southwest in the future. I've got all the confidence in the world in it. I've always said, "The next big city is going to be built around co-generation." You get two shots at that steam, high pressure to make electricity, and low pressure to heat your houses and cook your potatoes. There is no end to the amount of industry we're going to attract with co-generation.

I just see it coming. Here we sit on the Snake River, with the water and the climate—well, it's a Garden of Eden to live in. With no water south of the Snake, and every gallon of it spoken for, here we are still dumping millions of acre feet into the Columbia and right into the Pacific Ocean. I can see big things for this Snake River Valley. I don't know how big, I won't be here to see it.

No, it doesn't bother me that the idea might be controversial. I can sit here and try to outguess the future. It's coming. It's coming. I just think we've got something unique and I want to see us put our shoulder to the wheel and take advantage of the opportunities as they come. And they're going to come.

There will be a few people who damn me. But they all want jobs, they all want industry, they all want to see things expand and grow, they all want to make money on their investments. That's why you're going to see land values double, triple, quadruple, even in my lifetime, from here out. There is no question in my mind about it. Good land, with good water rights, is going to be real gold in the western part of America some day.

I just came from Tokyo, where you can really appreciate what land is worth. They just can't find it, it isn't there. The same thing will happen wherever we've got water, I'm telling you. You've got to have it to progress and to build around. There is no other way, and we've got it right here in Idaho.

**J.R. Simplot**

We have the water and land to irrigate twice the acres that we have today. You can't see it today, economically, but it's here. The land is here and the water is here. We are just scratching the surface. We preserve it, store it, keep it, and use it. We'll have to generate power, make it work for us. It will, because it's so simple. There is very little water south of us, nothing from New Mexico to the West Coast. We've got it.

*Rob Lesser of Boise was a founder of the Idaho Whitewater Association in 1979, organized in part as a response to Idaho Power Company proposals (which preceded those by Western Power Corporation) to divert part of the Payette River for the production of hydroelectric power. He has been active in Friends of the Payette, another organization concerned about the impact of power and other development proposals that affect the river. Lesser kayaks the whitewater of the Payette River, and also sells kayaks. He discussed the virtues of the river and the issues surrounding its use and development while relaxing on the bank of the North Fork.*

The Payette is such a fine place to introduce people to the sport of white water rafting or kayaking. People who go down for the first time have a real pleasant trip. It doesn't cause anyone to have a heart attack; people can just enjoy the outdoor experience.

I was blessed by being born and raised in the Boise area. I discovered the Payette in my backyard. There is nothing comparable to the chance to excel and constantly challenge yourself. We talk about making Craters of the Moon a national park, an yet the Payette qualifies with so much more to offer. This is world-class white water, no question about it. It has road access, late season challenge, and constant activity unmatched anywhere in the world.

Frankly, when I go off on expeditions to other parts of the world, I often say, "We could be on the North Fork of the Payette." A week ago, I was on the Clark Fork of Yellowstone, a spectacular scenic and very challenging river, but you have to walk around most of the rapids. You can't be on the river. It was three days of trudging through the wilderness. The boating was challenging, but ... we could have been on the North Fork.

Kayaking started to develop a following in Idaho in the early 1970s. People like Keith Taylor, Roger Hazlewood, and Tullio Celano from the Boise area had gotten together with introductions from Walt Blackadar from Salmon, who started kayaking in Idaho in 1965. The Payette was the home-town river, and kayaking developed on the main Payette and then the South Fork throughout the 1970s. Then people started rafting and whitewater canoeing.

I lived in Alaska for seven years. There we had class one and class five water, but nothing in between. The Payette system has

*Rob Lesser*

class two, three, four, and five water—all excellent. This unique variety on one system is one reason that people protect the Payette.

The threats to kayaking are development-oriented. I advocate that we have to demonstrate a need before we develop power projects. Perhaps some decisions will have to be made around the year 2000, but in the meantime, we should expect the river remain as it is, since there is no demonstrable need for any development until that year. I view rivers in the state as a bank account.

If the original Idaho Power project, which was to divert up to 2700 cubic feet per second into tunnels in order to generate the power, were to have been accepted—or one similar to it—there would be no water in this river. The river would be irreversibly changed. I just don't see that as being necessary. There is absolutely no need for the electricity, and that is why Idaho Power did not go forward with the project. The Idaho Public Utility Commission would have ruled against it.

In my seven years of interacting with Idaho Power on this issue, I realized that it was not cost effective. The extensive tunneling could easily overrun its projected costs. Development is an ongoing and positive aspect of our advancement as a civilization. But equally important is conservation, the development of consciousness, and not being wasteful. We have to become wiser users.

There aren't a lot of kayakers. The fight to preserve the river system is a concern of all the citizens of Idaho. Friends of the Payette is a broad-based organization of chambers of commerce, fishermen, float boaters, kayakers, senior citizen organizations, and others. There is more to the defense of the Payette than kayaking.

People return from a trip on the river to their home states or countries and show their slide shows. They talk about it and it becomes a quest for their friends. The Payette is something they sure as heck don't have in Ohio.

*Among its other responsibilities, the Idaho Public Utilities Commission grants licenses to operators of electrical power utilities. All western states and their constituents were involved with an appeal to a decision handed down in California by the Ninth Circuit Court. The court ruled that the State of California could not deny water rights granted to a power company by the Federal Energy Regulation Commission (a ruling since upheld by the U.S. Supreme Court). Perry Swisher of Boise, at one time a legislator for Bannock County, is a member and former president of the Idaho Public Utilities Commission. He reflected on this, and other changes in energy regulation that have had an impact on Idaho.*

The energy crisis of the seventies—the embargo by the OPEC countries, and the run-up in oil and gas prices—brought about PURPA (Public Utility Regulatory Policy Act). These things led Congress to look for ways to meet our energy needs without being totally at the mercy of oil. The PURPA law was one response to that concern.

This act saw to it that you could get energy where you could find it. That is, the utilities no longer had a monopoly on generation of energy. So if you had a high-line canal, or a stream with a long drop, wood waste from a forest product, or steam from a food-processing boiler, the utility company had to pay you as much money for that juice as it would have cost the utility to build a new plant of its own.

That was called "avoided costs." That was the foundation of the PURPA plants like the one at Barber Dam on the Boise River. On the Idaho Power system, there are about sixty such projects. All together, they come to over one hundred megawatts. That is a little less than half of one of the Valmy, Nevada, coal units. So the policy has added electricity.

There's some electricity out there in Idaho that is not under PURPA contract price. Simplot puts out about fifteen megawatts at his plant in Pocatello that are not signed to a PURPA contract. Potlatch at Lewiston generates thirty megawatts. Just the PURPA numbers alone don't tell the whole story on all the new energy. In addition to that you have industries that are internally generating their own power and not selling it under the PURPA act.

The number of projects isn't that high with the other utilities in the state. But the amount of generation is relatively just as high. In other words, there are fewer small hydro plants, but a higher proportion of industry-based power in the east and north parts of the state.

At the outset, most of the projects were hydro projects, although one of the first systems to go into production on Idaho Power was Tamarack, below New Meadows.

It is six or seven megawatts and just hums away at about 90-some percent efficiency. It is more reliable than most utility plants, and it has been running now for a good seven years.

The hydro was what got people excited and got things moving, but for the long pull it won't be hydro. It will be the industrial boilers. It will be renewable wood waste and other waste. It will probably be steer manure in the Gooding area. It will be onions in the Wilder area. Methane-based or wood-based boiler fires will be the major part of it over the long pull.

There should still be concerns about hydro power projects. If you are an organizer for an environmental organization, it's a good idea to jump up and down about the Salmon River. The reality is that there are so many review agencies involved in the licensing process, that I don't know of any small hydro projects in the Salmon River. I know of some big ones below the Salmon put in place

*Perry Swisher*

before PURPA that have had some adverse environmental impact.

In the Great Basin desert country, where Boise is, the impounding of water is not a negative event. While all of southern Idaho except the Bear River drainage is in the Columbia River Basin, southern Idaho's climate and water management outlook share crucial characteristics with those of the Great Basin. We have altered our desert climate by the incremental retention of water that otherwise would have gone out to sea, an advantage not shared by Utah, Nevada, and southwestern Wyoming, which comprise the rest of the Great Basin. We are not messing up fish runs of anadromous species. Rather, dams mean the retention of water that otherwise would be gone. If you think of the small hydro projects as you would think of beaver dams, then you'd be thinking of them in the right context.

There are proposals for "run-of-the-river" projects. I don't think they're going to go very far. I would be surprised if the proposals on the North and South Fork of the Payette ever fly. They cause some bad things to happen with the other uses of those two rivers. You won't see run-of-the-river anywhere on the Salmon drainage. I think on the Boise River system we will see little or no run-of-the-river projects. You may see better use of impoundments already in place on the Boise River.

I think that Idaho's biggest concern over water is not a new concern. We need to protect water from being sucked out of the state by the enormous economic and political power to the south of us. That is to say, Los Angeles is becoming an incredible pile-up of people with requirements for energy and water. After the 1990 Census, at least one in five, or maybe more, members of the United States House of Representatives will be from California.

We have our work cut out for us when we get an idiotic appellate decision like the one just handed down from the Ninth Circuit Court. This concerned the states' role in managing water under the Federal Power Act. We have our work cut out for us to protect not only the hydro energy that we can make cheaply, but also in the long pull, protecting the water itself.

Electricity doesn't recognize state lines. It's more a question of management and strategy. If you try to play dog-in-the-manger under the federal commerce clause, you're going to lose. That ought not to be what we do. We ought to see to it that this resource, which is here because of the nature of the country we live in, is as much a resource for us as sunshine is, or used to be, in Los Angeles. We should not have it loaded up and hauled away any more than Los Angeles would have voluntarily allowed its sunshine to be done away with.

Idaho put into motion some of the actions needed to preserve its interests. The first time was in the early 1960s with a constitutional amendment providing for a State Water Plan. It is doing it now as a part of the Snake River adjudication process, which will say who has the right to use what water when.

Still, the dangers ahead are the same dangers that are behind us. There is the danger of going to sleep, or getting distracted by something of no consequence and allowing the resource to get ripped off while nobody's looking. That's the real danger—inattention. That's always the danger.

Inattention caused the loss of hundreds of miles of rail that used to haul our farm commodities to market, because everybody was busy sitting in front of the TV set hearing Ronnie-baby say, "Everything is fine." Nobody was looking. That is the kind of inattention I mean. If the public or its leaders fall asleep, or become more interested in abortion than water, then somebody walks off with the resources while you're out doing demonstrations.

People like Governor Cecil Andrus and Attorney General Jim Jones are so far apart on so many issues, but when you hear that first splash of water, they get their

*Swan Falls Dam*

act together. I would say that the quality of the work being done by the political leaders exceeds the support base out there in the populace. There is a high level of informed-ness on the part of public officials. It used to not be that way.

I think the environmental groups have the ability to preserve rivers like the Payette, but I think they succeed when there is a mix of people involved—not just the environmental groups alone doing the jumping up and down. There is a lot of overlap of interests. You find that people who don't support the environmental groups specifically do support protecting the Payette River, for instance. Some of the categorization of interests is misleading. The press gets confused sometimes.

The fights you see going on between the "cattleman" and the "environmentalist" are pretty deceptive. There are only certain cattlemen fighting certain environmentalists. Some of the best environmentalists in the state trying to protect habitat are private ranchers whose families have fought with federal agencies for eighty or a hundred years. But that's not well known.

I think water is a separate question from other public issue debates. It is unique. You will find that some people borrow their facts on water from people who live in Portland, whose socks never dry out. The attitude of the Lower Columbia power establishment toward the country east of the Cascades is not based on reality. It's based on assumptions that don't travel much farther up the river than Grand Coulee dam.

There is a tendency now for Idaho people to imitate the quiche-and-crawdad circuit in Portland, and to repeat the mindless positions of the people on the Lower Columbia, who do not know that every acre foot of water retention in the Great Basin can benefit the ecology of the Great Basin. But that's not understood. If there is an area where we're going to have a little trouble, I think it is that people in Boise and Helena purchase their ideas at the centers of power in Seattle and Portland.

Those ideas are that any dam was a mistake, and that every smolt has to make it all the way up to Yellowstone Park and back without any human interference. The assumptions include the fact that the Army Corps of Engineers and the Bonneville Power Administration are the pre-eminent people in carrying out policy and making policy. The record of both those agencies in the creation of colossal public policy mistakes is so bad that I wonder how they continue to assert themselves without blushing. But they do. The people who put WPPSS together, the people who dammed the salmon off from their spawning beds, the people who ignored the effects of all of impoundments downstream: They are still looked to today to tell us what to do next. They ought not to be looked to. They are masters at consensual error. We ought not ever take policy direction from them again.

I think those agencies have too much influence on some of our leaders. Those agencies have too much voice. I would say that Idaho Senator Jim McClure is a good example of someone who once deferred to them, and no longer does, because experience has taught him that the Army Corps of Engineers will step on him if it has to. I'm not pessimistic in that regard. I think sophistication with respect to public policy is growing. I'm not worried about the future; I'm just dumping on you a little bit about the past.

I may be a futurist, but I'm not a prophet. I can't tell you what's going to happen to me for the next twenty-four hours. I have no business telling you what I think is going to happen in the next one hundred years. There is a lot of self-indulgence on the part of people in jobs like mine, partly because we're asked all the time. I don't know what's going to happen. If people were predictable, they'd be dead by now. Some predator would have eaten every last one of them, so I don't try to. It's almost the duty built into human nature that whatever policy or plan or cookie cutter is manufactured by people like me, their obligation is to frustrate it over time. So even if I had an idea about what ought to happen in the future, I wouldn't tell you.

## CONCENTRATED RESOURCES

*The Creator probably constructed the earth with all the elements distributed evenly throughout it, then established all the rules of physics, heat, biology, and chemistry—and set them all in motion. After six billion years of boiling and freezing, spreading and crunching, life and death, layering and eroding, earthquakes and volcanoes, the elements and the minerals they form are no longer evenly dispersed, but bunched up and concentrated. Because of the complex geologic history of Idaho, there is an unusual abundance of such concentrations.*

*People of several different cultures have lived in Idaho. Each mined the particular resources that they found useful or valuable. Prehistoric people quarried obsidian, chert, jasper, and other rocks useful for making points and tools. Early miners came to Idaho for gold, and then silver. Entrepreneurs of the 1860s evaporated the waters in eastern Idaho hot springs and made salt. After World War II, when India and Brazil embargoed exports of monozite, a source of thorium, the Atomic Energy Commission turned to Idaho, where they found it in the granitic rocks of the Idaho Batholith. Today, Idahoans mine rich concentrations of phosphate, gravel, sandstone, garnets, molybdenum, clay, lead, silver, gold, and many other minerals.*

*Profitability determines whether a substance will be mined or not. There is, therefore, another rule that the Mining Association of Idaho referred to in the 1930s as the "tragedy of low grade ore:" If the price of the mineral is lower than what it costs to mine it, it is not "ore," it is just another mineral. If the mineral is not concentrated enough to be economically developed by the technology and other conditions of the day, it is not worthwhile to mine.*

*A list of minerals concentrated in Idaho would be a long list. Some of them once had value, but no longer serve the needs of society. Others have little value today, but may emerge in importance with scientific, technological, aesthetic, or medical needs of the future. Idaho has concentrations other than minerals; the particular history of the land and the life that used to live on it has resulted in special accumulations of animal and plant fossils. Idaho geologists and paleontologists discuss just a few of Idaho's resource riches.*

# Gold And Silver

*The glory days of gold and silver mining in Idaho are certainly not over. New geological information about where gold is found, and to what degree it is concentrated has been combined with new methods to mine and refine it. Although the concentrations are far lower than they were a hundred years ago, gold remains a valuable commodity and will continue to be mined.*

*Part of the business of the Idaho Geological Survey is to provide the mining industry with information that will help it find valuable minerals in the state. Dr. Earl Bennett, its associate director and the state geologist talked about gold and silver.*

The key to finding ore deposits is what you know about the rocks and the geology. If you don't have a map showing where all the various rock units are, you are kind of blind. We now have about forty percent of Idaho mapped with fairly detailed geological mapping. One of our jobs is to fill in the holes.

That is why the state and U.S. Geological Survey's programs of geologic mapping are popular with mining companies. They like those maps. They look at where known ore deposits are, and figure out the relationship between them and the rocks. It is the basis for exploring for new deposits.

"Gold is where you find it," as they say. Many of the gold deposits responsible for our current gold rush were known in the past. They were mined at the turn of the century up through the 1920s or 1930s. But the old prospectors only mined narrow little veinlets. Modern mining companies look for "halos," zones on either side of the veins where there is widely disseminated gold (ie, in very low concentrations). They mine by bulk mining methods. That is how most of the gold mining in the United States is being done now.

Idaho, like Nevada and other parts of the West, is undergoing a tremendous gold rush. This is the largest gold rush since the 1930s. Today's prospector geologist, unlike the old prospector with his mule and his gold pan, comes to town in a helicopter or four-wheel-drive pickup with a fully equipped analytical lab not too far away.

He can't see the gold in the deposits he finds. It is measured in parts per billion. He has to use chemistry to actually see if gold is in the rock. These very low grade gold deposits are amenable to heap leaching. This is a process of using cyanide to leach the gold from the ore. The technology can extract very small quantities of gold from very large tonnages of rock. This is the impetus behind the new gold rush.

*Earl Bennett*

The magic numbers for Idaho are that you have at least ten million tons of rock that each contain five one-hundredths of an ounce of gold. In other words, you have to mine twenty tons of rock to get one ounce of gold. You have to have very large tonnages of the rock in order to get enough gold out to make the process pay.

Active mines in Idaho right now include Coeur d'Alene's operation at Thunder Mountain and Pioneer Metals' operation at Yellow Pine. Hecla will start at Yellow Pine very shortly. Nerco Minerals operates the DeLamar mine in Owyhee County. Idaho Gold started the Champagne mine near Arco this year, and will start another one at Buffalo Gulch near Elk Cily in 1990. They all use heap leach technology. Each of these mines will produce twenty to thirty thousand ounces of gold per year.

Remember, you've got to mine twenty tons of ore to get every one of those ounces of gold. Meridian Gold made a recent discovery at the Bear Track property just north of Salmon. This is the largest gold discovery ever made in Idaho. It may produce more gold than Boise Basin did, which was three million ounces. It alone has been a tremendous impetus for speeding up the gold boom in Idaho. It is still possible to become very wealthy from mining gold. There is no doubt about it.

Faulting is the process that controls where we find most gold deposits. Faulting is related to the stretching, or extension, of the earth's crust. When various forces pull the crust of the earth apart, it makes cracks in the upper part of it. Then, the hotter, more mobile middle part of the earth is free to move up closer to the surface using the fractures as conduits. The cracks then become mineralized.

The molten rock itself probably isn't the thing that does the mineralizing, but when it gets fairly close to the surface, its heat sets up huge hot water convective cells in the ground water system. That hot water is free either to extract gold out of the molten material itself or from surrounding country rocks that may be cold but may carry gold and other minerals. The water will extract the minerals and move them into the favorable faults. When it all cools and solidifies, you end up with ore veins and ore deposits. This has happened several times in Idaho's geologic past. Most of the gold deposits in the central and southern part of the state are related to those kind of structures.

The gold deposits in Idaho are generally very shallow. If you go down fifteen hundred feet you have found one that's really deep. In the late 1800s miners only went several hundred feet below the surface. They got what gold ore they could handle with primitive metallurgy, and then quit.

Some of those deposits have never been mined since. That is another aspect of today's gold rush. Companies are looking at those old deposits, not to see if they can go deeper, but to make an open pit to remove all the gold-bearing ore that's left in the area. Although the deposits are low grade, they are minable. They are near the surface, so you can use heavy equipment rather than go underground. You just scoop the ore up with big shovels, haul it over to a pad, leach it, and extract the gold. All this can be done at very low cost compared to underground mining.

The Silver City area in Owyhee County is enjoying as much of a gold rush as the area between Boise Basin and Bear Track Creek. The faults in Owyhee County are the young seventeen-million-year-old basin and range ones. That region is still stretching. Gold mineralization there is different than the older type of deposits in central Idaho, but they are still amenable to bulk mining. The very low grade of ore is compensated for by the very high tonnage.

A number of companies staked claims in southeastern Oregon and over into Idaho all last winter. So the gold boom is going on from DeLamar on into the

Weiser country. All of this means a great deal to Idaho. If we develop the mines, we have employment. Mining develops a tax base. One of the major sources of tax revenue right now for Valley County is from the two heap leach gold mines at Yellow Pine and Thunder Mountain. If Bear Track Creek comes on line, Lemhi County, somewhat depressed, will improve its tax base.

There are benefits from exploration ventures alone. We figure each exploration project represents about half a million dollar investment within the state. In 1988, we had sixty-eight exploration programs under way, then jumped to eighty-two in 1989. That was forty million dollars spent before there ever was a mining operation. That is a good investment for Idaho, considering that people are just looking. If they develop the property, that is a much bigger bonus. As long as the price of gold stays in the $400 per ounce range, we'll see continued exploration and development of Idaho's gold deposits.

When we turn to talk about silver, we talk mostly about the Coeur d'Alene district, our most famous mining area, which has very old ore deposits located near the Osburn fault. That silver is probably 500 million to 800 million years old.

The silver minerals in the Coeur d'Alene district are tetrahedrite, a complex association of sulphur, silver, antimony, and several other metals in minor amounts. It is a totally different kind of mineralogy than that of gold. Other minerals are galena, which is lead sulfide, and sphalerite.

The Osburn fault formed when two pieces of the earth slid twenty miles past each other. The Lucky Friday mine, one of the big producers in the District, is about twenty miles from the Bunker Hill mine. The Osburn fault is in between those two properties. Long ago, before the movement of the Osburn fault, the Lucky Friday ore deposit would have been right across from the Bunker Hill. The Osburn fault has a very long history. It probably goes back millions, perhaps billions, of years. It may still be active today.

The Osburn fault had nothing to do with the mineralization in the Coeur d'Alene district. The actual processes that generated the mineralization in the Coeur d'Alene district are much older than the latest fault movement. The fault just moved things around a little bit. The Coeur d'Alene district is the only place that we find this type of silver mineralization in Idaho. The silver veins are relatively narrow, but they go down to great depths. The only other place that we find this is in nearby Superior, Montana.

There are various theories as to why those are the only places, and this is one of the questions geologists will be looking at for years to come. One theory is that the mineralization probably formed in the old sedimentary basins in Precambrian time, a billion years ago. The mineralization was confined within layers of rock and was trapped there ever after. That is what they are mining now at the Troy mine in Montana. Some of those deposits were intensely deformed and folded. The rocks bent into very tight folds, then later the rocks fractured. The silver, lead, and zinc-bearing mineral moved out of the original stratiform (layer-like) deposits into the vein deposits. That's one theory. It happens to be mine, so it's probably the correct one!

Others think the veins may be simple hydrothermal deposits. Molten material could have come from the lower part of the earth's crust as part of a big hot water system. Still another theory is that metamorphism cooked the whole package of rocks. Heat and pressure might have moved ores out of the surrounding rock and into these veins. This is a plausible explanation also. Nobody really knows.

In the Coeur d'Alene district, all the major mines are now over a mile deep. That's a lot of rock to be working under. There is a tremendous amount of stress in the ground. One of the problems in the district is rock bursts. The rocks literally explode at that depth, especially when man is down there making tunnels through the rocks and changing the stress field within them.

All of the mines monitor their underground workings. They watch for stress build-up in the rocks. When they see a build-up coming which might result in a rock burst, they close that part of the mine until the stress is relieved. The Hecla Mining Company has just gone to a new mining method in the last two years called an "underhand long-wall system." They hope it will allow them to mine much deeper and not worry about stress build-up at great depths. It would also increase their productivity substantially. That would reduce their costs per ounce of silver. Other mining companies are watching them pretty closely to see how well it's going to work.

The deepest mine in North America was the Star Morning mine, which closed several years ago. That mine was 7,900 feet from top to bottom, the same depth as the deepest part of Hells Canyon. The company was in relatively good ore when they ceased mining operations. Mining stopped because Hecla felt they could go no deeper and keep the operation economical. The underground facilities and conditions at the bottom of the shaft were very difficult.

The rock burst problem may be a limiting factor on how deep one can go in the Coeur d'Alene district. Hence the interest we have in the long-wall system and how it's going to work out. Perhaps the mining engineers will invent new ways to go deeper. If you can solve problems and still extract silver that will make you money, you can keep going down past 8,000 feet. If you get to a point where the grade of the ore isn't good enough to make a profit on it, then the mines will end.

All mining districts have a finite life; they eventually end. The Coeur d'Alene District has the largest recorded silver production of any mining district in the world. A few years the total went over a billion ounces of silver. That is phenomenal when you consider that they have been mining only a little over a hundred years. The first lode discoveries were in 1884. Since that time we've removed a billion ounces of silver. There are only three or four other districts in the world with records close to that. Two mines in Mexico, and one in Peru have come close to a billion ounces. Those mines started during the Spanish Conquest in the 1500s. The Coeur d'Alene district eclipsed them in a little over a hundred years. That is a lot of rock—and a lot of silver.

# Phosphorus

*Roscoe J. Bolton, a Senior Geologist with the Monsanto Company in Soda Springs, Idaho, mines phosphate ore. Phosphorus was discovered in Idaho in 1903, and miners were shipping ore to the West Coast by 1911. One reason for its economic value is that our society likes to eat steak, of which twelve and a half percent by weight is phosphorus, iron, and calcium. Cattle ingest the phosphate from alfalfa and other feed.*

*Monsanto ships the ore by truck on a private haul road to its plant two miles north of Soda Springs. At the plant large electric furnaces convert the phosphate ore to elemental phosphorus. The company ships the phosphorus by tank cars to various burning plants in Long Beach, California, and St. Louis, Missouri, where it is converted to phosphoric acid and combined with other elements to provide useful compounds.*

About 450 million years ago shortly after the beginning of the Paleozoic Era, there was a shallow sea reaching from the Idaho-Wyoming border nearly to Boise, and extending north and south along the coast of the ancient American continent. It was a low area into which streams flowed. Sediments accumulated in this shallow trough-like region. The sediments accumulated to such a thickness that their great weight caused the trough to subside.

In Permian time, roughly 285 million to 245 million years ago, there was a smaller sea that extended from northern Utah to about Butte, Montana, and westward to near Boise. Under the sea were warm upwelling currents that brought in nutrients, phosphate in particular. The phosphate replaced calcium which occurred in small pellets of calcite rolling back and forth on the sea floor with the currents. That is how the phosphate layers were formed. This process was very slow.

Today phosphate is being formed off the coasts of Baja California and the Bahamas. When the phosphate in Idaho was deposited, North America was near the equator. It was hot and arid—just right for deposition of phosphates.

The layer of phosphate was originally flat because it was deposited on a continental shelf. But about 150 million years ago, the North American plate collided with the Pacific plate. The pressure caused some layers to move east from where they were. It was "overthrust," in other words. The overthrusting caused folding. So now we

*Roscoe J. Bolton*

have beds that dip from horizontal to near vertical.

We have mountains here today because about 17 million years ago there was a period of block faulting. This means that there was a series of earthquakes during which a block of earth on the west side would drop down while the block on the east side would rise up. Then there would be erosion. The two formations above and below the Phosphoria (the Wells underneath and Rex Chert above) are more resistant to the erosion. That layering sequence more or less protected the Phosphoria from being eroded away.

The Wells formation below is mostly sandstone. The phosphate ore occurs in a lower ore zone about forty feet thick and an upper ore zone about fifteen feet thick. About eighty feet of waste shale separates the two ore zones. There are a few waste seams between some of the ore zones. Some of the zones have a higher grade ore than other ones.

We are now mining the lower ore zone of the Meade Peak member of the Phosphoria formation. It is roughly forty feet thick. We mine it by facing it up in roughly twenty foot lifts with a Caterpillar tractor, which has a slope board arm on it. The arm adjusts so you can knock the ore down. Then we pick the ore up and haul it to the ore pile with scrapers.

Mining mainly takes place on ridges because that is where the ore is closer to the surface and is economical to mine. Ore in the valleys may be covered by five hundred feet or more of alluvium and can not be economically mined with today's technology.

# Gravel

*Idaho was the site of the world's two largest floods. Most geologic processes occur slowly, over thousands and millions of years. In contrast, these floods were catastrophic, sudden, and occurred in a period of days and weeks, not millions of years. Dr. Hal Malde, retired geologist, U.S. Geological Survey in Colorado, was the geologist/detective who discovered how the stacks of boulders found throughout the length of the Snake River canyon came to be there.*

I was working in the Snake River area with Howard Powers, a senior geologist who was working on volcanic rocks while I was working on the sedimentary rocks. It fell to me to pay attention to

*Hal Malde*

the surface aspects of the landscape. After a while we realized that the debris (scattered boulders and gravel) in places like Hagerman was a consequence of the overflow of Lake Bonneville, and not from the old Snake River simply washing over some lava flow that happened to reach the canyon at an earlier time.

We came upon a Stinker Station billboard, down near King Hill. It was in a field covered with uniformly sized one-foot boulders of this debris. The billboard said, "Petrified watermelons. Take one home to your mother-in-law." So we started calling the flood debris "melon gravel," and it stuck.

One thing that has perplexed me is why the flood remained undiscovered for so many years. There were very competent hydrologists and geologists working in this area who published a great deal of information. Harold Stearns, an early Idaho geologist, thought the boulders came from individual lava flows. It is easy to see how one could make that interpretation because downstream from lava flows there are boulders derived from that lava flow. I don't think I can remember any more just how it all seemed to suddenly fall into place. But it did.

Suddenly I realized that the erosion and the distribution of the boulders and the large alluvial fans spilling out from Pocatello were all related and contemporaneous. I tried to find how these features stretched along the canyon. Then I tried to describe in a report I wrote in the 1960s how all of these things were put together to make a coherent story.

Most geologists' lives in the field are made up of 95 percent just getting from one outcrop to another. The other 5 percent might be spent at making a significant observation. And then, after years of looking, suddenly it is there. It is like solving a detective story. Things fall into place.

Great Salt Lake is just a small remnant of the immense lake that existed during the ice age. We call that older one Lake Bonneville. It was comparable in size to one of today's Great Lakes and was over one thousand feet deep at one time. It was so large and heavy that it depressed the crust of the earth under it.

The surface of Lake Bonneville, like other lakes in the Great Basin during the ice age, fluctuated widely in altitude because of changes in climate. The lakes would fall when it was dry and rise when it was wet. Lake Bonneville went up and down many times. When it reached its highest point, about fifteen thousand years ago, the lake found an outlet at Red Rock Pass near Preston, Idaho.

Once a breach had formed, the lake cut rapidly down. It eroded the soft material that was in its path, and discharged a large part of its water down the Snake River of that time. The lake fell three hundred feet before the flood finally came to an end.

Red Rock Pass is a complex area. It is the only possible place over which the lake could have discharged. The area is complicated by some old landslides that might have been contemporary with the flood. Or they could have happened after the flood. Some of the effects of the flood may have been obliterated by those landslides.

In Hells Canyon there are some high gravel bars about four hundred feet or higher above the Snake River that are attributed to the Bonneville Flood going through. There is also flood debris in the Lewiston area where Hells Canyon enlarges and becomes a basin. It is distinctive because the rock came from Hells Canyon. Stratigraphically, it is overlain by material from the backwash of the Spokane floods. So there are deposits of both floods in the Lewiston Basin. This tells us that the Bonneville flood is older than some of the Spokane floods.

The canyon today is similar to the way it was at the time of the Bonneville flood. It was wide in the Twin Falls area and downstream. Upstream from Twin Falls to Milner, near Burley, it was narrower. The configuration was a circumstance of earlier geologic history, when lava flows had diverted the flow of the Snake River. But the flood greatly modified the canyon. In the stretch where the narrow canyon joins the large canyon at Twin Falls, we have fourteen miles of chaotically eroded landscape. The flood eroded a large quantity of material.

Shoshone Falls is a relic of that time. There probably was a small step in the canyon floor before the flood. But if you look at the resistant rock which forms Shoshone Falls, and trace it downstream, you can see that the surface of that resistent rock becomes lower and lower in the canyon. My guess is that the flood caused that small step to retreat a mile or two upstream. The flood made the 210 foot step that we have now.

Twin Falls is another of the discontinuities created by the flood. The flood enlarged the lower reach of the narrow canyon which extends downstream from Milner. Twin Falls happens to consist of lava flows of basalt, but the same general erosive action of the flood is evident there.

The rock that was being eroded had to go someplace. From Twin Falls downstream, there is a vast quantity of debris—melon gravel. You find it deposited primarily in wide places along the canyon. The first big enlargement of the width of the canyon is at Melon Valley. It contains considerable debris that was eroded from this particular area. An even larger basin with gravel deposits is at Hagerman. Then another fifteen to twenty miles downstream is King Hill, a very large basin. There is a truly enormous volume of the gravel there.

The boulders are quite large. Their sizes were probably determined by the jointing characteristics of the lava flows from which they came. The lava flows are exposed in the cliffs of the canyon. It is broken up into joint blocks, or columns. Those limit the maximum size of the boulders that might be possible. Even so, there are boulders ten to fifteen feet in diameter in places between Shoshone Falls and Hagerman.

Currently a graduate student at the University of Arizona is trying to determine precisely how long it took for all that water to fall from the lake. He uses information about the shape and roughness of the channel, and what got in the way of the water. But on the basis of simple arithmetic, we can estimate that the flood lasted at least eight weeks. All the water probably didn't go out at the same speed. Considering that, the total flood may have lasted a year.

If we compare the Bonneville flood to the very famous Missoula (or Spokane) floods which formed the Scablands of Eastern Washington, we find that the two floods were really different. Lake Bonneville's big overflow was a single event. The lake level never again rose up to that level, and there was no more flooding.

*There was more than one Missoula flood. The largest was larger by twenty times the Bonneville flood, and crossed North Idaho. Dr. Roy Breckenridge of the Idaho Geological Survey traced its path. The floods explain why there are vast accumulations of gravel in certain places in North Idaho.*

In late Pleistocene time, the last glaciation in this part of the world, large masses of ice were advancing southward from Canada into the northern Rocky Mountain states. One major lobe came down the Purcell Trench, a large trough between Bonners Ferry and Sandpoint. This ice mass progressed southward to just past where the city of Sandpoint is today. This huge glacier blocked the flow of the Clark Fork River in Idaho near the towns of Clark Fork and Hope. The Clark Fork River drained a huge area of western Montana. The glacier lobe caused over five hundred cubic miles of water to be impounded in glacial Lake Missoula.

At its maximum the ice dam held water more than a thousand feet deep at Clark Fork. It would have been nearly seven hundred or eight hundred feet deep at Missoula, Montana. The ice was very unstable as a dam. The dam suddenly failed, releasing water down what is now the Lake Basin of Lake Pend Oreille and a second route down the Little Spokane River past Newport, Washington.

The main path of this large flood came through Rathdrum Prairie, down through where the city of Spokane is now, and pulsed down into the Columbia River. It was blocked near Grand Coulee by another ice lobe and poured down through central eastern Washington, creating what we call the Channeled Scabland.

At first geologists thought this had happened only a few times. But by studying the layers of the gravel deposits, we now think it happened many times, perhaps as many as forty or more multiple outbursts. The best dates we have now place floods between 18,000 years and 11,000 years ago. Some of the loess (silt) deposits in central Washington show that it may have happened in the glacial period even before that.

The figures on the size of the flood are so awesome, it's really hard to describe. The maximum discharge was on the order of twenty-plus times the total flow of all the rivers in the world all put together. That is

*Roy Breckenridge*

pretty hard to imagine. There is nothing like it in history that we can relate to.

Many features of the flood can be seen today. The river valley was there before the ice came. But when the ice dam blocked the river, sediments started accumulating in the lake basin. Today the dominant features up in the Lake Missoula Basin are what we call varved lake beds. They are very fine, thinly laminated clays and silts. You see them all up the valley of the Clark Fork. At the outburst area itself, this huge mass of water, with its current and velocity, carried large boulders as well as finer material.

When you look across the river from Clark Fork you see a gravel bar that was built by the outwash of the Lake Missoula floods. People driving down the road see rolling topography in the fields. These are actually giant current ripples. We usually see them on the shores of lakes or at the beach, where the ripples are quite small, inches in size. But there are several hundred feet between the crests of the giant ripples. It tells you something about the mega-hydraulics that resulted from emptying the lake.

The gravel pits outside Sandpoint down the Pend Oreille River are built up of flood gravels that were flowing down a secondary channel, the Pend Oreille, to the

Little Spokane River. You can see large steeply dipping foreset beds that are inclined in a downstream direction. The size of these crossbeds is another indication of the huge currents, velocity, and volume of water in the catastrophic floods.

The floods left us with a number of resources. Pend Oreille Lake approaches twelve hundred feet deep. The valley was there before, but the ice and the flood scoured the basin to this greater depth. The Rathdrum Aquifer Spokane Valley gravel is one of the largest sole-source aquifers in the United States. Spokane and many of the small towns in the region get all their water out of this huge aquifer. It has been called an underground river. Of course, the water moves between the gravels left by the Missoula floods. The aquifer supplies domestic water, irrigation and agricultural water, and water for the aluminum and power industries.

Sometimes we forget about construction materials as a valuable resource. Sand and gravel are necessities for building. Nationwide they exceed the worth of precious metal mining. You have to be in a place where you don't have such gravel available to really appreciate it. Besides the interesting story of glacial Lake Missoula and the floods, everyday life of people who live in the area is involved with its result on the landscape.

## Hagerman Horse Fossil Bones

*Fossils are the remains of plants and animals that lived upon the earth in ages past. Their remains or imprints are found within layers of sediments that accumulated because of the presence of oceans, lakes, floods, or just the blowing of the wind. At Hagerman, Idaho, there is a bed of fossil bones layered within the sediments of the floodplains along Lake Idaho, a lake much older than Lake Bonneville. There are so many bones, and of so many species, that the Hagerman Fossil Beds National Monument is referred to for short as a "quarry," and mined for its rich scientific treasure.*

*At the quarry is a concentration of the bones of Idaho's state fossil, the*

*Ted Weasma*

*Hagerman Horse. This particular animal was a now-extinct zebra. Since it grazed in an open forest and grassland environment, it may have had stripes as protective coloration the way African zebras do today. Paleontologist Ted Weasma works for the Bureau of Land Management and studies the zebras and other creatures that lived by the shores of the old lake.*

In order to preserve a fossil, you have to bury it. When an animal dies, the bones usually lay out on the surface where carnivores can attack them. Temperature changes between day and night cause the bones to break apart, which in turn allows bacteria to attack them. So if an animal dies in the desert today, the bones will be destroyed in about three years by natural processes.

At Hagerman, there existed a very long-lived lake and stream system. For millions of years an animal that happened to die in that particular area would have its bones buried and preserved instead of laying out on the surface. That is why they were preserved. We don't really understand why all the horses are in one particular spot in the quarry.

The sediments at Hagerman were all deposited in or along the shore of Lake Idaho, which existed between four million and two million years ago. It extended from Twin Falls, Idaho, all the way to Adrian, Oregon. It was a very large lake system that lasted for a long period of time. We're not sure if it was one extremely large lake or a series of lakes all connected together. But the fossils throughout are all very similar.

It is highly likely that what occurred at Lake Idaho is what is occurring in Africa today. In times of drought, horses and other grazing animals congregate around a watering hole. They eat up all the local vegetation. Then they die in that area, where they are buried and preserved.

Streams fed into the lake and flooded each year, depositing sediments in the lake and covered up any animals that might have died. The tremendous variety of fossil wildlife includes frogs, turtles, fish, birds, beaver, otter, shrews, voles, mice—all the way up to horses. There were also giant ground sloths, about the size of large bears, camels, llamas, and mastodons. The mastodon was probably the largest animal that grazed at this particular spot.

We know quite a lot about the North American horse, or zebra, *Equus simplicidens*. It was a side shoot of the horse family, found throughout North America. The best collections, however, are found here at the Hagerman Fossil Beds in Idaho. The original discovery was in the early 1920s. The first Smithsonian expedition came in 1929, did some excavations, and returned in 1930, 1931, and 1934. They took tremendous collections back to Washington.

There is a great bone bed here for this particular species. There is no other place in the world that has the quantity or quality of specimens for this horse. The skull is very large compared to its body. It looks a little bit oversized. That is very true in modern zebras, too.

There are many other species here, too. But they are known mainly because of this horse, which is now the state fossil. The display at the Hagerman Historical Society is an exact replica, not the original bones. Most paleontologists today will not destroy a bone to mount it. We make exact replicas and mount those.

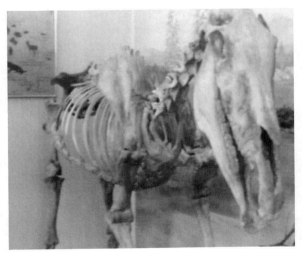

***Hagerman Horse***

This keeps the original specimens for further research and study.

The small mammals are considered extremely important because they tell us a lot more about the local ecology. The zebras and camels were grazers that roamed over a large area. They do not tell us much that is very site specific. The shrews, voles, and little pocket mice on the other hand, don't graze over the whole of North America. They stay home. These small animals tell us about the temperature, the climate, and the vegetation of an area. They are very specific about what they eat.

Between four million and two million years ago, which is the age of the Glenns Ferry formation, in which we find the fossils, there was a cooling trend going on through North America. The changes in the animals during that span of time help us understand what was going on. The area was getting drier because the Cascade Mountains were rising. They cut off the marine currents coming from the ocean. It had not been a tropical, but probably a moderate Mediterranean-type environment—a little warmer and moister than what it is today.

We don't have a good idea why the horses disappeared from North America. Llamas and camels also disappeared. There are some indications from archaeological sites that horses were still here during the Pleistocene glacial epoch. They might have been hunted by early man. Whether early man hunted them to extinction, there is not enough evidence to tell us.

One of the unique features of the Hagerman Fossil Beds is the fact that a lot of our discoveries are not made by excavations. They are found right on the surface. Wind and water erosion during the winter every year expose new fossils on the surface. I often find turtle shells, fish bones, rodent jaws, bird and other bones buried in good concentrations. I picked up a complete beaver jaw earlier this year. We found two different beavers here. One was equivalent to a modern beaver, and the other was smaller. So it is a very fine location for the paleontologist.

Another unique thing about the Hagerman Fossil Beds is the way the ants move small mammal bones to the top of their ant hills. It is a way to control the temperature of the hill. Paleontologists love it because they have all these little guys collecting for them.

## Fossil Leaves Of St. Maries

*Fifteen million years ago or more a flow of lava dammed up the St. Maries River. The lake had a short life, because as all lakes eventually do, it filled with silt. It may have existed only two hundred years, but certainly no more than one thousand. The silt filled the lake to a depth of about twenty-seven feet. The siltation process happened so fast, the silt covered and preserved anything that washed or blew into the lake and sank to the bottom.*

*All remained as it had for millions of years. Then, in 1971, Francis Kienbaum of Clarkia, Idaho, was bulldozing the side of a hill while building a snowmobile track. Large chunks of clay with well-preserved leaves fell from the bank. Kienbaum named his track the Fossil Bowl and entered into a partnership with the University of Idaho to study and preserve the fossils. Dr. Charles (Jack) Smiley, University of Idaho, emeritus professor of geology, supervises the project and visits the Fossil Bowl frequently with students and scientists from all over the world who are attracted to this strange concentration of colorful leaves, ants, and trout.*

The topography was just about the same then as it is now. There has been little change in the last fifteen million to twenty million years. The forested hills are what we call "basement." These are the Precambrian basement rocks of the whole region. They are metamorphic rocks that are over 1000 million years old. The low flat valley bottom, where the lake was, is now a grassy plain on top of the ancient lake deposits. It extends about twenty-five miles down the present St. Maries River Valley.

During Miocene time, lava flows poured out from cracks in the earth's crust to form the Columbia lava plateau. Some of that lava dammed this river valley to form the lakes. It was probably dammed several times by lava flows of different ages. This particular lake bed resulted from just one of those episodes of lava damming. Like any reservoir created by modern man, it began to silt in. We estimate the lake existed for a span of about 750 to 1,000 years. Finally, the outlet stream going across the dam cut down far enough so that the lake just disappeared. And we have the sediments with the fossils preserved inside.

At the beginning, the lake was deep enough that the bottom was stagnant. It was poisonous and lacked oxygen. Sediments accumulated very rapidly, so that it created a rather unusual type of preservation for fossils. That is what we've been digging fossils from—these unoxidized lake deposits.

Climatically there has been great change since Miocene time. The world climates were much warmer than they are now. The Cascade Mountains were not elevated yet. The storms coming from the Pacific came here to the western slopes of the Rocky Mountains, which were elevated. As weather systems climb up over higher elevations, there is greater precipitation. Naturally there would have been totally different vegetation here then. Today we find that type of climate and vegetation in the Carolinas and Georgia and Tennessee. We find it in the Yangtze River Valley of south central China and in southern Japan. Those places have a hot, muggy climate in the summer and mild, very short winters.

Global climates cooled. We don't know why. They cooled to the Pleistocene ice ages, when glaciers came to the Northern Hemisphere. The Cascade Mountains rose. That caused a rain shadow between the Cascade Mountains and the Rocky Mountains. It became drier. Now there are cool, rather severe long winters. We get mountain clouds in summertime, while in the lowlands to the west, there are few summer clouds and it is very dry. With that kind of change, the vegetation has to change, too.

*Charles (Jack) Smiley*

Very rapid deposition of lake sediments brought about this very fine preservation of fossil fish and fossil leaves. There was an anoxic situation on the bottom of the deep lake—no oxygen. This means that there were no scavengers down there and no bacteria. When the fish died their bodies settled on the lake bottom. So did the leaves when they were blown into the lake. They just sat there on the lake bottom. There was no change of any kind—chemical, organic, or physical. The water did not even move. So everything remained as well preserved as if they had been dumped into a pond yesterday. There has simply been no change. That is what is so striking about this deposit.

There are thick volcanic ash layers in the lake bed, and a lot of thinner ones, too. In between are thinly layered lake deposits. We get our fossils in these thin layers. Our best guess right now is that small storms muddied the lake, after which the mud settled to the bottom. Some of the thicker layers represent larger storms, which brought more mud into the lake.

Most of the leaves we find are blackened, but once in a while we find the original colors of green, red, or tan. Down at a lower level of the lake deposits, we find fish. Most of the fossil fish are small sunfish, but at the level where we found white volcanic ash, we found a trout, twenty-eight inches long and intact. That's the biggest fish we have found.

We have found swamp cypress, or bald cypress now found in the Everglades in Florida. This type of conifer once grew all over the Northern Hemisphere and is now extinct except on the eastern coast of the United States. Its close relative, the coast redwood of California, was also all over the Northern Hemisphere at one time. Still another close relative, the dawn redwood, now grows only in China. Each of these grew all over the world, but are now restricted pretty much to small local habitats.

We found an extinct member of the beech, closely related to the modern beech. I identified it as a new genus, *Pseudofagus*. At the base, the petiole of the leaf has a flute nut still attached. That nut is most like the nuts that you find on the modern beech. The leaf is very similar to the leaf of modern beech, but the nut is so unique that there is nothing living like this today.

We find the leaves of a tupelo—*Nyssa*, a tree now growing in the swampy areas of the southeastern United States. There are magnolias. We have bayleaf here—laurel.

We also get insects in the lake bed. Some of them have their original colors preserved. So far we have found four different kinds of fish, and about 120 different species of forest plants.

So far we have found no mammals or water birds. We haven't found a single feather. This is unusual because in other Miocene lakes there are birds. We know there were frogs, salamanders, beaver, horses, and bears around in those years in the western United States. Why not in the Clarkia deposits is just a question we don't have an answer for.

We visited a place similar to this one in China a couple of years ago. They have deer that are preserved just like our fish, with the skeletons intact and the carbon outline of the body all over the skeleton. They have frogs and snakes. Why not here? We just don't know.

One of the trout we found shrunk in size. When we first found it and exposed it to the air, it measured twenty-eight inches long. We had to break it out in pieces. When we got it to the laboratory, the water-saturated clay lost its water, and the pieces shrunk. It shrunk thirteen percent. It made a nice fish story.

We have found other floras of this approximate age elsewhere in the world, but they are not preserved like these. We can compare the chemistry of these old leaves with modern species of the same genus, and get a better sense of how close the relationship is. The insect damage shows that they fed on the plants in certain ways. Just from knowing the type of damage and the specific leaf, an insect specialist can tell what insect did the chewing, even though you can't find the insect.

A complete study of all the different kind of plants here would include a comparison of ancient cellular anatomy with modern cellular anatomy, morphology of the leaves, and the range of variations. We would do a computer analysis of all the data on each species. We've done it for only two species so far. One study was a master's thesis at the University of Idaho and took three years and involved four or five other people.

So we have many years of research here just waiting for the people who will be interested in doing this sort of thing. Someone might call me to say, "Jack, I want to work on world maple fossils. Do you have some?" I would say we have four species, two of which have never been described any place else in the world. Bit by bit, the work will get done and get published.

The St. Maries fossils are very significant, scientifically. It's not a good amateur collecting site because the specimens easily break up into nothing. So it's not significant economically. But it is the only place in the world where you can get the combination of preserved features in a single species. Some places have the cellular anatomy of a species, but not chemistry. Or leaves, but not fruits, or chemistry. Here you can get it all. Most of the plant species we find here are the most common kinds of plants found in these types of deposits around the world, so this site is pretty classic. It is commonly referred to as one of the few world-class fossil localities of its kind.

*Courtesy of Charles Smiley*

**Fossil Leaves**

# *Wilderness*

## THE EVOLUTION OF AN ENTERPRISE

*The mountains endure for the centuries, but human values change by the decade. What was once thought of as backcountry is now wilderness, a politically established management designation made by the U.S. Congress. The once elite big game hunters who went there by the handfuls have been joined by hunters who go by the thousands. In the past, lack of access and information kept mineral and other resources effectively locked up. Today, there is an abundance of information and access, and "locked up" has become an epithet of protest against the designation of lands for wilderness status.*

*One of the first people to create a commercial enterprise in Idaho's backcountry wilderness was Leon L. "Andy" Anderson of Challis. Anderson built "Middle Fork of the Salmon River White Water Float Trips" in 1946, the first business to sell excursion float trips down the Salmon River. Jack Simplot and three others went on the first trip, Barry Goldwater of Arizona on the second, and Bill Harrah from Reno, the third.*

When I started out, Jack Simplot had bought a ranch I recommended to him. He flew four little yellow Air Force boats into the ranch. He wasn't able to return for about a month afterward, so I took one of the yellow boats, rigged it up as well as I could, and took out in it. That was a trip that was almost too much for anybody to try and make. Alone, going down the river, I could hear the rapids ahead of me. I would pull in and walk down to see them. I would figure out which channels I could detect to get through them. This continued clear on down to the confluence of the Middle Fork with the Main Salmon. I took about ten days to just work my way down. There were a lot of times I wished I had never started, it was so scary.

When I got back home I thought to myself, "If you're going to run that river, commercialize. Stay with it for a while." I packed the boat down to the Middle Fork and took out again. My wife Melba went with me. She was the first woman to ever go through that canyon. We made it. It was spooky all right. I turned right around and I went again alone. I wanted to learn it.

At the time, nobody else had really run the river successfully. Quite a few started up above Camas Creek, but they tore their boats up. They were trying to run it in wooden boats. They walked out. One of them was Dr. R. G. Frazier from Bingham, Utah. He was a river runner and he had two or three friends who were. (Incidently, he was Admiral Byrd's doctor when he went to the South Pole.) He went through on rubber boats, little Air Force yellow rubber boats like the one I had.

Pretty soon Joe, my brother, came over and said, "Well, let's take that boat through." We had to know quite a bit about it to get us all through there. We had three boats, and he brought a couple of men who worked with him and the boys. We had our experiences, I'll tell you. Everybody was just paddling. We would get all mixed up—somebody paddling the wrong way would just spin around the rocks.

One time Dr. Frazier offered me a map. "I'll draw you a map to show the right way to hit some of these rapids, so you'll be safer," he said. He sent the map and a letter, but it didn't mean a thing to me after I got around the first turn. I just went ahead and fought it out.

When I started out there were no airfields on the river. People were scared to fly in because nobody had an airstrip. It was all pack horse. We packed our boats, the people, their duffle, our supplies, everything. That was quite a bit of work, packing them in, you know. I have pictures of a pack string you can't believe—about eighteen head of horses, packed solid for a party of eight. They call them the "good old days," but they weren't the good old days. That was a lot of work.

There was no road into Dagger Falls for years after I started. We had about a fourteen-mile ride to the river, the people riding, too. A lot of them had never been on a horse. But we had good horses that knew what the trail was and where they were going. We just put them on the horses and told them to let the horse follow us. We got by fine. We had to stop a time or two and let people get off and stretch their legs. That old saddle got pretty hard on them before they got down to the river. None of them seemed to complain about it really, because they had a chance to see things. The pack trail is a pretty trail. Nobody gave us much problem.

I was the first person to take paying customers down. I had no trouble at all getting magazine people to go with me. My float trips and I were written up in twenty magazines. A fellow by the name of Al Brick with the Sun Valley Company was an adventurous photographer and wanted to go. He made the film for Twentieth Century Fox. I heard from foreign countries after that. People got my name.

I figured I could make a business of running the river because it was so remote and nobody was running it. I thought it had a possibility. I kept after it, building up my advertising. One of the first who went with me was Barry Goldwater, the senator from Arizona. I ran into him when I was at Scottsdale in the winter. I talked to him about the river. He said, "I want to go. I don't care how wild it is. I'll go with you." The next spring he did, with some family and a couple of other people. By that time I'd gotten away from little yellow Air Force boats and had seven-man boats that I rigged up with good frames. He made a color film of the river for me and gave me a copy for a Christmas present. I had that for advertising. I'd travel in the wintertime with my projector and screen and show pictures to sportsmen's clubs and chambers of commerce. I built my business up and

*Courtesy of Andy Anderson*

**Andy Anderson**

built it up good.

I ran it for paying guests every summer for twenty-seven years since 1946. That was my summer home. It couldn't have been too hard work or I wouldn't have done it. But I got old, too; that was against me. I finally sold out and decided I better quit because I was getting so I wasn't active enough to jump in and out of the boats. It got to be all work then.

Making it a wilderness changed it because of the volume of people that can go. Thousands of people want to go into all the different wilderness areas. That is what made the big difference.

No, I'm not happy it was made into wilderness. I wasn't real happy about airfields when I first started out. I knew those airfields were going to bring in a lot more people. And they did. Of course, they made it a lot easier on us, because I could fly my equipment and people instead of packing them in. It helped and yet it didn't. It was seven years after I'd started to run the river before I saw another boat. It wasn't overcrowded then, and it wasn't overcrowded for quite a few years. But when they made it this wilderness and advertised it that way, there are just that many people who want to go to a wilderness regardless.

There are way too many people on the river now. There are so many that they don't have campsites for them. They've had to eliminate some of the outfitters who were going in there on account of that. They can't eliminate anyone who takes their own boat and goes. There is a drawing as to what days they get, but they can't eliminate them. A lot of people can run it.

Yes, I'm afraid I have taken my last trip down the river. There are times that I get to thinking I'd like to go again. I wouldn't want to go until after school starts and when the volume of people leave. They'd spoil it for me really. I had it to myself so long. I've got a hankering to go again. My sons Ted or Terry now take me anytime I want to go. I don't know. I'll be eighty years old next birthday. I get to thinking how awkward I've got. I don't know whether I'd like it or not. You get to liking leisurely, lazy stuff when you're sitting around in chairs. As you get old they say it's the golden years, but I don't think so.

Those years on the river were my golden years. You bet.

*The Wilderness Act was passed in 1964, carried on the floor of the Senate by Idaho Senator Frank Church. This legislation created a new classification of protection for federal lands. Its goal was to preserve wild lands from development, road construction, and motorized traffic and equipment. It also governed fire suppression efforts. The wilderness itself was identified as a primary resource. When the act was passed, it also designated several pieces of land as "instant" wilderness areas such as the Selway-Bitterroot in North Idaho. Additions to the wilderness system require an act of Congress. The Frank Church-River of No Return Wilderness was added in 1980.*

*Prior to the passage of the Wilderness Act, the Forest Service protected de facto wilderness under a system of "primitive" areas. The Central Idaho Primitive Area later became the Frank Church-River of No Return Wilderness. The primitive area system, created in the 1930s, protected lands from logging and road-building.*

*Ernie Day of Boise is one of the people who organized wilderness and preservation campaigns in Idaho, and whose effort and conviction had an impact felt across the United States.*

I first fell in love with the Sawtooths while on our honeymoon, when we stayed at the Clark Miller Dude Ranch in the Sawtooth Valley. I spent a lot of time hiking out of Grandjean mostly, and developed a real feeling for the Sawtooth Mountains. Then I saw a certain map. It was an aerial picture on a scale that was unbelievably large. The map showed proposed road systems up these canyons. My new love was going to be raped by this road system. That was when I became apprehensive and dedicated to the preservation of the Sawtooth wilderness.

It was a Primitive Area at the time, as ragged and rugged as you can find, but it is also the most tender area you can imagine. Erodible granite won't stand any abuse. It is exceptionally fragile. We would have lost the number one wilderness asset in the whole state of Idaho if these roads were built.

Probably some Idahoans always realized that the outdoors was a finite situation. Prior to the sixties and seventies, it was still like the frontier of the West. The land seemed so vast. If you didn't like a place, you moved on. After the war, people finally realized that we were taking something for granted which shouldn't be taken for granted. Almost everybody that you talked to, even the people who developed the minerals and the grazing and the logging, said, "Let's keep it like it is." But it is impossible to keep it like it is and keep overgrazing, overroading, overlogging, and openpitting.

As that became apparent some people thought, "We better do something about this." Some of us realized we had to have statutory protection of wilderness. We could not rely on the signature of the Secretary of Interior or Secretary of Agriculture as we had done since the mid-thirties when the Idaho Primitive Area was designated. That designation could have been abolished by the stroke of a pen. Some of us didn't feel too secure with that.

That's when the real battles for wilderness started in Idaho. It started nationwide about the same time.

It was a very dedicated group. They were not all Idahoans. Some of our best advocates from the inception were folks who had lost something someplace else. That is one ingredient that almost all conservationists have—they have lost something first, and they don't want to lose anymore. We had a few people from California, which many Idahoans resented.

**Ernie Day**

Nonetheless, those folks had already lost one round someplace. When they got here, they thought this place was too good to let go by default. Thank God we had them. We did have a core group of locals who were for the Wilderness Act. They wanted to make the Primitive Area a Wilderness and even to make it a National Park. We worked for a long time to get this designated a National Park. It wasn't because I was enthralled by that idea, but because the protection would be much greater.

The Idaho Wildlife Federation was the first large group to back the Wilderness bill in 1959 or 1960. There was a small core of people who realized that we had to get help from the east. We served as a beacon that these eastern people homed in on.

The early core group promoting preservation and protection came from the hunters and the fishermen. That's not really surprising because many of them had realized for a long time that good habitat is essential for good game. Hunters and fishermen were more knowledgeable about it. This was their bailiwick.

Our strategy was based on a gut feeling that most people did want to keep Idaho the way it was, and we tried to get that message across. Those people coalesced behind the original Wilderness Act, and later pushed for six specific areas: the Selway-Bitterroot, the Sawtooths, White Clouds, Hells Canyon, the River of No Return, and Middle Fork of the Salmon.

Probably the most outstanding of the group was Bruce Bowler, a local attorney. There was Frank Jones, who was a printer. One of the most effective was Mort Brigham of Lewiston, who became self-employed due to the issue. We were all self-employed. The issue didn't play too well with the corporations even then. A bit later, Ted Trueblood joined with us. He wasn't part of the original few for the Wilderness Act itself, but he was one of the main players in the Frank Church-River of No Return issue.

Had any of those four people been working for somebody else, I think their bosses would have called them in and said, "Cool it." But you couldn't tell Frank Jones that, and you sure couldn't tell Bruce Bowler what to do. He is the number-one-all-time conservationist. Nobody has written as many letters to as many lawmakers as Bruce Bowler. Trueblood was known on the national scene as an editor of *Field and Stream.* That's the way it worked. I never felt endangered. I may have sold a few less houses to people because I was not recommended, but that was early in the game. I really didn't feel I was making any great sacrifice although my blood pressure went up quite a bit frequently. I must admit that.

We formed a little group we called the Idaho Wilderness Users Committee. That's what the effort stemmed from. We sought help from the Wilderness Society, a national preservation group, and its Olaus Murie, Howard Zahnizer and Stewart Brandborg.

We showed slides around. Our message fell on pretty deaf ears every place except with Frank Church. I spent some time on the board of the National Wildlife Federation. When I was a delegate, I sat next to the delegate from Illinois. I used to sputter occasionally about all the fights and problems we were having. He would say, "You should be so lucky. We lost all that years ago." In Idaho, we have not only the resources, but the time to save it. The bad examples in other places were important too, because they made us more dedicated. You just had to make certain that this didn't happen to Idaho.

I don't like to call it a "group of four" because we had friends all over the state. We headed it up because we were in Boise. We had evening meetings and we stuffed envelopes. We did all the things you had to do. Senator Frank Church early advocated for wilderness. That was courageous for him. Some of his closest associates thought it was political suicide. Thank God Frank Church championed wilderness. In the last days of the Wilderness Act battle, when Clinton Anderson was ill, Church carried the Act to its completion. In 1964 it was signed, a window in history, and thank God it happened. Later it culminated in the River of No Return Wilderness, 2.3 million acres. It is still the largest coherent wilderness in the United States outside of Alaska.

We were semi-successful. We about half finished the job as far as acreage is concerned. But as my friend Martin Morache used to say, "We have the hay in the barn." With the 4 million acres we have, it's some of the best. There are still many precious places that need to be secured. There are 9 million acres of de facto wilderness in Idaho right now. A lot of it is in trouble, at least 3 million should be saved. They are in areas from the north through the southwest. I could recite the whole Christmas list if you want it. I think you understand. There is much more to be done.

Perhaps we were more powerful than people realized. The Idaho corporate structure has boards and interlocking directorates. We were quietly doing the same thing, but it wasn't quite as obvious. We grew. First we had the Idaho Wildlife Federation, then the Ada County Fish and Game League, which is where many of us cut our teeth. Then we received help from the Sierra Club, the Wilderness Society, the National Wildlife Federation, and Audubon. We got help from any organization we could. We wore hats with them, too. So actually we were playing the same type of corporate game on a much lower scale. We built a constituency, which was what we were after. We still have many more: Kelly Creek, Mallard Larkin, French Creek, the Smokeys, the White Clouds, and about thirty-five other places of real merit.

The White Cloud-Castle Peak fight came later. That was the most spectacular one, of course. Governor Andrus to this day says that fight was one of the main factors in his election as governor in 1970. And it should have been. There were seven different gubernatorial candidates at the time. Cece was the only one who had the smarts and the guts to come down on all fours against ASARCO's proposed open pit molybdenum mine at the base of Castle Peak. That was a pretty good political line, I guess, because he was elected, and then re-elected by the greatest majority an Idaho governor has received.

The White Clouds was the showpiece—Castle Peak was so fancy and ASARCO was such a villain. A vast open pit mine was a thing that would coalesce people. It was the glamour issue. There were an awful lot of people involved in that fracas.

The White Cloud and Boulders are not designated Wilderness, although they were saved from ASARCO's open pit mine. The main reason was that the bottom fell out of the molybdenum market. ASARCO gave up on fighting it. Later another molybdenum mine was developed on the other side of the Salmon River. We didn't fight that and Andrus didn't fight that. It is not a thing of beauty, but you have to make some choices on priorities. The one up Thompson Creek is not doing the violence that the one at Castle Peak would have done. In our second century we are gaining a little in our ability to differentiate values in Idaho.

Some of my attitudes will never change. Wilderness is the core of the whole conservation picture. Without a large enough core of wilderness for the present and the future, we have lost the battle.

When I first went to Alice Lake with my kids, we saw five people there on a weekend. The last time we visted there on a weekday there were over fifty people there. That presents another problem. How are we going to manage the wilderness? The idea of management is antithetical to the idea of wilderness, but we must do it. One answer is to get a broad enough wilderness base to spread out the use without destroying the resource.

To this day I'm ambivalent on whether the Sawtooths should be a national park. If it meant running macadamized fingers up all these favorite canyons of mine, I would oppose it vigorously. I think now I'm satisfied with it the way it is. I don't care if a road goes to an open mine or is a road for tourists; in some places, roads simply aren't desirable.

*Cecil D. Andrus*

Courtesy of office of the Governor

I don't think that's a selfish point of view. Personally, parks are the flip side of my character. I spent sixteen years on the State Park Board trying to take care of recreation for macadamized people. Wilderness is a flip side of that. Idaho, God bless it, is big enough and good enough to have both. That's wherein lies the tale.

*The big issue in the gubernatorial election of 1970 was whether the ASARCO mining company was going to develop a molybdenum mine or not. The incumbent, Republican Don Samuelson, supported the mine, and said, "The good Lord never intended us to lock up our resources." But Democrat Cecil Andrus was opposed to it, and won the election. Later, when Jimmy Carter became president in 1976, he asked Cecil Andrus to come to Washington as his Secretary of the Interior. Andrus returned to Idaho in 1981 and was elected governor of Idaho again in 1986. The camera crew took him away from his duties to the nearby Boise River where the urge to fish eventually began to compete with the requirements of the interview.*

My position on the White Clouds came from common sense. It made no sense to destroy a beautiful area that was still pristine—just the way God created it—for a mineral that was in surplus worldwide. It wasn't needed. The price was so low it wasn't even an economically viable project in its own right. To destroy that area for no reason at all, or perhaps for the economic gain of one company, was ridiculous. It didn't happen then; it wouldn't happen today. That took place in 1970, twenty years ago. I think people are stronger today in their resolve to protect those pristine areas in Idaho than they were in 1970. But that was a major issue even twenty years ago.

I didn't know there were such strong feelings for that issue. I won't say I was new to the political scene, but I knew what was right and I knew what was wrong. I took a position that was thought to be wrong by the industrial people at the time. Since then it has been proven to have been the right position. I didn't think of it in political terms at that time.

I take it as a compliment to be known as the first environmentalist governor of a state. I think it's true. I ran as a concerned citizen in 1970. That was the first gubernatorial campaign in America that revolved around protecting portions of the world in which we live. Since then Colorado had an environmental race. It has become a little more popular. It's an educational process now. The public throughout America are more concerned about the environment than they were some years ago. Toxic and hazardous waste is a big unseen villain out there in the future of our second century, and people are concerned about it.

There is a critical balance that we have to reach for in the tug between jobs, development, and preserving. We don't always achieve it, but we have to reach for it. The first thing is to make a living if you are to sustain your family, educate your children, clothe them and do the responsible things. But equally, you have to have a living that's worthwhile. Every once in a while you've got to be able to get away, take your favorite fly rod or your rifle and go to the outdoors to relax and enjoy life. We put a value on that. To some people a wilderness experience is a king-sized bed in a Holiday Inn. If that's their attitude, they shouldn't come to Idaho.

There is always an argument as to whether our policies are balanced, or right or wrong, too far over one way or the other. History is the only way to judge whether we were right or wrong. We have to do what we think is right, and hope that it turns out that way.

The term "environmentalist" causes confusion. People see the word "environmentalist" in different ways. I think we're all conservationists. We want to protect and preserve some portions of Idaho. In other areas we want to develop them, but we don't want to destroy them. I think the conservation community is 99 percent of the people who live in this state. Whether you're a farmer, rancher, industrialist, or whoever, even if you don't use certain areas on a regular basis, you want to know they are there for us and our children.

I think most Idahoans at times feel small or insignificant when they're out in the backcountry. They're concerned about beauty, they're concerned about having it available. There is nothing more peaceful than sitting in the warm sunshine and watching the river go by. At the same time, you are close enough to get in your pickup and make the shift change at the sugar plant at Nampa, or Micron, or Hewlett-Packard. We have the best of both worlds.

Frankly, I don't get to fish as much as I used to or would like to. My workday is quite long and intense, so when I get out with that fly rod, my mind is relaxed. I concentrate on where a fish should be, on presenting the fly in a proper manner to attract that fish. I don't hear a telephone ring. The pressures go away, just like when I'm elk hunting. I can walk through steep canyons and ridges and it's just exactly like it was when Columbus discovered America, centuries ago. It makes you feel quite insignificant in the overall picture.

ANDRUS: Let's go fishing. I assume you just want me to do what I'm going to do. Only my back is going to be to the camera. I'm going to fish the far bank slowly. Then I'm going to come up on this side of this water up here.

CAMERAMAN: At some point I will probably get in real close.

ANDRUS: Shout instructions. I'm married, I'm used to that. If you get in close, I'd screw it up. Oh not bad Andrus! That was a good cast. You get one every once in a while. I forgot Ricardo still has the tape rolling over there. I'm in trouble, I've got to watch my language.

CAMERAMAN: When you're out here, what do you think about?

ANDRUS: Your mind is constantly looking for the fish, where they will be... very relaxed... tells something about the lifestyle in Idaho. I'm watching that little fly all the time. See that rock right over there? There ought to be a trout right.. behind that rock right there. Oh, he didn't come up. So he isn't! I can be out here all day long and do just exactly what I'm doing right now—not even catch a fish—and have a ball. It's like... There is one rising right there...doesn't really matter whether you catch anything. I release most of my fish anyway, unless I happen to pick up a trophy fish... and most of those I release...being out here is being a part of the world. I don't know how you can explain it...you can feel it, but you can't explain it. Hey, there was a good cast! You missed the best one of the day, right there.

CAMERAMAN: Of course, it works that way

ANDRUS: Ricardo, are you shooting over there? Watch that cast! Oh! My stars, man! I would like to see a big old German Brown come jumping up here right now....

*Courtesy of Tom Morris*

**Tom Morris**

*Tom Morris is a lifetime resident of St. Maries who practices law and has been involved in public debates about the designation of forest and wilderness lands.*

My grandparents homesteaded this country. When they came it was covered with virgin stands of white pine timber. There was very little wildlife—no eagles, fish osprey, blue heron, or elk.

One of the first plants of elk was done in 1919. My father assisted in that plant. They brought elk to the Bovill area by train from West Yellowstone in 1919. They built a low fence they thought would hold them while they fed them for the winter. They let an old cow out of the boxcar, and she took two bounces and went over the fence. So they closed the door and built a higher fence. They kept the rest of them corraled there most of the winter and fed them. They let them out in the spring. That herd of elk, together with two or three other plants, produced our current large herd of elk.

The 1910 forest fire and the logging operations of the last seventy years have resulted in supplying habitat and food for wildlife. Logged-over areas produce great food sources for elk, deer, bear, and other animals. Sound logging practices are compatible with wildlife production.

I was raised here and went through St. Maries High School. I wanted to see how the other half lived, so I attended and graduated from the University of California. I passed the California Bar; however I couldn't wait to return home, flew out the next day and have never been back except to visit. I love this valley and expect to stay here the rest of my life. In California, there was no place to live and just enjoy life. Californians cannot enjoy their cities for fear of being assaulted, and they are afraid to leave their homes at night. In St. Maries we don't have these kinds of fears.

My definition of multiple use is utilizing our forests and land with many uses, not just one. A good example of the variety of uses is the way it is with the St. Joe River and its drainage. My grandparents, myself, my children and my grandchild have all waded, boated, and swum in the river. Since 1900 it has been a working river where tug boats pull booms of logs from the upper reaches of the river to the sawmills on the lower portions of Coeur d'Alene Lake. The mountains have been logged continuously and are still furnishing logs for the mills. At the same time, the river provides excellent fishing, camping, picnicking and pleasure boating. People have been able to live and work in the area and still enjoy hunting, photography, berry picking, and the woods in general. All of these uses have been going on during my lifetime.

If this area were designated wilderness, there would be no roads built, no motorized vehicles, and the grazing of livestock would not be permitted. There would be no jobs. If I didn't have a job, my kids wouldn't have been reared here. They wouldn't be able to stay here to enjoy this quality life. You either live here or lock up the state of Idaho for Easterners to come out and take float trips down the Salmon. For the most part, to enjoy the wilderness, one has to hike many mountain miles carrying supplies on one's back, and the average Idahoan does not have time or the money for this.

I feel that certain areas should be locked up, but only the very small portion that is unsuited for growing merchantable timber. I feel that the high country, five thousand feet altitude and on up, is not suited for growing timber. Some of that country could be considered wilderness and kept for the backpackers. I couldn't go up there and hike in now, most people can't. Just a few young people, or people who have the money to take the time off to do it.

The average working person only has the weekend to go up and enjoy it. That's what the people here do. That's what most of the tourists who come here do. They use their campers and take their children up the river and feel that they're in wilderness. To them that's wilderness. I see nothing wrong with viewing it through a camper window. We do it every weekend we get a chance—go up in the woods with our little camper, and spend the time picking blackcaps and huckleberries or photographing wildlife.

This town is like any town with three thousand population. I suppose there are limited opportunities. But if we can get some guarantee of an allowable cut of timber, we will be able to keep the mills and the timber industry active, I think we will have a good future. But we cannot put up with not knowing if there will be a timber supply tomorrow. Spotted owls and other impediments are holding up timber sales for years and years and causing towns like St. Maries to become smaller and smaller.

In one logging operation nearby, there are ten men employed on the landing itself. Then there are truck drivers and support staff. In the whole operation there are probably one hundred men, which would represent a hundred families, and this is just a small part of our industry. The other part, about a mile downriver, is the plywood plant, which has several hundred men and their families living off of it.

I don't know of anyone who wants to see our streams muddied. Contrary to some people's beliefs, the logger isn't some vicious, bulldozing, chainsaw maniac. He likes his rivers, and he likes his streams, and he likes them clean. That's why we live here. I represent loggers, so I'm in the woods all the time. Loggers want to be proud of their work when they get through, they want the country to look good. They have grandkids coming up, and they want them to be able to live in Idaho and have jobs. You cannot lock up the country and have jobs.

*Ted Anderson is the son of Andy Anderson. He learned how to run the Salmon River from his father, and was a part of the business until his father quit. A "river ranger," he works for the U.S. Forest Service as supervising forestry technician.*

**Ted Anderson**

I'm the river manager. I'm the fellow who takes care of the river and has the boats and other equipment to do the job. Yes, I still consider myself a river runner. It is, in a lot of respects, a unique occupation. There are not that many people in the world that run rivers and white water. The Middle Fork is my main river.

The first trip I made with my father, I was about sixteen years old. That was back about 1945. We went looking for a fellow who had drowned trying to ford the river. Apparently the horse fell over. The family heard that Dad had run the river, so they asked him to go down and look for him. But it was too early. In the cold water it takes about two weeks for bodies to come back up. He told them he thought it was too early, but they wanted him to go anyway. So we went and didn't find the body.

Dad was sort of a pioneer. He moved into the Meyers Cove area out of Challis in about 1938. He had been working for the U.S. Fish and Wildlife Service and decided to go into the packing, hunting and guide business. He and my Uncle Joe were down in here hunting when the Second World War broke open. They didn't know about it for two weeks until they came out.

His customers were people who liked to hunt and fish. Dad would advertise in *Field and Stream* and *Sports Afield* to get sportsmen types down here, saying, "You're going to get wet." There were just a few people to start with, and now we put about eight thousand people down the river between June 1 and September 3rd.

Today it is more of a camping type experience than the avid sportsman type. About the time they put the road in, commercial outfitters from out of state started bringing in individuals just for camping and the fun of running the rivers. Prior to that it was the true sportsmen types who wanted to fish a pristine river that hadn't had that much action on it. We really didn't gear our advertising toward the everyday citizen type.

We gave up the business, I guess, because when we ran the river, it was kind of a unique experience, your own thing. When the crowds started to move in, you felt, well, like everything was going to pot. I had been in and out of the service, and worked with Dad off and on. We phased out about the time that business started to pick up.

A lot of people like to fish. With the amount of use that we have now, the Idaho Fish and Game Department has implemented a "catch and release" fish-for-fun program in the Middle Fork in order to save the Middle Fork cutthroat. The population of the fish has come back real good. For awhile it was going downhill.

The fish started dropping off in the 1960s right after the road was built into Dagger Falls in 1959. Access was easier to the river and fishing was pretty heavy. It was around 1972 or so that they implemented "catch and release." They claim the fishing has improved and is holding its own. So that's good. When the salmon run at Dagger Falls on Fourth of July, you can sit there and watch them jump the falls. Farther up you will occasionally see one spawning. It is not like it used to be, but there are still a few. I think it's starting to improve.

I didn't get in on the initial part of the river planning. When they first put the management plan together in 1973 (Recreation Management Plan, Middle Fork Salmon Wild and Scenic River), I wasn't working for the Forest Service. They had gone through a public involvement process around 1972. At that time everybody was griping about the "pack-in pack-out" policy on garbage. Outfitters were going to take quite a cut in customers because the plan was going to cut the size of the party you could take and the number of launches per year. The commercial outfitters were the biggest users. Private users were just getting started, but not to the point where they were involved in the program. Before that, the outfitters just did what they wanted to do.

I started the fire pan program. It wasn't quite as difficult as pack-in pack-out garbage, because that program had already started, and people could see the benefits of it. When we started the fire pan program, my crews would go into the campgrounds and destroy all the fire rings and clean them up. In ten days they would come back and there would be just as many or more. No one used the same pit. People always moved over and built their own. They often had foil and garbage in them.

So we decided to try the fire pan. They had started doing that at Grand Canyon, which was where I got the idea. At first, we let people dump the ashes in the river. But there was too much debris from the campground in it. Poptops and aluminum foil started showing up in the river. The outfitters were the ones who said, "Why don't we start carrying it out?" We found out that if you reburn your ashes every night, by putting them back in the firepan, then build another fire on top of them, they just keep burning down to a fine powder or ash. This made it easy to carry your ashes with you, so we started the pack-out policy.

When a resource starts to degrade and go downhill, there needs to be some restrictions. The Forest Service now has a process called "limits of acceptable change" in campsites and other areas. We haven't started the study here yet. I hate to say it, but we may be at the point where we have to "sacrifice" some campsites in order to maintain the rest of the river in a pristine condition.

The first day you leave Boundary Creek on a float trip is hectic because parties are passing each other. But once you hit your camp the first night, they space out better. Everyone seems to hit the water about the same time every day at about ten o'clock and float until about four. So you can feel alone on the river. If you take about six days, the average trip length, you cruise along about the same speed as everyone else. Potentially we could have about a thousand people a day on this river stretched out over 198 miles if every permit opportunity were filled. So the system is working real well. The folks who built that system in 1972 did a real good job, with a lot of thought and planning in it. You have to give them credit—the outfitters, the private individuals, and the Forest Service people who worked to put the plan together.

Oh, yes, I think wilderness designation was the best thing to happen. It sets it aside so that you can keep it in some kind of wilderness condition. The country is so rugged and so vast. There is no commercial timber, so it should be set aside for recreation, hunting, fishing, boating, and backpacking. I think it's a real good idea. But people may love it to death. Once they learn about it, then they'll move in, and it's pretty tough to keep it in the condition that you're commissioned to do.

*In the fall of 1989, a group of hunters from Pennsylvania went out on an elk hunt with a professional outfitter and guide. Tom Cope brought his son John Cope and came with his friend Barry Macken. On their second day of the hunt, the group saw one dead elk on the way up a mountain, and then about twenty elk at a distance. Their guide had seen three cougars. They sat around the fire that night and discussed the events of the day.*

JOHN: I found out one thing today. If you see elk close and don't run after them, you should try to get a shot at them. Because they're gone. They carry the mail in a hurry, I'll tell you. With whitetails I've shot in Pennsylvania, it's a matter of running them up and getting a better vantage point and getting a shot. You can forget that with elk. They're a big animal but they sure can move. Smart animals. Noisy animals, when you finally get close to them. But they are definitely a challenge to hunt. They don't frequent the lowland, that's for sure.

We came to Idaho when we were told by somebody, I don't remember who it was, that Idaho has a better kill ratio for elk. There are fewer hunters per population. Idaho doesn't get as many elk killed as Colorado; it doesn't have as many hunters as Colorado. Then we knew two young men who were guides for Boulder Creek Outfitters who we knew from back home. They recommended our guides. Last year we hunted whitetail with them. One thing led to another and now we are hunting elk with them this year.

BARRY: I came out with Tim Craig two years ago on a cougar hunt. I just liked the country. He was a good outfitter and showed me a good hunt then. I heard they have some big trophy bulls here, so that's why I'm here. This land reminds me of the last wilderness, really. It is not like Pennsylvania, that's for sure.

TOM: Just seeing game in the wilderness environment is worth it. It is a reward in itself to just be here. If you got a shot or an opportunity to kill one of those beautiful creatures is really not that important. Just being out there and having the opportunity is what is important.

Your guide naturally wants to find you an animal you came here to find. I'm sure he gets satisfaction from having that happen. But just having the opportunity to see wildlife in it's habitat... Even though we didn't get to see the cougars, we know that they were there. We got to see those elk that we saw,

**Barry Macken and Tom Cope look for elk**

C  O  N  V  E  R  S  A  T  I  O  N  S

134

even though we didn't find any bulls today. Whatever is available to see in the wilderness is worth it—that is the reward for hunting. I guess maybe that's the main reason why we come here.

Naturally I would like to go back with what I came for, but I still have a sense of satisfaction, being able to be out here and experience it. I really don't go home with a bad feeling if I go home empty-handed. Some people might. We've always been able to see game when we came out West. We saw more elk today than we did on two previous elk hunts.

BARRY: My wife supports my trips out here totally. I spend a lot of time on my business and she thinks I deserve it. She encourages me to go. She went with me to Costa Rica last year when I went sail fishing. She didn't go out on the boat. She doesn't hunt.

TOM: My wife doesn't really doesn't complain, does she John? She realizes the value of my just being out here with our son. Naturally she is glad to get us back. She worries about the hazards that are involved in being out in the wilderness, although if you go with an outfitter, the hazards are significantly reduced.

Most of a person's problems are people problems. To get away from that, the telephone, and the routine to the solitude of the mountains is one of the other motivating factors of why we come out here. There are a lot of things all wrapped up in one: the hunt, closeness to nature, solitude. I did reflect when I was up in the mountains about the pioneer days—what stamina it must have taken to pioneer the West. There is no vacation like hunting. It's totally unique.

BARRY: I agree with you one hundred percent. And I'm ready to hit the sack.

# *Recession*

## THE EARLY 1980s AND ITS AFTERMATH

*In the early 1980s the United States experienced a recession, and Idaho's major resource and commodity industries simultaneously experienced a collapse in demand and prices. For each industry the collapse was the result of events mostly external to Idaho, a familiar source of economic troubles in the state's history. People began to leave the state as mines and mills closed and growth rates in urban areas sagged. At the same time, the environmental movement was affecting the way public land agencies conducted their business.*

*Professor Michael Dinoto, an economist at the University of Idaho, discusses the state's economy and the adaptations underway as a consequence of the crisis.*

The economy sort of peaked out for Idaho in the mid- to late-1970s. In the early 1980s there was a major recession not only nationwide, but in Idaho. We saw precipitous declines in mining and forestry that were almost catastrophic. Those industries have not even recovered to mid-1970s levels. The resource base in effect ceased to be there.

Industries that were growing, such as microelectronics, began to become dominant. Coupled with that was a movement toward certain kinds of service activities, specifically in tourism—Sun Valley and "Sun Valley North," which is what we call Coeur d'Alene. It is a very sharp move away from a long pattern of industrial activity.

The massive downturn of the early 1980s put Idaho in a very poor position budgetarily. Money was just not going into the general fund. The legislature had no money to do much of anything. Now that there is more money, the south can be more responsive to the north. (People in the north have not always felt that they have had their fair share of

*Michael Dinoto*

highway funds.) Hopefully, communication and interaction will be better.

A lot of the industries that are important now have a presence in both north and south. Coeur d'Alene and Sun Valley are recreation and tourist oriented. If the state legislature does something for tourism, it will impact both north and south automatically. The microelectronics industry has a major presence in Boise and in northern Idaho. If you do anything to help the industry in general, you will impact both north and south. Regionalism or sectionalism should be somewhat diminished.

I share some of the alarm over a shift to service-oriented jobs. There has been a change in the real personal income of Idahoans. The service industry is like a dumbbell. There is a concentration of people at the low end and a concentration at the high end—a lot of jobs waiting tables and a lot of jobs programming computers. You lose people in the middle and there are a lot more low paying jobs than there are high paying jobs.

I don't really believe that you can do anything about the occupational structure associated with the job. You're going to have that build-up of minimum wage kinds of jobs. There is no way to avoid it. When you look at the tourist industry there is a low amount of capital per worker for a waiter or waitress. It's quite different from the kinds of capital stock that you have for a smelter worker. This changing kind of capitalization affects worker productivity and worker wages.

Idahoans used to view themselves in the 1970s as a recession-proof robust economy. We used to brag about it and use it as a recruiting tool. The 1980s brought an end to that particular myth. It emphasized a backwater kind of mentality or opinion of the state. It was not only external, but internal.

The current growth is shifting views around again. The emphasis is not on resources. The emphasis is on other aspects. And it seems to be working as far as changing the opinion of others as well as our opinion of ourselves. We're looking more toward things other than taking what was on the land. That is a very nice—and very productive—change in attitude.

*One of the leaders in the recovery from the permanent changes in the structure of the mining economy of North Idaho is Harry Magnuson of Wallace, the president of H. F. Magnuson Company, and the chairman of the Idaho Centennial Commission.*

My grandparents first came to the Coeur d'Alene district in 1890, and we have been here ever since. My grandfather was an immigrant miner and worked in the mines. The family has been involved in mining in various ways. We have all been dependent upon it as an industry for the last hundred years.

I have heard my parents and my grandparents talk about the area

**Harry F. Magnuson**

as it was first settled. Immigrant miners supplied most of the labor. Various ethnic groups settled different parts of the valley. Mullan was were the Finnish people stayed. There were the Burke Irish. Gem, which was halfway to Burke, had the Scandinavians and was called Swedetown. That is where my grandparents first settled. Welsh people settled Cornwall. There was an Italian settlement in Kellogg. It stayed that way for fifty to seventy-five years. In the last twenty-five years, the ethnic groups have become pretty well integrated in the valley.

My grandfather was involved in the labor problems in 1899. He was placed in the stockade in Kellogg. They tried eleven of the immigrant miners for blowing up the Bunker Hill Mill. He was found guilty and sent away for eleven months. That decision was appealed and reversed, so he came back. There still are a number of the original families, but we are getting fewer as time goes on.

This mining valley has had its ups and downs for a hundred and four years. But this one is different. There has been basic restructuring in the last seven or eight years. It is going to be a different industry, and this is going to be a different valley.

Restructuring was forced upon us by the drop in metal prices and very aggressive foreign competition. It involved becoming more efficient and cost-effective in order to stay alive. It is very evident that jobs have been lost. We have to produce silver and metals at a lower cost. We need more production that comes through technological changes, better equipment, and greater human productivity. We have had an excellent response from our labor force.

In the 1950s and 1960s we had about five thousand or more employed in the Silver Valley mining industry. There were twenty to twenty-five mines working in the district and twenty-five mills operating. People stayed here, shopped here, played here, lived and worked here. Now people are more mobile and travel up and down the Interstate. Today we only have about five operating mines and about five operating mills.

We have had so many good people in the Silver Valley. They hung on as long as they could, but were forced to go elsewhere to make a living. We lost some of those good people. Those of us who live in the valley see that unless you prosper and unless you make a profit, you cannot stay in business. Civic leaders, community people, and employees have tried to bring that about.

These last eight years since the closing of the Bunker Hill plants have been particularly difficult, not only in the financial aspect of things, but also in the physiological and emotional aspect. It has been difficult to cope with an area that has been hit so hard and has been down, down, down. Some of the basic structures—government, schools, churches—start to come apart. We have a strong group with strong fiber living in the community able to pull together and work together.

We are not waiting out the silver market. I think we have learned to live with it. We are hopeful that it will get better, but we have to do what we need to with the framework of what we have.

We have had some difficulty within the local silver industry coming up with a program that might resolve some of the price problems. One segment says, "Let the free market run its course and it will." But it is a long wait for that. I believe we are the victims of low foreign wages and a victim of Third World monetary problems and international finance: low-priced dollars and high-priced Japanese yen. Those things are caused externally, not locally. That being the case, perhaps we ought to have some kind of assistance. One suggestion was an import tax to equalize costs.

But the industry has not been unanimous with our recommendations. As a consequence, we have not been able to get help.

We were all shocked when we were first confronted with the closure of the major Bunker Hill facilities. The initial plan was to think that somebody would take care of us. Time went on and nothing was done. Then we thought the government would take care of it. That did not happen. I finally joined a group that set out to restore some of the Bunker Hill facilities. That is a long process and we have been partially successful.

Simultaneously, it became evident that we needed a broader economic base. What is the best thing that we have? Well, of course tourism comes to mind right away. We have a beautiful community, a mining history, and a beautiful area. That is what tourists like. So we have moved in that direction.

We also formed an economic development corporation to lure new industries. It is a long-term process, but we have made some progress. We have a beautiful place to live and the finest quality of life. We have the infrastructure in place and a wonderful community with schools and churches in place. It takes a little while.

Idaho is going to have a lot more people. That is not good. You would like to keep Idaho just like it is. But we seem to measure progress with growth. I do not know whether you can have progress with just improved economic activity and without growth. If growth and progress are measured together, it is inevitable, so we are going to have a lot of growth. Growth comes with changes and I am sure a lot of that is not good. That is why Wallace will be a good place. Our quality of life in Wallace has not changed.

With growth you get more population and crowdedness. With that comes a variety of problems. You can see it in Coeur d'Alene. Ten years ago it was a quiet little summer place. It has not grown too much, but enough to have changed all of that. It is no longer a quiet little summer place, but a bustling community about ready to break loose. That is quite a price for change.

*The adjustments that Idahoans are making to the world around them include the clean-up of the debris left by older industrial practices that damaged the environment. The largest Superfund site in Idaho is in Kellogg, where industrial contamination finally affected the health of the children who lived there. Jerry Cobb, Senior Environmental Health Specialist with the Panhandle District, is responsible for the removal of lead-contaminated yards of the children who live in Kellogg and Wardner.*

Mining began in the 1880s when they discovered gold and silver in Shoshone County. Mining

***Jerry Cobb***

developments sprang up throughout the county. The Bunker Hill Galena lode was discovered by Noah Kellogg near Wardner in 1895.

Like other heavy industries, the mines and mills discharged their waste products onto the ground or into nearby streams. It was one price we paid to ensure a continuous supply of precious and industrial metals for a growing country. Nobody wants to give up the good life that the metals and their alloys have brought us. Today the mines continue to produce under much more strict environmental regulations.

In the 1920s and 1930s many new processes were developed that resulted in a lessening of the waste discharges. In the 1960s environmental awareness began to grow. Regulations required mining companies to stop discharging raw mill waste containing heavy metals and processing chemicals into the South Fork of the Coeur d'Alene River. Until this time people referred to the river as Lead Creek. Mine tailings, which included lead, zinc, and silver, and other metals, are like a rock flour, and the river ran the color of milk. You couldn't see the bottom of the creek.

In addition to the discharge of tailings into the streams, air pollution from smelter emissions impacted the cities and towns around the Bunker Hill smelters, which discharged lead and sulfur dioxide. Barren areas and soil contamination are widespread in the western end of the county.

In September 1973 the main pollution device (bag house) at the lead smelter was severely damaged by fire. This resulted in dramatic increases in air lead emissions. The fire was determined to be responsible for a rise in blood lead levels of children living near the smelter. In 1974, when the target threshhold for protecting children from the adverse effects of lead was 40 ug/dl (micrograms per deciliter of blood), the average blood lead in 201 Smelterville children was 65 ug/dl. In 1988 and 1989, surveys found that the levels were reduced to an average of 14 ug/dl. Meanwhile, the target threshhold was lowered to 25 ug/dl in 1985. In 1989, blood screens for 275 children in Kellogg, Smelterville, Wardner, and Page show that 2.9% are at or above the target threshhold.

There is no known physiological use for lead in the human system. As we get more sophisticated in testing, we find more impacts at lower and lower levels. The health effects include delayed cognitive development, reduced IQ scores, and impaired hearing. The Centers for Disease Control said in 1985 that "lead in soil and dust appears to be responsible for blood lead levels in children increasing above background levels when the concentration in soil or dust exceeds 500-1,000 million parts per million (ppm)." In Smelterville and Kellogg yards, the lead concentrations are 3299 ppm and 2580 ppm respectively. Nearly ninety percent of the yards have soil lead levels above 500 ppm.

The Bunker Hill mining and smelting operation closed in 1981, and except for the mine, has remained closed. A survey of blood leads in 1983 found that twenty-five percent of the children still had a blood lead level at or above 25 ug/dl. Based on that, the area was placed on the National Priority List as a Superfund Site in September of 1983. The site is a twenty-one square mile area, and includes Kellogg, Pinehurst, Wardner, Smelterville, and Page.

Superfund is a program enacted by Congress in 1980. It allows the government to do clean-ups designed to handle the specific needs of the site. The people who were responsible for creating the problem are first offered the chance to do the clean-up, but if they refuse or can't be identfied, money from a fund created by taxes on chemicals and crude oil, "Superfund," pays for it. Meanwhile the governement tries to sort out who was responsible and takes the potentially responsible party to court to recover the cost of the clean-up. If the court finds that a responsible party refused to do it, they have to pay treble damages. It's an extremely powerful law, one that makes a lot of industries very nervous.

As part of the Bunker Hill Superfund project, we removed or capped soils at public parks, play grounds, and along some road shoulders in 1986. In 1989 we removed the soil in residential yards and replaced it at eighty-one homes and at two large apartment complexes. More is planned for 1990. We are taking soils with concentrations of lead greater than 1000 ppm. This will help break the pathway between children and soil lead.

The process of removing lead is expensive and time consuming, but great progress is being made. Community response has been positive and sustained. Blood levels have dropped dramatically, and cooperation in residential yard clean-ups has been excellent.

We've spent the last week out visiting with about twenty home owners identified as having soil lead values above five hundred to a thousand and who have children less than three years old. They're very happy. They say it's great to get it over with. But if you look at the community as a whole, the entire community, you see different reactions. Some of them are just flat tired of hearing about lead. Some agree with it, some don't. Some people who aren't particularly concerned with the health issue worry about the economic impacts of lead in the yard on future home sales and insurability.

If you own industrial property, buyers want an environmental audit. They want to know they are essentially free of liabilities for some contaminant that they did not put there. I think the community by and large would like to see it over with. They want to get on with developing the community.

There are a lot of clean-up successes. In 1973 the Bunker Hill forester Ed Pommeraning began a program to revegetate the hills. They built a nursery in an abandoned area of the Bunker Hill mine, planted seedlings, and planted over 400,000 trees each year for three years.

Air quality has improved. Blood lead averages dropped. The water situation has improved. The new gondola project, which will be the largest gondola in the world is under construction. I think the perception of the community is changing. Of course, a lot of that is based on how you present yourself. If you sit and hang your head and say, "Oh, poor us," you're perceived one way, and if you stand up and say, "Yes, we had a problem, but we identified it and we're fixing it. And while we're fixing it, we have other things available to enjoy." Then people say, "You're right, you have

*Ramona Arnold*

had a problem, but you are working on it. By the way, you have an awful lot interesting things to see and do here."

*One of the residents of Wallace who has other ideas about how federal funds should be spent is Ramona Arnold.*

I think this project stinks, if you want to know my opinion. I thought there was a better place to put this money than into something like digging up yards. There are a lot of young people who would like to go to college and could use that money. An awful lot of young people in this town could certainly use a YMCA.

Why isn't this money put toward something that everybody can use instead of this hit or miss project? There is all kinds of lead in the valley, there always has been. We've always learned to live with it. There are not that many two-headed people here!

They are only removing it here and there; they are not doing it right across the street, they're not doing the hillsides. In the summertime you can see where it just turns white. You have got to take it from the whole area if you're going to take it from one place. The next windstorm that comes in brings it right back again.

I was born and raised here. I can remember when there used to be trees down from old Bradley Hill. There were great huge big cedar trees down in there. It was beautiful. Then they sawed a lot of those cedars down, used them, and put the slag pile in. So the trees had to go. Ordinarily they would have died anyhow. Then the trees on the mountainsides started dying, little by little. I can remember when there was quite a bit of timber on the mountains. But I can also remember the kids then being as smart as they are right now today.

So I haven't seen the lead problem. When you live in an area such as this, you are told, "Wash. Clean yourself up. Wash your dirty hands before you eat. Wash yourself before you go to bed, especially your feet." That was just the way we've always done it. So I don't think it's anything unusual for there to be lead in these areas. I think it's a waste of federal money.

**John Ensunsa**

*Idaho farmers experienced the shock of the early 1980s in their own special and personal ways. Farmer John Ensunsa of Castleford is now the director of the Southern Idaho Family Farm Hot Line that has assisted farmers in Idaho, Utah, and Nevada.*

My father came to this country when he was seventeen years old from Spain. He was a Basque and herded sheep for a few years. Then he started farming and retired in 1972. I had moved back to the Twin Falls area in 1966, so we started farming some of the ground he was farming and added to the operation after that.

I got too big, too fast. When I took over the operation in 1972 we were just renting 240 acres. The prevailing economic thought at that time was to borrow as much as you could and string out the terms as long as you could. You could pay for it down the road with inflated dollars. The prevailing thought was that land was never going to get cheaper. At that time farm prices looked good and the farm economy looked stable. Farmers were optimistic. Lenders were optimistic and lending money. Money was available and there to be used. So I took advantage of it.

I bought this eighty-acre farm from my father, another 240-acre farm on contract, and rented an additional 640 acres. Things were good while prices were up. But then two things happened. Commodity prices failed. As a result, land prices devalued considerably. We paid a thousand dollars an acre for that farm in 1975. Then in 1985 we appraised it for six hundred dollars an acre. A big loss in our net worth.

At the same time, our lender had trouble. They got into trouble right along with the farmers. In fact, our primary lender closed their doors. When our debt became due, there was no way we could pay it, so we were forced to go into a Chapter 11 reorganizational bankruptcy. We let the 240-acre farm that I had been buying go back to the owner and cut down the operation to this eighty acres that I'm still buying. There is also a little bit of rented ground that I can handle by myself. So we cut down on labor, and trimmed it down as much as we possibly could to get by.

My father saw the first part of it and passed away in 1985. He never did say what he thought. He was worried for me, I think, because he could see what was happening. Neither one of us liked what we saw, but I know he felt it. But he said, "You just have to do what you have to do."

We had an irrigated row-crop operation. Our main crops were alfalfa hay, sweet corn, and grain corn. We raised a lot of commercial dry beans, some contract garden beans, wheat and barley.

I fought confronting the truth. I fought it as long as I could. It's human nature. You see the problem, you understand the problem, but you won't admit it's there. So you fight it. I'd go out and work from daylight until dark. I would find things to do just to keep myself busy because when I'd stop working, reality would creep in. I suppose the full reality sunk in when we filed our Chapter 11 reorganizational bankruptcy. It was our last alternative. We had used every alternative that we had by then, and it was the last resort.

You spend a lot of your time and your thoughts building your dream. When the dream disappears, it takes away all of your incentive, all of your desires, the thrills that you associate with working toward a goal. I think that was the biggest loss—to lose the dream.

A lot of credit goes to my family—more than me—for holding things together. They are very understanding, patient, kind—the whole thing. Working with the Hot Line and being with the Hot Line people has been a great help to me as far as holding things together. A lot of the scars that were created are still there. Those wounds open up, and you have to talk to people, be around people who understand what you're going through. The encouragement and help you get from them means a lot.

I'm by far not healed up from this thing. Sometimes you can talk yourself into being strong. "I'll play the cards the way they were dealt me. We'll go on, this too shall pass." But other times you sink into a depth of despair that is really hard to get out of. It's a feeling of failure, I suppose. The failure is what hurts the worst.

We have two children. And no, I don't want them to farm. Well, I shouldn't speak for them. Neither of them wants to farm. They were home in high school when we were going through financial problems. What the farm meant to them was that Dad worked seven days a week from daylight until dark. He was tired and grumpy most of the time. We didn't take vacations, didn't go on picnics, didn't go fishing. So that was the idea of farming that was instilled in their minds. They were smart enough to realize that there are better ways to make a living, more enjoyable ways to make a living.

With the Hot Line, we first try and establish communication. If we can get the person talking about their problem, that's the first step. Secondly, we try and deal with their attitude. We try and let them know that some of the problems affecting them aren't really their own fault. A lot of farmers say, "Hey, this is all my fault," but it isn't. There could be hailstorms or the recent Hawkins Bean closure. There are a lot of external forces that are completely out of a farmer's control. Yet they affect his ability to make a profit. We try and get that through to that farmer.

On a personal basis, we try and get the farmer to establish priorities in his life. When I was building my operation, that farm became my god, in a sense. My life revolved around that farm. It shouldn't be that way. We try and get a farmer to list his priorities that mean the most to him. When they really think about it, that farm will come out somewhere down the list. It surely doesn't come out at the top.

I spend from March through November farming. I also sell insurance part time for the Farm Bureau Insurance Company. I enjoy it. It wasn't a let-down for me to go to work with Farm Bureau. I enjoy being in contact with the farmers. It would probably be less desirable if I were in the city and working in that element a little bit more.

We've run into some people for whom the farm has been their whole life, the only life they know. The aren't trained to do anything outside of farming. They don't have anything to fall back on. They have to take whatever menial jobs they can find. It is very degrading for these people to have to do that.

The farm family is the biggest loss that's been suffered. The farm will be here, it's bound to be here. But the farm family—the loss that they've suffered, the stress that's been put on children and on the marriages, divorces, suicides that have resulted from it. That's the loss that we'll never be able to measure. The family is the casualty, not the farm.

*The constituency for the nation's public forests has grown dramatically in the last twenty-five years. National legislation, changes in public perceptions, and structural changes in the forest products industries have all demanded that planning and operations be carried out substantially differently than they were before. Jim Weathers is a region manager for Boise Cascade Corporation. He compared the newer ways of forest planning with the old.*

In logging planning, there are a lot more things we need to consider today than we did ten or twenty years ago. Many of them are requirements put on us by the Forest Service, which provides a lot of the timber that we use. For example, elk calving restrictions didn't exist ten or twenty years ago. But because we are more aware of the needs of wildlife, Forest Service contracts have built-in provisions that restrict logging seasons to times when they will not conflict with other uses of the forest.

A lot of economic changes have been brought to bear on the way timber is sold and harvested today. For one thing, the Forest Service puts up much shorter contracts today than they did years ago. In the past the norm was to allow the purchaser five years to complete harvest on that timber sale. Today the standard is more like one or two years. You have a shorter planning horizon, and you have to be able to react quicker to changes in your timber supply.

**Jim Weathers**

We also run today on much lower log inventories than we used to. That is primarily because logs are much more costly and the carrying cost of the inventory is greater. It used to be common to have three, four, or five months worth of logs in inventory at any point in time. It gave you a lot of flexibility to deal with problems that might occur in your woods operations. Today it is not unusual at all to have a mill running with one or two or three weeks' worth of logs in inventory. All that requires a lot more detailed planning and scheduling.

One advantage of having a shorter period of time to operate on timber sales is you're always closer to today's market. If you have a decline in the market, you probably haven't bid an excessive price for that timber. That is one of the primary reasons the Forest Service has gone to shorter contract terms. It was to get away from some of the speculative bidding that was done in the early 1980s.

A Forest Service contract today is probably one to two inches thick if it's got a road package with it. There are many clauses that the Forest Service has added to protect the environment. It almost takes a law degree to understand the complexity of the conditions and terms under which we have to operate on a timber sale. It's not uncommon to have a quarter of a million dollars in deposits on timber sales and mid-point payments that require you to pay for half of the value of the timber sale half-way through the contract term, even if you haven't harvested the timber.

These are some of the financial criteria that we have to build into our planning process when we schedule a sale, because we literally can and do have many millions of dollars tied up with deposits and mid-point payments as well as advance road work on timber sales.

We have been very active in the federal forest planning process that is currently under way. That process was required by the 1976 National Forest Management Act. Each forest had to put together a ten-year management plan and get public input to help decide land-management issues. Boise Cascade, along with the rest of the wood products industry, has been very active in participating in that public input process through our technical foresters as well as concerned employees who feel a vested interest. We have a group of our mill employees, called the Northwest Timber Workers Resource Council, who participate in the forest planning process to represent their peers—the people that they work with in our facilities. So at all levels of our company we've participated in that process to try to find a proper balance and to make sure that multiple use in the forest continues.

Sometimes the final plans come out very differently than the way the forest has been managed in the past. In areas critical to our needs we find declining timber availability coming out of those plans. For example, the Payette National Forest contains some 2.3 million acres. In the prior plan there were about 800,000 acres out of the 2.3 million allocated to multiple uses including timber production. But the final plan allocates only 431,000 acres to long-term timber management. While we worked very hard to ensure that we would have a better balance and that more of those 2.3 million acres would be available, the results were far different than what we were attempting to achieve.

The company in Southwest Idaho has gotten smaller as less timber is available for our industry. We had to shut down a sawmill in Barber, just out of Boise, and a sawmill at McCall several years ago. We used to have a sawmill in Emmett, now we just do the finish work. That is how we've had to accommodate.

But the planning process included all the interest groups, the people interested in wildlife, timber, mining, fisheries, and water quality. The Forest Service challenge was to accommodate all of them and strike a proper balance that reflected all of the wishes and needs and desires of the users of our public lands. I think many of us are still headed in different directions.

We see more consensus and compromise and dialogue with people who have local knowledge of the issues, rather than in courts that may be many miles away. Many lawyers for both sides don't understand the issues and concerns on the ground. There is some improvement in that area, but we're still seeing an awful lot of litigation, appeals, and legal challenges. I'm not sure the worst is behind us yet.

The wood products industry may get smaller in the next five to ten years. I don't think the timber is going to be available to sustain our business here in Idaho as it exists today. How much smaller, that's hard to speculate. I don't see the serious problems in Idaho that they are facing today in Oregon and Washington. Idaho is somewhat insulated from some of those problems, and while we may get smaller as an industry I don't think it will be catastrophic like it may be in other parts of the country.

The biggest issue facing the state of Idaho is the ultimate resolution of the roadless areas of the state. How that is resolved will determine how much land is allocated to wilderness and how much to multiple use. There are some people in the state of Idaho whose stated agenda is that not one more tree shall come from a roadless area. I don't think that view represents the mainstream view of preservationist organizations in general. I think they genuinely believe that we need more additions to Wilderness, more protection for fisheries, streams, and water quality, and less logging. The question is where is the balancing point.

*Duane Hagadone is an entrepreneur from Coeur d'Alene, the owner of the Coeur d'Alene Resort, a large lakeside hotel and recreation complex. He often identifies himself as being from North Idaho, a region that shares its time zone with Spokane, Washington, directly to the west, instead of with Boise, Idaho, directly to the south.*

I look at the relationship between northern and southern Idaho as one of the major problems we have. Frankly there is very little parallel between the northern part of the state and the southern part. When you eliminate the political environment—which is very important to us—there isn't all that much that ties us together. The business communities in North and South Idaho realize this. I see more and more interest in getting together a little more and sharing our concerns. We had the legislative caucus here a month ago. It's always good to get the legislators from the southern part of the state up here to see what our problems are, which are quite different than the problems of southern Idaho.

**Duane Hagadone**

In business, these differences have not been a serious problem to us. The biggest difficulty is communicating with the legislative community so that we have the proper legislation to operate competitively vis-a-vis Washington and Montana. Other than that, we really get along quite well.

Transportation has been a real problem. I feel the advent of Empire Airlines has been a big help. It now offers in-state service from Coeur d'Alene and Lewiston to Boise. That's certainly been very helpful, but under any scenario it's a long day to go to Boise for even an hour's meeting. There is no way you can make it in less than a day and that's by air. If you're looking at the automobile it's a long two day, or two and a half day trip. That hurts communication. But I see that improving year by year.

We'd like to think that the hotel has played quite a major part in improving relations. Most state conventions were held in the Boise area or the Sun Valley area. Now we have gotten on that circuit. Many conferences will rotate. Just about every major convention that is held in the state is now being held in the north. To the surprise of many, the attendance records have been extremely good. It has gotten the southern people into the northern part of the state more. I think the northern people get south just because of the fact that most meetings take place in that area. I have been shocked at the community leaders from southern Idaho who have come to a meeting, that have called me and said, "You know, this was the first time I've ever been up here." They tell me how beautiful it is.

Spokane, which is a relatively large city just a half hour away, is very important to us. It's the trading center. Most of our wholesale supplies are purchased from Spokane and flow through Spokane. It used to be that all of our medical services came out of Spokane, but now we have the Kootenai Medical Center, which has helped. We now have a regional shopping center, which will help us.

I have always been a cheerleader for northern Idaho and have really tried to look out for our area. But we still lose millions and millions of dollars in retail sales to Spokane, which hurts our tax base, hurts school funding and all of the necessities that rely upon that tax base. Many people work in Spokane, but enjoy the beauty and lifestyle of northern Idaho and choose to live in our area.

I've had the opportunity to watch this area grow, and have studied our basic industries of mining, lumber and agriculture. Those industries are good solid industries, but they certainly would not be classified as growth industries. I doubt you will see new employment in that area.

The only other natural resource we have is our recreational beauty. That ties into tourism. It offers tremendous potential for us as we move into the nineties. I think North Idaho and the Inland Northwest is truly one of the last frontiers. People have had very limited interest in coming to North Idaho. As the hotel continues to grow in stature, with golf course, ski activity, and additional rooms, it will compete on a national basis for meetings and conferences.

Most leads for new industry have come through the exposure of coming to the hotel and saying, "Wow, this is a wonderful place to live." Tourism is the fastest growing segment of the world economy today. It has more potential than any other. It's a great industry, clean, doesn't need a lot of support from schools and things of that nature, gives us exposure and advertising that we need.

We had the front-page cover of the *Los Angeles Times* in the August travel section. Since then, real estate sales in northern Idaho have been almost at boom level. Most Realtors will credit that page and a half in the *Times*, and their million and half circulation. I see tourism as the leader. It's amazing the interest that people have in getting out of the big cities. Unless you have a draw for them, they don't find places like this.

We've got people with concerns about too much growth here. We've had that for the last thirty years. You're always going to have that. People say they don't want to become another Lake Tahoe. I don't see that happening. There can be quality development. To some people who were here twenty years ago, the lake is overcrowded. Guests who come today are shocked at how little traffic there is. It's all relative. The thing to realize today, for individuals or businesses or communities, is that you can't stay status quo. You either move ahead in life or fall back.

It's been sad to see many of our youngsters who have wanted to return to Coeur d'Alene, after an education in North Idaho, not be able to find employment and have to leave the area. I want to see good solid growth. So I think we can have growth, but certainly not ruin the area.

Anytime you live in a beautiful area, you do attract a larger number of environmentalists. We have a lot of retired people who have come to Coeur d'Alene who want no growth. They have made their money and they're active to see that there is a balance.

There is not a lot of commercial land in the prime areas left. There will be real trouble in trying to get lake shore property rezoned from residential to commercial. It will happen from time to time, but it's just not going to open up into a total Waikiki Beach or something. I don't see in the next ten or twenty years any need for a tremendous amount of new hotels and recreational activity. But you've got to have some.

There is tremendous competition in all types of business today, whether it be recreation, tourism or mining and lumber. You've got to be on your toes to stay in business today. You just don't open the door every day and and let everybody come in until you've got a full house. It takes a very professional business approach and a well-rounded team—all the way from city government to county government to state government to the community leaders, all working together as a team. I think we have that unification here in North Idaho.

I'm very proud to be an Idahoan. I was born just three blocks from my office. I can look at my family residence out my window, and I take pride in telling people I have come a total of three blocks in my life.

# Commerce

## PREREQUISITES FOR PROGRESS

*It is not just an accident of history that Idaho was the last of the states to be entered by EuroAmerican explorers, but a logical consequence of the mountain and desert barriers surrounding the state. How could a place like Idaho ever build a permanent community of interests and a dependable economy? It was hard to get to and harder still to get through. While there were "resources" in Idaho, they too were guarded by mountain sentinels. The good soil on flat terrain was in areas without water, while the water was in the mountains or guarded by some of the steepest canyons on the continent.*

*The first economic impulses in the state—the fur trade and the gold rush—reflected its lack of obvious potential as a permanent place to live. Trappers by the hundreds and miners by the thousands blew through the state with no intention of staying, building, or developing. But while that breeze was blowing, the food production industries lodged like so many little seeds in the more welcoming environments of river valleys and grazing ranges. When the gold rush was over, those support industries remained because they managed, with the help of railroads, to find other markets for their beef, lambs, grain, fruit, and vegetables.*

*Since then, one industry after another has scraped itself together into a more or less permanent existence—silver mining, timber, tourism, microelectonics, nuclear energy. The food producers industrialized with the help of federal irrigation projects until Idaho became a national powerhouse in beets, seeds, potatoes, dry peas, lentils.*

*In order for these industries to become the basis of a permanent society in Idaho, there were certain prerequisites: there had to be resources to develop, there had to be labor to work the mines and build the roads, railroads, canals, and dams, there had to be innovation in finding markets, there had to be capital investment with a very long-term view of returns, there had to be research and scientific breakthroughs, there had to be sympathetic government interest and support, there had to be transportation of people and goods, and there had to be the will to diversify, branch out, and take risks. These prerequisites are needed no less in Idaho's future than they were in the past.*

# Resources

*Beaver was the first of many Idaho resources considered valuable to EuroAmericans. Howard Dutton of Pocatello is a member of the Portneuf Muzzleloaders and Fort Hall Replica Commission. He studies and collects paraphernalia of the fur trade in Idaho and the Northwest.*

When the trade first started, the fur companies tried to build forts where the Indians and trappers could bring the furs. But if you had a fort, everybody had to travel a long distance to it. Later on, they established a rendezvous system. Everybody would bring the furs to rendezvous. At each rendezvous they would set the place for the next one.

The rendezvous was mobile. It might be in the middle of prime beaver country. Everybody close could haul one big shipment of goods out at once. Just haul all the pelts in one trip, and that was it. There was no upkeep on a fort, no permanent employees all-year round. It was a good system. It became an occasion to look forward to, a celebration. The mountain men and the Indians would get together and have a week of hell-raising.

Everybody would bring furs and trade for goods out of St. Louis. The goods were often necessities of life—simple things like a flint steel to start a fire, or a shirt. They didn't always wear buckskin in the summer time. Buckskin was awful hot and they liked a good cotton or wool shirt to wear.

At the rendezvous or the trade stations, it was just like going to the store nowadays. You could go buy a rifle, more traps, powder or shot for your rifle, a new blanket. Since the rendezvous was just once a year, you had to be careful to take care of your equipment. It would be kind of thin pickings in between.

Most trappers got started with a company which would recruit back east and around St. Louis. They would start off indebted to the company. The company would furnish every man with six traps. Once they got free and clear of debt from the company, they would go out on their own. These were called free trappers, indebted to no one. They would trap on their own and set their own price at the rendezvous. The free trapper was the elite of the mountain men. He was on his own. Quite an individual, some of them. Pretty cocky.

When there was a call for volunteers to trap, a variety of people responded. People came from all parts of the

*Courtesy of Howard Dutton*

**Howard Dutton**

country, from all walks of life. It was kind of a duke's mixture. At some of the long sessions around the fires at night, people were reading Shakespeare. Some of them were very well educated. Others couldn't read or write their names, but, on the other hand, could speak five or six different Indian languages and get along with people. There was a lot of talent out here in the mountains of the West.

Trappers covered virtually every stream, every river. There were very few places that these men didn't reach in their quest for these furs. Toward the end of the fur trade, when the source dwindled, they had to go farther and farther afield to find them. Therefore, they did cover a lot of country.

They pretty well trapped the beaver out in some places. There was not only the Indian looking for them, but the white man, the English. In the eastern Idaho area, there was a lot of competition between the Americans and the English. The English wanted to keep the Americans east of the Rocky Mountains. Once they came west of the Rocky Mountains, the British would go through an area and take every pelt they could find, when they had a chance, just to keep the Americans out.

Daily life all depended on the season of the year. During the trapping season, there were some long days put in. Each man was initially issued six traps. He would go out and set these traps, probably in the morning, and check them at night. There was always the skinning and preparation of the hides. It wasn't any good to catch them if you didn't take care of them. The pelts were stretched on a willow and fleshed on the back. They were different sizes and colors. The thicknesses were different according to the time of year they were taken. They folded them twice and put them in bales, loaded them on a horse. From rendezvous they were taken to St. Louis.

In the wintertime there were some long leisurely days when people just holed up. This was the time for story telling, for reading, for games, for just lounging around and enjoying the long winter evenings.

## Labor

*The silver industry of the Coeur d'Alene Mining District hired wage laborers willing to work in the heat and hazard of underground mines and smelters. Unlike laboring gangs in South Idaho, who were imported to build a dam or canal or railroad track and then sent elsewhere, the miners and loggers of the north aspired to be permanent residents of communities where they could raise families. They had to fight for humane working conditions, safety, and fair wages, which they did by means of union organization and action.*

*Union efforts were resisted by the Bunker Hill Company and other mine owners and led to "the troubles" of the 1890s, one of the most violent episodes of labor-management conflict in United States history. In the first decades of the twentieth century, the union movement had to overcome the bitter memories of these episodes and then the "red scare" of the 1920s. The successor to the Western Federation of Miners was the International Union of Mine, Mill, and Smelter Workers, which revitalized during the 1930s.*

*Three union men discussed some of their early experiences with group action in the mining and lumber country of North Idaho. Pete Piekarski of Pinehurst, Elwin Shultz of Kellogg, and Art Norlen of Cataldo began their working lives in the late 1920s and later, and continued active throughout the 1950s, a peak period of union membership in Idaho.*

NORLEN: The greed that developed was responsible for some of the violence in the 1890s. The companies were trying to get as much as they possibly could for each dollar paid out for labor. They had to find all the shortcuts they possibly could. It was a class struggle—you can't call it anything else—between the working class and the owning class of the industry. That is what it amounted to.

I don't think the full story about the Troubles will ever come to the light of day. The operators can share the blame with the union. There is no doubt the union was to blame for some. The union made some terrible mistakes in the early days. So did the operators.

PIEKARSKI: The companies kept up the propaganda about the Troubles. Everyone was scared of unions because that propaganda had taken hold of the district. Old timers told me there was no such thing as talking union in the mining district. This lasted until about the late 1930s. After the organizers from Mine-Mill came in, some union people went to work in the mines around here, and people got over that scare, finally.

*Art Norlen*

NORLEN: What brought the union here was the need for a union. In 1927 or 1928, when I first came to this district, union was a dirty name. I would sit down at a lunch counter and there would be a working man next to me. I'd ask him, "Are you a union member?" He would say, "No, I'm not." They were afraid to admit that they were union members.

The companies had a hiring agent named George Edminston they called "the king." He worked for all the mines except Bunker Hill. When I went to the king to get a job, the first question was, "Have you had any mining experience?" I answered, "Butte, Montana." He said, "Come back in two days." I went back—no work. I couldn't get on. I thought, "My gosh, this is something else!"

I went to Wallace to help a guy tar a roof on a building there, and we talked. He loaned me a pair of cowboy boots and a cowboy hat, and I went back to see if I could get hired at the mines. I went by the name of August Nelson, a name with the same initials, which I had on my belt buckle. I didn't know English well enough to take on a southern drawl, but I did pretty well, I guess, because I convinced the man that I was harmless. He asked, "What mining experience have you had?" "I haven't got any." And he hired me.

My first experience with collective bargaining was in a cedar camp in the spring of 1929. There were no showers, no way to wash clothes, no nothing. I used to take a bath and wash my underwear in a creek.

We had a meeting and decided that we wouldn't work anymore unless we got a bathhouse. We decided that we would strike the next morning and refuse to go work unless we at least got a promise of a bathhouse. I went out and stood in front of the shop. Pretty soon here come three Finlanders who couldn't speak English. All the rest of the guys went to work, having forgotten about the fact that we were going to get a bathhouse. That left me the spokesman, the first time I was a spokesman for any demand that labor made.

We got ahold of the boss. I wasn't sure of myself, but I kept a straight face and told him what we had decided at the meeting. He said, "My gosh! I've been fighting for that myself all this time. I'm glad you guys helped me do this." I was all perked up and he said, "I'm going to town today and see the general manager." When he came back he brought with him a man that stayed with us that night and did all the figuring for what it would take to install a water heater and bathroom and laundry and the whole works.

*Pete Piekarski*

Later I went to work at Bunker Hill, on level number 23 which was at the bottom at the time, about four feet below sea level. About the second union meeting I went to, the shop steward had quit the job. Some bright guy got the idea that, "We have a new guy here who can handle that job." Then he mentioned my name. I said, "My gosh, I can't handle it, I don't know enough about this. I don't know the people, I don't know their work, so I don't know anything." "Well, that makes no difference, we'll help you." So I was railroaded into that job. Pretty soon I got to be chief shop steward of the Bunker Hill mine.

I didn't take up many grievances unless they were a violation of the contract. I really rode those to a finish. It was always important to me to make the company live up to its contract.

SHULTZ: I was twenty-one years old when I came here in 1938. People like me that came from somewhere else were actually easier to get into the union than those who were educated in the Kellogg school system. Laboring people hadn't done their homework and didn't put people on the schoolboard so they would have some control over what was taught to their kids. Believe me, there was no good labor stuff taught to our kids in school.

I had started out in a non-union place, so I had a good reason to see what the need for unions were. There had been no vacations, no eight-hour days, no health benefits, no insurance. I plainly saw the need. When I finally hired in where there was union, I was amazed to find these things already there.

When I first came to Idaho the Depression was still on. I cut wood and and worked in harvest fields and then tried to make a living on a stump farm. I finally learned that I couldn't make it that way. Relatives working at Bunker Hill urged me to give up on the stump farm. I finally did and went to work for Bunker Hill at the smelter.

As soon as I hired in, the first man that handed me a union card, I signed it. All I did was just attend meetings and learn what was going on for a while. I finally got into the lead refinery, which was one of the rougher places to work in that smelter. They didn't have a union steward on the shift that I worked on. We talked union quite a little bit in the dry house, and on the job. The guys got together one day and said to me, "Why don't you become our steward?" There was a rather informal election, and I got to be the union steward. Probably my main function in unions was handling grievances. That was where most of my experience was.

*Elwin Shultz*

I'm most proud of getting people to work together to obtain for themselves that which they have earned, as near as possible. Any kind of unified action brings this out. For example, we had a lot of problems on our shift. When there was a no-show, we had to work shorthanded. We didn't let any of the work go, just doubled up and did it. If two or three guys were missing, you had to do the work on the run, practically. That didn't set too well. I said, "Let's do something about it."

The contract called for grievances to be settled right then and there. Management was supposed to make every effort they could to settle it before the problem went to arbitration. This problem affected the whole crew, so the whole crew stopped working. The shifter (crew boss for a shift) couldn't settle it, he didn't have the authority. They got the next level of management there, and he couldn't settle it. The next level of management just told us all to go back to work, that we could arbitrate. But the guys didn't go back to work.

The next thing you know, the kettles were all getting filled up with no place for the lead to go. They had a real problem. They were going to have to close the blast furnace down. They fired me right then and there. The guys still didn't go back to work. Pete here was in the crane, and he was one of the grievance committee members. Since we had to have the grievance committee in order to settle that grievance, they got Pete down out of the crane. That, of course, slowed the blast furnace up considerably and they had to put the relief crane man up.

The upshot of the whole thing was that they unfired me, put us all back to work, and agreed that there would be fourteen men per shift. If they tried to get a man to work over from the previous shift, and they couldn't do it, or they couldn't get a call out, then we would work shorthanded. I don't think there was ever a time that we worked shorthanded after that.

PIEKARSKI: My grandfather and my father were very union-minded. I was a smart kid, so I didn't listen to Pa. When I got out to Idaho my ambition was to own something. Polish people had a tradition of wanting to own land. I bought a stump farm. I used to walk up and down the property line and say, "That ain't mine, this is mine." After twelve years I got it worked out of my system.

I got on at WPA (Work Progress Administration), where my dad worked, too. He and some others had a lot of trouble with two bosses there, and these bosses were afraid of my dad, who was six foot two and a half inches tall, all bone and muscle. The bosses decided to pick on his kid and get even with the old man. One day they called me over and said, "You've got to get busy, start earning your keep around here or we're going to 402 you." That meant fire. I said, "I'm doing just as much as anybody else." They said, "You either shape up or we're going to get rid of you."

My dad was just fighting mad when I came back to the crew. He wanted to go beat 'em up and my brother said, "Pa, don't do that. All you'll do is get yourself fired, and it won't do any good."

So that night after the shift was over, the whole crew surrounded the big shot. I thought they were going to kill him. They said, "By God, if you're going to pick on somebody, pick on somebody that's a little older. That doggone kid doesn't know from anything. Incidentally, he is doing just as much as we are." So that was my first experience with group action. I started putting two and two together. What Pa had been telling me was right.

Later I got a job at Cabinet Gorge, but I could see there was no family life. I went to Kellogg where there were steady jobs. When I got on the job, old Pop Pruitt, a union steward, signed me up for the union and said he didn't want that to be the last they saw of me.

So I went to the next union meeting. They had a battle going on. They had a phony (laborer more sympathetic to management) who was an alternate on the negotiating committee. The phonies wanted to put him on again because one of the regular negotiators was leaving. The battle was to keep him off the negotiating committee. All the rules I had ever seen was that the alternate automatically goes on. But Pop Pruitt and others spoke against him. I trusted his judgement, and when the vote came up I voted to keep him off the negotiating committee. That immediately identified me with the progressive element in my mill. Thank goodness it did.

In my union days at Bunker Hill, I'm most proud of some of the grievances that I participated in where we won safety measures. We showed the company that when they sign the contract they damned sure are going to give people what the contract says.

I was proud of the (1960) strike because it showed the tremendous potential that people have. Without people you have nothing. The song Solidarity says: "In our hands is placed a power greater than their hoarded gold." That's what I believe of people.

NORLEN: If you sum it all up, what has caused us to be two-car families today? And live in decent houses and work eight hours? The unions. They have urged industry along by their action to modernize facilities in plants. We have come a long way.

Unionism caused some struggle. There is always that. While you try to improve your benefits, the other side is trying to take them away. It's a constant struggle.

PIEKARSKI: Gains between management and labor see-saw back and forth. Over a historical period, the gains of people who work have been more than their losses. That's why I'm so optimistic about the future. If they don't blow this world up with atomic bombs, eventually the laboring world will come out with a lot better deal than they have now. When they drive us back, we forge forward. We always forge forward a little further than we were driven back.

That even goes with Right to Work, which is a learning experience for labor. Eventually labor will have to see to it that people are elected into Congress, and overthrow the section of Taft-Hartley that gives the states the right to enact Right to Work. Those things are just like kidney stones, they're painful but they'll pass.

# Transportation

*Idaho was the home of Varney Airline, the first commercial airline company in the United States. Varney Airline began carrying the mail for the United States government between Elko, Nevada, and Pasco, Washington, with headquarters at Boise. Chet Moulton of Boise started flying in 1927 and became a flight instructor for the U.S. Army after Pearl Harbor. He reflected on how it all grew.*

*Chet Moulton*

My first memory of Varney was with the building of the airport where Boise State University now is. There was no commercial airline anywhere in the nation at that time. Flying was all handled by the military. The site for the airport was an old dump along the Boise River where the city hauled its trash. There were lots of sloughs and tules and birds down there.

A man named Cyril Thompson was primarily responsible for starting a program to make that area an airport. He was head of the Idaho American Legion. This was all before the federal government would help air carrier airports. There was lots of interest in the project—some good, some bad, some negative, some positive, but nobody had any money.

So Cyril organized the American Legion to go down there as free labor to do this job. They asked for volunteers. I was a young man from the Midwest, and I volunteered for two summers to drive a truck and haul fill. It turned out to take longer than they had anticipated because of the volunteer labor and the nature of the swamp. There was no modern equipment like today. As soon as the runway was about 1200 feet long, the pilots started to practice and get ready for the opening date for the mail.

When the airport opened in 1926 they had a big hullaballoo show and started flying. They had a pretty good turnout of mail. Then after a couple of years, United bought them out and built a taxi-through hangar for DC-3s and a couple of other smaller two-engine aircraft. When the DC-4s came along, they would not fit into the old hangars, so the airport made plans to move out south of the city, where it is today.

The first planes used by Varney were Swallows, biplanes with open cockpits, so the pilots sat outside in the rain and darkness. They had a number of mishaps and soon changed to a little better airplane. The mail and any passengers would be put in the front of the airplane, ahead of the pilot, where they used a big rolling curtain made of metal to cover them up. They shut it down and locked it, so there you were in the dark with the mail setting out on a flight to someplace.

When I flew in an open cockpit plane, I had to put on a sheepskin-lined suit in cold weather, a helmet and goggles. You had to have something on your head or your hair just cut you to pieces at one hundred or two hundred miles an hour. Your eyes couldn't stand that either, so you had to have goggles.

There were no radio aids. There were a few beacons with rotating lights every fifty or sixty miles. There was no way to make any kind of communications with anybody except yourself. You had to have your own experience and make up your own mind about which was the right decision and right direction. When I flew to Boise from the north, I always hesitated coming through the area north of New Meadows at night. That is where the big change in weather patterns occurs separating the moister north and the dry south.

There was that big deep Hells Canyon. No reservoirs then. Big changes in altitude. You could see lights occasionally, but at ten thousand feet there wouldn't be much. There would be that creeping something that comes over you that you would like to get closer to those lights, and see cars and things. But of course, it was the last thing you should do. The best thing I can say is that that is one of the most lonesome feelings that can come over anybody—to be a pilot at ten thousand feet at night, flying over rough mountains and heavy timber with no radio, no lights, and no means of help whatsoever.

There were a lot of jokes in those years, even after United bought out Varney. They used to say that the pilots would mail Sears and Roebuck catalogues to each other, since the government paid for mail delivery by the pound, and the joke was that the catalogues paid for the gas for the planes.

The engines of the early planes weren't as responsible as later ones. One plane went down at King Hill out on a rocky lava butte, and another one somewhere else. Terrible losses. You must remember they were going up at night as well as daytime, summer and winter.

But it is like most things in life. There has to be somebody to go first. Take the boats that first crossed the ocean. Most people would be scared to death to get on them, yet they opened up the world. Varney had a great vision of the future. He and others just liked to fly, wanted to get into it. Once into it, they would starve to death in order to stay with it.

There was a lot of resistence to commercial mail service. It was a brand new thing. It was amazing how many people in the service clubs and chamber of commerce argued and quarreled about the futility of this kind of silliness.

When we built an airport at Kellogg, one of the county commissioners said, "There is no way you are going to get me in one of those fool things. I'm going to stay where I can keep both feet on the ground." Well, the day we opened the airport and there was a big to-do, his wife brought a cakepan full of dirt from their garden. She said, "He said he was going to keep his feet on the ground, so here is some ground from his yard. Now he is going to take a ride with Chet." When we got up into the air, I wanted to show him how you could look from Kellogg over into the St. Joe drainage and made a little turn in the airplane. He about tore the ceiling out. So I had to slide the airplane into its turns to let him see the valley.

Everything seems to go through a scare-'em period. There can't be any improvements without trial and error and some failure. But everything in life seems to be this way as it creeps and grows and comes into being.

## Research

*The sheep industry is one of the longest-lasting enterprises in the history of Idaho. In 1916 the United States established its first Sheep Experiment Station near Dubois, Idaho. The station has pioneered in range management methods and selection procedures. Research has produced new breeds of sheep, like the Columbia and the Polypay, with better wool and more lambs. Reducing predation and improving the ranges is also a research priority. Hudson Glimp is the director of the U.S. Sheep Experiment Station and discussed some current research objectives.*

The most important part of our program is to realize first and foremost that we are in the land-use business in the western United States. This has great implications. We have multiple uses for our land here, much of which is public land. We therefore have recreational uses, wildlife, fish, camping, and hiking. We have livestock—both cattle and sheep. We are primarily in the sheep business here at the station, although we now have cattle and goats in our range research.

One of the things we recognize is that as this desert land environment becomes more harsh, the diversity of plant species becomes much greater. On this range in Clark County, Idaho, for example, we have identified over four hundred plant species. When you have the huge diversity of grasses, weeds, and shrubs that we have, it's very likely that multiple uses are the most efficient use of that plant community.

Sheep prefer to graze the high country. They tend to graze the shorter grasses, weeds, and some shrubs. Cattle do not like shrubs. They will eat some weeds, but they much prefer grasses, the taller coarser grasses that sheep

*Hudson Glimp*

don't care for. Elk prefer a more intermediate type of diet. Antelope prefer the sagebrush and the shrubs that the sheep and cattle tend not to eat. Moose will eat the taller, wet marshy grasses and plants. Sheep won't even go in a marshy area. Cattle really prefer the grasses rather than the types of plants the moose eat.

The dietary overlap between the moose and the sheep is only about 15 percent. Between cattle and moose, it is about 30 percent. It's about 30 percent between cattle and sheep. And these are quite different plant species that they are eating. So, a better understanding of that as well as the animals' nutrient needs for performance will allow us to work the proper species mix to continue to improve the land as well as efficiently utilize it.

One of the ways to find out involves this heifer in a new program that we have. She has an esophageal fistula in her throat. When we turn her out to graze, we can put a bag on her and take the plug out. Ninety-nine percent of the time, the plug is in, but one percent of the time, everything she eats will drop into that bag, and we can analyze the different plant species that she has eaten. We analyze the chemical composition and determine what her demands are. We can then relate that to what is on this range. The optimal mix may be different in another part of the state than it is in Dubois. But if we understand the preferences of an individual species and compare it to what the plant community is, then we can work that mix together. We study sheep the same way.

We are talking with some of the wildlife specialists who have responsibilities for deer and elk and even bison, and have measured their food intake.

Another area of range nutrition research is the problem of undesirable species. There are many plant species that are very undesirable. One of them is called leafy spurge. As this plant grows it puts out a toxin that kills all other plants. Out here, it costs about one hundred dollars an acre to kill it chemically. Well, we can't afford that. In addition, we don't want to use the chemicals.

I see in the future the use of less and less chemicals. We should use them less and less. To spray along streams and in riparian areas is to risk contaminating the water supply for humans and for fish. We have to find other methods of controlling these kinds of plants.

It just so happens that goats dearly love leafy spurge. Sheep will also eat leafy spurge. Goats will also seek out spotted knapweed, another nuisance plant, and graze it. So we are looking at the way goats, cattle and sheep might control these weeds and toxic plants biologically.

We are also studying the genetic selection that causes multiple births. We want to develop animals that have greater productivity and adaptability to this environment. The most important genetic trait is adaptability. An animal must first be able to survive where it is expected to be. Then it must thrive, it must reproduce, and it must grow.

I see a younger generation of ranchers coming on now that are equally as concerned about the environment as their cousins in town. I'm not saying all ranchers are good, just like all lawyers are not good. The good rancher realizes that the last thing in the world that he can do is rape his basic resource. If he wants to stay in business and wants the next generation to be in business, he has to take care of the land.

There was an attitude in the 1880s and early 1900s that there was more land out here than they could ever use. If they ruined one piece, they could just go on to the next. Some of that happened. But now that operations are more sedentary, people know that this is home base, this the only piece of land we can graze. If we don't take care of it, that is all there is going to be.

*In the 1960s the sheep industry was looking for improved profit from the sale of meat more than the sale of wool. They asked station researchers for a sheep with higher lifetime production, more twins, ability to lamb more than once a year, and other features. What they got was the Polypay, a name chosen for a sheep that will pay at least three times a year—one wool and two lambing crops. Reed Hulet of Wendell is a sheepman and a member of the American Polypay Sheep Association.*

I started being a sheep inspector around 1970 and did that for fourteen years. When I started we had about seventy-five range operations that I inspected in the southern Idaho area. When I retired from that, there were half that many. It was partly economic reasons and partly range problems.

*Reed Hulet*

Our problem now is range usage. We have so many people now who want all livestock off the range. They want wilderness, parks, and all of the kinds of things where livestock are not allowed. With many people wanting all livestock off the public land it looks like there are difficult times ahead for sheep, since most of the sheep in Idaho are raised on the range.

I had been raising Suffolk sheep for a number of years. Our main market for those were range operators. We knew that in the West, the greatest number of sheep are raised on the range, and my brother (Dr. Clarence Hulet of the U.S. Sheep Experiment Station) and I knew we would need a sheep that worked well on the range. It would need to have more lambs than what we were getting, have more milk so it could feed that higher number of lambs, and have an acceptable quality of fleece.

My brother also thought that out-of-season breeding with more than one lambing per year could result in over a 200 percent lamb crop. At first I wasn't so interested in that, but now I've found that lambs add up pretty fast when you get an extra lambing in a year. Quite a few people have achieved over 300 percent lamb crops from accelerated lambing.

Before the Polypay we found it almost impossible to get more than 140 percent no matter what we did. The Polypay broke that barrier greatly. We get 180 to 200 percent lamb crops for once a year lambing, which we feel is a profitable production.

The pluses are that you get more pounds of lamb and more product to sell. This is the big thing. But along with that, the Polypay is a very easy-to-handle sheep with a good disposition. They have good white wool. They have flocking instinct and can be herded very successfully. In a farm situation this is important also because guard dogs are much more effective when the flocks don't scatter all over.

Polypays have been introduced into most of the states of the United States, perhaps not into Florida or Alabama or other extreme southeastern states. A county agent from Arizona, a Navajo, obtained some Polypays that we raised and liked them so well they came and bought a truckload the next year. They liked the spinning quality of the wool and the production and said they got along very well on the range. Polypays are in Hawaii and Alaska, Canada, Mexico, and Guatemala. We hope to send some to other countries soon, too.

Is anything ever perfect? No, they aren't perfect. They don't have armor plate to defy the coyotes. Development needs to continue. They need stronger milking ability, and could have multiple births more consistantly than they do. The wool could be improved. Time is required to attain those things.

The scientific procedure says you can improve faster if you select for only one objective at a time, but we haven't done this. We've tried to work on all of them continuously. We have put more emphasis on productivity than we have on some other things, so we are turning to more emphasis on wool at this time.

Polypay is a medium wool sheep. It grades, as a rule, between fifty-six and sixty-two spinning count, which makes nice blankets and sport clothing. It is not fine enough for worsted clothing, fine suit material, or dresses. It's good for knitted material. Coarser wool goes for the coarse outdoor clothing and carpets.

Sometimes it is difficult to get range men particularly to switch to the Polypay. These are families who have been into sheep for several generations and their attitude is, "If it worked for my father and my grandfather, it will work for me." In the East where most of our customers are new to sheep they are more willing to try something different. The fact that the Polypay has more lambs is attractive to them, and they take to it. As time goes by, the traditional families here will start wondering why their neighbor is shipping more loads of lambs than they are. It works eventually.

I suppose it is ironic that the people who oppose sheep on the public land and who go into the wilderness wear a lot of wool. It is something like, "If we get rid of the farmers, we'll go into the store to buy our food." Animal agriculture is needed, really needed. Natural products, fibers and foods, are better for us, I believe, and we need them. I'm a believer in animal agriculture.

*Hulet's Polypay Sheep*

# Higher Education

*The University of Idaho at Moscow is a "land grant" university established in 1889 by the territorial legislature of Idaho. Its mission is to undertake the kind of research needed to help develop the resources of the state. Since Idaho's resources lay in its mines and forests and rich agricultural land, the University of Idaho traditionally focused its research to aid those industries.*

*Dr. Elisabeth Zinser, who arrived at the university as its new president in 1989, discussed the potential for the expansion of the university's mission in the progress of the state and her first impressions of Idaho.*

One of the most important features of the University of Idaho is its land grant research mission. One of the reasons I came here was the potential to develop the university even more fully by applying the land grant concept in some very creative ways to bring technology and knowledge to people in the diverse regions of the state.

We are focusing our research efforts in at least six new areas that we believe have great significance to the state of Idaho: water resources, aquaculture, biotechnology, materials science, microelectronics, and hazardous waste management. Each is a new center for interdisciplinary research and advanced education, as well as technology transfer to industry. We have the opportunity to develop national recognition for the university beyond that which we already enjoy.

*Courtesy of Elisabeth Zinser*

***Elisabeth Zinser***

For example, we want to make a contribution to the commercial fish industry in the Twin Falls area. We have made a commitment to develop a small, highly specialized wet laboratory on the Moscow campus where a team of inter-disciplinary scholars work together with those at Washington State University. Technology developments and findings from the laboratory in Moscow will be transferred to the south of the state for further development by industry.

Another feature of the aquaculture project is its development in a socially responsible manner. The laboratory is in a location where the Palouse water system is fragile and not well understood as yet. We have kept the laboratory small enough so that the impact on the Palouse water system will be small. In addition we have committed ourselves to study the Palouse system in order to understand it better. We want the development process to improve our knowledge of this and other water systems.

We intend to develop other programs with that same philosophy. This is certainly appropriate when land grant universities across the country are revitalizing their mission. Development in agriculture, forestry, mining, engineering and other areas have traditionally been part of the land grant environment, and we're looking for new high-technology developments to come from those and related fields.

Modern telecommunications are more sophisticated than ever before, making it possible for the University of Idaho to offer services far beyond anything it has offered before, despite its remote location. We are sending more and more of our people into other areas of the state. We recently sent two key faculty members to Idaho Falls, where their expertise can be applied to scientific and engineering work there. And we aim to expand our capabilities in simultaneous telecommunications between such sites and the faculty on the Moscow campus.

I am extremely impressed by what I am finding in Idaho. I came here because I am an adventuresome person. I like being part of a state, a place, and an institution on the move and eager to do things.

The reverence that people feel for the land in Idaho resonated for me right away. I very much cherish the land, and wanted to come to a place where people are very serious about balancing the use and preservation of our natural resources. That was a value I already had. I began to appreciate quickly the special role our university and state can play in this area.

I've enjoyed visiting some of the lumber mills and forests, and seeing some of the University's forestry experiment stations. I am deeply impressed by the increasing sensitivity that the forest and wood products industry has toward its responsibility to help preserve the land and replenish the trees that they use for economic development. That is very encouraging to me.

Living in Idaho will probably move me in the direction of being more moderate in my thinking about some issues. Growing up in California in the 1960s gave me a somewhat liberal orientation to many issues, although I've always measured opinions and candidates on examination of the merits.

Some areas of the country tend to be swallowed up in a very conservative or very liberal orientation. In Idaho the range of orientations to issues are bracketed much more broadly, which forces a more intellectual approach to solving problems and resolving one's own opinion in a more rational thoughtful way. Moreover, living in a state with 1.2 million people, we learn to argue about issues while maintaining respect and friendships.

I guess I had so much pre-warning about sectionalism in Idaho that I wasn't terribly surprised to find it when I got here. Some of the regionalism is negative, but regionalism comes from the diversity of the state as well. None of us want to diminish the diversity of the state. We want to celebrate it more than fight it. In fact, we could use far more diversity in the integration of other cultures in our state. If we can move to a positive attitude about how diversity helps rather than hinders the state, we will be better off. Commitment to basic, common goals for Idaho leads to unity, along with improvements in transportation and communication systems.

Right now is one of the most adventuresome times in the life of Idaho. Everyone is consciously geared to moving across the threshold of the century. It creates an excitement about what the next stage of things will be. With that comes a new level of commitment and a desire to be a part of building the future. Idahoans appear to be very tenacious and persistent people who are going to get what they want when they put their minds to it. There is a fresh opportunity for innovation and engagement, for unity of purpose in diversity, for making a better life for Idahoans while contributing in unique ways to solutions to perplexing national and global problems. Research and education are essential ingredients. I'm glad Idahoans value both.

# Diversification

*Diversification of the economy has been a conscious goal of the state and many of its communities and enterprises for many years. However, diversification is also a strategy for individual enterprises, such as Don and Pam Heckman's ranch near Whitebird. They still trail their cattle to higher country in the early summer, but the business involves a great deal more.*

DON: These cattle are going onto the Nez Perce National Forest. We start on the first of June with a portion of them. We usually have three turn-out dates. This is the last date. This bunch is about 145 head. That will make a total of about 403, I believe. This particular drive goes the farthest. It is a three-day trail from the ranch to get where they'll be dropped, and ends up in the Gospel Hump Wilderness Area. That's a rugged, rustic area, but there is some good pasture. The season is short and it costs a lot to get there and use that country.

We've worked out a rest rotation system with the Slate Creek District of the Forest Service. The people at Slate Creek have been real tuned in to grazing. They're good people to work with. It isn't a complicated rotation, but it took a lot of hours to work out on paper. It's complicated to manage.

Going into a Wilderness area makes a difference in how we do things. One of the resource managers, before the Wilderness classification was given to Gospel Hump, said there was no wording in the law to prevent grazing there. But you have to do a job that looks like you haven't been there. That's almost impossible. You

***Don and Pam Heckman***

can't do trail maintenance work with a chain saw, you can't even haul salt with a motor vehicle of any kind. It is a lot different than operating in a multiple-use area.

Operating costs are considerably higher for a couple of reasons. The Wilderness area is farther back. It costs more just to get the cowboy in and out. His supplies have to be packed in on a pack horse. The death loss is greater in there. I call it death loss. Maybe we just don't find them all. So people might ask why we are in there. The the main reason is that in the scheme of things we graze from our deeded land to the Gospel Hump Wilderness Area. That is all our area, so that's why it works well. If grazing fees go up significantly, that would probably put an end to it. It isn't going to take too much more to turn us around. We will reduce the numbers and hope to continue on the multiple-use area.

We'd like to be diversified more. We mainly raise cattle and our own hay. Over the years we have occasionally raised wheat or barley. We've also sold timber. When a timber sale was made in the past, there was no consideration other than the size of the timber that would be cut. Thank God my parents didn't allow small timber to be cut then.

Now we thin the timber to enhance the stand. We seed tame grasses back on skid trail roads and landings. We're increasing our carrying capacity for cattle as well by thinning the timber. We're actually increasing the growth of stands that were stagnant. We are enthused about that. Pam watches for new seedlings. We hire a forester to work with us. Pam and I were jointly named Idaho Tree Farmers of the Year for 1989.

One other thing we've done is outfit big-game hunting on our place. We're probably going to go into that more because we don't have a lot of other options left.

Our cattle are cross bred. Back when I was a boy growing up, we had straight Hereford cattle. I like good cattle of all breeds. I've helped class bulls of various breeds at bull sales. Right now we're into natural fed beef. People like leaner animals with less backfat. We're having better luck right now with cross bred cattle.

PAM: From some of the research that I've done, the consumer now wants more natural beef, drug-free beef, low-fat beef. I don't feel that there is as much available for them as they would like. I feel proud that maybe we're on the cutting edge. It's a little scary out there, I guess. You really don't know all the ins and outs, but it is exciting to me. Don and I feel strongly about having a good, healthy, honest product. We want the same thing the consumer wants. We're not in the business just for the money. We want to put the best that we possibly can out there. That's the bottom line.

Consumers don't concern me as much as some of the people in between. Packers and retailers are the hardest people to deal with. It's all new to them. They don't want to take chances like we do. Don and I and his folks are known for taking chances and trying new things. The consumer is not the scary part. We were invited to a seminar held by a natural beef retailer in Colorado. He brought retailers and consumers from all over the United States together. It was an eye opener to me because we got to sit down and talk to retailers who stood behind the counter from consumers in New Jersey and Texas and New York and Seattle and California. It solidified in my mind that the demand is out there. Our industry is not really meeting the need.

I think our heart is in it. It is new ground. We are all having to learn new channels, even make new channels. It's exciting, but you don't always do it right.

I guess you wouldn't call me a typical rancher's wife. I'm more involved in business, in a lot of public relations and promotion. The idea of a rancher's wife is that she is on a horse. Whenever everybody else is on a horse, I'm with an accountant, an attorney, or doing book work. But I also run my own business in addition to maintaining the houses on the ranch, which Donny's grandmother and mother didn't do because they didn't have so many then. I have a contractor who works under me, and I oversee all the work. I do a lot of the work myself, which I find real satisfying. It's just another job that has to be done.

DON: My grandfather was from Nebraska. In his young years they came to Idaho to the Lewiston area. He worked in a sawmill and then got a small ranch. He had a desire to have a larger ranch. It was when times were really hard. The banks had quite a few ranches they had taken when so many people went broke. They were looking for operators to buy them. In 1933 Granddad went to a ranch up from the mouth of the Salmon River about three miles. My dad and uncle were around twenty years old then.

There were no roads in that country and it was pretty tough going. All the work was done by pack horses and pack mules. I ride in some of this country and see where homesteaders and ranchers have been and I don't understand it. At any rate, they grubbed out a living. It was real tough, I'm sure, because from the sales sheet of their first year, they got two dollars and fifty cents a hundred for thirty-three head of cattle. They were a hard-working family, and they expanded.

*Driving cattle to the summer range*

Granddad didn't care much for the farming around Lewiston. He had worked for a lot of the large farms. He was a teamster, drove the thrashing machines with the big horse hitches. He liked working with cattle and being in the rugged part of the country. He told me many times that he was born a hundred years too late. If there was an easy way to do something he might do it the hard way just to do it.

Then times got mechanized. I worked with the small equipment as a kid. We got larger. We probably grew from three or four thousand acres to about thirty-five thousand deeded acres, plus a lot of leased land. Pam and I have been active as managers for about twenty-three years. Of that, the last ten have been the toughest. There have been good times in the ten, but it has tightened, and there is no room for error. You either have a real high or a real low. I'd rather go back to my first ten or fifteen years. There are so many things that can happen real fast to you now.

Nationwide, ranching had it really tough for five years in a row. When you lose neighbors you wonder if you're going to go down yourself. You keep thinking next year is going to be better. A normal down cycle usually averages out between two or four years. But you have to be a gambling-type person or you wouldn't be a rancher anyway. You're pretty hardy and ambitious and all those things that go with it. I've had a little trouble being optimistic part of the time. It's better now, we're rambling along.

PAM: We see big changes coming. New government policies are going to affect private land in this area. We've become such a major recreational area. When you have a big influx of people, they may want things different. There are going to be some real tough challenges. If you make your living off of the cattle industry and ranching, you have to be diversified.

DON: I hope that this family ranch can continue. I'm the third generation. My folks and grandfolks before me had that same theory. Dion, our oldest boy, and his wife live on the ranch now and work with us. Our younger son, Dean, is away going to school. I hope those guys have a feel for the land, too. I hope they continue. They're capable of it if they don't get discouraged with all the demands. It is a lot of responsibility. They would have to make adjustments. I sure did. I made some mistakes along the way. There is a lot of competition in ranching. There are some dark spots. But it's not rosy anywhere you're at all the time.

I like to think that if you're good to the land, it will be good to you. If a drought year comes, you have to work toward the averages. In stocking rates, I like to feel that we don't use the land right down to the last mouthful of grass every year. I like to leave some. The same with the timber.

## Capital, Innovation, Government, Self-esteem, New Markets...

*Robert Smylie was the Governor of Idaho from 1955 through 1966. He was responsible for some of the first initiatives taken by state government to diversify the economy and create new attitudes and resources in Idaho.*

Idaho used to be a lot like a developing Third World economy. I think that we managed to get reasonably financially independent of our Third World condition along about the early 1950s. We had set the conditions for this early on with the establishment of some laws in the 1930s that permitted horizontal chaining of banks. That was really a decision that we were going to end up with four or five statewide chain banks with each having an economic presence in every major market. That gave the Boise banking establishment sufficient muscle by 1950 to be able to handle reasonably good-sized commercial accounts on their own. They didn't have to talk with San Francisco or New York. Originally we used to have to go to New York to get anything financed. Right after the war it was always San Francisco. By 1960 at the latest, the Boise banks could pretty well put a big loan line together.

This is oversimplification, but the Depression started in Idaho in 1892, and we didn't get out of it until about 1950. Take the war years out. Nothing ever came on-stream all at the same time. Timber was down, mining was down, or agriculture was down. Historically these irrigation projects had to go through the wringer at least once, sometimes twice, before they began to get enough water out of them to show a profit. So it was about 1950, I think, before we really got our ducks in a row.

It was a matter of growing up. If the United States had had a Marshall Plan for its territories, they would have sent a lot of money out here for us to grow up on real fast. But they didn't have any use for us for that purpose. They just wanted two votes in the Senate.

Resource development was a typical concern of western states as they developed their constitutions. There were quite a few of the people who wrote that constitution who had come here from California and Grass Valley through Nevada. Many parts of our constitution bear great similarity to the resource parts of the Nevada constitution.

The extractive industries—mining and timber—did well on that constitution. They made it a good constitution. It promotes the security of promised advantages, and that it did. The extractive industries were all we had, so it maybe made good sense to take care of them.

The United States is not supposed to meddle in the state's purely domestic affairs. It was supposed to defend the republic and conduct foreign relations. The state governments could, once they achieved statehood, regulate commerce inside the state, enact their own labor and tax laws. They generally ended up benefitting the establishment.

The first thing we did (as governor) was organize

*Robert Smylie*

a Department of Commerce and Development. Characteristically, the legislature decided that they didn't have any money to spend on that sort of thing. We figured out a way to begin without an appropriation. About 1957 they began to be of the opinion that it was going to make some sense. From there on they were willing to appropriate very modest amounts of money. They would have been appalled at the appropriations that we now make for Commerce and Development. It was an altogether different state then than it is now.

There were quite a few believers then. They were in the "guest accommodation" businesses. They were pretty active and supported this sort of thing. I don't think the grocery store people really thought it made any difference. They didn't see the trickle-down effect of the tourist dollar. It was difficult to get a handle on defensible statistics. The idea of appropriating money for this purpose got locked on pretty tight and was going fairly great guns just about the time that Governor Andrus and his first administration decided that it had to be done away with. It was making things too big too fast.

We went backward, of course, and that was a mistake. If you are in business, you have to stay in business and keep the store open. We would have been better off and wouldn't have had so much catching up to do if we'd been doing advertising all that period of time.

International trade under my administration really started with the wheat business. We decided there must be some way to get rid of all that wheat up in the Palouse. We did quite a bit of traveling to Tokyo and Yokohama and Osaka in the interest of merchandising some of that wheat. This was in the 1950s and Japan still had some coming back to do after the war.

But wheat caught on, and we developed quite a market for American wheat there. I think it still exists. Earlier we would have gone through the United States government to do that, on the theory that the foreign relations of the United States are to be conducted by the United States. But trying to do a little business over-the-counter was just trying to make a buck.

The Wheat Commission was one of the first efforts in that direction. The Potato Commission was the original commodity commission, but it was primarily addressed to the domestic market. The Wheat Commission, which came in 1959, was a pioneer in the West. Other states followed us. If we could have gotten away without telling anybody that we were doing it, it would have been better. We would have done more business. When we got into competition in Tokyo, we started not doing as well.

A bunch of the wheat growers had the idea in the first place. They didn't start out by thinking about Japan. They thought about the fact that a self-funded volunteer effort would be a good thing in trying to merchandise what they grew best, which was soft wheat. They looked at world markets that consumed a lot of starch. One thinks of Japan and rice. Shortly after that, they sent a mission there to see if they could cook up something. They did some homework about what they could do that would fit in the Japanese market. They must have done pretty well because they were fairly successful.

Grain that had gone east to the Mississippi and down the river to sea now went to Portland. That was the first thing that happened after the Port of Lewiston came on-line. We started bringing wheat all the way from North Dakota down U.S. 12 to Lewiston, and sent it down the Snake. That was a fairly abrupt turnaround. However, the port is the one thing that happened in my time that hasn't made as much of a dent as I thought it would. We used to think that when we put that road over the Lolo Pass, together with the port, that there would be a dramatic turnaround. But there hasn't been. There is lots of downriver traffic, but not much upriver traffic.

One of Idaho's strengths is a magnificent work force. Always has been. Idahoans have, generally speaking, responded very vigorously to inspired leadership when they got it. But they haven't gotten it very often, in my judgment.

I think Idaho's lack of self-esteem kind of colors our whole history. The only political figure of consequence, really, that we ever produced was Senator William Borah. Historically, the political parties attempted regularly to organize his destruction. They were never for him. I suppose it's because somebody like that really couldn't come from this place. We have had a tendency to tear down our people that achieved greatly. Some of the reaction to Mr. Simplot is in that same picture. That's slowly fading, but not with any haste.

The first thing I learned about being governor was that I had to want to be governor first. To want to be governor, I had to be believe that I could be. And believing it myself, I could get other people to believe in me. Idaho has never really carried that message to the world.

I think the first attempt to advertise our virtues as a destination resort came in 1955 or 1956. We were already halfway home to the Centennial by that time. Early on, we treated Sun Valley as though it didn't exist. It was there, but it was not really a part of Idaho. We just never did brag about ourselves. It was only after World War II that we began regularly to publish a highway map. That was not any way to encourage people to regard us as a destination resort.

In my estimation, this was just a pure inferiority complex. We felt that we really couldn't do those things. Everything we tried to do cost money. We could always use that as an excuse for not doing it.

I think the problem of the next century is going to depend on how big we can really be. How many people we can really afford to have here. It is a fragile hunk of real estate. Too many people could very easily mash it into the ground. There are probably finite limits to how big we can grow.

*The Port of Lewiston*

# People

## IDAHO INDEPENDENTS

*Idahoans like to describe themselves as individualists, preferably "rugged." No Idahoan is very typical, but many have lived, and still live by choice, in challenging physical circumstances, surrounded by magnificent natural spaces in which people and their works are a relatively small component. Urban dwellers, while not in those spaces on a daily basis, nevertheless identify themselves intimately with the Idaho outdoors. They have an affinity for the presumed independence of spirit and style of western life as it is really lived on ranches, farms, and in very small towns.*

*Tim Nettleton is the sheriff of Owyhee County. Nettleton gained widespread recognition in 1988 when Claude Dallas, a man who lived an isolated lifestyle alone in the desert, murdered Idaho Fish and Game officers Bill Pogue and Conley Elms when they confronted him about poaching. As Nettleton sat in his office and then flew over part of his territory, he talked about his work.*

I took the job because I was a broke kid looking for something to do. You might say I got involved in the wrong thing, I don't know. I was raised in this country and the size of it doesn't bother me. I'm used to it. I'm completing my eighteenth year. It's about 7,600 square miles, 110 miles along the south border and 117 along the west.

Seventy percent of our population lives in the northwest corner. Our response time there is classically under ten minutes. The majority of calls there are answered under two minutes. But we get calls from the backcountry where we measure response time in days.

People have to help themselves to a certain degree. When they're waiting, they do the same thing they do in town—ring their hands and wonder where the cop is. But people pretty well know how to handle themselves and take care of themselves.

The crimes are still the same as they have always been. You take a cow that doesn't belong to you and take it home. The way they take it home is different. The invention of little gooseneck trailers for pickups has been a factor in this. Illegal slaughter is the biggest cause of direct loss of livestock.

The people who do it are usually the ones from the city. They drive down the road, shoot a cow, do a sloppy job of butchering. It's probably the same people that, for the most part, are illegal game takers.

I really can't say I dread certain kinds of calls. There are some you don't like, but when a call comes in you handle it. That's your job. The toughest case, looking at it professionally, is where two good honest people have a water or land dispute, and they let it turn from a civil fight to a criminal fight. Those I don't like because you've got honest people involved. You have to talk pretty straightforward to them to keep them from damaging each other.

How do I feel about the Claude Dallas case? It hasn't changed since the first time I got a call that Bill Pogue might be missing down there and shot. It was "Lord, why me?" It isn't finished yet. It probably never will be put completely to rest. It was just one of those things that was bigger than what we needed and could handle.

It wasn't that complicated a case criminally, but the publicity that it drew and the fever that it built up made it a big case. He was a selfish little man who murdered two game wardens. It was that simple. The case did have a good following. The thing got blown out of proportion the first day or two. Probably part of it was our fault in not getting to the press quickly enough with the proper information.

I don't look at them as close calls, but I've had a couple of weapons pointed at me. When I think back on it, it didn't bother me that much. But now I think, "How stupid I was to stay in there."

People around here talk about my driving and flying. That's probably putting me closer to a close call than anything else. I enjoy flying. We've done jobs out of that airplane that were vital. A couple of hours in the airplane can replace a couple of days.

*Courtesy of Glenn Oakley*

**Tim Nettlton**

Both times when people pointed guns at me, what went through my head was whether it was going to hurt when it hit, and who was going to tell my wife and what they were going to tell her. It's kind of silly what goes through a guy's head at that time.

The idea that people down here "wear their own law" just depends on how you look at it. We've got ranchers who are remote. Even the best flying time to them is two hours. I don't think you would classify it as taking law into their own hands, but they do know how to take care of themselves. If they didn't, they couldn't survive in that country.

It's a boon and a bane to me. Generally they do not report suspicious activity. They don't talk to me or tell me things unless they think it's real serious. There are a lot of times I could help them if they would make more of an effort to contact me. We've had cowboys almost kill themselves getting horse wrecked. They're big and tough, so they don't need the sheriff to help them get a helicopter. So they ride out in the back of a car. One man spent six weeks in the hospital. We could have got him there six hours quicker than what he got in, which was about twelve hours. That cost him about three more weeks in the hospital and several more days off work. He broke his kidneys loose when the horse fell on him. This is typical of my ranchers out there. They are self-sufficient, hard-working people.

We have drugs in Owyhee County. I would say that, as a percentage of the population, we have just as much drugs as anyplace else. It follows a population trend. The best money that was made on corn was when they hauled it out in a bottle during Prohibition days. Socially and morally, a lot of the citizens in all counties look at drugs as they did alcohol during Prohibition. I don't agree with it, but that's the way the citizen looks at it.

We've got one other problem in combating drugs here. On the one hand, we get to the schools and do a lot of good by establishing personal relationships with the kids. On the other hand, trying to do enforcement work in interdiction is difficult. Everybody is related. A lot of people know that their cousin is using drugs, and want him to stop, but they won't help me do it. They just can't cause that fight in their family. So, interdiction is quite a problem.

If you don't have a good wife behind you, you can't do this job. She has never stayed home and worried. She knows what the job is and what it amounts to. Being in farming and ranching before this, she knew the dangers. I honestly don't feel that I face physical dangers here greater than I did farming and cat skinning and ranching. It's rougher, they tell me, on the heart and nervous system. She takes it well.

One time a bad pursuit started down at Homedale. I was coming home from Boise over by Nampa. Back in the days when we had the radio, she answered the radio and telephone at home. She knew that she was plumb safe because I was too far away to get involved in the pursuit. To make a long story short, there were five cop cars down there, and mine was the sixth one. The last thing she heard on the radio was me telling the other officers to move over, I was going to take him. Then the radio went dead. Of course, after a pursuit that's what happens—nobody talks because there is nothing to talk about. She sat there and listened. Pretty quick we called for one wrecker. She knew that if I was going to take him, that his car would be wrecked. When we called for one wrecker and no ambulance, she figured nobody must be hurt and his car must be out of commission. So she went to bed. Didn't even wait to find out what happened until I got home.

Some people say I have a Matt Dillon image. That's fine for what the public thinks, but that's not the way things are, and it won't work. If the public wants to pin that image on me, I don't mind. There have been times, to be honest with you, when I've probably used that image. You've got to be ready to use your fist and your guns, but you don't need to. I hope not to ever have to.

I've never fired a weapon. Well, maybe I've had to scare a couple of people to see how far and fast they could run. As far as a good barroom brawl, I've never been involved in one.

My family, the Joyces, came in 1863. The Nettleton side of it got here in the 1870s with the railroad. The Joyces took out a homestead, which is one of the oldest ranches that continues in the family. They started in 1864 to grow produce for the mines at Silver City. They just bent with the country. I was raised on a ranch, not that particular one, though. That ranch ended up in my uncle's hands. But I worked the old Joyce ranch.

They came down and spent the summer of 1864 near a meadow. They spent the first year in a little dugout. They took the meadow to start the fruit and vegetables for the mines. And that was home for about four or five years. Then they built rock barns. An old bunk house is the only building built in one piece. Everything else was built as you go.

I wish my kids could live in Owyhee County, but I'm glad they have the moxie to go where they can make a buck. The economy of Owyhee County right now is mostly dependent on agriculture. The Delamar Silver Mine, Envirosafe, and the molding plant in Homedale are the only outside employment other than agriculture. Agriculture is terrible. There is no money in it.

*Roger Lewis is a (sort of) retired farmer who lives near Twin Falls. He comes from a pioneer Idaho family who arrived in Idaho to help build one of the first large irrigation dams and then stayed.*

**Roger Lewis**

The way we got here? Well, I had three uncles who lived in Arkansas. They heard there was a job in the Seattle area and managed to get on a freight train headed west. They got to Spokane and picked an old soggy newspaper up out of the street. It said there was a construction job down where they were building a dam on the Snake River at a place called Milner. That sounded good to them, and since they didn't have anything on the other end, they changed routes. They all got jobs at Milner doing one thing or another. They were not skilled, by any means.

The one who turned into the electrician was my uncle Art Boone. He was going past the powerhouse that they'd built at Milner, which was downstream from the coffer dam. Something had just happened and blue lights were arcing all over the place. The electrician was scared spitless,

*Robert Lewis and his bee bath*

## ROGER LEWIS' "FAILED" BEE BATH INVENTION

In the early days we didn't have to contend with Chalk Brood, but then it moved in like a plague. The leafcutter bee larvae would get infected with little black spots, spores. A few bees can infect a whole field. When the bees move out into the field and start visiting the flowers, each flower gets some spores. The next bee comes and picks up the spores and takes them with him. It was just devastating the bee boards. It just about put the alfalfa seedgrowers out of business.

So people started scrounging around for ways to do something about these Chalk Brood spores. And various people invented things. I suppose there were a dozen or more up and down the valley. I thought I might as well get into the act, and rigged up this thing here. It really didn't work, because the bees didn't cooperate.

Originally, you put the full bee boards in a sealed box about the first of July. The way the bees get out of it is through a hole. They head for the light. That's the nature of the bees.

So I hooked up a tank of sodium hydrochloride solution to a Volkswagen windshield washer and a timer. The whole thing would turn on in the morning about nine o'clock when heat normally builds up, and the bees become active. The bees would collect, and then about every fifteen minutes, the timer would come on and spray them for five minutes. The motor here would turn this elastic belt and it would bring the bees out here. When the belt turned to go back, it was supposed to dump the bees on the ground. There they would dry out and hunt a new home, and pollinate the alfalfa. Any ordinary human being who understands gravity would think, "Well, the damn bees will fall off." They didn't cooperate. They would latch on and ride around the belt and go through the process again and again. Net result: mostly dead bees. I finally decided I was licked, so I gave up on it.

But I still think it was a great idea, and I might prove on it yet. I might do away with this belt, put a plopping mechanism in here that would turn like a trip, and go bang. That would knock the bees off. But I haven't got around to it yet.

and just crawled over to the corner. My uncle came by and looked in the door. He got a stick, reached in and pulled a switch that stopped everything. So they made my uncle the head electrician. That's how things were done then.

He was naturally kind of handy with that kind of stuff. Later he was wiring houses. He didn't have any license or anything, but he wired a lot of houses around here.

My folks all lived here. My father came out shortly after my uncles came. His first job was working on the Bank and Trust building. That was about 1906. He worked in town for several years; I was born there. He always had a yen to be a farmer, but there were two things against him: he had never been a farmer and he didn't have any money. But he tried it anyway.

He got a little old farm that was thirty-nine acres out west of here and was clearing the sagebrush. There was still a lot of sagebrush in those days. It was owned by a bank when he bought it. He was clearing it, and then my mother got sick and died when I was about twelve. That put an end to everything. He had to pick up and move to town and go back to working in a grocery store. It was quite a traumatic era.

Later he remarried. About the year before I graduated in 1929 they decided to move back onto this farm, which he had been renting all this time. About rented farms: the weeds seem to do better than anything else. We moved back and had chickens and turkeys and all kinds of good stuff. We were doing pretty good, but quite a debt piled up in those years. He ended up losing it. He moved over onto another farm and helped turned it into a golf course over east of here.

Most of my life I've worked here and lived in town. I worked after school and on Saturdays during my high school years in Kinny's grocery store. The last year I worked for Hayes High Grade Hatchery. Chick Hayes, he just recently died. I was what was called a chicken picker, mostly. The chickens that didn't want to hatch real good, you'd assist them. They weren't the choice chickens, usually weak. About half of them died, I think. But anyhow, they got a few more chickens out of the hatchery.

I got enough to buy a suit that cost eighteen dollars to graduate in. That was the main goal in taking that job. Then it was scarce times. I moved back to the folks' place and we raised pigs. Dad butchered them and he would peddle them in town.

The highlight of that era was the time I walked to town and got ahold of twenty-five cents. On that I could shoot one game of pool and have one milk shake. One time I found an extra quarter in my pocket. That doesn't sound like much now, but I was out of high school and times were tough. This was about 1932.

Jobs were horribly hard to come by. That fall a friend's brother was running some threshing machines. He lived up around Milner. We went up there and worked behind those old, dirty bean machines and mucked up and did all kinds of flunky work. But it was a job. It got us by. Later on I moved out here and started working with my uncle on the farm. He wasn't rich either, but it was steady work.

I was a friend of Rolly Jacky, who lived north of the hospital. He was one of ten kids. Rolly was my age; there were others younger. We would go over there and play ball and one thing or another. There was this little redheaded gal hanging around, and I forgot how to play ball after a while. I sort of got more interested in her. Didn't have any car at the time. I just walked about two miles to see her. We were married in 1936.

We didn't have any place to live. Didn't know what we were going to do for sure. We went to Salt Lake and we hunted for a preacher. We thought we could just call one up and there he'd be. Most everybody was out playing golf Saturday afternoon. We had a few camping supplies and I had bought this old Chevy and we'd piled in and headed out. Everybody always said you could always get married in Farmington, just down the road toward Ogden a ways. Well, we missed it. We kept a-going and finally got to Ogden. We were bushed. It was eleven o'clock at night. I said, "Fern, you sit right here. I'm going to find somebody, and we'll get married." I found a justice of the peace. He said I had to bring a witness so I went out in the street and hailed a likely looking couple. We got married and drove out of town about two miles and pitched camp. It's lasted fifty-two years.

The farm problem is mostly prices. We keep talking about farm subsidies. Most farmers feel like they've been subsidizing the consumers for years. The prices for groceries are one of the lowest in the whole world. I don't know what the answer is. It takes about three cents worth of wheat to make a loaf of bread. Now you figure it out.

I tried to retire, or half retire, and somehow or another it just didn't work for me. I'm just too interested in trying to do the best for my land and my crops. So, much to my wife's disgust, I started farming full time. I hire a lot of custom work done, so it isn't like I dig every shovel of dirt myself.

I have two grandchildren. The main thing in life is to be happy and feel a sense of worth. I don't know. My oldest grandchild is a girl working in Seattle for a marketing firm. I guess she's doing pretty good, but she thinks she ought to be doing better. She's hunting for another job that'll pay her a little bit more. But she's earning more than I ever made for umpteen years. That's inflated dollars, of course. My grandson is going to school at Pacific Lutheran this year. I doubt if he will be coming back to Twin Falls.

Anything that works out for them is okay by me. You can't live your kid's lives, and you can't follow them around either. I've seen people try that. It doesn't work.

Well, I actually think that the "good old days" are right now. Anytime you look, there are a lot of good things about right now. It has always been that way, I believe.

Twin Falls now is exciting, I think. There is quite a change going on. There is more manufacturing. They are pushing tourism, which is a mixed bag, as far as I'm concerned. At times I think Idaho has enough people. But then I think that's kind of selfish. They shouldn't lock the gate after the last Californian gets here. But sometimes I think they ought to lock it before the last one gets here.

*Roy W. Bryant, Jr., is an elementary school teacher with eleven students, all of whom shared a one-room schoolhouse near Lowman, in Boise County, and who managed to survive his first year of teaching there. Lowman is a mountain town on the South Fork of the Payette River about twenty-five miles from Idaho City, the county seat, and fifteen miles in another direction to Garden Valley, the site of the nearest junior high school.*

Before I came here, I was teaching in a school in south Texas, thirty-five miles south of San Antonio in a little town called Natalia. There were twelve hundred people in that little town and almost that many stray chickens and dogs.

We came here primarily to get back to green trees, snow, and the Northwest area. South Texas didn't have a lot of nature that I wanted to look at besides horny toads in the back yard and snakes in the driveway. We came to the area more than for a one-room school house, but it was a nice thing that happened.

To tell you the truth, a one-room school house was a total surprise. Before I came, I applied to about eight school districts in the area and nailed it down to about three that I thought were possibilities. I thought this one was the least likely to call me. My wife came and looked at it, and I looked at it, and we liked it. Before we left they called us and said, "It's yours if you want it." So we took it. We went back to Texas to pack and hated every minute of waiting to get back here. We liked the pot-bellied stove. We liked the remoteness. It was being self-contained. We have a computer, a copy machine, a microfiche, a VCR, and a TV—almost everything in microcosm that you have in a big school. Only you don't have to share with anybody, you don't have to wait for one of the two TVs that the whole school has. It was nice to know that what you've got is yours. You can use it whenever you need it. That appealed to us, too.

There is a lot of flexibility here. In any other school you're going to be involved with other people. Scheduling is going to involve other classrooms and other teachers. You can't just make your own schedule. They tell you what you have to teach the kids and when. In our setting we aren't nailed down to having to do it at a specific time directed by what everybody else is doing. We can make a schedule to fit our own needs. I like that. It's kind of nice.

When they hired me, they told me they used to have a kid do the janitor work. Of course the kid graduated. I thought it would be a great job for our son, who was thirteen this last January. He'd like

*Roy W. Bryant, Jr.*

that and he could earn himself a little money. As the year went on, it kind of wore on him. His schooling began to need more attention. It's Mom and I now. Maybe one of these days, he'll take it back over.

We have to have two recesses. We found that when we let all the kids out at the same time, the big kids and the little kids couldn't get along. This way we don't have as many fights.

In teaching, we center on basic skills—trying to make sure our kids not only know how to read, but know all the skills connected with it. They can apply them to the other subject matter. We get them ready for Garden Valley when they will hit seventh grade. In most schools it is something of a shock, and kids feel like they're suddenly on their own. Our kids are kind of spoiled with a lot of individual attention.

I get ready in the morning and rush to get my son to the bus stop at the South Fork Lodge by 7:20. He rides the bus to Garden Valley. I get to the school about 7:30, turn the lights on, and hope I remembered to turn the heater on the night before. If not, it's "Frost Bite Falls." This morning I had to clean because I didn't do it last night. Then I get the writing assignments up on the board, and get everything ready for the kids. It isn't too much trouble because it's so routine. Everybody knows exactly what they're going to do every day.

Mrs. Felty, the teacher's aide, helps if anything slacks off one way or the other. If I am involved with some of the kids, she goes and fills in and keeps the kids on task. That really helps. In that regard, it's better than in some schools. We go into approximately a two-hour block of language arts: spelling, writing, English, reading, every kind of language arts skill—all in the morning while the kids are fresh.

Then we usually have health class, then math, where every kid is at their own level and works in different books. It's a matter of finding out which kids are having trouble where. You teach this little bunch something and that little bunch something and keep everybody going. The hardest thing is remembering where they're all at. Somehow we do it. I don't see how it would work without a teacher's aide.

Kids never forget a thing, which is great. They tell you if you forget the pledge or whatever. They know their routines; that takes care of itself.

This is a job where you are going to do a good job on your own or it doesn't get done. The administration apparently assumes that you're going to do a good job, or they wouldn't hire you. There are twenty-five miles of bad road between where we are and where they are. We do stay in contact by phone because of the setting.

To be honest, at the end of nine months, every teacher is getting a little tired. Summer does a great job of rejuvenating you. By next year it's wonderful again. Right now the reality of gathering wood all winter wears you down a little bit. You look forward to summer and starting over next year.

*Bob Johnson, retired editor of the* Salmon Recorder Herald, *lives all year long at Williams Lake, south of Salmon, a place where many of his neighbors can visit only on vacation from their year-round homes in California.*

I came into this area in 1939. My family bought a cabin down by Shoup on the Salmon River. I was just a senior in high school at the time. I came back in 1962 and I've been here since then.

I had been working at the *Salt Lake Tribune,* where they put me on swing shift on different desks, one desk one night, one desk the next night. It got me completely out of reporting and writing, so I came up to Salmon. I went down the river and spent two years free-lance writing, traveling the backcountry, and doing photography. I wrote about river trips, historic places. I interviewed hermits and people along the river.

I lived in San Francisco and no one ever spoke to you. I've been in Las Vegas, and the bartender won't speak to you. At the *Tribune* I worked nights and never got to get out to talk to people, really. At Salmon and Challis you can sit down next to a total stranger and he'll start talking to you. People are friendly.

The reason I live here is that I like mountains. I like Williams Lake and I like the people. I have a lot of friends who come up here and fish. There is less hurry here, a slower pace.

I think that people have in mind to retire, but they develop a work habit. So when they retire they don't know what to do with themselves. They go back to work. I have friends who have retired and can't cope

**Bob Johnson**

with it. Myself, I have enough interests that it doesn't bother me. I have about two thousand books up here at the lake and my apartment downtown. I've been doing a lot of reading and I can read for hours.

I think people have a kind of anti-government feeling in this area for historic reasons. I think the type of individual who came in and settled this country was an individual and didn't want any controls. I thought with the old generation dying out there would be a change in that attitude. But the people who came here came for the same reason, to get away from controls and big cities. Today you still have that feeling. Anytime the Forest Service or Bureau of Land Management calls a meeting, you've got a crowd that's crying, "No!"

When I worked I kept track of government. I did a lot of work on my own. Even though the community was anti-government, they criticized me for having so much about government in the paper. I said, "Well, that's the only way you're going to find out what they're doing." Not that I was pro-government, it was just for better balance.

As editor and one-man staff of a weekly you have to know all the desks, if you want any speed at all in putting out a paper. If not, you could certainly get swamped. In an average day, I went to work at eight and worked until about five-thirty. I'd go home, get some supper, and then go to a city council meeting or a planning meeting or a school board meeting or one of the dozens of meetings there are. Salmon, I found, was a town that was over-organized. I used to say that if you ran across three people on a street corner, they would elect a president and a secretary and set up meeting dates.

We used to go in after the paper was out, a bunch of us from the *Recorder Herald*, and we'd sit down and play pitch. That no longer occurs. The people we played pitch with have died off. Now they've gone to these dart games. The bar business in Salmon, which was one of the biggest businesses at one time with seven bars, is now down to one bar that has live music. So times have changed.

I don't go into the bar much anymore. I used to go simply because I found out more information in a bar than I could in the sheriff's office. I got a lot of tips. The business of gossip is rampant. I often wondered what they were saying about me when I wasn't there. Bar information gave you a start. Then you had to check it out. If somebody drowned or was in an airplane crash or somebody beat up his wife or anything, you could find it out at the bar faster than you could find it out from public officials.

I think the outdoors is an escape. A lot of people tell me how lucky they think I am. They come up here and spend a week or two at the most. Then their cabin is empty the rest of the year. People come up here to hunt and fish and get away from the big cities, the hustle and bustle. But that's where they make their money, and that's where they're stuck. Because in Salmon, unless you work for the government, the wages are low.

Lots of people come here and want the same things they have in Los Angeles. Better roads, better water system and more services. But the county commissioners are not going to give them anything. The city will patch a hole occasionally but that's about it.

*Phyllis Laird is a wool grower living in Dubois, Clark County. She took over the management of the ranch she operated with her husband, Roy E. Laird, after he died. She is a former president of the National Wool Growers Auxilliary and once took the balance of her husband's term in the Idaho Legislature.*

**Phyllis Laird**

My grandfather, J. D. Ellis, and another man owned this ranch before my husband's father Edward D. Laird and his brothers bought it in 1902. My grandfather was the original settler. My mother, Annie Laurie Ellis, came here and cooked on the horse ranch when she was thirteen. They didn't have sheep then.

I was raised in this country when I was little girl, but I went on to live in Portland. I came back one summer to visit my father, and I met my husband. I went on to college and four years later came back and married him in 1929. Life was wonderful, although I was a city girl, the greenest of green. I taught school in the same room I went to school when I was six years old. Before teaching in Dubois, I taught in a one-room school at Birch Creek, a three-room school in Medicine Lodge, the first three grades in Jacoby, and then back to Medicine Lodge, where I had all six grades.

We rented a house from my husband's brother-in-law and sister and lived there the first few months. Then we went and lived on the mountain during the summer. It rained a lot. If you want to see people with straggly hair, be on the mountain when it is raining. That fall we bought a house in the north part of town and lived there a few years. Then we moved that house together with another one.

We used to use teams on this ranch, and still did the first five years after my husband died in 1963; now we use automobiles. We used teams that first summer I was married. I was out in the Pine Butte area. We were lambing on the range in those days. In those days the little creeks in the forest didn't have bridges on them. Sometimes it was hard to get your lambs across. My husband was quite a long time getting them across. He wanted me to stop to lead. I was riding on my horse back and forth, and there were a lot of little lodgepole pine in the way. I thought I would just tie up the horse and walk back and forth. It would be a lot easier. When my husband got there, I started to cry and said, "I can't find my horse!" He said not to worry, we would find it. We made a mark and went around until we found it.

This is a bad year to ask how we are doing. We had a disastrous storm. I lost a hundred or more lambs during that storm and forty or fifty ewes. I shouldn't have been lambing then, but the herder that I had last fall decided that he wanted to. He left two or three buck lambs in with the ewes. They breed a bunch, so I started lambing in January and February, which I don't ordinarily do.

I pray a lot, I tell you. It's going to be tough this year. I also lost five cows and thirteen calves. This was the worst loss I've ever seen because of weather. You must remember, my husband was a better operator than I am. I haven't learned much in the twenty-five years that he's been dead.

He was sick about six years before he died. He didn't want me to be left with it, and we sold one band of sheep. We were in the process of turning over one of the ranges with it, but we didn't get the job done. The buyer changed his mind after my husband died.

A lot of people say that it's poor to raise sheep here because we feed hay so long. I went in on hay in November this year, which is unusually early. Usually you can keep them out until the first of February. Cows usually go in about the first of December. But this year has been a long year of hay feeding.

I didn't sell it when my husband died because it was my living. What else could I do? I always anticipated that I would sell it. At my age I would like to, except that I love the land. You know, you kind of marry yourself to something. I do anyway.

It gets expensive. A couple of times I've almost sold out, but the months of hay feeding often stop the buyers. But there are lots of advantages. I bring off good lambs. But a lot of people around here bring even heavier lambs than I do. When I was at the Wool Growers meeting in Las Vegas, I met the man who gets the lambs I sell, and he said, "Mrs. Laird, those are dandy lambs. They grow out with feeding them in the winter." I was real pleased with that.

I do own a condo at Sun Valley. I wanted a duplex, but I got a condo. I rent it out. It's my second home, so I'm not going to rent it all the time. I want to be able to go over there and swim. I don't ski, but I love to swim. I like the sociability. There are lectures and theater in Sun Valley. We don't have that here in Dubois.

One of my girls has taken an interest in the ranch, but the boys, grandsons, don't see the profit in it. Maybe they will some day. If I had my husband, I would do it all over again. We were happy. I have always known that I am not rich in money—but rich in family and friends, which counts the most.

*Dean Oliver won eight world championships in rodeo calf roping plus three titles as world champion all-around cowboy. At age eighteen he first attended the Snake River Stampede in Nampa in 1947, watched the action, and decided he would try for a career as a rodeo champion himself.*

To be in the rodeo takes a lot of hard work and years and years of practice. I started when I was twenty years old and by the time I was twenty-five was roping pretty well. It took a lot of trying, a lot of mistakes, and a lot of relearning things I had learned wrong before I became good enough to compete against anyone. There

**Dean Oliver**

*Courtesy of Dean Oliver*

was a guy around here named Jake Dyer who showed me a few of the right things. You learn as you go and pick up things from watching other guys. You have to pay your dues.

I was just working for wages when I started. I never did really dream of being a world champion, especially since I started so late. But you get to roping well, and it just happens. Having things click at the right time played a role too. I found a really good horse. I may not have won more than two world championships if I hadn't gotten Mickey when I did. With him it was easy. They say you are lucky if you have one horse in your lifetime that perfectly fits your style of roping. Mickey was mine.

You are a little bit nervous when you go out. You get a little bit keyed up. I think you perform better. If you're kind of dead, so to speak, you might rope that way. When you get on a bull you're taking your life in your hands. Some of them will hurt you. You have to really be alert. You are trying to win and you get excited when you're ready to go.

I liked it better than a nine-to-five job because you are your own boss. You do have to be prepared to give up quite a bit since you're not home that much. You have to think of yourself as an athlete and stay in training just like in professional football and baseball. This means staying away from drinking and smoking, or at least taking these things in moderation. You have to practice when you would rather be doing something else—hunt, fish, golf. You are away from your family spending most of the year in an automobile, motel rooms, and cafes. I often traveled 75,000 miles in a year.

You've got to have an understanding family who is behind you. If they're not, it puts too much pressure on you to win. Nobody can win consistently that way. Every time you go out, you can't be having those kind of worries on your mind, you just can't hack it. When you have children in school, you have to settle for having them with you only during the summer months.

A typical week or two on the rodeo circuit in the mid-sixties could get pretty hectic. For example, one of my weeks began on a Sunday, when I had just got done at Calgary. I came here to Nampa, which started on Tuesday. I was here two days, roping Tuesday and Wednesday, getting done sometime around ten o'clock at night. I got on an airplane and flew to Salinas, got there early in the morning. Up there I would rope in the afternoons, then fly back here for the nights. Then go back to Salinas, and do the same thing. After that I would go to Salt Lake, then Ogden, and then Cheyenne. All this within about ten days. I was probably sleeping three or four hours a night on a plane. You're so busy going, and the money's so good, you don't really get too tired. You're just kind of keyed up and ready to go. You drive when you can, because you've got to get your horse to some of those events.

You hate to give it up, but when you can't win, it ceases being fun. If you start losing your reflexes and the ability to make good runs, it isn't fun. Also, it's very expensive. A guy who has won a lot of money and made his living doing it doesn't want to go just to hear his name called. Anyhow, I didn't. I want to feel like I've got a chance to win some money.

Rodeo really isn't that hard unless you're in the riding events, which can be hard on your body. You take a beating from the bucking horses and bulls. In my events, which are the timed events, it's actually fun. About the only way to get hurt in calf roping is to have your horse fall or something like that.

What most cowboys consider the best rodeo is where you can win the most money. Calgary and Cheyenne come into that category. They have more ropers, so there are more entry fees. That adds more money. But my best rodeo is really right here at Nampa. I've won Nampa ten times. Sometimes I can't believe that a person can win that many times, especially in his hometown. I've won Calgary and others about three or four times.

The sport of rodeo has changed a lot since I became a professional cowboy and has changed even more since I retired. When I was going down the road and winning a lot, my best year's winnings would total around $30,000. Nowdays, a cowboy can win that much at the National Finals Rodeo alone. There are a lot of lucrative endorsements that cowboys can make today that weren't available when I was champion. Hat and jeans companies sign up cowboys; soft drink companies are entering the picture.

Another thing that has changed is the fact that the champions are much younger than they used to be thanks to junior high, high school, and college rodeo programs. The middle-aged guys were the winners when I started rodeoing. Today's world champion all-around cowboy Ty Murray was just twenty years old in 1989 when he won nearly $135,000, not counting endorsements and bonuses.

Rodeo has never really been accepted as a sport event like golf or football on the sports page. 'Probably most cowboys that win a lot are not well-known outside the circle of Western rodeo people, although there are some exceptions. In other sports some names are a household word. Everybody knows Joe Namath. A cowboy has to be an athlete just as much as those guys. When you ride a bull, you are really doing something.

# Biography

## BUILDING FROM SCRATCH

*Thousands of pioneers, thousands of builders, thousands of visions have gone into the making of the state of Idaho. Fame has come to many of Idaho's leaders, sometimes within the traditions of a family, at other times, in the memorials of towns, communities, or state history books.*

*Two traits that Idaho builders, famous or not, had in common was the vision of a brighter future and the will to work hard to achieve it. In 1990 Idaho celebrates its Centennial of Statehood. It is still such a young state that people in many fields of endeavor are starting at the beginning. That being the case, it is still possible to imagine just what it took—and still takes—to build Idaho.*

## William H. Clagett

*William H. Clagett, the chairman of Idaho's 1889 constitutional convention has been characterized as the right person in the right place at the right time. His grandson Fred Clagett continues a family tradition of leadership as mayor of King City, Oregon, and is preparing a biography of his grandfather.*

William H. Clagett was born in 1838 at the family farm, Weston, in Prince George's County, Maryland. The farm has been in the family for three hundred years. His father, Thomas Clagett, was the eldest son of the family and theoretically stood to inherit that farm.

However, Clagett's father picked up in 1850 and moved his family from Weston to Keokuk, Iowa. The family still in Maryland says Thomas thought there was too much intermarriage among the Clagetts and wanted to get his family away to meet other people in the world. Others say that Thomas thought the county was not big enough for him and his father, both very strong-willed men.

The Clagett kids attended the Keokuk schools and became acquainted with the Clemens family, who lived about ten blocks from the Clagetts. The Clemens kids were the same ages as the Clagett kids. Samuel, later known as Mark Twain, was about the same age as William's brother George.

Fort Sumter was taken on April 14, 1861. Two weeks later William, by now known as Billy, married Mary Elizabeth Hart. He immediately prepared to leave with his brother George for California, and joined a wagon train. Mary stayed in Keokuk and planned to meet him later. Billy and George traveled by wagon, while

Sam Clemens and his brother Orion left in July on a stagecoach.

The Clemens brothers got to Nevada in three weeks, while the Clagetts took over four months. They met the Clemens brothers in Carson City, and stopped there. Shortly after, George Clagett was killed by falling from his horse. In December Sam Clemens, Billy, and two others took off for the Humboldt mining region north of Carson City to try their hands at mining. Meanwhile Mary Clagett and Orion's wife prepared for their trip west.

While Billy Clagett was in Nevada he practiced mining law and also served in the territorial legislature in the house and senate. Mark Twain was the press reporter for the legislature at the time for the local newspaper, the *Enterprise*. After Nevada took up statehood in 1864, Clagett was elected as a senator from Virginia City to the Nevada legislature.

When the Nevada mines started to wind down, there were stories of gold discoveries in Montana. Clagett and his family picked up in March 1866 and took a wagon for Montana. They seem to have had contacts with Indians and the trip apparently was very peaceful. Their first child had been born in Unionville in 1863. The second child was born in the wagon just after they reached Idaho at the Snake River. They named her Idaho and she was called Ida throughout her life.

*Courtesy Idaho State Historical Society #1102*

**William H. Clagett**

In Deer Lodge, Montana, he was again a mining lawyer. About 1877 he went to Deadwood, Dakota. That was the year my father was born. They remained there until 1882, which was through the peak mining period. Billy had two landmark mining cases there that made him famous. They pertained to how to define rights when a quartz vein is discovered on the surface and is followed underground.

Billy Clagett served in Congress as a territorial delegate from Montana December 1871 to March 1873. He introduced the Yellowstone Act in the House of Representatives two weeks after he was sworn in, which created Yellowstone National Park. He also had a great deal to do with the Mining Law of 1872, which is still on the books.

In those days women were a subjugated lot, but Mary took an aggressive part in women's activities and church organizations. The Clagett family were traditionally Episcopalian, and she took part in establishing churches in new mining communities. She was also active in the business of bringing culture to the mining towns. She tried to bring gentility and diversity.

Deadwood was a traumatic experience for the family—as it was for a lot of people. The cemetery there is full of children who died in epidemics. The Dixon family lost two of their children there. The Clagetts lost only one child out of nine, which was really an achievement under the circumstances. There was a major fire in the town, a major snowstorm, and floods—all in just a few years. As best as I can read the tea leaves, they had a pretty traumatic time.

Mines went up and then down. Except for mines like the Homestake, things began to fall off. Living was just not very good. So Clagett went to Portland, where there were other Keokuk people. Since there was no business for a mining lawyer in Portland, Billy, probably on a temporary basis, went to North Idaho while Mary stayed in Portland. But they never got back together again. He headed for the Coeur d'Alene mines in 1884, and built a home for the family in Osburn, but Mary didn't want to go back to a mining community. Their children were in school in Portland, whereas there was not much for schools in the Coeur d'Alenes in those days. Later Ida did some teaching in Murray.

One of his major law cases was the Bunker Hill argument in 1885 as to what kind of rights to a strike could be claimed by grubstakers. The opposing attorney was Weldon Heyburn.

*Courtesy of Fred Clagett*

**Fred Clagett**

Clagett was popular as a speaker on legislative and mining issues. He had developed strong feelings about monetary policy. The country had a financial panic in 1893, and by 1896, Billy was a full-blown Populist.

The peak of his career was when he was elected to chair the Idaho constitutional convention. Following that, he ran twice for U.S. senator, in those days chosen by the legislature. There were heartbreaking losses for him when he didn't make it.

As best I can read it, he had hoped to see his election as a means of getting the family back together. The kids lived alternately between Portland and Osburn, and he went to Portland on occasion. I don't know that Mary ever went to Osburn. She was deeply affected by the difficulties in Deadwood.

During his later years in the Coeur d'Alenes, his mining law practice apparently dropped off. He was in poor health because of diabetes. About 1898 he moved to Spokane where Mabel and Ida lived. He died at Mabel's home in 1901.

## Clagett And The Constitutional Convention

*The issues debated at the Idaho Constitutional Convention are issues that still have life at the Centennial of Statehood—resource development, water rights and priorities, private property rights, separation of church and state, and many more. Professor Dennis Colson of the University of Idaho calls William Clagett the "Father of the Idaho Constitution."*

I'm fond of saying that Clagett is many fathers to Idaho. If you compare him to the convention that drafted the United States Constitution, you see that Clagett played roles that were played by three or four different people at the United States convention.

Like George Washington, Clagett convened and presided over Idaho's convention. George Washington's reputation was essential to the constitution. If he had not been willing to come and chair that convention, that constitution would never have flown. Clagett had that kind of prestige. He was known as the Silver Tongued Orator of the West. In southern Idaho they called him the Grey Eagle of the North. He had a tremendous reputation that he loaned to the convention.

He made the committee appointments. He had, therefore, all kinds of influence on the design of the constitution and the allocation of committee responsibilities.

*Dennis Colson*

James Madison was the scholar and theoretician who designed the Unites States Constitution, a whole new theory of government. Clagett was the innovator for the Idaho constitution. He did it as chair of the convention. He drafted and proposed several sections. Clagett wasn't nearly as extraordinary as Madison; after all, it was so much later. But for the Idaho setting he did what Madison did.

Clagett's best known innovation related to jury trials. Going back in common law, if you were entitled to a jury, that meant a jury of twelve people and a unanimous verdict. Clagett wanted to reform those two provisions so that in civil trials only three-quarters had to agree on a verdict. This represented a sort of majority control. In the criminal setting he proposed a five-sixth majority verdict. This was so you couldn't hang a jury by the power of just one vote.

He single-handedly got these provisions put into the Idaho constitution. He did it by playing different roles. First as president of the convention, he took his jury reform proposal to the judiciary committee. That made a lot of sense because in the United States Constitution the judicial article has some provisions about juries in it. But at the Idaho convention, the judiciary committee were all lawyers. They were conservative, protectors of tradition and the enemies of Clagett's reform. That committee debated for three days and fought to a draw. Six to six.

Clagett took his section over to the Declaration of Rights Committee, where James Shoup from Custer County was chairman. Shoup was not a lawyer and had no ax to grind. He said, "Sure, I'm for reform." He put it into his committee report, which meant when it came to the convention floor there was a presumption for its passage because the committee had approved it.

Clagett had gained a tremendous procedural advantage because he was president and able to move things from one place to another. So there he is—being like George Washington manipulating it, and being like James Madison because he designed the reform and brought it to the convention to be accepted.

Then Clagett was like Gouverneur Morris of Pennsylvania who was a great persuasive orator. Clagett was, too, and would give somebody else the gavel to talk. He did this every day. When it was important to be in the chair, he was in the chair. If it wasn't, he gave somebody the gavel and he went down amongst the delegates and he argued until he was blue in the face.

There is a story about a miner who said, "I walked fifty miles to hear Billy Clagett speak because his silver never depreciated." Clagett would be something like television figures today who are a major presence because they are in our living rooms on TV. Clagett was comparable to that a hundred years ago because of his speeches.

Clagett didn't need a campaign or a case to have an occasion for a speech. It was his nature. He loved it, he excelled at it. He did it whenever he got the chance. People knew him for that.

He spoke more from the floor in this convention than any other delegate. And he is the chair! Now George Washington never spoke in the debates. But Clagett wanted to be out there. He was a great orator and advocate.

The final way Clagett is very much a father of Idaho had to do with the issue of state's rights. Today we are in an era of Sage Brush Rebels and New Federalism. They are all ways of emphasizing or re-emphasizing state sovereignty. A hundred years ago, Clagett was our hero. He said that Idaho had the power of any despot on earth. He said that the U.S. Constitution placed almost no limitation on what Idaho could do. At the U.S. Constitutional Convention Luther Martin was that character, the anti-federalist, the states' rights advocate. Clagett carried the same torch.

Clagett was not only the most important person, but the most important in four different capacities. His service at the Idaho convention was the pinnacle of his career. It was good that Idaho could give him the opportunity because the state was as important to him as he was to the state. It was a magical coincidence of circumstances that brought them together.

Polygamy was very much tied up with politics, as it was in other states. The main debate over the Mormon question at the convention came up in connection with the article on suffrage, or voting. Mormons had not been able to vote in the Territory since 1885. By 1889, Mormons made up 25 percent of the people in the territory. And not one of them could vote. Their interests, of course, were obviously not represented at the convention.

The convention time and again went on record being anti-Mormon. There was no question that Mormons were going to be disfranchised in the constitution. Both the Republicans and the Democrats agreed upon it. Everybody, except a delegate named Peter J. Pefley, the mayor of Boise, thought that Mormons ought to be outright disfranchised.

The question was how much power the legislature would have in the future to keep the Mormons disfranchised, to keep their heel on them. The Republicans wanted to allow future legislatures to do anything it wanted to disfranchise anybody. Voting in Idaho is at the mercy of the legislature. The Democrats were willing to disfranchise Mormons, but didn't want to give the legislature this extraordinary power to disfranchise in the future.

The Republicans who wanted this legislative power were concerned about two things. They were concerned about an invasion of Mormons. There was a constitutional committee from the U.S. Congress traveling the west in the summer of

1889, chaired by a Senator Dorsey from Nebraska. He and his party took the floor of the Boise convention to speak. Every one of them said the most important thing they had to do to get Congress to accept Idaho as a state was to bring in an anti-Mormon constitution. They inflamed the circumstances that already existed.

As a result the Republicans were very anxious to come in with a very strong, anti-Mormon section. This committee reported that they had heard while they were in Salt Lake City that the Mormon church was organizing an emigration into Idaho. As soon as statehood was achieved, there was going to be such an emigration into Idaho that Mormons would capture the new state the moment it was born.

The other thing that they were worried about was a revelation. Polygamy was the lightning rod, only the surface of the issue. Everybody could agree that bigamy and polygamy were bad. It could easily be outlawed or criminalized by statute. But what the delegates were worried about was that the Mormon Church would have a revelation excusing its members from adhering to the doctrine of plural marriage. That would take them out from underneath the statutes and put them in the polling booths. This would facilitate emigration—the "overrunning" of the new state by Mormons.

So they thought the legislature had to have the equipment to respond to anything that the Mormons could do in the future—or else be run over almost immediately.

The section regarding legislative power over the franchise came to the convention floor. The chairman of the responsible committee was James Beatty from Alturas county. He proposed a compromise that the legislature should be authorized to disfranchise any people who were within groups that the constitution already disfranchised.

The compromise was supported by the Democrats because they said the legislature would otherwise be able to disenfranchise Masons and Catholics. Aaron Parker from Grangeville said there were good honest Catholics up in his country. He did not want the legislature to be able to disfranchise them at some time in the future. Other delegates referred to the Idaho legislature as a "biennial mob." They didn't trust this biennial mob that could go down to Boise and disfranchise people. Delegate Reid argued, "You labor men, you think you're alright, don't you? Just wait until you're part of a union that disfavors Chinese immigration. The legislature is going to want them, and they're going to disfranchise you."

So that was the compromise. It was written in a hotel room in the Overland Hotel, the prominent boarding spot in Boise at the time, where many of the delegates were staying. There was a meeting between some people from outside the convention and people inside the convention. Beatty, oddly enough, wasn't there. But other members of his committee were. It is almost certain that the outside members were the congressmen who were still in town and that they were proposing this compromise.

Later at the convention, Beatty proposes this compromise and all the Democrats rushed to it. They loved the compromise. And Clagett stands up and says, "This compromise did not come before the Republican caucus. I think our Democratic friends have hoodwinked our Republican colleague, Mr. Beatty. I think we should call a halt to this." Then he spoke a bit about why the Mormons were a threat and said, "I move we adjourn and hold a caucus." And they did. When they came back, Beatty was all over himself to withdraw his compromise. It must have been the longest and most disgusting day in Beatty's life. He kept saying, "It wasn't my language, I didn't mean it, I was doing it at the behest of other people on the committee." Beatty was a very proud man, and he had to eat words because the Republican caucus said "no" to the compromise. Clagett is the one who stood up on the convention and called a halt to this compromise nonsense. He was holding the reins. So we have a section in the constitution which authorized the legislature extraordinary power to disfranchise people.

It stayed on the books a long time. Even though that part has been removed, the Mormon question can today still be seen all over our constitution. It hasn't been purged of the anti-Mormonism.

After the convention, Clagett had a falling out with the Republican Party. He never was on the inside because he detested professional politicians. He was so pure in his principles. He had great flare and wanted to state things on great principle, be pure and loyal to them. The party at the time was run by Fred Dubois and Willis Sweet, a young lawyer from Moscow. They had a political ring that controlled all the appointments. When the National Republican Party wouldn't get behind a silver standard, to the detriment of the Coeur d'Alene mining interests, Clagett became disenchanted. He became a Populist, ran twice for the United States Senate, and was defeated both times.

Clagett mastered the convention as much as any one person could with all these maniac lawyers there. It was a very unruly convention because the lawyers and a couple of the non-lawyers were very strong willed. Clagett presided over the Republican caucus at the convention, so he had that additional opportunity for influence.

Clagett was shrewd, but also fair and quick. Our constitution has often been amended but never revised. My general impression is that other states are far more anxious to tinker with their organic law than Idahoans are. Some sections have been amended eight or nine times, but most of the document has never been tinkered with. We seem to like our document the way they drafted it. That is why it is so important to look at the circumstances and the people that drafted it.

# Ira Burton Perrine

*The story is that I. B. Perrine first saw the deserts of Idaho blooming with crops as a vision glowing in the flames of his campfire one night. What he saw eventually became the Magic Valley, so named because the application of irrigation water to the deserts above the Snake River turned them green within a matter of a few weeks—like magic. But the magic was merely the conclusion of years of physical labor, public relations, fund raising, litigation, and the creative application of energy.*

*Perrine settled at Blue Lakes, transformed it into a dairy, orchard, nut and berry farm, built roads down the canyon walls, operated ferries and stages, conceived the Twin Falls Project, raised funds for it, filed for the rights to the water of the Snake River, and platted the Twin Falls town site. He often harvested more produce than he could market. Before refrigeration was available, he had to rush his peaches and other fruits to any market he could find before they spoiled.*

*I. B. Perrine's daughter, Stella Haight, who now lives in Boise, recalled her father's life.*

*Stella Haight*

Dad's folks lived in Lebanon, Indiana. He was one of eleven in the family. His father wanted him to be a minister. But he wanted to come west. When he came, he lived with his aunt and uncle, the Griffins, in Hailey. He began to work in the mines, but then decided he was too small. Besides, he thought the miners needed milk. So he went and bought some milk cows and drove them up to Hailey. In those days, there were no pastures or bailed hay, so the poor cows didn't have anything to eat. He drove them down toward Shoshone Falls looking for a place to pasture them.

Charles Walgamott, who later wrote a book about it all, told him about a place down on the Snake River that he thought would be a good place to graze his cows. Dad drove them down there, and liked it so well, that he and his partner started to build a road out. They lived in a dugout to begin with. It took them seven years to build that grade. Some of it had to be blasted. Of course, Dad had gotten his education on blasting up in the mines in Hailey, so he knew how to use dynamite.

The Indians used to go down there to make arrowheads and spend the winter. When Dad went down, there was a white man and a squaw living at the west end of the ranch, where they were placer mining, and he bought them out.

Coming down the grade, you would see these two beautiful Blue Lakes sitting there on the bottom of the canyon. They were blue from the reflection from the sand on the bottom of the lakes, like two gems. It was warm in the winter because the rock walls kept the heat in the canyon, which was good for the fruit trees later on.

In order to keep the grades, Dad at first did not let automobiles down, just horses. Later, he built a home at the top of each grade, and put a family in there.

They charged people to go down the grade when he opened it up to automobiles. It took a man, a wagon, and a team to keep those grades operating. That's where the money went.

Dad wasn't afraid of work. So he set out not only to feed the miners, but the other settlers in the Twin Falls area. The strawberry patch was his first crop. They picked strawberries and put them in the boxes, then on a boat to cross the Snake River, then on a horse to go to Oakley and Albion. There was a saying, "You don't see I. B. without a shovel over his shoulder." He had to build ditches to irrigate the trees and plants.

He got in contact with a nursery back in Iowa. We figured there were as many as thirty thousand trees at one time down at the ranch—apples, peaches, pears and plums. He even had some nut trees—black walnuts and English walnuts and Japanese walnuts, and almonds. He had a Chinese gardener called Kitty, who did all the gardening. Even peanuts, cotton and tobacco were growing down there.

*Courtesy Idaho State Historical Society #1861*

**Ira Burton Perrine**

When you have trees you have to have bees to pollinate the blossoms. He started an apiary. He built a home, now called Brook Lodge, for the bee man. Some lady from New York was down there one time, a tourist. She looked up at Dad and said, "Oh, I see you keep a bee." But he had thousands of bees!

When Twin Falls came along, that was a market for the fruit. He would tell people around Jerome to come down and load up. He didn't charge them anything. They came down and picked fruit, took wagonloads of fruit off of the ranch.

Dad had orchards of different kinds of apples. When the Delicious apple was first started, it took too long for an apple tree to grow. So my father got some Delicious buds and grafted them on to other kinds of apple trees. He had Delicious apples in half the time. He had both Red and Yellow Delicious.

He built a prune dryer and dried prunes. He didn't know what to do with the second-class apples, so he built a cider mill and made cider. Well if you keep cider too long, it turns into vinegar. So we had about a dozen fifty-gallon barrels!

He took prizes at the worlds fairs, even in Paris. One medal I have is from Paris in 1900, and others are from other fairs. Dad kept up with the new fruits through Luther Burbank, who he met on a train trip. He sent to California for all the smaller fruit plants. There were raspberries, grapes, blackberries, loganberries, boysenberries, gooseberries, currants. Mother had her own little garden up along the ditch. She had rhubarb, asparagus and gooseberries. They planted white mulberries to keep birds out of the cherry trees and to keep droppings from staining the wash on the clothes lines.

He built a ditch to take water out of Blue Lakes to make an artificial lake. Dad decided to fill it up with water, and put some fish in there—catfish and perch and sunfish. I don't know where he got them; he must have sent away somewhere.

Down at the end of the ranch is Auger Falls. The Snake River runs on the south side of the canyon and then turns to the north side. It goes through a very small channel and kind of augers through it, so they called it Auger Falls. The sturgeon used to come up there, but they couldn't get over Auger Falls. Dad would drive his wagon and horses to the southside to the river, take clothesline, wild eels for bait, and big hooks. Some of those fish were so big, it took a team of horses to pull them out of the river and put them on the wagon to take them to the market in Shoshone.

When the Twin Falls Project went under construction, he had to have a ferryboat. Then later, a bridge was needed. He asked mother, "Which will we have, a new home or a bridge?" It was a big conflict between them, because she wanted a house. But he built the bridge in 1911.

He opened up and ran a stagecoach route from Shoshone to Shoshone Falls. He worked for Union Pacific, and would meet the tourists in Shoshone at the train, where he had a livery stable, and drive them down to Shoshone Falls and the ranch. Mother would put on a big meal for them. Averell Harriman was down there one time for a visit when he was about nine years old, and Thomas Edison, who sent him one of his first record players in 1900.

Dad and William Jennings Bryan became real good friends. W. J. Bryan and his wife Mary and daughter Ruth came down and would visit. They stayed a whole week at the ranch one time in 1906. He wrote a book on China while he was down there. They were good friends.

Mother was the daughter of Amanda Bartholomew and Don McKay, who had a hotel in Shoshone. She started giving her apple blossom parties. She would invite the ladies of Twin Falls and other towns down to lunch in the springtime. At the first one, as the women crossed on the ferry, the wind came up. Here were all these high-faluting ladies with their big hats and bunches of flowers. Everything went upstream, hats and flowers and all!

I imagine Dad's greatest achievement, and the one he was most proud of, was the Twin Falls Southside and Northside Irrigation Project. He got water up on that land and made it bloom like a rose. Twin Falls, Burley and Buhl, all those little towns up there, Jerome.

Dad always loved the ranch, although he didn't spend too much time down there, but he always came back to it. Mother really ran the ranch and took care of it. She had a good bookkeeper who took care of hiring the men, the workers and paying them wages.

Dad was acquainted with Stanley B. Milner from Salt Lake, who did placer mining down at the ranch. Dad got him interested in irrigation. They decided to build Milner dam to back the water up. Dad didn't only want to back up that reservoir but he wanted to go clear up to the beginning of the Snake River. They organized a group of men in an investment company and got Paul Bickle, an engineer, to survey the canals and the towns.

He got acquainted with H. L. Hollister in Chicago. They were good friends all their lives. Hollister and Milner believed in his ideas. Investors and bankers like Walter Filer, Peter L. Kimberly, and Frank Buhl from Pennsylvania, put up money for these projects. They built hotels, too. The Northside Inn in Jerome was one.

Dad did not own the Perrine Hotel, but the cement that went into the blocks of the Perrine Hotel was hauled over through Blue Lakes Ranch from Shoshone.

Dad was a thinker. He would think out these projects. If an idea would not work, he just changed his ideas. If one idea didn't work, he would go and work on another one. The last one that he didn't get to finish was one down on the Bruneau. He wanted to carry water out there and open up the Bruneau. But he didn't live to see this done.

My two brothers weren't interested in fruit. My oldest brother Burton liked fish. He opened up a fish hatchery down there. They sold the land around the artificial lake to the Twin Falls Blue Lakes Country Club, which has a clubhouse and golf course. Burton's fish place was bought out by the Blue Lakes Fish Company, now owned by the state.

Dad was always on the lookout for something different, something that would help people. Is there such a word as fortitude? When he got an idea, he followed through and saw that it worked. One way or the other.

## William Borah

*At Statuary Hall at the United States Capitol stands the image of Senator William E. Borah to represent the state of Idaho. His career as a senator and statesman from 1907 to his death in 1940 exemplifies the tradition of political independence still admired in Idaho. The dictates of his conscience always preempted party platforms and labels, and he never followed the party line just because it was there.*

*As a Republican, he was not anti-labor, he opposed corporate monopoly, he supported civil liberties during World War I when that was not a popular thing to do, he championed the diplomatic recognition of the Soviet Union in the 1920s when that too was not popular, he tried to get aid to farmers suffering from the decline in*

*commodity prices in the 1920s, and he opposed the reelection of Herbert Hoover to the presidency in 1932 because Hoover opposed direct relief to the needy. Borah was a leading isolationist opposed United States' involvement in European wars throughout the 1930s. His many critics called him a "spearless leader," accusing him of doing nothing, spending his energies on negative critiques of the initiatives taken by others. Nevertheless, by the time Jess Hawley of Boise met*

**William E. Borah**

*Courtesy Idaho State Historical Society #2252*

*the Senator, Borah's reputation as a great orator and one of the most influential men
in the United States had long been secure.*

Senator Borah was a great friend of my grandfather and my father. My father
was his personal attorney for about twenty years in the latter part of his life, and he
was quite close to the Senator.

I met Senator Borah when I was a young boy. When I went to law school at
Georgetown University in Washington, D.C., I met the Senator on several occasions.
The most vivid recollection is from 1939 when I was invited to his apartment on
Connecticut Avenue for Thanksgiving Dinner. A number of Idaho people were
present, including some people from his office and Joe Burge from Hagerman. We
had dinner in his lovely apartment with Mary
Borah. I recall thinking that I was in an
aviary. There were half a dozen or more
canaries that just flew through the room. It
was quite unusual.

*Jess Hawley*

The Senator discoursed at length about
the Japanese. He didn't seem to be concerned
about the expansion plans of the Japanese in
the Far East. Instead he thought our relations
with Japan were not friendly enough. He
thought the Japanese were dying to be friends
of ours, and that the United States should
cultivate a more friendly attitude to the
Japanese. The Senator died in January of
1940. The following year the Japanese
displayed their friendship to us at Pearl
Harbor.

Borah was rather an austere person. Of
course, I was in awe of him; he had that
enormous national stature. He was very
friendly, however, and went out of his way to
ask me to dinner. He was a perfect gentleman, and his wife was a lovely person.

He spoke in a conversational tone. Although he was the greatest orator of his
time, he spoke to us in a soft, confidential, conversational tone. He didn't orate
privately. He pronounced his consonants and he didn't sluff words like lots of
westerners do. He cultivated a western appearance and wore a broad-brimmed hat.
He had a heavy head of hair, which he wore long, down to his collar. He spent lots
of time outdoors, but I never saw him without his bow tie.

When he did orate, he was extremely articulate. He had a marvelous baritone
voice, and a commanding appearance. He looked and spoke like a senator. I was
certainly impressed as a young man by his performance on the floor of the Senate on
the one occasion I had to observe him. He did extensive research before he gave a
speech. My father said he wrote out his speeches in longhand and memorized them.
He began as a trial lawyer on the frontier. That gave him the training to think and
speak clearly on his feet.

When I was in Washington, President Roosevelt importuned him any number
of times to go along with New Deal legislation. Borah did go along with some of it,
but when he was opposed to a piece of legislation, generally on constitutional

grounds, he was stubborn. When he argued against Roosevelt's constitutional amendment to add justices to the Supreme Court, he gave a three-hour argument which beautifully marshalled the law and the facts. He spoke without a note for all of that period of time and held the attention of most of the senators.

I don't think that "spearless leader" was a fair assessment of Borah. His reputation was that he had not espoused any major piece of legislation. He was a powerful orator, and had great influence and respect in the United States Senate. He certainly spiked a lot of major legislation. He fought the Versailles Treaty, believing it had sown the seeds of war. He was certainly prophetic in that. He fought President Wilson's appeal to have the United States join the League of Nations. He fought any number of Franklin Roosevelt's New Deal legislative proposals and was very successful killing some of it. I think he was happy with his role in the Senate and doubt that he had any second thoughts about not sponsoring any major pieces of legislation.

For over a decade he was chairman of the Senate Foreign Relations Committee. He had enormous responsibility in that position although he never left the territorial limits of the country. That was a little strange because it was not unusual at the time for senators and congressmen to travel to foreign countries.

He pulled it off because he was intelligent, had been in the Senate for a long time, studied a lot, and was always intensely prepared. I think he made up for travel by reading and studying. He had contacts with diplomats all around the world. He did what he did by sheer force of personality and intelligence.

When he believed he was right, he voted accordingly, irrespective of political or other consequences. That was the trait I most admire, more than the oratory and intellectual ability, which were obvious. He did not try to have different images of himself for the international, national, or Idaho audiences. I don't think he would change just to suit someone. I suppose he had an inner fire. His great ambition had to come from within.

When I was in Washington, there were two things Idaho was known for. One was the Idaho potato, and the other was Senator Borah.

# Vardis Fisher

*Vardis Fisher wrote essays, newspaper columns, poetry, and thirty-six novels and major works. He wrote about himself, about Idaho, about the history of humanity and the human spirit. "It is only through the study of history and its implications that humans may fully understand themselves and reform themselves if they wish," he said once in an interview.*

*Born in Annis, Idaho, in 1895, he studied or taught at the Universities of Utah, Chicago, and New York before returning to manage and write most of the celebrated Idaho Guide, a project sponsored by the federal government to employ authors during the Depression. After that, he remained in Idaho, and lived at Hagerman.*

*Fisher died in 1968, and is remembered by many people who agree that his accomplishments came about because of the reach of his vision and the labor of its execution.*

*He talked about his background in Antelope Valley, Idaho, in a videotaped interview with John Milton in 1967, who published the full interview in* Three West: Conversations with Vardis Fisher, Max Evans, and Michael Straight*.

My immediate line apparently started moving west in the early nineteenth century, on both sides. Those closest to me in background came across the plains with Brigham Young in the great Mormon exodus. All my people on both sides were then, and as far as I know today, are Mormons.

I was born in eastern Idaho, on a real frontier. It was the habit with Brigham Young to send settlers out in all directions from the Salt Lake Valley. My father and one of his brothers were two of a small colony sent to the Upper Snake River Valley. I was born in a one-room cottonwood log shack with a dirt floor and a dirt roof.

My father was rather introverted, I think probably a schizoid type, who felt that he was crowded if he had a neighbor within ten miles. When I was six years old, he had forty acres in an area where his father had homesteaded. He loaded us all into a wagon. He had two old horses, a bake oven, and a few things like that, and headed up the South Fork of the Snake River. He didn't stop until he was about thirty-six miles from his father's place. There was no neighbor, except the one across the river, within ten miles. That was just the kind of place he wanted. There were no schools, and I never got to go to school until I was twelve years old. My mother, who I think

**Vardis Fisher**

Courtesy Idaho Historical Society #77-90.1

\* Published at Vermillion, South Dakota, by the Dakota Press

C O N V E R S A T I O N S

didn't go beyond the fourth grade taught us, the three children, as well as she could up to the time when she felt she could teach us no longer and had to get us to school. It was real Western pioneer life.

I both liked and detested it. I suppose I was born a rather sensitive child. There were so many things there to terrify me and my brother and my sister also, but my sister less, being more like my father. There were also many beautiful things there, the wealth of wildflowers, the wild fruits, the birds. People who read the book *Silent Spring* don't realize how many birds there used to be in those years. All that sort of thing did go deeply into me as a child.

I took my B.A. in Salt Lake City. I would probably not have gone to graduate school, and I probably would not be sitting here to tell you, if I had not had a great teacher in Utah. I had assumed that I would get a teaching certificate to qualify for high school teaching, which I did get and which I have. After I got my first degree I think I would have gone out teaching in high school, because I was married then and had a wife and child, if this professor had not said, "You're not going to do anything of the kind. You're going back to Chicago this summer to take the summer course back there. After you come back I'll give you a job in my department." Well, I had never foreseen that anything like that would happen to me. There was no saying "No" to him. I didn't have any money, I just had to go back to Chicago and do all the work I could that summer on my master's. I came back and taught the next year in his department. Later he said, "You're going back down and get your doctorate." Well, I didn't have anything to say about it and so, one way or another, I went back to Chicago and got through.

*Fisher left Utah and taught at New York University in New York.*

I came west. I left New York University because I felt I had to make a choice between teaching and writing books. The chairman of the department allowed me to teach all my courses in the afternoon so that I had my mornings completely free for writing. I decided after a while that that was not fair to the students, because I would

## SELECTED WORKS OF VARDIS FISHER

Vridar Hunter (Autobiographical) Tetrology
  *In Tragic Life*
  *Passions Spin the Plot*
  *We Are Betrayed*
  *No Villain Need Be*
Federal Writers Project
  *Idaho: A Guide in Word and Picture*
  *Idaho Encyclopedia*
  *Idaho Lore*
Testament of Man Series
  *Darkness and the Deep*

*The Golden Rooms*
*Intimations of Eve*
*Adam and the Serpent*
*The Divine Passion*
*The Valley of Vision*
*The Island of the Innocent*
*Jesus Came Again: A Parable*
*Peace Like a River*
*My Holy Satan: A Novel of Christian Twilight*
*Orphans in Gethsemane*

pretty well work myself out in three or four hours of writing before noon. I didn't feel that I was up to my job in the afternoon.

I also felt that this daily load of teaching would erode finally, the interest in creative work, and that it was a diminishing return there. I had to make up my mind.

About that time the Work Progress Administration started the Federal Writers Project [to publish a guide for each state]. Out of the blue I had an offer to be the Idaho director, which I was for four years. That took care of 1935 to 1939.

My four years there were very busy years for me, as a matter of fact. I was still quite an innocent person when I took that job. I thought this was to be a serious spending of the taxpayer's money, so I took my job seriously. I was determined to get the *Idaho Guide* out first. Of course I did. It became something of a national sensation. The Washington office tried to stop the *Idaho Guide*, they didn't want it published first because it would be an embarrassment to all the big states that had so much more money in their projects, and such huge staffs.

They sent a man out from Washington, and they called me long distance several times, saying, "You must not go ahead." I had this huge advantage in that J. H. Gibson from the Caxton Printers in Caldwell, Idaho, said, "We'll publish this book." Wahington did send a man, a distinguished novelist, to come out to stop us from publishing that book. We took him to Gibson's home and got him drunk. I put him on the train, sent him back to Washington, and we went ahead and published the Guide.

I guess I'd had six novels published when I took that position. Then I worked about sixteen hours a day. I gave the board what I was paid for on that project. I did more than my eight or nine hours a day. I did all the research for *Children of God*. That's about all I got done in those four years on my own writing.

*One of Vardis Fisher's colleagues as a newspaper columnist was John Corlett of Boise, retired editorial editor of* The Idaho Statesman.

Vardis was writing his *Idaho Guide* in the late 1930s, and I began working for the *Capitol News* in 1935. I must have met him somewhere along in that time. When he started writing a column for the *Statesman* in 1941, I remember meeting him for real.

Vardis was a man who was hard to get used to. He had eyes that bore into you and a nose that was kind of shoveled off a little bit. He could kind of throw you back, but to be truthful he was fine with most everybody, there is no question about that. He had a lot of friends, just common ordinary friends.

Vardis Fisher was an intellectual, a scholar. He had words coming out of his ears, a tremendous fellow. But basically it would all depend on how he felt. He might take a look at someone and size him up as a phony of some kind. Then he would really take after him. I always thought that Vardis liked to psychoanalyze people. He would look you over and decide what made you tick. I think he enjoyed it.

I think his unhappy childhood affected him all of his life, as far as I can figure out. I never did talk to him about it. When you read about it in his autobiography, you understand it from A to Z. It was a hardship. There were no real expressions of love from his parents, especially his mother. Yet, undoubtedly, she did love him. But this did not come his way. As I understand it, that's where he got the word "orphans." Orphans were those people who lived in some hardship but did not get the compassion and love that most people get. He wrote about orphans in portions of his work.

His home at Hagerman was a cozy place. When he told me he had built it all himself, I was just flabbergastered. I remember mostly his working place, which was at a lower level of the house, but had windows that looked out on his tree-filled yard. It was tremendous; I'd never seen anything like it. This was the first time I'd ever seen a novelist at work. I don't know what book he was working on at that time, but when I walked in he showed it to me. He sat in his chair by his typewriter. The walls and the ceiling were cluttered with 3 x 5 cards, thumbtacked all over. He was doing his research. When he ran into something, he typed it out on the cards. He knew where every one of those cards was. Whenever he started writing, and needed something, he just picked out the card. And away he went. I don't know how many typewriters he must have gone through. He wrote fast and grammatically perfect, seldom, if ever, making a mistake.

*John Corlett*

His big idea was his *Testament of Man* series on the history of mankind. It was one that had never been explored. He was looking at history, spirituality, Christianity, and other religions that had taken men off course. He thought mankind had been swayed by Christianity and by all kinds of religion. He said religions were made up of myths, legends, symbols, parables, and were not historically founded. They were founded by prophets. He would never back away from those ideas even though people kept after him all the time. He figured that we missed the boat somewhere down the line by getting into all of this stuff.

At the same time I think that he had a lot of spirituality in him, and some Christianity in him. At an early age he read the *Bible* from one end to the other. He said he read it several times when he was growing up out on that little old farm at Burns Creek. The Old Testament and the New Testament are a covenant with God. Then he named his series the *"Testament" of Man*, and I'm not sure whether he wanted us to think of it as a covenant with his type of God or not.

I think it worried him that his books didn't sell well. I said to him one time, "Why in the world don't you write a popular novel? Get into some romance or gothic or something, and make some money?" He just settled back and said he simply would not compromise. He wouldn't prostitute his art and the way he was writing. And he never did.

His books are not popular. Scholars one of these days will go through his work and find out exactly what he did. For the *Testament of Man* series, he read about two thousand books, everything he could find. Imagine reading two thousand books just to write a series of books over a period of twenty years!

As a columnist, he dealt with all kinds of subjects. He got into trouble with the *Statesman*. I recall talking to Margaret Cobb Ailshie, the publisher, who was upset because he brought in religious matters in some of his columns. He was working on his *Testament of Man* series at the time and was immersed in the research for it. He didn't question Christianity, but he got into religion and she just didn't like it.

One would never, never edit any of his columns, never touch one single word. That was one thing he did not understand. At the *Statesman* when they first tried to edit his column for length to fit the page, he just had a fit. So they sometimes had to run it onto another page. He would tear your head off for editing, he didn't want anything changed.

He wrote essays, poems, letters—it's amazing what he wrote—historical novels. Of course, he also wrote bad notes out of outrage. *Time* magazine was continually depreciating his books. I thought it was terrible what they did. When he wrote a book called *Pemmican*, *Time* called me up (I was a stringer for *Time* then) needing a photograph of Vardis right away. Vardis didn't have a telephone, so I hired Bill Bach as a photographer and we got in my car and drove to Hagerman. We got there a little after eight o'clock at night and knocked and knocked on the door. Finally he came, he had been asleep. I told Vardis what *Time* wanted. He growled. I said, "Vardis, they just want the picture of you for a review of your book." He finally consented, and Bill sat him down to take a series of photographs which I sent in. When the review came out, it was terrible. The book was about Hudson's Bay trappers up in the Canadian country. I didn't think it was so bad myself, but *Time* just took him down. Vardis wrote me a scathing letter, taking me apart. I replied to him immediately to tell him it wasn't me, that I was just the messenger. I thought for a while that he was disappointed in me, but we finally got back a little bit better. I only saw him once in a great while after that.

I never did read any of his original *Tetrology*, four fictional works detailing his autobiography. I recall scanning *In Tragic Life*, the first of the four, in the Idaho State Library, but I didn't cotton to it. But I did read it all in his expanded autobiography contained in the last volume of *Testament of Man*, *Orphans of Gethsemane*, which contains nearly one thousand pages. I was among the more than two hundred persons who subscribed to the last four books of the series in order to assure their publication.

His autobiography is worthwhile to read. It describes an era, a man who had a lot of tragedy in his life, how he worked, and what he did. I'm impressed with the research—the two thousand books. All of his historical novels demanded similar research in a smaller amount. But he wrote fast, and kept writing all the time. It was part of him. I wished I could do that.

# Gracie Pfost

The top vote-getter in Canyon County politics during the 1940s was a Democrat, a woman, the county treasurer: Gracie Pfost. Because of her power to attact voters in a strong Republican county, her party was eager to have her run for Congress for the First District. In her first run for it in 1950 she lost by 783 votes. In 1952 she won by 581 votes, the year Eishenhower carried Idaho by a margin greater than 25,000 votes. In the next election, she won by 9000 votes, and her margins kept getting bigger and bigger after that.

Born in a log cabin in Arkansas in 1906, she came to Idaho as a child when her family settled in the farm country around Meridian. She left high school before she graduated, met and married Jack Pfost at seventeen, returned to Link's Business School at his encouragement, and eventually obtained a job in the Canyon County auditor-recorder's office in 1929 at age twenty-three. Her political ideals were probably formed during the Great Depression, as she made out checks for the dependent and the unfortunate. She became indignant over the social and economic injustices that the Depression exposed. In touch with real people with real problems in the real circumstances of their lives, she never forgot it.

She campaigned with unforgettable style, her red hair suited to her high-energy enthusiasm for people. Her campaign slogans included, "True prosperity is not measured by spending, but by earning," and "The power to tax is the essence of the very power to enslave." Her issues included the support of labor, aid to education, improvements in social security and farm subsidy laws.

Like other Idaho congressional representatives who knew their Idaho politics, she got herself appointed to the Committee on the Interior and Insular Affairs, where she could promote irrigation projects, mining, and public lands legislation of particular importance to Idaho. She fought for the construction of the "high dam" in Hells Canyon, a federal power project that was part of a program for basin-wide development of the Columbia River and its tributaries.

The only woman Idaho ever sent to Congress, Pfost was proud to be a woman, worked hard for "increased recognition of the power of the woman's vote" within the Democratic Party, and never ran an uncontested election. She worked hard, paid attention to detail, accomplished her legislative goals, and managed public relations brilliantly. She died in 1965 at age fifty-nine of Hodgkin's disease. One of her colleagues in the House of Representatives was Ralph Harding of Pocatello, who served from 1961 to 1965.

**Ralph Harding**

She was really almost a woman of the frontier. She grew up in Nampa. She was in the Canyon County courthouse at a very young age. I think she was a little girl sitting on a fence when Jack Pfost rode a horse down the lane and saw her. She was very young when they were married, and there was great love between them.

I would describe Gracie Pfost as a Calamity Jane type who was on the frontier and saw these marvelous changes come along. She lived in Idaho when we first got automobiles and when it was really a pioneer state. She was always excited and enthused about life. Always trying to help people.

I got to meet Gracie through Democratic politics. She was the Congress lady from North Idaho while I was elected from the Second District. We became friends during the campaign and then worked together for four years in the United States Congress.

In 1960, the Republicans put up a candidate to run against her named Erwin Schweibert, the mayor of Caldwell. He was a good man, a big man, and popular. He had the business community's support. He structured his whole campaign on the basis that Congress is a place for a man, that you need a strong energetic man back there. During the Lumber Jack Days up in North Idaho, log rolling was one of the sports that the lumber jacks would engage in. Gracie challenged Erwin to a log rolling match, and she dumped him in the water in a hurry. That finished his campaign. Gracie proved that she was a better man than he was. She wasn't afraid of anything.

When I ran in 1960, I didn't have any chance to win. I was too young. The Republicans called me the brash young bookkeeper from Blackfoot. I won in a real upset. Well, Gracie Pfost became my mentor. She taught me about Congress, introduced me to all of the powerful committee chairmen, told me how to do things and what things not to do. She really was my teacher for my first year in Washington. After she taught me, we worked closely together. She ran for the Senate in 1962. Later it was diagnosed that she had Hodgkin's disease. I used to go see her in the hospital in Baltimore at least every week. I helped organize and spoke at her funeral service in Washington. I dearly loved her. She was a very special person.

She was a very, very effective congresswoman. Everyone was Gracie's friend. People would vote for legislation merely because Gracie Pfost sponsored it. This was in the early 1960s when there weren't a lot of women in Congress.

Our offices were ten doors apart in the old Cannon House office building. We saw each other every day, and worked very closely on

*Gracie Pfost*

Idaho projects along with Senator Church and Senator Dworshak.

I remember some of the luncheons that we used to have. I can see her eyes flashing and see her talking. Senator Church and Senator Dworshak and Gracie and myself discussed matters pertaining to Idaho. Henry Dworshak, a Republican from Burley, was a great man, a former newspaper man who probably looked more like a senator than anyone else in the U.S. Senate. He had a great sense of humor, and he used to tease Gracie. But he could never get ahead of her. She would come right back and have a retort for everything. There was always this good-natured teasing going on. Senator Church and I used to sit back and wink at each other and watch them go at it. They had a lot of fun. We had those Idaho Congressional lunches every Tuesday without fail. We wouldn't bring guests. One Tuesday we would have them in the House of Representatives, and the next Tuesday in the United States Senate. Gracie and Henry, they had a great respect for each other. We had a great time together.

It was much tougher being a woman in Congress than it is today. Everything was done on the basis of seniority. Most of the women in the House at the time had followed their husbands. Their husbands had served in Congress and already had name recognition. They weren't taken as seriously as Gracie was because she had gone out and won her election on her own. It was her own ability, her own desire, and her own determination that got Gracie elected.

People used to call her "Hell's Belle." The government wanted to build a huge dam on the Snake River down in Hells Canyon as part of the Bonneville Power System. Idaho Power and the private power companies opposed it. Gracie was in there fighting for the "High Hells Canyon Dam" to the very end. She was a champion of what she thought was best for the people. She went all over Washington making speeches for the Hells Canyon project, so she won the nickname of "Hell's Belle."

Some of the congressmen who knew I had worked for a potato company in Blackfoot would see us coming, and they would jokingly say, "Well, here comes 'Hell's Belle' and the 'Idaho potato.'" We were quite a pair.

We were working together for a project called the Burns Creek Dam in the early 1960s. It was very much opposed by the power companies. The Utah Power and Light Company was the main opponent. Yet it was overwhelmingly supported by all of the irrigators and the city of Idaho Falls. This dam was being considered in the Interior Committee. The power companies had enlisted a big strong man from the coal-mining regions of Pennsylvania, by the name of John Saylor to be their champion. He was a good orator, attractive, and would get up and make these orations against the Burns Creek Dam. Then little Gracie would come along and just cut him down to size in a hurry. She would say, "Look, we know you're speaking for the Utah Power and Light Company, John. I don't know why they had to go clear back to Pennsylvania to find someone. They wouldn't be able to get someone from Idaho to come back here to oppose a project that was good for all of the people of Pennsylvania." After a few minutes of listening to Gracie, John Saylor would silently walk out of the room. I saw that happen in several hearings. She wasn't afraid to go up against someone who was bigger in stature, better educated, or better financed. Gracie was a champion of whatever she believed in, whether it was Burns Creek, Hells Canyon, loggers, miners, farmers, teachers or children. She was truly a champion of the common people.

We spent many hours talking about Idaho projects and what we could do in the best interest of the state. She wasn't motivated by money or power. She was a very dedicated good Christian lady. She was someone who wanted to make the world a little better place to live.

It happens quite often that people will vote for an efficient lady in their county and send them to the courthouse for some local county office. But it isn't often that they will send them to Congress. She is the only lady to ever serve in Congress from Idaho. She was a champion of women's rights and equal pay for women. In every way she felt that girls should have the same educational opportunities and be rewarded equally with boys. I felt exactly the same way, but my feelings were strengthened in favor of equal pay and equal rights for women by my many conversations with Gracie.

## Frank Church

*Frank Church was born in 1924 in Boise, and aspired early on to influence the foreign policy of the United States. He succeeded. First elected to the United States Senate in 1956, he was elected three more times. Church served in the Senate until 1980, when he was defeated. He had become chairman of the Senate Foreign Relations Committee, had run for president of the United States in 1976, and through his investigations of intelligence agencies and multinational corporations, had influenced deeply the policy conduct of his country.*

*Like Gracie Pfost, he too desired membership on his house's Committee on the Interior and Insular Affairs. As a member of this committee, and various subcommittees, Church advocated public works and public lands legislation important to his constituents. In 1964 he co-authored, sponsored, championed, and led the floor fight for the Wilderness Act; in 1968 he authored and championed the Wild and Scenic Rivers Act. Both of these are cornerstones of wild lands preservation. In his honor the Frank Church-River of No Return Wilderness in Idaho bears his name.*

*Church died in 1984 of cancer at age fifty-nine. One of his closest personal and political associates throughout his life was Boise attorney Carl Burke, who managed Church's campaign for student body president at Boise High School and all the ones that followed.*

At the time we thought his first race was a tough one. He ran against a young man named Bob Barber, the captain of the football team. Usually the captain of the football team won in those days. Fortunately for Frank, and probably unfortunately for Bob, the team didn't have that good a record. So Frank squeaked through and became president. We had a lot of fun together in high school.

He was a young officer in the United States Army, after going through Fort Benning. Later he was assigned to military intelligence and served under General McClure in the Chinese theater. He saw that it was a big world, with a lot of different cultures, a lot of different languages, different kinds of thinking. He recognized that we were not an island unto ourselves.

When the Japanese surrendered, the question was whether all the Japanese troops in China would obey the order of the emperor and actually surrender. There was a huge army at Nanking which had remained undefeated. The Americans were not certain how the Japanese would respond. So they decided to send First Lieutenant Frank Church in to see if he could make it. He and the pilot flew in an old DC-3. The pilot landed the airplane at the Nanking airport. There on the runway stood regiments of Japanese soldiers at attention. He got off the plane, looking about fifteen years old. The Japanese general handed him his sword. So Frank Church took the surrender of the Japanese army in Nanking.

When he was a law student at Stanford, the doctors told him he had cancer and had only a few months to live. It looked like the end of things. He had married by then, and they had their son Forrest. He was treated at the Stanford University Medical Center and bombarded with x-rays. He was very ill, but kept hanging on. One day they concluded they had killed the cancer. But he had made his plans for good-byes. It obviously built character. He came out of it a stronger person with a lot of will.

Frank thought that if you're going to get into politics, you should dive in and not go up the ladder step by step. There were some opportunities in 1956 in that there didn't seem to be any Democratic candidate that had a clear chance to beat the incumbent, Senator Herman Welker. Frank agonized, but he decided to do it.

It was a very feeble beginning. We didn't have any organization of any kind. We cranked out our announcement on old machines. It was a long night. We had

*Frank Church and Carl Burke*

about a thousand copies to mail. We put all the stamps on, then walked down to the old Post Office in Boise. Frank looked at me and said, "Well, Carl, we've crossed the Rubicon." And away we went.

We were a bunch of amateurs, very naive. They were the days of innocence. We had no paid staff, a very modest budget. I don't think we raised more than fifty or sixty thousand dollars. We produced our own homemade television commercials. One day he called me from Utah. He had been campaigning all day in a Utah county, thinking he was in Idaho. People never did tell him; he just kept right on campaigning.

The Democratic convention in 1960 was in Los Angeles. That was his first opportunity to speak to a nationwide audience. Frank's speech talked about the type of person the party should have: young, vigorous, with a new vision of the future. There was only one such person running—Jack Kennedy.

Our delegation from Idaho was deeply divided right down the middle between Johnson and Kennedy. Frank strongly supported Jack Kennedy from the beginning, and that was his opportunity to say so without mentioning his name specifically.

I think his decision to oppose the Vietnam War was one that naturally evolved. He had a strong aversion to America committing itself to the internal affairs of other nations. He felt that we had made great mistakes in the past and were never really left with friends. On someone else's turf, we never had a clear-cut view of what our objectives were. He felt that Vietnam was a mistake, and he said so at a time when that was very unpopular to say.

We began sending military advisers to South Vietnam in the Kennedy administration. That just kept escalating. At first, everybody thought it was okay that we send military advisers everywhere, as part of our self-interest. But it became quite clear that the government we were supporting in South Vietnam was corrupt. They had stolen from the people, and it was a virtual dictatorship. It was not a country you would be very proud to assist. But this escalation kept going on.

At first Church supported President Johnson, as did the great bulk of the Senate and House. Then he was one of the early leaders to part with the president and members of his party, publicly. He took his message and his views around the country.

It was a huge risk. There was a recall campaign. A lot of people did not think his loyal opposition was patriotic. They felt he should back the flag 100 percent. Frank felt strongly that what we were doing was against the best interest of the United States, and said so. He was attacked unmercifully for years by those who felt he let the country down, and that we should all be united.

Those kinds of attacks hurt; they affect family and friends. But he withstood it very well, and went on to win in 1968. I think people who did not agree with him on this issue felt he was being candid and honest, not riding the fence. I think they liked that in the Senator. He had to have Republican support in Idaho to win, and he got a lot of it over the years.

He felt that one of his greatest accomplishments was trying to preserve the rare wilderness and wild rivers in the United States. He was one of the authors of the wilderness legislation, which was twenty-five years ago. He loved the outdoors, thought that it was something majestic and magnificent, and needed preserving

I never knew Frank to take advantage of any situation for his personal gain. He never made much money and didn't leave much of an estate. But he had opportunities. One of the first government bail-outs was for the Studebaker

Company. It was in financial trouble, and had a lot of employees. Four days before the final vote, Frank knew how it was going to come out. The stock was selling for about two dollars or three dollars a share. We laughed about the idea of buying some stock at such a low price, and then watch it go up in value.

Of course no one bought any stock or even told any friends about it, anywhere. The stock did go up in value, it doubled or tripled within a few weeks after Congress took the action. He had enough sense of ethics and propriety not to be swallowed up by that kind of thing.

He also felt that neither the FBI nor the CIA should violate American criminal law. He found considerable evidence that they had been. Both Republican and Democratic members of the committee agreed to the conclusions to be drawn from the evidence of the investigation, so it wasn't a one-man committee. They uncovered serious hidden efforts by the CIA to assassinate people and government leaders in other countries, to overthrow those governments without the knowledge or consent of the Congress of the United States. He felt that this was not appropriate, and tried to bring it to light with those hearings.

Those hearings lasted a lot longer than he had anticipated, which is why he got into the 1976 race for the presidency so late. The hearings didn't end until sometime in March when other candidates were already way out in front.

He surprised everybody. He was the first one to beat Jimmy Carter in any primary. He beat him in Nebraska, in Oregon, and in Montana. But the key was California. We had a terrific organization in California. Some of the top people in the state were in his camp. Then Jerry Brown, governor of California, decided to run for President. That was the ball game. Without California we could not have the kind of convention support we needed to prevent a first ballot victory for Jimmy Carter.

The 1980 Senate race in Idaho was a tough race. Probably one of the dirtiest races I've been involved in. At least from our perspective it appeared that way, with charges from all kinds of outside sources. Committees that been formed to defeat Church kept up a steady campaign against him. It was a real hate campaign for about two years on television. They tried to portray him as unpatriotic. They tried to make people think he was not the chap he was made out to be, that he really had no integrity. It was unfair.

He took the loss much better than I would have. He didn't cry, but went on with his life. I think he was disappointed; it was an awfully close race. Ronald Reagan was running and won with quite a landslide in Idaho. The difference between Church and Steve Symms was about five thousand votes, a close election under the circumstances. I always felt we should have won, should have done things better. Maybe we would have.

The Panama Canal probably played some part in the defeat. A lot of people have always felt very strongly about that emotional issue. I suppose in today's world people say maybe Frank was wrong. I don't think he was. Eventually you cannot control a major waterway in another country. I was sure we were never going to permit Noriega to block the Panama Canal. The question was about who should have the ownership of the canal facilities. Half of the Republicans in the Senate voted for the treaty. So it was not a party issue as such. It was almost entirely a local Idaho issue. It was not an issue in most other states anywhere. No one felt it was that important a matter. The issue was manufactured, in a sense, blown up and distorted. It put blinders in front of many people's eyes. They believed Frank was no longer the one who should represent them.

He was about the least jaded person I've ever known. One time he was invited to the White House for dinner. Limousines were rolling up, but Frank drove his Kaiser, the old campaign car from the 1956 campaign. He had a hard time getting in, because no one would believe a United States senator would arrive at the White House for dinner in a beat up Kaiser. Later he had an old yellow Mustang that he drove to the Senate every day.

Frank and Bethine Church had one of those incredible marriages. They were not only man and wife, they were the best of friends. They had the same goals. She campaigned as hard as Frank. She admired him, he admired her. I never heard them raise a voice against the other. There was a remarkable calmness between the two.

Right off the bat in high school, they were in the starting gate. No one even thought anything else. The war years were tough on them. When Frank went overseas, she didn't hear from him for quite a while. She didn't just sit alone; she had other boyfriends. Frank had to come and woo her back.

*In 1947 Church married Bethine Clark, the daughter of former Governor Chase Clark. She now lives in Boise.*

Frank and Carl Burke and Stan Burns and all their friends argued, had fun, and debated. I remember we were eating ice cream cones when we heard about Pearl Harbor. All of a sudden we were trying to decide what it was going to do to our lives. There was never a time, from the time when I first met him when we were both in student government, that I wasn't one of the debaters in the group. We would all meet and we'd argue and we'd talk and we'd raid Mom's icebox. On Sundays she always thought she had enough roast to last to Monday, but it never did because of the many sandwiches that went out during the debates while we were sitting on the kitchen counters.

I knew politics from the time I was little, so what I contributed was Idaho politics. Pop, my father, was always interested in the issues of the day. I knew the state. If someone would say, "Well, such and such won't make any difference," I'd say, "I think it will affect a lot of people, and they will be mad about it." Then we'd argue that back and forth. I always said I was the politician and he was the statesman. He always had a long view of the world, and what was going to happen, how we should live in it, and how we should shepherd our resources, whether they were children or the

*Courtesy of Bethine Church*

**Bethine Church**

elderly.

Frank had not had much experience when he first ran for office. It was painful for him. He was really shy. All of his life he was shy. You'd never dream it, but down underneath, there it was. In the mornings, when we first started to campaign, he would say, "Bethine, when you see the first hand for me to shake, push me out of the car." I said, "You know, if somebody sees me doing that, they'll think I want to be senator and not you. Then you will be in really deep trouble." He said, "No, do it carefully. When you think we should start, let's start." But he needed that little impetus. Once he got started, he loved it. Toward the end of that nine-month campaign, he would set himself a goal of five hundred people a day to shake hands with.

A lot of the women who are involved with men in politics really don't like it. I really liked it. That was part of the great thing we had going. I love politics, I love people. When he was defeated, it was very relaxing to change our lifestyle and think of other things that we never had any time for. We didn't drop off a cliff, like lots of people do. We had a good time.

During the Kennedy days, people would comment about how John Kennedy would come in and Jackie would have soft music playing and really good company to talk arts or books. I said to Frank one time, "Don't you wish I would do that instead of saying, 'Now why did you vote like that today? Tell me about the debate.'" He said, "No, I couldn't stand it. I have to have a way to get it all out." I could tell when he was working on a position, because he'd work on me for weeks. He would try variations on it to figure out how he felt about it, try to feel comfortable with it. When it felt comfortable in his mouth, then he could write it. Someone once said he wrote like he spoke and spoke like he wrote. That is a rare thing, I understand.

Selling Robinson Bar Ranch (to avoid the appearance of a conflict of interest while he was working for the establishment of a wilderness designation on adjacent lands) was a hard thing to do. Frank didn't own the ranch. One of the most vitriolic letters that I have ever read was by someone who said he had lied about the ranch, and that was the reason he wanted to support wilderness. Beulah, my mother's half sister, and I owned the ranch together. My family homesteaded there just before the First World War. It was part of our family. It had its own natural hot water and all the family memories. We were married on the front porch there. Beulah was married there many years earlier. But I just don't live with regrets.

Frank never used to tell jokes. Instead he would tell of real events. When we were campaigning once, he got bitten in the nose by a dog down in Malad. He would tell the story that it was a Republican dog.

During the 1976 presidential race no one expected that Jimmy Carter would come to a certain big banquet in Omaha. But we had accepted. By the time we got there, Carter had been advised that we were coming, and maybe he should come after all. But he wasn't on the program. Half the Democrats were mad. Backstage we were trying to decide what to do just as he arrived. Frank said, "Are there any Idaho potatoes anywhere?" An inventive young kid with our campaign went out and got a big basket of Idaho potatoes. Carter got up and made some comments about Frank, "this young man," running for the presidency as though he were aspiring for something too big for him. It was sort of demeaning. Frank countered by saying that he wanted Carter to see some Idaho peanuts. He handed him the basket, and the house broke down. I think that's why we won the Nebraska primary. Sometimes it's those little things that events swing on.

Frank always said he hadn't expected to win election the first time in Idaho. No Democrat had ever won the second time in Idaho. He thought it was remarkable to win the third time. He said, "Bethine, one of these days my luck is just going to run out. If I were William Borah and from his party, I could probably be senator till the day I die." When we started the 1980 campaign, he said, "Look, we're not going to talk about this again, but I don't think we're going to win this one. We have a lot of people who have a vested interest and who care deeply. We have to give it the best shot we can. Let's do everything just like we've always done it. Let's do as much as we can within our physical capacity to do it. Then when it's over we will have no regrets." I said, "Right on." That's what we did. I did the hardest campaigning I have ever done. I never felt like I'd ever let him down and he never felt like he'd ever let me or his constituency or his friends or his family down. When it was over, we went to bed at peace that night. We weren't kidding when we woke up in the morning the next day and thought, "Well, it's a new day. We're going to do something different, and it's going to be wonderful." At the concession speech, a young reporter asked Frank, "What are you and Bethine going to do now?" To my surprise and everybody else's, he said, "We've decided to stay together." It just blew away the crowd.

Sure, Frank got frustrated. Everybody gets frustrated. There are two kinds of legislators. One is the person who wants to accomplish something, who has a goal in mind. The other wants to throw a lot of things in the hopper and doesn't care what happens to them because they can say, "I introduced such and such. It's a shame it didn't pass." Frank didn't like that. I watched him and John Kennedy lose a floor fight by one vote. It was a worthy fight because they made their point and they lost by very little.

But he liked winning. He would go into every battle, like the early wilderness fight, where he knew that every word might be hanging him, with a passion to persevere and to make it. He wanted to win the battle. When you look at the record of his passed bills, it's quite phenomenal. The most controversial thing he ever did, the Panama Canal Treaty, was only won by one vote. I think he was always a bit surprised when things came out as well they did because the fights were so hard.

He cared so much about peace. He said, "Every citizen who loves his country, it's freedom and good life; every parent, whose children yearn for their day in the sun; every American who believes our national heritage still represents the last best hopes on earth, must become earnestly engaged in the quest for peace."

He once said, "Bethine, my career has been a case of swimming upstream—like a salmon. It was hard, it was always a fight." He took on the hardest ones, and I was proud of him for doing it.

*One of Frank Church's sons, F. Forrester Church, is minister of All Souls Unitarian Church in New York City.*

I grew up in the household of not a great man, but a great father. Somehow he did not bring the burdens of his office home with him. It was not a difficult environment to grow up in at all. It was very relaxed and comfortable. Only after I left home did I begin to realize what an important figure he was. Our closeness was due to the fact that he had been primarily a father in my early life, and then that I could respect him immensely and try to emulate him in my own life.

He followed in the great tradition of independent-minded statesmen from the West who had a tremendous grasp of national and international issues, and became principal spokespersons for the foreign policy of our time. Foreign policy so often was dominated by the eastern establishment, but Church and William Borah were both independent voices, countering the old cliques and clubs of the East.

My father introduced religion to me by quoting Thomas Jefferson who said: "It is in our lives, not in our words, that religion must be read." He had no patience whatsoever for pious cant, for people who said all the right things and whose lives were cesspools. He had tremendous respect for any person of integrity and honor, regardless of that person's specific religious beliefs. For him the core of spirituality was ethical behavior, one's fundamental respect and reverence for life.

From the very beginning he refused to enter into the kind of smear politics that have become so prominent and successful today. At the end of his career he was fed up with what politics had become. He could not prostitute himself, change who he was in order to simply be successful. Fortunately in his early political years, negative politics and the mudslinging were not nearly as prominent as it has become in recent years.

His twenty-four years in the senate took a certain toll, not in themselves, but because the Senate changed in those years. In his first race, the primary against Glen Taylor in 1956, he spent ten thousand dollars and won. In 1980 he lost, spending three million dollars.

Earlier, he would have two or three primary committee and sub-committee assignments. He could study the issues and rely upon his own understanding. He could work hard in an area, develop an expertise, and become an important spokesperson. Later he would be serving on thirty or more committees and subcommittees. Staff members did so much of the work. Senators become like Ping-Pong balls, knocked back and forth from one committee room to another, wondering, "If this is Tuesday, it must be price supports." He found that environment demeaning and frantic.

Then meanness entered politics when people discovered that it was possible to beat a good person by telling lies. His whole approach in politics was never to respond to untrue accusations. At a certain point he discovered that by not responding, people assumed they were true. It made the entire life he had aspired to from the time he was a sixth-grade civics student in Boise in

*F. Forrester Church*

some ways cheapened and diminished. He himself was not cheapened and diminished, but I think it did wear him down. It made leaving at the end of twenty-four years easier than would have been the case at any earlier point in his career.

Given his prominence, the thing that impressed me most about my father was his sense of freedom, his easy and unforced way of moving through the world, his elemental kindness and a compassion, his great, good humor. All this combined with a terrific gift of service and knowledge.

The month before he died, I once more appreciated his courage and humor. There is a great line from G. K. Chesterton: "Angels can fly because they take themselves lightly." Even in the face of death, he took himself lightly. He had tremendous humility in many ways. He saw that life was a gift and not a given, and that we should live in such a way that our life will prove to be worth dying for. He was able to look back with great peace about his life. And then he was overwhelmed by the love that was shown to him those two times he faced death.

From his death, I learned again that death is a sacrament, not something to be feared, but something to be honored as the hinge upon which life turns, a natural passage. His last words were uttered to a cousin who asked him, "How are you, Frank, I mean spiritually?" My father looked up and said, "You know, it's very, very interesting."

## Joseph Garry

*In 1953 the United States Congress decided that the relationship between American Indians and the federal government should end, that traditional treaty arrangements should be terminated. This new "termination" policy began when*

*Robert Dellwo*

*Congress began to target the tribes that would go first, and then bought and sold Indian lands, forests, and other assets. The policy began to set the Indian peoples adrift from their tribal identities and to force them into conditions of poverty more severe than what they already experienced.*

*The leadership of one man stands out in the subsequent resistance to the policy. He mobilized Indians and their leaders, managed a campaign of information and lobbying in Washington, D.C., spoke for the aspirations of American Indians, and within five or six years turned Congress around. The man was Joseph Garry, an Idaho legislator, Coeur d'Alene Indian chief, and the president of the National Congress of American Indians. One of his close associates was Robert Dellwo, an attorney from Spokane, Washington.*

I ran across Joe Garry way back in 1937. When I was an undergraduate at Gonzaga University, one of the nuns from DeSmet was trying to inaugurate an arts and crafts cooperative. I was interested, so I went out there as one of the speakers. Joe was there, too, as one of the speakers. He was about ten years older than I. I had never run into an Indian who gave such a fine talk and such a fine impression. He was in favor of this project. I marked him as an Indian leader to come and it turned out that that's what he was.

I next ran into him some years later, in 1950. I took over the various tax cases of the Coeur d'Alene Tribe. By then I was practicing law in the city of Spokane. That was in the late 1940s and early 1950s. The Internal Revenue Service sought to attack the exemptions that Indians had on income from their trust lands. I picked up all the Coeur d'Alene cases. Joe was not chairman at the time, but he himself was one of the litigants. He was being charged by the IRS for not reporting his trust income for tax purposes. There were eighteen or twenty such cases on the Coeur d'Alene reservation, and we won refunds in every single case. Those were celebrated cases. And Joe was active in them: the Nicodemus case, and the famous Quinault Capoeman case, which went clear to the U.S. Supreme Court.

Joe was very active in those, even though he was not a lawyer. As a lawyer, I relied on Joe. He had an expansive knowledge of Indian law. He was nearly always

**Joseph Garry**

*Courtesy of the Coeur d'Alene Tribal office*

right. For instance, in this case, the legal opinion of the senior partner in my law office was that that income was taxable. But Joe disagreed. We found out he was right in winning those cases. Those cases rule to the present day. Indian trust and land income is exempt from federal income tax.

A year or two later, I became the official tribal attorney. And a couple of years after that, he became the tribal chairman. I served with him until his death.

Joe became the national leader in the fight against termination. Without him, termination would have occurred for most tribes. It did occur for some tribes: the Klamaths, the Menominee, and others. It almost occurred at the Flathead Reservation, where I was born and raised. But it didn't occur because Joe Garry went there and led them in their fight against termination.

Senator Arthur V. Watkins of Utah and his "Watkins Committee" had come out to sell the Flatheads on a termination bill. There were two leading speakers against it—my father, who broke ranks with the white community on the issue, and Joe Garry.

The Watkins method was to have a big meeting with the tribal members and offer them the large financial benefits that would result from the liquidation and sale of their tribal lands and forests. That is how Watkins would get a favorable vote. Then that vote would become a mandate to introduce a termination bill to end the tribe. The Flatheads rejected it.

Watkins had been to the Klamath reservation, and won by a small majority. Joe showed up a month later and called the tribe together. Under the constitution they needed to have a certain number for a quorum. Joe got them to reconsider their termination vote. But the pro-terminationists walked out and killed the quorum. For that technical reason, Joe lost the fight in the case of Klamaths.

Without Joe's leadership, termination of many more tribes would have occurred. The Colville termination issue kept coming up every session of Congress. Joe organized the opposition. Several of us appeared at the congressional hearings.

As a result of his successful killing of the termination movement, a different policy arose. Congress finally recognized that Indian tribes are here to stay, as an identified people and as part of our pluralistic society. He changed the philosophy of America toward Indians.

Back when I first became active in Indian affairs, people told me it was foolish to promote Indian programs because "termination is just around the corner. In ten years there won't be any recognized Indian tribes." It turned out that the tribes survived. The Menominees reorganized and became reinstated as a Tribe, partially because of his leadership.

So Joe Garry killed the termination program and he obtained the recognition that Indian tribes are permanent identities on the political and social face of America.

As part of that, he accomplished several developmental programs. Many tribes won claims judgments from the United States, some of them for millions of dollars. The Coeur d'Alene Tribe had won a claims settlement of four and a half million dollars.

Up to the time of Joe Garry, most tribes would make a per capita distribution to the members of the tribe. Everyone would get a large payment, and then the money would be gone. Joe set up a program for the Coeur d'Alene claims judgment that became a pattern all over the nation. Only a small portion was distributed on a per capita basis. The rest was programmed into housing, economic development, and land restoration. He started a land restoration project that has almost doubled the trust land base of the Coeur d'Alene Tribe.

The program he inaugurated was copied by other tribes. It became almost mandatory as part of the legislation that goes with these judgments. Congress now says the judgment will not be available until the tribe comes forward with an acceptable program for the use of the funds. What they meant was similar to what Joe had started in his own tribe.

He recognized that Indians needed both economic and cultural security. He became a champion of economic development, land restoration, and educational programs.

He leaves in his path really three things: the idea of tribal perpetuation and identity, the need for education and for economic stability for the tribes. He accomplished much of his agenda on these programs.

You ask why a person becomes a leader. Look at other family groups, like the Kennedys. Very often the answer is in what we might call familial indoctrination. Joe Garry's ancestors were leaders. His grandfather was Spokane Garry, one of the chiefs of the Spokanes. He was very active in the late 1800s in the negotiations and parleys, in which the Northwestern tribes ceded most of their lands to the United States. He was born into a family of leadership. His relatives, the SiJohn family of the Coeur d'Alenes are active intelligent Indian leaders. Because of his abilities, he stepped forward. Because of his literacy on Indian issues, tribes carried him forward and recognized him as their leader all over the United States.

Like Jack Kennedy, Joe Garry led by involving other people. Joe had very capable Indian leaders around him. They constituted a kind of "national Indian cabinet." He would involve me for example. He would call me and say, "Bob, I want you to appear at the National Congress of American Indian convention and give a lecture on Indian taxation." I would be happy to do that because that was my field. He deliberately involved guys like me, bringing us into Indian affairs. I noticed he did the same with many, many people. He enjoyed the political life.

Perhaps he did not achieve such happiness in his personal life. His only child was born brain-damaged and is presently in an institution. He loved her very much and with great concern cared for her.

He was hitting his peak when he went through five or six years of deteriorating health. That robbed him of any further political career. As he was losing his ascendancy throughout the nation, he was defeated in a race for re-election as president of the National Congress of American Indians. Behind the scenes, I think it was because of the health factor. He was no longer able to dynamically carry forward the mantle of leadership.

One time we were standing on the back steps of the Capitol. Bobby Kennedy was having his picture taken with tourists, but he came up and asked to have his picture taken with Joe.

I think the Kennedys trusted him on ideology, trusted him not to propagandize them. He was not just a lobbyist out to get everything he could. He was there to exercise discriminating leadership on behalf of Indians.

If he had had another twenty years, his friends and admirers thought he might have become the Martin Luther King, Jr., of American Indians.

*In Washington, D.C., with the National Congress of American Inidians, Joseph Garry worked with Helen Peterson, a Sioux who was its executive director. Peterson had been the director of the Mayor's Committee on Human Relations in Denver when she attended an NCAI meeting and met Indian leaders Ruth Muskrat Brownson and Darcy McNichol, who persuaded her to be the new NCAI director when the position became vacant. She is now retired and lives in Portland.*

I went to Washington in the fall of 1953 with an agreement to stay six months, help pull the annual convention together, and help the organization regroup. I ended up staying there eight and a half years. That fall I met Joseph Garry.

I began work in September just after Congress passed the worst and most anti-Indian legislation since the Allotment Act of 1887, House Concurrent Resolution 108, or HCR 108. It declared it to be the policy of the United States to terminate the special relationship between Indians and the federal government as rapidly as the circumstances of each tribe would permit. Certain tribes were named in the policy resolution including the Confederated Salish Kootenai on the Flathead reservation, Turtle Mountain Chippewa, Menominee of Wisconsin, Klamath of Oregon and others. This terrified the Indians.

*Helen Peterson*

I began from scratch to put together an annual convention with the help of Indian leaders who were meeting in Carson City, Nevada, that September. With advice and consultation with them, the 1953 convention was set for Phoenix in December at the Westward Hotel. Joseph R. Garry, who was then chairman of the Coeur d'Alene Tribe, came and ran a very dignified and sophisticated campaign to become president. I'm sure that Joe Garry had been heard of before, but I had not been close enough to the National Congress of American Indians to really know his involvement prior to that.

The support and confidence of Indian groups in the Northwest was an important part of his campaign. His tribe was a small one, but Joe Garry was a very, very impressive man. He had great leadership quality and it was not surprising that he won rather easily.

The National Congress of American Indians had been started in 1944 out of an awareness by Indian leaders of the need to consult with each other and work together to lobby and protect themselves, exchange information and gain strength. In its early years the NCAI was dominated by Oklahoma Indians. Joe Garry's presidency from 1953 to 1960 changed the pattern of leadership away from this dominance and shifted it to the Northwest tribes.

When I went to work in September there were three tribes with their dues paid. Eligibility to vote was always based on whether dues were current and paid according to the constitution. Joe visited many tribes, particularly the little tribes in the Northwest. He explained the crisis in Indian affairs that the termination policy represented. He brought the NCAI to the least and the smallest as well as the largest tribes in the Northwest. In those six years membership (from the Northwest and elsewhere) grew to about one hundred and eighteen tribes. The National Congress did indeed become a national organization with national stature. With that kind of stability it was a respected voice, and still is to this day the most important Indian gathering of the year.

Joe made the issues real to the tribes of the Northwest. They gave him massive support in NCAI, and that brought it to that point. He stopped serving when he made a run for a United States Senate seat in Idaho that year.

Joe loved his family. He was a very earthy man, despite his commanding presence. He was always hospitable, always generous, always concerned about youth. He thought a lot about training young leadership as well as having respect for seasoned leadership.

Joe called the bingo numbers and presided at the bingo games of the Coeur d'Alene people to raise money for NCAI. It seems difficult to believe these days that a dollar could mean so much or that thirty dollars could seem so big. When funds arrived at Washington, we used to go with him to his Catholic Church to give thanks. He was a devout Roman Catholic. He gave thanks for these hard-earned contributions that his family and friends in Coeur d'Alene would send in.

I doubt he is ever given enough credit for his leadership in the 1950s. It was the most critical time of this century in Indian affairs. I think it's not remotely understood how critical his leadership was.

*Jeanne Givens of Coeur d'Alene, who served in the Idaho legislature from 1984 to 1988, is his niece.*

This is from a small book that my mother wrote about her memories growing up in Lovell Valley. This is the part she wrote about her brother, Joe. It's called "Thank You, Joe."

"The memories I write are about the twenties and the thirties. Joe was eleven years my senior. When I was in my growing-up years, he was already an adult, and on his way to a preparation of better things to come. Joe was tender, kind, and generous with me. He was somewhat different from the rest of my brothers. He was gentle, studious and hard working.

"In his efforts at educational pursuit, he went through difficult times. He rode horseback wearing a sheepskin coat to attend Tekoa High School through rain, snow, and freezing weather. Dad sometimes took him on a wagon when the roads and the weather were too bad. The roads in the twenties and the thirties were not paved or even graveled. Many times on horseback, he went over the railroad tracks to escape miring in the mud of the road, taking pancake

**Jeanne Givens at Cataldo Pageant**

sandwiches for school lunch.

"Even with his difficulties in attending school, he was active in school activities. He played high school football, basketball, and participated in track meets. He attended school in Tekoa for two years. After that, his aunt Sabine Polotkin sent him to Gonzaga Prep, where he was able to finish high school. He then attended Haskell Institute and Butler University.

"Through the years that Joe had gone away to school, his associates were national Indian leaders, United States senators, congressmen, governors of states. Joe retained his full Indian self. He never forgot the power of Indian chants. He never once forgot his native language. His stature, dark skin and his Indian accent he considered assets, not liabilities.

"It was Joe who made me realize that, in our later years, no matter how successful we become or who we are, there are hard, strong tugs that take us back to our sweet, bitter roots. When his health started to fail, many of his days were spent at a Spokane hospital. His wife would urge me to come and visit him—in Indian. Our visits sometimes were filled with laughter as we told each other stories in our native language. The memories of people we knew, their love and their simplicity, and the memories of special events flooded back.

"Joe passed on January 31, 1975. We mourned our brother and buried him with love and pride. The love and pride was not only for him, but for the love and pride also of our parents, for our grandparents, and pride in all Indian people who seek justice, betterment and somehow, bring with them a little bit more of happiness for their people."

Joe's father, Ignace Garry, the last chief of the Coeur d'Alene Tribe, was a strong influence on him. Joe understood the burden and responsibility that went along with being elected by the people to be the chief. He was raised in an extraordinary family. Ike, Henry, and Francis SiJohn were his brothers. Celina Garry was his sister. They were a very colorful group of brothers and sisters. Henry taught history at the college level. My mother worked at the American Indian Center in Spokane. Ike worked as heavy equipment operator. Francis worked on the Spokane Reservation.

Joe worked for the Bureau of Indian Affairs soon after college. He did express frustration with that bureaucracy: they weren't getting the job done, they weren't upholding their trust responsibility to tribes, they were inept, they were just a mindless bureaucracy. That was his big frustration. If you look at people who get into politics, there is something that propels them. Often it is frustration and anger. I think that he thought that the Bureau of Indian Affairs could definitely do a better job, and that as a tribal chairman he could hold them accountable. That frustration helped steer him in the direction of tribal government.

When I was younger, about eight years old, he was running again for the senate in the legislature. In the old days, the political parties used to have caravans throughout the district. I was invited to go along with my uncle. This was my first campaign experience. Many cars lined up together and we went to all these small towns in Benewah County and lower Kootenai County. In the group were people like Cy Chase of the Idaho Senate and Congresswoman Gracie Pfost. We went into Avery, which is a very small town, and Uncle Joe began drumming. My job was to do the dancing. People would come out of their businesses and their shops and I would just be dancing.

We went over to the Senior Citizen picnic at Harrison, Idaho, and he would always capture everybody's attention. He was a dramatic person and he would begin his speech speaking in Coeur d'Alene or Spokane or Kalispel. He would say, "Oh, excuse me, I forgot, I must use English with you."

My first experience with my Uncle Joe involved politics. I saw a man who was able to walk very well in two worlds. At an early age I realized that you can accomplish things for your tribal people. You can accomplish things for the state as well.

Some of my favorite memories are hearing the brothers drum, Ike and Francis and Henry and Joe sitting down and drumming. They had a special tone and sound, unique among Indian drummers.

Physically, he was a tall man, at least six foot tall. As he grew older his hair was pure white. It was beautiful white hair. He had dark beautiful skin the color of copper. He had a dignified way of introducing himself to people. Once people met Joe Garry, they knew that they had met a strong leader.

I can relate very well to his experience in the Idaho legislature. One of the things that he did while he was in the state senate was to give a demonstration of Indian stick games. If you can imagine, on the first floor of the Idaho Capitol, they set out the sticks. Indian people on both sides sang stick game songs. He wanted to give that demonstration because they were considering a bill about gambling. He wanted for the Indian stick game to be exempted from the gambling bill. He was a good communicator. He could take something cultural and show non-Indians that this was important to us. He used his communication skills to educate non-Indians.

One of his lasting legacies is that he pushed very hard for federal housing. The housing situation on the Coeur d'Alene reservation was horrible. People were living in shacks. Joe Garry fought to create decent housing. Now people have a good roof over their heads and some decent housing. He was willing to work on the very basic kinds of issues, housing, health care, education.

He was an active supporter of the civil rights movement. He saw that the gains that blacks in America were trying to make would spill over to benefit Indian people. He knew Robert Kennedy when he was attorney general, and advised President Kennedy, although I don't know how much of the advice Kennedy took. He worked well with the regional senators from the Northwest, Scoop Jackson, Warren Magnuson, and Tom Foley.

The Flathead Reservation, in Montana, still exists. The Colville Tribe still thrives and is growing. They do because of those battles against termination. When you see safe and sanitary housing on an Indian reservation, I can clearly say that Joe Garry had a part in making that happen. When you see poor Indian families receiving prenatal care, it's because Joe Garry worked hard to explain the special kind of health problems that Indian people have.

Joe Garry was guided by his faith and his religion. He had a lot of tough times. I'm sure he felt the loneliness of the defeats. He was re-elected to the Tribal Council often, but when he ran for Congress, he did not make it through the primary. I'm sure that his faith in God helped him through these difficult times. He was a very spiritual person.

Perhaps his most painful experience was in tribal elections. There were people who would oppose him. He would never say publicly that he was bothered by it. But we know that it must have bothered him. You want to have unanimous acceptance of what you're doing, what your policies are and the kind of way you're guiding your tribe, but knew unanimity is a hard thing to achieve.

Joe Garry was a nationally recognized leader. He dedicated his life to government and the improvement of Indian and other people. He was special to us because he made gains in the life of Indian people. Like many good Idaho leaders, he had humble origins. He retained that humility and humbleness. What kept him grounded was his Indian spirituality, his sense of being Indian.

## Joe Albertson

*When the wreckers came to dismantle Joe Albertson's first supermarket at Sixteenth and State Streets in Boise in 1982, many Boiseans came by to collect one of the old sandy-colored bricks. When the new store opened to replace it, Albertson customers gathered in the aisles for reunions and parties. Between the first store in 1939 and its replacement, Albertson had built a supermarket empire of four hundred stores that reached into sixteen states.*

*Joe Albertson of Boise, like so many other enterprising business founders in Idaho, built it all from scratch.*

I learned how to work in 1909 after we came from Oklahoma to Idaho when I was three years old. We landed in Caldwell, Idaho. It had been raining and the mud was clear up to the curb. That was the first thing I saw when I looked out the window.

Later I worked on the ranch. I mean worked. My dad was a nurseryman, and he took a relinquished homestead in 1909. He worked for Talcott to provide extra money so we could buy cows. We kids and mother took that land and took out the sagebrush. The sagebrush in those days was six or seven feet high, so big it was hard to get out. The roots were spread out, mushroom-like. They used a big iron rail. When you pulled that through the field, and you could pull a lot of brush out. Some of it had to be grubbed out with a hoe. Doing that made blisters on your hand—made it hard to milk.

We got up at four o'clock in the morning to milk the cows. We had Jersey cows. I had the strongest thumb and first finger that you ever saw. Six cows, night and morning. Then you went in to change clothes, walk three miles to school, grade school. When school was out, you didn't play around, you'd come on home, change clothes, and started your chores again. You have pretty good work ethics when you do that for a few years.

I started to work for Safeway in 1927. That was on Ninth Street, where Johnson Floral is today. The Chesapeake Cafe was right on the alley, and there was a hardware

*Joe Albertson*

store nearby. I was with them for twelve years. I was four years in western Kansas, in the heart of the Dust Bowl. We got sick and tired of moving, and came back. I never felt so damned good in my life as when we saw the Rocky Mountains.

Safeway was going to punish me, I guess, and gave me the store in Emmett, Idaho. I thought they had a damned boom on in Emmett, compared to Kansas! The first thing I did in Emmett was start a price war. We were just happier than a chipmunk in a barrel of nuts. My wife and I both loved it; we got along with all the people and the sales volume went up.

I was moved from Emmett over to Meridian in August of 1932. Stayed there until the first of May 1937. Then I was brought to Boise. They gave me the new Safeway store where Home Federal is on Eighth and State Street. We opened that store, and were there until October. Then Safeway moved into Ogden, Utah. I supervised sixteen stores there. I stayed with them until the first of April 1939, then came up here.

After twelve years with Safeway I thought, "I can do better than that." L. S. Skaggs was a friend of mine—he was in Denver when I was in Kansas. We would talk and got pretty well acquainted. Well I had forty-five hundred dollars saved up, but I had to raise more. L. S. Skaggs had 45 percent, and his auditor had 10 percent. So that made him majority owner, which was all right with me. But he told me I had to put up 80 percent of my own money. I said I would get it somewhere.

We started out with twenty-five thousand dollars and my share needed to be about nine or ten thousand. I went to my wife's aunt, Bertie Estes, who is dead now, and she loaned me five thousand. I gave her a note and said, "I'll pay you interest on it."

So we went to work. We opened a store. Safeway had six small stores in Boise at the time, and they publicly announced in the *Statesman* that they were going to put us out of business. When you have all your life savings in, and you have your back up against the wall, you're going to come out fighting, hard. They launched a price war on dry groceries. We ended up grossing 4 1/2 percent on dry groceries. It was due to the people who traded at the commissary in Mountain Home. They wouldn't even trade with them, they came to Albertson to buy.

We operated through the end of the year and made sixty-five hundred dollars profit. Safeway lost big. I could put that into more forceful language but I'll delete it. So, they took inventory, and I know they were very, very surprised. As soon as their inventories were off, the price war ended just like that.

We made our money from service meat, the magazine racks; we made our own ice cream. I was the only guy who knew how to make it. I didn't go to bed for two days before we opened that store. We had the scratch bakery and the donuts. One night before Halloween, I stayed up with that donut machine all night, so I had enough donuts for the kids. We were fortunate, we tried to hire good people.

The most important things to know about running a store are that you must have the merchandise priced so that people who are ready and willing to buy are ready and willing to pay. Plus give them all the good service you can give them—tender loving care, we call it. And work like hell.

I worked about eighteen hours a day. There is a lot of work to be done, but if it is organized, it is very easy to accomplish. You organize a store by listening to your people. They are in contact with the customer. So, if you listen to your employees, they'll tell you how to manage a store.

A good employee was one with desire. Desire to learn all he could about the job that he was given. Desire to excel in it, so that when a promotional slot opened up, he would be ready for it, and then move on and progress with the growth of the company.

In locating a store, the trick is easy accessibility. You have to make it easy for people to get off the highway and get into your parking lot. I picked a lot of locations still used today. In fact, I had to do everything because we were just small. One way that I chose a good location—you can't do this now—was drive around in the car. If you see a new elementary school, or houses going in, or tricycles on the sidewalk, or diapers on the line—all of those things meant mouths to feed, so we would put in a store. It worked, but it won't work now because they don't use clothes lines anymore.

Customers have very much changed over the years. One thing that is different from 1939 is the progress that has been made in manufacturing. Take cake mix as an example. It used to be that you bought flour and sugar and so on, and baked a cake from scratch. That's no longer true. You can still do it, but very few do. You have Duncan Hines today. There are all kinds of cake mixes out there. People just take their pick. It makes it easier and quick. A new bride starting out could get Duncan Hines and almost guarantee a nice cake that would please her husband. So why wouldn't she?

There were a lot of things that happened that I still get "blamed" for. We had what we called the Big Joe Ice Cream Cone. That was two big scoops of ice cream on a cone for a nickle. We had kids lined a block from each side of that door, waiting to get their ice cream.

One Easter, the American Express guy called me up and said, "Joe, I'm stuck with five thousand baby chicks. What am I going to do with them? I can't sell them in your meat department. They are too young." I said, "Well, if you want to, send them up. I'll see if I can get rid of them." He had to do something with them. It was just before Easter. We didn't advertise in the *Statesman*. I went on the radio. The kids lined up for blocks, waiting to get free Easter chickens. The first one said, "What am I going to feed him?" Well, we had overlooked that. But we scrounged around and we found a one hundred pound sack in the back room of "Baby Chick Start." We packaged that up in little glassine bags for when a kid said, "What are we going to feed them?" I think we sold them for a quarter. About a year from then, I got pictures back from some of the folks of kids with grown chickens. They said, "We like to trade with you, but all during this growing up period, all we could hear was "chirp, chirp, chirp."

Oh, there have been mistakes I made throughout the history of the company and its growth. But there is a saying that, everything being equal, one will never go broke being right 51 percent of the time. And that's right.

My job is fun. I'm here every day. I get here about eight or nine o'clock and go home about four or five. I gave up golf about nine years ago. Warren (McCain, the chief executive officer of Albertsons) and his crew take care of running the business, but Warren and I visit quite a bit. I give Warren credit for running the store now. He's done a magnificent job. Outstanding. When you go along the twentieth year of increasing dividends every year, and profits, that's the name of the game. He has had all of the recognition that probably can be given—Merchant of the Year and many other awards that he's gotten. He has earned it.

We try to take care of our people. They're very valuable to us. We have stock options.  We have turned out quite a few millionaires.  When we went public, I said to Aunt Bertie, "I'll pay your loan off with the interest or I'll give you common stock.  It's your choice."  She said, "I'll take common stock!"  It was a good choice, but she didn't live long enough to enjoy it.

My wife said that the first she heard about my going into the food business was in chemistry class at the College of Idaho.  She said I said one day, "I'm never going to be a farmer.  I'm going into the food business.  Come hell or high water—depression or boom time, people are going to eat. In depression there will be salt pork and beans, and in boom times there will be steak."  I haven't changed my mind.

Working long hours takes a lot of understanding on the part of your family, mainly your wife.  I would say I was very lucky, because she has been a great help.  The fact that she put up with me for sixty-one years stands on its own.

Although I'm not a farmer, we do have a little farm.  We farm over two thousand acres of land now, and it makes money.  My wife and I go down there every Friday after lunch and come back Sunday after lunch.  And she doesn't have to do one thing down there if she doesn't want to.  No housework, no cooking, washing dishes, nothing.  Just go down there and relax.  She loves to go down there.  Light the tamarack in the fireplace and listen to it pop.

# INDEPENDENCE OF EXPRESSION

*While paper mills, farms, and food processing plants have become less and less labor intensive in recent decades, the production of art has not. Putting on* Oedipus Rex *still requires the same number of actors it did two thousand years ago, four hundred years ago, and three years ago. Musicians still need to rehearse and practice, a painter still needs to apply the paint to the canvas by hand, and a writer still has to convert the thought to the page by hand. Despite word processors and other helpful innovations, art is still "handmade," labor intensive.*

*The labor intensity of art in a society whose economy has gone beyond handmade production methods has implications for artists of all kinds everywhere, not just in Idaho. Few can afford to be artists full-time. And living in Idaho has certain implications for artists as well. Idaho offers diverse opportunities for isolation and natural beauty, for time to reflect or go to school, or for living the engaged life of a city or small town.*

*Scholars differentiate among the fine, the folk, the high, and the low arts. Artists may be known or unknown, their works valued by thousands of people or just the members of their families or small towns. What they all have in common is that they deem it worthwhile to transform their visions and ideas into shapes or forms or sounds or objects, and they deliberately arrange their lives to do it.*

*Jerry Luther is the Hooey Man from Sagle (near Sandpoint).*

I came up in the low income area of Los Angeles. I was bright, creative. I worked my way up, like you do in Los Angeles. You jump companies. By the time I was twenty-seven I was regional manager of Muzak & California Communications with an office in the Disneyland Hotel. Then I got interested in management. I went to school and made what Peterson in *Up the Organization* called an "upward arabesque." I got into general management.

I had in my heart a desire to live where there were big trees and clear water, where it was beautiful, where there was no layer of fuzz over the city. It took fifteen years, and learning to make puppets, to do it.

I left the Los Angeles business communication scene when I was thirty, around 1969 or 1970. I made my first jump to Santa Barbara, one hundred miles north of Los Angeles. There I had my first interaction with the alternative world. I heard ideas about going back to the land.

Then I went up to Sacramento and stayed a couple of years. I regrouped, got a trailer, stored food, and got all the things you need to go back to the land. I thought that I would raise musk oxen and weave things. But you are not allowed to have musk oxen! The only people allowed to have musk oxen were the Indians.

So I went from Sacramento to Spokane, Washington. I went there because it was next to the drop-off point for coming up here to the woods. I stayed there for about seven or eight years. I started doing woodwork. I became what was known as the Hooey Man, a vaudeville character and a woodworker. A lot of my friends who were doing the back-to-the-land thing settled in Sandpoint.

So I would visit them. Sandpoint was the first place I ever did the Hooey Man routine, in the community center right downtown. I went from Spokane to Oregon for a while, for about three years, and joined the community movement. At that time, those of us that had left industry without cash, who had few resources, joined the Oregon community movement.

I burned out on the community movement, like a lot of people did. We were all the same age, there was no one with any money, we didn't have any farm skills. My wife, Becky, and I worked apple picking and would go to craft fairs. After one apple season, we went to a healing gathering in North Idaho. We were seeking a home and Becky said, "Let's go to Idaho. It's a beautiful place, a wonderful place."

So we packed everything up, in the middle of the winter, January twenty-third. We had a couple of thousand dollars cash and a handful of tools. We pulled in here in the middle of a hideous snow storm, right around the side of the cliff here, overlooking the lake. It was beautiful. The house had a three car garage which we

*Jerry Luther the Hooey Man and his dancing ducks*

turned into a shop and a great view. That's how we got our start.

When we first got here, naturally I had long hair and braids. I was very hippie looking, very alternative. We had a blue van that still had pegasus horses painted on the side from the time I was doing puppet shows out of the van. The local people probably thought we were dealing marijuana or something.

It took us about a year of going down to the local bar, where our son would get on and off the school bus every day. We would sit and talk to people. They learned to like us and enjoy us. They came up to our shop and saw that we made these funny folk toys and traveled all around. After a couple of years, people began to trust us.

Keeping things going requires guts and creativity. That's what is beautiful about this place. The spirit of North Idaho is that you have to really reach inside of yourself and your resources and be creative to make it work.

We make about thirty-five hundred things a year, anything in wood from a six hundred dollar jewelry chest to twelve dollar ducks. We travel to about twenty art fairs around the Northwest. Three of them are at Sandpoint, Coeur d'Alene, and Boise. That is how we make it.

We sell to stores. We have a mail order business now, and a brochure that we send out. A lot of it is on a wish and a prayer. We make things that we like and that other people like. We haul it all in that trailer behind our truck and we take off. We end up someplace where we don't know who is going to show up. We set up our booth and people come by. We say we are from Sagle. They say, "Where is Sagle?" We say, "Near Sandpoint." Now our letterhead says, "Sagle, Idaho" with "near Sandpoint" in parentheses. That's how we do it.

My life is full. I am doing my own demo video. A wonderful dancer is choreographing routines for me. My accountant is an artistic person, a wonderful guy. I get to talk business with him. One of my best friends is now a county commissioner who used to work for the library board. I get plugged into what's happening at the library. School kids come through our shop here. I get to go visit schools.

It would be hard to have the diversity and richness that I have in my life in any other place. In other places you tend to get more and more specialized. I'm above all a generalist. I love to do a lot of things. And I think that is the way it is happening here in Sandpoint. But I still am a businessman. Business is one of the bases for our success. I keep good records and I manage well.

There is an interesting mix of people in Idaho, from my perspective of eight years. There are old established families, where logging, ranching, and farming were the heart of their existence. Then a whole bunch of us swarmed up here in hordes, about ten or fifteen years ago. Some of them are still saying, "Who are these people?" There are a lot of us saying, "Who are they?" But I see more and more of us getting together. I see their kids liking our kids. I see them enjoying some of the things we do, in building and decorating.

I personally feel well accepted, but I have a funny act. People like a funny act. My wife and I were part of the alternative group that didn't want handouts. We didn't do food stamps. We wanted to make it on our own, pay our taxes, buy our land, go to school, go to meetings. I think a lot of colleagues in my industry have the same temperament. There were years where people left the city and got on welfare. I am resistant to that, because room for economic survival is thin up here. There is not a lot of room to carry people who can't carry themselves, other than older people or handicapped people. The land is difficult, the roads are tough, the weather is tough. This is one of the least populated parts of the United States. If you can learn to deal with all that, you can earn your place.

In my industry, some people are obsessed with trying to define what art is, and what craft is. But it is hard to find the time to think about that. We make things here, and sell there. That is work. That is what makes money, what keeps the kid fed, what keeps us going.

We find that a lot of things that sell the best are under fifty dollars. That makes us production artists. Some people find the two words mutually exclusive. But my friends who are successful in Idaho are production artists. They make things that people can afford. It is very difficult to make one thousand dollar items and send them off unless you're established from a Los Angeles or New York base. It is important—and okay—to make something for twenty dollars. And okay to make a lot of them. Repetition is okay. I practice my vaudeville act over and over. The act may only last five or ten minutes; and there are tens of thousands of people who feel better because I do it.

Courtesy of Barney Hill

**Barney Hill**

*Barney Hill from Emmett is a Cowboy Poet.*

I write cowboy poetry because it's fun, mainly. I started writing poetry because I've always been interested in the stories that my mother and old-timers would tell. My wife's granddad was born here in 1880. He had some fantastic stories. But whenever you try to retell a story it never comes out quite right; so what I did with some of my poetry was to take the basic idea of a story and try to make it a kind of history. Some of them come from personal experiences.

I think cowboy poetry is popular in Idaho because most Idahoans are very much individuals. Whether they truly understand a cowboy's way of life or not, they are still individuals with an appreciation for someone else who is an individual. It doesn't matter if they're river rafters, kayakers, cowboys, or whatever. I think people just appreciate each other in Idaho, maybe more than in some other states.

I've never had critics or anybody just come and tell me what I was doing was wrong. I'm a terrible speller. My wife gets after me all the time about that. My English is pretty poor and she is very good in English. Whether or not it's poetry, I don't know. I put together words that rhyme. Some poets put together words that don't rhyme and call it poetry. I reckon it is, but I always figured it's supposed to rhyme.

I imagine Shakespeare, Keats, and Shelley and some of those people had critics when they were writing what they wrote. I'm sure not comparing myself to them because there is no comparison. I think that if a person appreciates cowboy poetry, then they should listen to it, if they don't like it, then they shouldn't.

# COLD TURKEY
## by Barney Hill

I used to chew tobacco,
lower lip ahangin' loose.
Oh I love to fill it full
of that Copenhagen snoose.

I went out to check the stock
one cold and windy day,
and the horse that I'as aridin'
was a half broke little bay.

Well I dug my can out of my pocket
when much to my surprise
I'as about to fill my lip
when it blew right in my eyes.

I just dropped everything.
My eyes they burned and itched.
My pony knew there's something wrong,
so he swallered his head and pitched.

I started to reach for something
to try and hold me down.
Didn't do no good cause
I'as alayin' on the ground.

I couldn't move my leg,
I had a busted knee.
and I'as asittin' on a thistle
and it was ajabbin' me.

I had three teeth a missin'
and my eyes was swollen shut.
And on my little finger
I'as asufferin' from a cut.

I had some busted ribs
where that horse had stepped on me.
I couldn't find a place that didn't hurt
and I still wasn't able to see.

Well I quit a-usin' tobacco.
They'll get no more of my wealth.
You see, I believe that surgeon general
'Cause it sure was harmful to my health!

I think there are a lot of people who can write poetry. Probably anybody could write cowboy poetry. I do think that amongst nine or ten other cowboys, they're going to know pretty quick whether I'm a cowboy or not just from the conversation around. To me it's important that my cowboy poetry is heard and appreciated by my peers. If somebody is trying to write cowboy poetry and they're not cowboys, they're going to get found out pretty quick.

Every cowboy poem has to have a basic honesty about it to be authentic cowboy poetry. It's hard to just take a subject someone brings to you to make a poem out of it. You get away from being authentic, because you weren't there and didn't see what happened.

I had a story told to me the other day about a fellow who roped a washtub up here while several others were gathering some cows. He started dragging it toward this other guy riding a green horse. There was quite a wreck anyhow. They said I ought to make a poem out of that, but I wasn't there. It would be awful hard to do.

I think most cowboys like to take a look at themselves and laugh about their experiences. It's like slapstick comedy; it's funny when it happens to somebody else. It might not be funny when you're getting bucked off a horse or drug under or have a bull run over you or knock you down or something, but later on it is. You can retell that story and make it funny. It's the same thing that makes slapstick comedy, or getting a pie in the face, so popular over the years. We all like to tell these experiences, whether we put it in poetry or just sit around the coffee shop and tell about the last time we got bucked off a horse. And we make it sound funny because it sure does hurt when it happens. Other cowboys can appreciate that, but they really don't care to hear about how bad it hurt. They do appreciate the funny part.

Speaking for myself, because I can't speak for anybody else, cowboys do have different values than a lot of people today. We like simple things, a simple way of life. When you get down and start being serious, you're just plain afraid people are going to laugh at you.

*Art Troutner is an inventor and architect from Boise. He was a founder of the Trus-Joist Company and, at the time of the interview, vice president of T.J. Intertnational, its successor company. He discussed his work at one of the houses he designed and built near Hagerman.*

Good architecture is a combination of both art and engineering. I like to call it poetic engineering—engineering that is art. The simpler the engineering is, the more poetic it becomes. The simplest solution is often the most difficult to arrive at.

I don't think there is an Idaho style of architecture. Most of it comes from California. The condominium style of California has been a big influence in most of the larger cities and places like Sun Valley. Condominiums have a powerful style, but often the architect has more ego than natural talent.

In the old Idaho towns, local materials were used—like logs and dirt roofs. In isolated areas people may have used a lot of lava rock, which you still see around. In general, styles in Idaho have been imported from other places.

***Art Troutner***

This house was a combination of high-tech engineering and wood. It was made possible by the use of Micro=Lam©, laminated veneer lumber. You can make almost any size and any length, which is different than most of the wood that you use. The biggest drawback in solid sawn wood is the size of the defects in the wood. It is very difficult to grade out the defects and use the wood. The variability in the strength is very high.

With Micro=Lam© we found that the smaller the defect, the stronger it is and the less variability. We start out with a tenth of an inch thick veneer. The thinner the veneer is, the smaller the possible defect is. By spreading those small defects around, you get a piece of wood that is much more structurally sound than solid sawn wood. It opens up new vistas in engineering with wood. The box beams and other structural materials are made out of Micro=Lam©.

The beams are large, but they're hollow and light. Yet they are very stiff and strong. The beams are fifty feet long. You would never be able to get solid sawn structural lumber in that dimension.

In developing the idea, the site for the house is most important. One consideration here was to site the house where it would be remote from other houses.

We are on a cliff overlooking the reservoir. Part of the idea was to be able to get away from the traffic on the reservoir. But from the living room you can see the reservoir all the way up and down. So from part of the house you get away from it, and from another part, you don't.

I spent about two or three years coming back to this site. It was not all because of architectural considerations. But this site does lend itself to it. I just kept coming back to it.

I came at different times of the year. That helped to dictate the height of the house. I wanted to be able to have patios where you could be in or out of the sun. With the three points on this patio, any one part is always in the shade and part is in the sun.

I think the house in Idaho I like most is probably the Frank Lloyd Wright house in the Hagerman Valley. I have always liked his style. It fits the site very well. It is artistic. Most of his buildings were an art form.

I like to think that in order to put a proper building on a site, it has to improve the site, rather than detract from it. Some of the worst architecture is probably around Sun Valley, in the condominiums. You get huge areas of very severe buildings, all exactly alike, up in the beautiful foothills. It is definitely a detraction rather than an addition to the site. There is one building up there that is a fine building, though, the Sawtooth National Recreation Area Headquarters. It fits the site very well. The theme fits it, too.

The site comes first, but you also have to consider the client. That's why I like to build my own houses—I'm the client. But the site and the architect are both present in any building. You can't separate the two.

The most unique structure I was involved with was the Kibbie Dome, the stadium at the University of Idaho at Moscow. At the time it was the longest span wood structure in the world. It was the first to use Micro=lam© in that large a structure, a four hundred foot span. The length of the arch is about four hundred and fifty feet. It won the American Society of Civil Engineers Structure of the Year award when we put it up in 1975.

There is no stress for me in putting up an innovative building. Sometimes management gets a little stressed out, but I just have fun with it. A new structure has to meet fairly stringent engineering standards. The Moscow stadium was probably a little conservative in its design. You build in an extra safety factor, so each element supports another one. You can't have a total collapse of a structure of that type.

I was born here in Idaho, went to high school and college in Idaho. Ever since I got out of college, work has been the center of my life. I started Trus Deck Corporation with Harold Thomas very soon after I got out of college. It turned into Trus Joist. Inventing things is even more interesting than architecture, because it's more demanding. It has a wider horizon. I hold about forty patents.

The zeppelin was one project that, while it was a fun project, was sort of a flop. Ideas always start out as a flop. You have to develop them. That's the key—to be able to develop a product once you've decided that there is a market for it. It doesn't discourage you. You have to remember that the Germans during World War II fired off three thousand V-2 rockets before they found one that would work. Now that would be discouraging.

We're working now on several new products and manufacturing processes. We are working on a press that will speed up the process of making Micro=Lam©, and make it more economical at the same time. We're working on a whole new series of open-web joists. A lot of things are in the fire just now.

The amount of time to bring an idea to completion depends on the complexity of the product. If the product is very complex, then you find yourself making a lot of expensive junk. You try things and they don't work, you throw them away, and go on from there. In Research and Development we have to do that in order to accomplish anything. If you don't make a lot of expensive junk, you're not doing your job. It's hard to convince top management of that theory, but that's the way it is.

*Bert Russell writes about the life and history of the logging communities of North Idaho from his home in Harrison.*

*Courtesy of Bert Russell*

**Bert Russell**

I started writing when I was still in high school. I had no idea what I wanted to write except I wanted to write about the country I lived in—the area and the logging. I began to be aware of it and work at it. At the end of World War II, I went to Hollywood and took a class in writing. My dad knew I wanted to write, and one night he gave me a check for five thousand dollars, and said, "If you want to write, why don't you go do it?" So that's where I went.

Since that time my interest is in writing something I know to be true—the lives of people I've worked with, the place I'm in. I wasn't interested in money, particularly, except that I financed myself, published my own books, and sold them to get my money back and maybe a little on top of it, too. I've sold 17,000 copies of *Caulked Boots*, but that's the most I've sold.

As far as I know, my books don't have a wide appeal. The people who have grown up in this country recognize the area and the kind of people who were here. Perhaps I hoped they would reach a wider readership. But if it sacrificed a general readership for the local one, I'd rather have the local.

My stories are a result of my own imagination picking out the things in my background that I think are important. Some of them are like oral history books. You get information right out of the person you're talking to. I'm able to understand the kind of a story I'm getting and put it into words that make it into an interesting story.

The story I'm working on now is a story of a sawmill, the people in it, the ownerships. It is a story that happened in my own family. I'll use different names here and there, but that's what it is. I think reality is so much more interesting than fiction. You can't play with the facts—they allow us certain yardage all right—but you can't just dream them up. The family in the story went through the days when small businesses competed with big operators like Potlatch and Diamond Match. Those people ate you alive.

For example, my dad and his company were unable to buy white pine in

*Spirit*

## BERT RUSSELL'S CHILDHOOD AT A BOX FACTORY

In the box factory they hired kids like myself to nail box ends. In those days apple, pear, and fruit boxes were made of wood. Lumber companies could get rid of low grade lumber by having it cut up short for boxes. You could cut out the knots and flaws as you go. We kids made the tops and bottoms.

One time a fellow who worked there with us put his name and his address on the end of a banana case end. Everybody decided to join in. About six months later he got a message from the depot that his shipment had arrived. He got a complete stem of bananas. The news spread like magic. Pretty soon the boss came around and said, "The next one who puts his name and address on a box is going to get fired forever out of this outfit. Our customers are driving us crazy." So they put a stop to it. He scared all of us kids who worked in the nailing room. "We will throw you in jail." That was enough to stop us.

I was ten or eleven years old. There was no such thing as child labor laws. They could have hired you right out of the cradle if you had been worth it. It wasn't all bad. You could work for an outfit like that and be among men and learn what it is to work eight hours a day. There wasn't a break between being a boy and man. You were associating with men who were running the machines and you got broken in to that kind of a life.

Sometimes it was a little rough; if you got sassy they'd throw you down on the floor and spit tobacco juice in your ear. If you got sassy over that, they'd pull down your pants and take a wad of grease and shove it down and then they'd squish it around to make sure it got spread. There was a certain amount of breaking in to it all, initiation.

Of course, the first thing you had to learn was to swear. If you didn't swear, you were finished. By the time a guy eighteen years old takes you by the back of the neck and bangs your head on the floor and says, "Say 'goddamned,'" you say it pretty quick. It doesn't come out easy because you know you will go to hell for sure if you do it. On the other hand, this guy is banging your head. Well that was part of the initiation.

I remember one time—this is kind of wicked, you probably wouldn't want to use this in your program—the boss had hired two young women to come and work. They tailed machines. The men pushed the lumber, and the women caught it, stacked and piled it, and counted as they went. We had heard all kind of things about how women are built. But we didn't know. There was no such thing as naked pictures in those days. So we wanted to see what a girl looked like. They were older than we were, sixteen or seventeen years old. We were just little snots, as they called us. The company built an extra toilet for the women to use. It was in the part of the mill that sat over the water. So we went down there and saw to it that there was an old log that would float us pretty good under the building. We went down there and made a bunch of snowballs. We planned to throw and hit them, and listen to them squeal, and at the same time get a look.

As luck would have it, one of the guys who worked with us, an older man, tipped off the girls that we were going down there. So they never did use the toilet from that moment on. We stood there waiting with our snowballs ready. Just about that time, here came a bare bottom down on the men's side. We threw those snowballs and we hit that white butt as square as could be. There was a curse up above, and the butt disappeared. We ran over to the bank and up the steps into the building. When we got there, we rushed for the nailing room. Here was the boss, standing right there: "You're fired, you're fired, you're fired, you're fired." We all went home crying our lungs out. It had been our ill luck to hit him. He happened to be the one on the can. We never were able to satisfy our curiosity as to what a woman looked like.

But it was a great time to grow up. They made you grow up whether you wanted to or not.

competition with the big companies. It was "hands off" the white pine if you were a small operator. If you didn't want trouble, you had to stay out of it. You had to take sales that either didn't have white pine in them, or you had to sell any white pine that you logged to the big operators. It was pitiful, really. As a young man in high school, I used to tow a little bunch of white pine logs from Harrison to Coeur d'Alene with a gasoline launch and deliver them to Potlatch to prove to them that we were letting them have all our white pine and not operating in competition with them. They in turn would give me enough mixed logs of the same monetary value to take back home. I felt it was demeaning to my father that he had to do that.

The reason I wrote this book was because I felt that something needed to be said. I think something is happening nationally to our country. When you throw away anti-trust laws, and let the big companies combine with other ones, to the point where there aren't any little businesses, you don't have capitalism. You don't have competition. You have something that is going to destroy the nation. I believe that firmly and politically. We can't afford to do that to ourselves. It isn't right. You can't allow a guy, just because he has political pull and is bigger financially, to smash somebody else. It is the law. That's the reason I wanted to put the book into print. It shows how it happens.

I guess there are bad-apple characters in my books because I'm convinced there are a lot of bad-apple people. But there are sure a hell of a lot of good people too. I didn't make up those stories. I was seeking to find out what made people tick, the good, the bad, and the in-betweens. That is the fascination about people. There are no two alike.

*Bert Russell at 18*

*Penelope Reedy lived in Fairfield as this interview was made. She is the editor of* The Redneck Review *and a writer who now lives in Twin Falls.*

Solitude is being comfortable with yourself when you are by yourself. Isolation is being out of contact with things that are important. Idaho artists have been both comfortable and uncomfortable. I think some good work comes out of solitude, but I don't think isolation is very constructive, it's pretty negative. People have to find ways to make contact. Because of the isolation I experienced, I started publishing the magazine as a way to make contact. When I lived on the Camas Prairie, the mailbox was the most important thing I owned.

I call it *The Redneck Review*. In the beginning we called it *The Camas*. That was dull. The rarest issue was called *Sideroad*; there were only fifty copies of it. Local people in Fairfield bought it because they thought it was history. Were they surprised! We called it the *Fairfield Tractor Company* one year, thinking the title would encourage local people to read it. We did an *Operator's Manual to the Fairfield Tractor Company*, and another called *Guns and Grammar* one time. The idea struck me for the *The Redneck Review*. We sold out. Tourists coming through town on Highway 20 bought it. I've called it that ever since. People hear it and they laugh. It's an oxymoron—redneck and literature. It's being able to laugh at ourselves about who we are.

I look to the evolution of the magazine. It started out as a tabloid that we had professionally laid out and printed on newsprint. The next year we did the layout ourselves. Then we decided we wanted to do it in book form, so we used a

*Penelope Reedy*

mimeograph machine, had covers printed, and stapled it all together. One year we had it done offset and bought our own paper. We didn't understand about putting together signatures, so we just had the staple in the middle. It looked horrible. I've published some really strange-looking magazines over the years. A lot of that came from living out in the middle of nowhere. Camas Prairie is not exactly a metropolitan area. There were no other printers or people around. Every time we needed a piece of equipment, it was a one hundred mile drive to get something. Instead of driving, we'd look around to see what we could use to make do.

I see publishing as a means of allowing people to see themselves. That's what writing really is: speaking the unspeakable. Everybody knows things, but the artist is able to say it in a painting or with words. People can identify with it, because they already know it.

But art angers people. Sherwood Anderson angered people in his hometown with his book *Winesburg, Ohio*. Grace Metalius angered people with *Peyton Place*. The same thing is happening in Idaho now. People are finally saying what is true and what is real. It can be very upsetting because people tend to think they have the world figured out. When someone says what they know, we have to respond to it, to deal with it.

I see it in my work. I've been working on a novel for three years. It concerns three generations of women in southern Idaho. The things I'm able to say, I could not have said ten years ago. It is about simple things that really happened. But it upsets people when they read it. I published a couple of other stories, and it bothered people. They say, "You can't say things like that." I say, "Why not?"

The West was settled during the Victorian era. One of my professors remarked that Victorian values didn't affect Western women at all. They were too busy plowing and dealing with real life. I said, "Why were they plowing in dresses?" Women were looking for the genteel tea party. These women must have been miserable. For a woman to write realistically was not "nice" during that time, so women didn't. We find things now in journals that are more realistic. I grew up thinking it wasn't nice to tell the truth. But life really isn't interesting unless you do.

I'm not interested in reminiscences about how nice it was in the canyon and the cabin. I don't believe those things are true. It's something I discovered about sentimentality. Psychologists talk about denial systems. Sentimentality fits right into that. Some people have had hard lives, and they can't really say the things they experienced. So they write sentimental, nostalgic things.

I came across an extreme example in a newspaper three or four years ago. There is an organization called World of Poetry, which sponsors contests. The work that they publish is sentimental stuff. The winner of their contest this particular year was a fellow in the Idaho State Penitentiary. The poem was real sing-songy, hearts-and-flowers, a "people say life isn't good, but look around: everything is nice" poem. It was awful. I found out that this man was in prison for the mutilation and murder of a woman near Pocatello. The contrast between his life, and the agony that he was probably experiencing but denying, and the poem struck me. That is what sentimentality is; it hides things, and people hide behind it. I think if you scraped off the surface of those kinds of works, you would find a lot of anger, a lot of agony, and a lot of real difficult things. I'm not saying that sentimentality is all bad because it is, after all, a survival technique that people need from time to time, but I don't want to publish it.

I'm starting to receive works I call "conscious literature." The writers here are starting to see themselves and their lives for what they really are. They are starting to explore their emotional existence. Leslie Leek, who lives in Pocatello, published a book called *The Heart of a Western Woman.* Her stories deny the whole concept of the "Western woman." There used to be two choices in Western literature for the female character—the prim and proper school ma'am on a pedestal, or the "whore with the heart of gold." It always seemed that hunting and drinking beer on a mountaintop were male activities. Leslie's characters are women who are living real lives. On a first reading, without being used to that, you say, "Well, this doesn't seem real or right." But then you think, "I do those things. Perhaps this is my life." I think she has broken some good ground.

I've had very religious people tell me that because writing means so much to me, I should give it up. I've been trying to figure out why. If God gives you a talent, it seems to me, you're supposed to use it. I suppose this idea goes back to the work ethic—physical labor has meaning. You hear that writers and artists are "lazy," because their lifestyle isn't the same as everyone else's. You hear someone say, "He's probably never done a full day's work in his life." They mean with a pick and shovel. But writing is hard work. You don't just sit down and write. You revise and revise, and revise and revise. Nothing is an accident. I think science is more accidental than art. Many scientific discoveries have been accidents, just the reverse of what you might think. Art is a very conscious activity.

*William Studebaker is a poet and also teaches at the College of Southern Idaho in Twin Falls.*

I just started writing poems. In the old fashioned sense, I was strangely touched by the muse. I wrote what I thought were poems. I packed them around and showed them to people, and they all said, "That's nice." (I was about sixteen.) I wrote a whole stack of them—a big stack. Finally, I burned them all.

*William Studebaker*

When I went to the university, I signed up for creative writing, wrote a short story, a terrible short story. Then one day I was walking, thinking, "You're in creative writing and this is not going to work. How are you going to pass creative writing?" I was walking through some leaves on campus, and I started kicking them. I wrote a poem and took it in. The teacher gave me an A on it. And I thought, "Hmm, this is it. This is what I should do." So I started writing. Writing and writing and writing—a lot of poems. I published a poem, then went five years without publishing any more. But I kept on writing...that one moment was essentially it.

Then one day I was in the bookstore, and I picked up a collection of poems by John Haynes, an Alaskan poet, and read them. That was really a big step because he was writing very close to home. He was writing about Alaska, living in the wilderness and giving it significance that went far beyond the wilderness. I said, "I can do this, too. I can do this about my life. I can do this about Idaho. I can write John Haynes-type poetry about where I live, and people elsewhere will read it." As soon as I did that, I started publishing more and more.

I'm pursuing what I consider to be the essence of Idaho. The essence of Idaho is not what most people know. It's not what we put on our billboards. It's not what we advertise in our brochures. The essence of Idaho is what exists for the ordinary person who is out and about in the environment, community, the desert, mountains. It's for the person who is a very good observer.

One of my favorite lines is "my woman stands like Blue-eyed Grass." If you haven't seen blue-eyed grass at six thousand feet on a June morning, you haven't seen blue-eyed grass. I can't help it. I have, and it impressed me. It is a little tiny flower, and once you see it, you cannot not see it again. It's forever, but not on our brochures.

I have expanded my interest from Idaho to the Intermountain West. I think they are synonymous terms. Utah, Nevada, and Idaho are states that share a lot. They are ignored historically and still not very heavily populated. They are probably going to end up as government reserves of one sort or another. The Native Americans who lived here used the whole area and wouldn't recognize the borders. Art in Idaho is art in Nevada and vice-versa. Culture in Idaho is culture in Utah. So, I write poems about Nevada and Utah, as well as Idaho, with the same sort of fathering and husbandry.

It is my goal to write full time. But it's not my goal in terms of making money. I don't know of a poet in the United States who is making a living full-time writing poetry. They may be making money translating, teaching part-time, giving lectures, writing novels—or living on inherited money. So, it can't be a full-time job. But I do want to be a full-time poet. As soon as I find the means to make a living that would take less time than I'm spending now, or when my ship comes in, that's what I would do. I'd grab the dingy and go with half the load. There are a lot of people who consider themselves full-time writers because they write and teach writing. But I don't consider that full-time writing. I write and teach writing.

**AFTER TWO MONTHS IN
THE OWYHEE DESERT**
by William Studebaker

My woman stands thin as Blue-eyed Grass.
Around her, heat waves hug the shape she is
while her arm, waving, speaks across
the distance I must still travel.

The days I've been gone come from behind,
old dogs at heel, strong and quick now,
nose to the wind, looking for the scent
of a warm bed, a familiar hand.

Like the full song of the Mourning Dove,
her voice fills out what the wind misses.
All my years come to bay.
Distance closes between us.
And in her the desert ends.

A patronage system would help. I was on sabbatical once and wrote my best pieces. I had a check coming in; I had all day to think about writing; and writing takes a lot of thinking. A lot of it. A patron system would work, would help, would be beneficial. But it obviously has its problems. A patron probably has a birthday and would want a poem. When Robert Penn Warren was asked to be the first poet laureate of the United States, he asked, "Does this require occasional verse?" When they said it didn't, he said, "I'll take the job." He wasn't about to do occasional verse. The patron system has its drawbacks. I don't think poetry is different than other arts. I envy novelists, and I envy certain visual artists because there is money to be made.

I don't know if the climate of acceptance for artists has changed in Idaho or if the environment of Idaho's tolerance has changed. I think I've changed. I may not hear the derogatory comments as much as I used to. I may not pick up on the nuances that people throw out when I say I'm a writer, a poet. That's what I am, and I can't afford to be concerned about what other people think of me because I write. I've been told in earth-shaking tones that psychologists think poets are effeminate. What is that supposed to do to me? That's categorical of artists. I ignore it and go about my business, tune up my own car, build my own house, and I'll worry about being effeminate later.

I don't think Idahoans ever thought art was a luxury. That's a misconception. Artists have always been prominent in this state. People have never seen it as a luxury, but may not have had the time to spend on it that they wanted. All the territorial newspapers published poems. Lots of poems. It has only been fairly recently that our newspapers haven't published poetry. Every town had two or three newspapers—with all the art that went into the production of them.

Idahoans purchase quite a bit of art. It's their taste that I think is more the case in point. Idahoans are principally realists, pragmatic. They're not cultured in the significance of abstractions. They don't realize how much time they spend dreaming, how much time they spend involved in abstractions themselves. They think that anything of value has an object in it, an identifiable object. The question here would be the kind of art as opposed to the amount or the availability of it.

I would like to consider myself the kind of artist who gets totally absorbed. But I can't be. I have too many children. I have jobs. I write because I must, whatever that means. And I don't think it needs to be explained. I write because I have chosen to write. I write because it rewards me. I feel good about a poem when I finish it. A poem for me is kind of a secular epiphany. It's an experience that awakens me to the reality of something that I wasn't fully aware of until I investigated it and delved into it—wrote a poem about it.

I'm going to make an effort to incorporate, as late as it is, more science into my work. Too many poems are rooted in medieval theology and philosophy. I see myself as aware of this, and wanting to make a shift to science metaphors that deal with things that are still in the environment. It's very difficult because the training in poetry takes you back to medieval concepts. It won't be the kind of science that is *science*. It won't be addressing science. It will simply be using the vocabulary. For example, I will assume that you know what a pion is. I use the word pion now for light, for glue, for subatomic structure. I will use the word quantum more frequently. I'll talk about quantum grammars. I'll use the notion of anti-physics, of waves verses photons. The assumption behind the work is that you too have to know science and have it be consciously employed by you. I think it will be easier for you than medieval theology. It will gain some sort of readership because I will be modernizing my metaphors.

I'm going to pursue my interest in the Intermountain West, using the metaphoric base of science, modern American language, and western idioms. I'm still going to try to say things that are significant about the Intermountain West, significant to people who know the Intermountain West, not necessarily to those who don't.

I've considered getting political. I think we've got some big battles to face in the West. Not to win or lose but to find the right answer. Bombing ranges, gold mining, nuclear plants, coal-fire generators, water rights—all of those are big issues for the West. Writers, artists, and poets have to have a social-political stand. I'm going to be moving in those directions.

*Rosalie Sorrels of Grimes Creek is a storyteller, songwriter and singer, author of* Way Out in Idaho, *a collection of Idaho folk songs planned for publication in honor of the Idaho Centennial of Statehood.*

One of the great things about the folk song collection project is to find out how exotic Idaho is, with all its pockets of people. It's hard to attribute a single characteristic to all the music. That's what the character of the music is: it is diverse, hard to describe. One of the things you notice in the ethnic group songs is a thread of yearning for the place that has been left. There is a continual reference to how hard it is here, but also how beautiful it is. Often the songs dwell on how you have to hold on to the things left behind, or you will be erased and forgotten in this hard place.

One of the first stops we made, as we began this odyssey through the state, was at Buhl. I saw a group of Czechoslovakian ladies, many of them dressed in traditional costumes. They made wonderful food, kolatchi and strudel. My favorite part was when they sang together, sixteen women, some second generation, who still speak Czechoslovakian. They sing their songs in the beautiful style you find in Yugoslavia. They don't have the full-throated sound of some of the singers I've heard, but they put their arms around one another and move together when they're singing, and sing in beautiful harmony.

They sang in Czechoslovakian: "Our pretty Czech songs are like those precious pearls, lovingly strung on a string. There is much beauty in them, and it's a great sin it should be so oppressed. This is our beautiful Czech song, so lovely, lovely begun. Just like a flower in

*Rosalie Sorrels*

the meadow grew our beautiful song. If ever our song becomes lost, then nothing else will remain. Should it once perish, all else with it will vanish. Even we, no more then will live."

The Basques have a lovely little children's song called "Aurrak," which is a word for children age seven through thirteen, or so. It says: "Children, you should learn the songs, and you should learn the steps to the dance, or it will be forgotten." Another one from the Mexicans has that same theme: "I am a poor Mexican with one sorrow, to be of my ways because I am alone, looking for a way of life for my children, for my mother, for my dear wife. The Gringos tell me every time they see me, 'Chicano what are you seeking?' I seek my life. Later they turn around and tell me, 'A Mexican always has a lost life.' I am poor and humble and I am not sorry to look for my wife. I am not ashamed. I sing my songs to all my compatriots, don't you forget that I am a Mexican. I'm a poor Chicano field worker, united with all my race in the United States, because poverty has brought me to this land, in the land where they say you find riches. I am poor and humble. I am a Mexican."

Ethnic songs have more sense of identity than songs from people more settled because identity is held as so much more precious. Czechoslovakians are not easy to tell walking down the street, but they gave up a country and a place to live to come to a place that's unforgiving in terms of poverty and geography. Those are the things they hold the tightest to. That is one of the characteristics of all the music of Idaho. Even the Indians still have that need to connect to something sacred, like the earth. Something solid.

The sense of passing things on from the old generation to the new generation is much stronger among ethnic groups than it is among mainstream middle-class people, who tend to care more about things and possessions. They lose sight of how important those things are, because they don't have a really hard time. Their times of deepest sorrow or trouble are only in certain parts of their lives. We aren't threatened by death and destruction, we haven't had a lot of war visit our country. But when you live in deep poverty, and suddenly find yourself faced with riots and possible death, the thing that can save you is the little fragment of song that you inherited from your grandmother. That's the only thing that will comfort you in the dark and the depth of despair. It's much more important than almost any number of things you could collect in your life. When you die, you remember the comfort that you received as a baby. That's how important those things are, and a lot of times they don't survive or live in an easy middle-class life, because nobody needs them.

Folk music is music that people use in their lives. That's what distinguishes it from popular entertainment and art. It's something that everyone knows, instinctively.

I don't think I write folk songs, except for a couple. I did write one song called "I'm Gonna Tell on You," which is a folk song. It is a children's song. People know it all over the country. They don't know that I wrote it, which is the first test of a folk song. If you know who wrote it and associate it with that person, it usually isn't a folk song. People write verses to that song all the time. Many people have adopted it. I made it up out of things my children said to one another. Mostly, "I'm gonna tell on you."

People don't sing most of my songs. A lot of people ask me to sing "Traveling Lady." A lot of women like that song and identify with it. They identify with it on their own terms and have no idea why I wrote it. If they did know what I meant by it, they wouldn't like it. They put their own story into it. They adopt it for their own use, but they want me to sing it. They project an idea of me onto me, but that has nothing to do with me. I sang it one time to a group of feminists up in Portland. They were all pretty young. Most of them were at that place of life where they couldn't wait to get out of their houses. They assumed that was why I wrote about my "big fine house I used to live in that I don't answer the bell to anymore." But I loved that house, giving it up was really hard for me. When I told them that, they were angry. Then they asked me what it was like to ride in a freight train. I said I had never been in a freight train in my life. Then they were really angry. They said, "Your album has a picture of you on a train." I said, "Yeah, but if you look at it closely, you'll see it's a big silver flyer, not a freight train." You don't hop a freight train with five children! None of them had five children. They couldn't relate to the role they had cast me in without knowing who I was. They felt like I had led them astray by writing this song and putting a picture of myself on a train on this album.

A lot of the songs that I have written are very particular to me. They're very personal and nobody else would ever sing them. Where I come back to the people in my performance is the story I tell which goes with the song. I always choose a story that I think that everyone will have experienced in some way or another. That's why people think of me as a folk singer, but most of my writing is not.

I will always remember a concert I did in Two Harbors, Minnesota. It was way the hell out in the middle of nowhere. It was the dead of winter, so cold, snow was up to my chin. I went to Duluth and got in a car with these people. It took forever through this cold wasteland to get to this little place.

## TRAVELIN' LADY
### By Rosalie Sorrels

I used to live in a big fine house
With many rooms and a wide open door,
And all of my friends came to visit me there,
But I don't answer that bell anymore.

I used to live in a big fine house
I had rooms for twenty friends or more,
Now I run begging from lover to friend
For a pallet on any old floor.

*Chorus*:
Oh I've gotten to be quite a rambler
Going by land and by sea,
And once it was aprons and dishpans and such,
But now I'm a travelin' lady.

Once it was me that gave all the parties,
I baked the bread, I spread the feast, I poured the wine.
Now I receive all my friends in a bar,
And none of the glasses are mine.

But the bars hold notions of freedom,
And drinking with friends or all alone,
I find being one with the wind and the rain
Fogs over the windows of home.

*Chorus*

There's no more rooms to retire to,
I've got to move, there's no place to stay.
I've nothing that's mine but my shadow,
If you need one, I'll give that away.

*Chorus*

There was hardly anything there—a post office and an Elks Hall, which was kind of a grange hall, a general store, and some little houses. But there was this big play hall, with a large log cabin, large-looking place, which was the pizza parlor and the public meeting hall. And that's where I did the concert. There were four hundred people there. I don't know where in the hell they found four hundred people. They got them from all kinds of little towns like that around there. They came through weather twenty-seven degrees below zero.

They stood in line for me to talk to. Nearly everyone of the four hundred wanted to talk to me and say they were so glad I came. Nobody ever does that. That concert was put on by a real character named Paul Iverson, who belongs to the International Workers of the World, a radical. He didn't have the money to guarantee me a fee, so he got an entertainment coalition put together—a ladies' sewing circle, a rabid feminist group from Duluth, the hockey team, and the Elks—and this IWW person put this concert on. They all got along great together, which doesn't seem possible.

I think folk music makes it possible for everyone to get together. I'm religious on this subject. I believe that if you eat the food that everyone in a place eats, the food that is peculiar to those people and particular to that place, and if you listen to their poets, not their famous poets, but their people's poets, and if you sing together and dance together, and listen to the music that everyone knows, you can't be enemies. I believe that's the way to save the world. The food that's particular to a place usually is because of what's there. You can learn to live with that easier than anything fancy. The music is the same. The words come about because they are the most necessary things. If you find the music that people who live there play, you can't hold hatred in those circumstances.

When I go away from Idaho, I'm like a chameleon. I'm happy in a lot of places. When I tell stories about Idaho, which I do in a lot of different places, people identify with me just as much or maybe more than the people of Idaho do. I'm talking about people who live on a farm or in a mountain cabin. They do that everywhere. I use my place in Idaho, my handmade nest, as my own frame of reference. The reason I'm able to feel comfortable is because I have this place to be in, in my head.

I don't know that I could ever have done what I've done without having this place to refer to in my head. It makes me feel very centered. It is like a taproot. I take a lot of strength from it. It's almost like being rooted wherever I go, just knowing that it's here. That's very important to me. It's probably the thing I use to center myself to relate to everyone.

*Dick and Barbara Young\* organized and operated the Salmon River Playhouse at Salmon for ten years.*

DICK: I practiced dentistry in Salt Lake City for a few years before we came to Salmon. I was single at the time and Barbara was singing in a choir that I was singing in also. We got acquainted and got married. Her folks had a nice ranch in Mud Lake, which is about halfway between Salmon and Idaho Falls. We wanted to come up, be a part of the ranch, and still practice dentistry. When we heard that Salmon needed a dentist we looked it over and liked it. That was twenty-eight years ago.

BARBARA: When we came here, I used to do a lot of singing and I worked with the music teacher at the school. I helped her with operettas and other productions. There seemed to be a hunger for that. Salmon is so isolated that we felt if something were here, it would be a drawing point not only for local people, but for tourists. We are, as you well know, rather distant from larger areas.

    I guess The Playhouse was born because Dick and I both came from backgrounds that liked theater. We used to take our children to Montana or Utah to different shows. We kept thinking, "Salmon needs something like this." For several years we looked for a facility to become available. When a church building came up for sale, we said, "Shall we take the plunge?" It was May 10, 1979. It was like jumping off a big ship into the ocean.

DICK: In May and June, we had to rebuild the church to accommodate a theater, get all the advertising out, build the stage and get the audience chairs. We found a place in Montana that was tearing an old theater down. They said, "Sure, come and get these chairs. You can have them for three dollars a chair. Just come and tear down all you want."

    So, Merrill Barney, who had been the Salmon High School drama director and always wanted a summer theater, and I took some U-hauls up there and spent two days tearing out benches and chairs. We put them in the theater here. It was exciting and busy those first few months. If we had looked at the costs to see if we could make it or not, I don't imagine we ever would have done it. But we just did it.

**Dick and Barbara Young**

BARBARA: We looked at the successes of

*Barbara Young died on May 25, 1990

C  O  N  V  E  R  S  A  T  I  O  N  S

the people in Montana and other places and thought, "We're so isolated it's a natural thing." We expected to make a killing, and it about killed us all. It was quite a shock to all of us. We had a love for theater, but when it came right down to the cost, the surprises came afterward. We didn't expect to get rich, but we thought that the community would help make it pay and expand.

DICK: A great many people in this community have supported the Salmon River Playhouse. We could not have stayed in business ten years if they hadn't. We have people who will sometimes see a single show two or three times. They just keep coming back and want the same seat every time they come. Many businesses have contributed to help the theater along.

We've never taken any government money. We have been independent all ten years. We are able to say what we want, do what we want, and do what plays we want. We don't have anyone to answer to, except ourselves. If we fail, we fail; if we succeed, we succeed.

A lot of funny things happened over the years. People can get very involved sometimes. In *Bus Stop* one night, at the end of the show the lead walks off the stage and is supposed to leave his luggage onstage. There was a fellow in the front row who stood right up and said, "Hey, you forgot your luggage." The whole house broke down. The actors had to walk offstage because everyone was laughing so hard.

A lot of times you just watch the audience instead of the show. If they're sitting on the edge of their seats, totally involved in the show and someone is sneaking in the door, they'll start pointing toward the door and say, "Look out." It makes it all worthwhile to see people become so involved they lose their sense of responsibility, you might say.

BARBARA: We've had a couple of directors say, "What's your budget for this play?" We were so naive we didn't even think about a budget. All I knew was that the royalty kept going up, the price of playbooks kept going up.

Being realistic, re-using materials, and not thinking there is a Santa Claus who will pick up the tab is important. But in order for a community to keep a theater going, you have to delegate. You have to depend on people but not bore them or burn them out on the same task, year after year. That takes work all the time. When we have been short an actor, I have hit up somebody on the street to come over and audition. Some of those people who have been real first-class capital letter introverts, have changed their personality through that experience and they loved it.

It is difficult to say what our hits were because plays appeal to different people. We did *Our Town*, and there were those who raised their eyebrows about that. Others said it was the finest show we had ever put on. We promoted that show as *Salmon, Idaho, Our Town*. Those familiar with it, loved it.

*Annie Get Your Gun* probably had more appeal; who can go wrong with Irving Berlin? It was well done and the fact that we could do it on our stage was a real tribute to the creative director. You never go wrong with *Miracle Worker*. I would say that *Miracle Worker, Annie Get Your Gun, Our Town, Arsenic and Old Lace*, and this last show that we put on, *Abbie's Irish Rose*, have been our most popular.

But then, how do you evaluate successes? Is it by the attendance? Every year our attendance has increased. If you go on that basis, the last play we did was the most successful, because we had the highest attendance. Yet a couple of plays—*Mousetrap* and *Angel Street*—were very well done, but had lower attendance because a lot of people don't like mystery plays. The quality wasn't any less than the others. It depends on the measuring stick you use.

DICK: Over the years, almost five hundred people from this little valley have participated in one way or another in the theater. We feel quite proud that we have been able to put together something where so many people have benefitted by it. Young people who had never been on a stage before because they were so frightened would start helping with the sets, just wanting to be around. Eventually they would take a small part, then large parts. Just seeing them grow has been well worth it.

We have been on our own in doing this. Due to Barbara's persistence we have been able to stay in business for ten years. We hate to see it stop, but there comes a time when it just can't go on any longer.

BARBARA: We shouldn't leave the impression that we have done this whole thing together, because we certainly have not. Eight or ten people have been with us from the beginning, including all our children. Several in the community have struggled and sweated and worried and been there with us. But the bottom line is that we're the ones who have to see that the insurance and taxes get paid on the building, but others are certainly supportive.

We approached the city for certain things that were necessary, but frankly were turned down. It was a shame, because a lot of businessmen and chamber of commerce men have the foresight to see what that theater could do for this town. Others do not. For those who were totally supportive, it has been frustrating. They can see, particularly as time has gone on, that there has been financial gain for this town.

We would like to see the Salmon River Playhouse go on, but we've reached the end of our energy, you might say. Four of our five children have moved. They've grown up and gone. They were among the more willing to give up their time and do things. Our oldest son, who is quite musical, did a great professional jingle for us. He recorded it in Las Vegas this year. Even though they're away, they still try to contribute. So there is this beautifully plowed field, and we would like to see it go on. Many people come up and say, "Oh, we hate to see this close. Won't someone take it over?" But there aren't very many people who are willing to commit to the work.

*James Ogle conducts the Boise philharmonic orchestra in Boise.*

I was the most normal roll-in-the-dirt, play-baseball, ride-your-bicycle kind of kid that you could possibly find. Yet early in my life because of the exposure I had to music, in my case through playing an instrument in a junior high school band, something touched me that caused me to want to pursue music and ultimately make it my life's work. I think that potential exists for every human being.

The sound of that junior high band was really exciting to me. I was fascinated by moving my fingers and creating a sound. I practiced because I liked the sound. I liked moving my fingers fast. I loved practicing scales because it was fun. I'm sure a lot of that had to do with the fine instruction that I received early on. I had some very talented mentors who helped me to develop. Another thing, and this may or may not be true for musicians in general, was that I was good at it. We all gravitate to things that we're good at. We get gratification from it and we get praised for it. In my school, the athletes certainly were well respected, but so were the people on the drama team who excelled, and so were the musicians. I received notoriety for it and it felt good.

There is an inherent problem in a symphony orchestra. It is so labor intensive that's it's very expensive to produce the product. When you take those eighty people, you have to pay them for the four or five rehearsals it took to produce the concert. By the time you get to the concert your costs are quite high. Even if you sold out the house, the cost of a reasonably affordable ticket actually represents less than half the cost of producing the event.

So we are constantly having to find ways to make up the difference between ticket sales and the cost of the product. In most businesses you consider yourself successful when you're able to sell your product on a large scale, but a symphony orchestra is just the reverse. The more often you play, the more money you lose. Consequently, the more intensified your fund-raising efforts have to be, and the more dependent you become on help from foundations and corporations.

The Morrison Center is unbelievable to play in. That this facility could exist anywhere would be a remarkable tribute to the community that had the good sense to build it. That it exists in a community of 100,000 or so people is really remarkable. We certainly give credit to the architects, but they would admit readily that, while you can measure acoustical phenomena to the nth degree, you can't really predict whether a hall is going to sound good or not or whether the musicians are going to be able to hear each other well onstage. It has a lot to do with being darn lucky, and in our case we were very lucky.

In every audience there are as many reasons for being there as there are people there. For some people, that reason is to have a nice evening out and to wear nice

*James Ogle*

clothes and to go out to dinner beforehand. Those are sometimes the people who are the most generous in helping to fund the particular arts event. We certainly couldn't exist without them. On the other end of the spectrum is the high school or college student in jeans and a T-shirt who those people who dressed up may be looking at with less than full approval. Yet that person may be there because of that particular Tchaikovsky symphony. Or just to get away from the everyday routine of life.

# DESIGNING THE MORRISON PERFORMING ARTS CENTER

*Ernest Lombard of the firm Lombard Conrad Architects in Boise designed the Morrison Center in Boise. The Center is on the south side of the Boise River with views of the foothills to the north.*

During the boom times of the mining days, a number of theaters were built with a great desire to bring the arts to Idaho. The patrons who made a lot of money in mining wanted to put the money into the arts. Today we still have patrons who feel it is important. Harry Morrison and his wife, Velma, stayed with the idea of putting money into the arts. Someone like that has to care enough to do it.

We decided to take a unique approach to the accoustical design of the hall, and the Morrison Center was the product. We don't have a lot of big plaster ceilings. We kept everything exposed. The ceiling is not the material that reflects the sound, but big precisely-located sound panels that reflect the sound. The ceiling just encloses the total volume of the space. By adjusting the panels, the room can be tuned for a full orchestra onstage or for a theatrical production.

Some of the materials in the hall are reflective and some are absorbative. The padded seats absorb sound and have an acoustical value which is there whether someone is in the seat or not. If a person is sitting in that seat, there is the same acoustical value becuse of clothing. So when you are practicing, the sound is the same as it would be if you were before an audience of two thousand people.

*Ernest Lombard*

The walls themselves are masonry and bounce the sound to the audience. The few surfaces are short and angled so they disperse the sound in a uniform manner. There are no places in the hall where you can't hear anything or only the high or low notes. There are no bad seats.

We wanted the Morrison Center to be a place of re-collecting and interacting of people. The lobby was designed to have a patron be presented to the river and the park and the mountains. You do see each of these in succession as you go to your seat. You can't avoid it. The balconies are such that if you are on one balcony, you can easily see someone on another one. No one can get a long ways away from you.

During intermission, no one stays in the hall. They all go back out in the lobby. This is very unusual for a performing arts center. Most people wait until things start again, or go to the restroom. Here, going to the lobby is a social event. Everybody is talking to everybody, looking and waving. That's exactly what we wanted to happen. People want to get out and see the views, enjoy the sight, and make the most of it.

Even though people love this place and like having it here, they don't necessarily spend a lot of time here. They feel better because they know it's here. If it weren't here, they would feel less enriched. I think that people feel the same way about the arts. They like it and maybe aren't always involved in it. But they feel better about their community and themselves because it is there.

Or to be enveloped in a wonderful emotional experience. Music is for everyone.

To me art is a very real and ongoing part of daily existence. It's like eating for me. I don't isolate the artistic experience from the life experience. For me they're too integrated to be able to separate them.

Idahoans seem to appreciate art. I'm one of the newer citizens of Idaho, having only been here not quite three years yet. If the response to and attendance at our performances is any indicator, I would say Idahoans enjoy the arts very much. We have enjoyed sell-out subscription audiences all three seasons that I've been here. Our pops concerts are very well attended. We do some unusual concerts, like Pops in the Park, that are sponsored by one of the local banks here, that draw huge crowds of people. I would say they are very interested in it indeed.

*Kerry Moosman*

For myself, the thing that means the most to me is the sense of personal gratification that comes from having done a really good performance and having that performance appreciated by the audience, having the audience indicate that by their applause. When I can accomplish that, I feel very appreciated and successful. You can measure it in monetary terms, but I think for most performers, or artists in general, appreciation for the work itself is how we measure our own successes.

*Kerry Moosman is a potter who lives and works in Atlanta, an old mining town.*

My family is from Idaho back five generations. Part of them were Mormons and part of them were gold miners. They came in the beginning and are still here. Some of them settled in the Payette Valley in the really early pioneer days. One of my great grandfathers was a weaver; that was the trade he brought with him from Europe to Utah. He probably could have related to what I am doing.

I went to school here until I was in the fourth grade. My grandparents lived here until 1982. I came back to spend time with them every summer. It has just always been home. There is beautiful scenery, quiet, opportunity to explore and look around, walk. There is a lot of old stuff that needs fixing up. There are friends, family, fun.

Having an interest in history has influenced my work a lot. I like to know what came before. I'm very curious about how people lived and what they did. I think that's why I make pots. It is a very ancient and time-tested vehicle of expression. Clay hasn't changed much in the last four thousand years. I've been able to develop a life in Atlanta that is more traditional. I don't have electricity. I burn wood.

I would like to say, "Yes, Idahoans appreciate art." However, they have space and natural beauty around them everywhere. There is not as much desire for art as there is in more urban areas, where there is more of a need for an escape. Art offers urban people that escape. In Idaho there is not the pressure of urban life. But it's a good place for an artist to work, because you can live fairly inexpensively in Idaho. There is a lot to inspire you, a lot of beauty. And if you spend a lot of time in the studio, you don't feel like you're missing a whole lot of action.

It takes a lot of physical exertion to paint, to carve. You use your whole body. You don't just sit there and "create." I've been experimenting with terra-cotta clays, which have a rust color from the iron in the clay. I've been firing them with different combustible materials, which is kind of fun. With one piece I used some newspaper. It might have been the lead or something in the print that created interesting silvery effects. Others were fired with horse manure, which gives them really nice beautiful blacks.

I've been playing around with different kinds of sawdust, hard woods, black walnut, and wood ash. They all have an effect on the terra-cotta and turn it different colors. Lots of room for experimentation.

The main tool for polishing clay is a little rock. This is the only rock that I have been able to make work. Polishing actually compresses the surface of the clay. There are many different ways of doing it and reasons for doing it. In the early cultures of the Stone Age, the Neolithic people polished clay to make it watertight. They hadn't invented glazes yet.

My stone has a good shape. It's something I can hold onto for some reason. It's smooth. It's been polished in a modern tumbling machine. I think it's an agate. For Indians, their polishing stones were very sacred to them. They were very cautious with them and handed them down from generation to generation. This one

Photo: Rick Jenkins

*Kerry Moosman's polished clay pot*

is getting flattened off at the end because I polish quite a bit with it. Some of the Indians use nice big stones that they can grab hold of and really get going. I've never been able to make a big one work. I keep experimenting with different stones, but this is the only one that I seem to be able to make do.

I just finished a piece which still has a little moisture in it. You take your little rock and start going over the surface to take out the little scratches and inconsistencies in the clay body. It compresses the clay and actually makes more of a glass-like surface. It's fun to look at ancient pots from different cultures, because a lot of them did this kind of stone polishing. Traditional potters in Africa, Mexico, South America, and the Pueblos of the American West still do a lot of this. It's a technique they can use without kilns. Most of the polished pottery is fired in pit fires. If you fire any higher than that, the polishing goes away. You have to be careful. It's a slow process; you can't be in a hurry if you want to polish clay.

Art in early Atlanta was more decorative. Emma Edwards Green, the schoolteacher, used to teach painting. The paintings that came out of her classes were mostly landscapes, all realistic. Art is now moving in many different directions besides realism.

Artists in the 1864 period were flexible. They painted furniture, headstones, houses. I think there has always been a need for artists in every culture. I think it might have even been easier back then. People liked to have their portraits painted. Now they don't so much.

Art is more functional now, because there is a real need for the humanness. In our culture we are more mechanized and impersonal. Art adds back some of that personality, some of that humanness. I hope that's what it does. That's what I want it to do. In the earlier days, people's lives were less mechanical. They had quilting and basketmaking. Art was more interwoven in their lives.

*Hazel Weston of Boise was president of Boise Music Week from 1948 to 1950.*

Eugene Farner of St. Michael's Cathedral was the one who started Music Week in 1919. Then other cities took up the idea and it spread all over the United States. It is still observed and handled by the National Federation of Music Clubs.

Music Week is a showcase for all the talent in town, beginning with little folk and right up through to the professionals. They get together and the beginners have a chance to hear what the professionals can do. People who can't afford to go to the expensive performances can see and hear what there is in Boise free of charge. And there is a great deal. Boise is full of talent.

I was on the board and then became president of Music Week. It had been a going concern for quite a while. The whole town was involved in it, and some of the

*Hazel Weston*

outlying districts. It was good music, and I wanted people to hear the very fine music that Boise had. I get very angry when some people infer that Boise is the outpost of some lost civilization. We have very talented people from all over the world here. For the size of the town, it is a very sophisticated city. I am proud of Boise.

People were proud of Music Week, because we had received national recognition for what we had accomplished. I don't think cultural organizations were as competitive as they are now, or as highly organized. Things were a little homier then.

We built outdoor stages, some in front of the Capitol. One year we had a ballet, and there was to be a drummer for one of the scenes. His drums were down under the stage, but when it came time for the performance, there was no drummer. No one would volunteer, so I crawled down under there and went after the drums. I am sure it was bad drumming, but at least we got through the performance.

One night we had an outdoor performance and it was cold. The orchestra was down front, and the director not only wanted lights on the stands, but also heating lamps at their feet. We scrounged up heating lamps. By the time they had put all that electrical load on the system, everything went. It was quite a scramble to get back into the performance again. Having it outdoors added a great deal of demand to the ingenuity and work and creativity.

Music literacy went way up, especially in the schools. The average Boise citizen does not ordinarily get to hear children's programs. But they go to Music Week and

*Marjorie Stevens*

they see and hear where their tax dollar is going in the arts, which I think is very important.

The more the amateur hears the professional, the more that the casual listener hears both, the more interested he becomes, the more selective his or her taste. It is a means of raising the interest of the whole town in what we have. That's very necessary. It helps raise the interest of the community in good music. Good music expresses the very best that man has produced.

*Marjorie Stevens and Gertrude Heimgartner, Quilters, Stoney Point*

MARJORIE STEVENS: My husband thinks it would be quite a bit cheaper to buy a blanket and be done with it. The pioneers used to lack materials and would take scraps of anything and make quilts. They could design a quilt out of scraps and make something pretty out of nothing. That's really an art.

When I first came to Stoney Point, I came as a country school teacher, and was invited to come down to the quilting club. My mother had taught me how to quilt before that—just making tiny stitches, as tiny as you can. Mine lacked quite a bit being tiny. But I practiced. I belonged to the club until I got involved with 4-H. I took a breather for a while and then came back.

Quilting is one of my means of relaxation. I like to visit with neighbors. We get to know each other well enough to be real friends, know each other's problems. We are somewhat isolated, so it's nice to get with other people and visit. I think we probably have the same stresses and strains that other people have.

Our friendship club was formed to help our neighbors. We would meet with the hostess and do whatever work she wanted done. And it turned out that mostly it was quilts, because we all liked to quilt so well.

*Gertrude Heimgartner*

A person can forget pretty much what she is doing. You keep your eyes on your quilting, but you visit with the neighbors. You become a part of the community that way. Our community is a close community, I think. Partly because it's one big family. There are quite a few relatives in it. Some of us aren't related very closely and we still feel part of the community.

We don't sell our quilts. At least I don't. They're too valuable to sell. They're nice for gifts but I wouldn't sell one for anything. They are part of me.

GERTRUDE HEIMGARTNER: Of course quilting is an art form! If it was just to keep you warm, you would put two pieces of cloth on each side of a cotton batting. We do it for pleasure. We don't get near the work done anymore that we used to do, but we're hanging in there.

I suppose the youngest of our bunch is in her late fifties. We don't have any members younger than that. I don't know what will happen when we're gone. Many younger women don't seem interested. And yet some have learned to quilt with us. They do a real good job, but it will probably die out.

Of the bunch that are here, a lot of them couldn't even quilt when they joined the club. They've gotten to be really accomplished quilters. I learned it at my mother's knee, because my mother was a seamstress. It's just trial and error. When some women start out they sometimes have to take their stitches out. They would be monstrous sometimes. It's hard to learn how to do it well.

I don't know how many chances we have turned down to make quilts for money. We decided years ago that quilting for money took the fun out of it. If we needed money we would get it some other way. One of the things we thought about was that when people start out, they don't quilt very well. If we were doing it for money, we couldn't very well have that. When we are all friends, each stitch counts. If someone can't quilt as well as another...well, those stitches mean just as much.

Years ago, the Stoney Point Quilting Club was the only way we saw each other. We looked forward to getting together every two weeks. We disband in the summer, then pick up in the fall and quilt until spring. After we lost our little country school, which had been the thing that held the community together, the club held us together. That's where we learn all the gossip and the real news.

How many quilts have we made? Oh, mercy! That is the one thing I regret about our fifty years of meetings. It is just a shame that we didn't write down every quilt that we have done. We would probably be shocked.

# *Potatoes*

## WHAT *DID* MAKE THE IDAHO POTATO SO FAMOUS?

The potato and Idaho are a pair of forged links in the minds of American food consumers—stronger than the link between Florida and oranges, California and raisins, and Wisconsin and cheese. This bond did not occur by accident.

The man who started the potato on its phenomenal career in Idaho was named Joe Marshall. In him was combined a committed and sympathetic attitude about delivering a high-quality product to the American housewife, a genius for advertising, a love of potatoes, and a generous personality willing to show other growers in Idaho the way to premium prices.

Before 1921, Marshall, like other potato growers, shipped his potatoes by rail to Chicago, the control center of potato finance and trade. He observed that once a buyer bought potatoes for resale, they were combined with potatoes from everywhere else and lost any further identification with the grower. Dissatisfied with the prices he was getting for his excellent potatoes, Marshall decided to go to Chicago in 1917 to sell them himself, and bypass the brokers. His label was Blue Diamond. He loaded his sacks onto a train car and then went to Chicago himself to await the car. He found restaurant and other buyers willing to pay a premium price for a better potato that they could not get otherwise. When the average price for a one hundred pound sack was forty cents, Blue Diamond sold for that and a dollar more.

One of Marshall's customers was Tofanetti's, a chain of popular restaurants. Tofanetti featured the Idaho potato on his menu and in the window of the restaurants, where potato displays attracted attention. His patrons liked the food, and the large fancy potatoes took up plenty of room on the plate with tasty, but inexpensive food. Soon other restaurants were buying premium potatoes from Idaho.

After World War I commodity prices collapsed. Huge surpluses remained unsold and rotting, a legacy of the Federal Loan Bank policy that had encouraged farmers to expand and produce food for the war effort. The agricultural depression of the 1920s was on. The Twin Falls Bank and Trust took over scores of farms unable to repay their loans. The bank asked Marshall to manage them and gave him the necessary capital. He used the opportunity to upgrade seed, supervise the care of the crops, and manage their sale.

Before long, the Federal Bank asked him to take charge of more than a hundred farms in similar circumstances in Pocatello, Declo, Aberdeen, and other areas. His objective was to help make the farmer solvent once more. In the process, Marshall broadcast his ideas of quality and control, and proved over and over that premiums were to be had for both.

Marshall transformed the potato farmers of Idaho into an industry. Jack Simplot later became one of its stars. Wresting control from the Chicago brokers was only one step in a long series of innovations, campaigns, and struggles. Marshall built potato cellars, innovated the use of consumer-friendly sized bags, and encouraged the use of certified seed in Idaho long before other parts of the country did. He promoted disease research, railroad responsibility, standards, farmer control, and advertising.

Joe Marshall and others helped create a state commission that would advertise the Idaho potato nationally. After a controversial battle over its constitutionality, the Idaho legislature passed a law authorizing the state's potato growers to assess themselves a half a penny for each sack of potatoes to spend on promotion. The Advertising Commission became today's Idaho Potato Commission. The first commission, with Marshall as one of its members, distributed brochures, placed ads in newspapers and restaurant trade journals, promoted the use of "potato flags" on potatoes when they were served in restaurants, had contests, and promoted "Idaho Potato and Onion Week." The effort, the budget, and the market all grew.

Joe Marshall's son, Charles Marshall of Jerome, also a potato grower, talked about his father's career.

My dad was born in a log cabin near Versailles, Ohio, in a little town called Frenchtown. They were very poor. They had about forty acres of timber. He said he remembered the mornings in the winter. When he would get up, snow would be on the blanket. They chinked the cabin with mud, but it would come out. He said they thought nothing of getting up in the morning and shaking the snow off the blanket. They were tough, but there was a lot of sickness because it was so cold and miserable in that country.

He left home when he was about eighteen. He went to Iowa and got a job, working for one of the Milner's boys—Elliot Milner. They liked him so well they sent him to their big ranch in Montana in the Bighorn area. After less than a year, he was running the whole thing. The company got in trouble in Texas with their rice plantation, so they sent him there for a year to straighten it out.

My first sister was born there. My second sister Alice was born when he went back to Montana. Then I was born in Idaho. He was planning to go to Mexico, and if it hadn't

*Charles Marshall*

been for my mother getting pneumonia and the Mexican Revolution, my youngest sister would have been born there. He never was satisfied.

Then the Idaho potato became his life. He always wanted to put into the bag better than what the picture showed on the outside. He had the famous Blue Diamond label. I never saw him tired. He would just go, go, go. Had a lot of energy.

Dad helped to bring the potato industry up and give it fame, not only in the United States, but all over the world. Even in Australia, they have Idaho potato menus. He just believed in the potato. He brought it to fame and it's still famous. It started developing about 1921 to 1922. We had nothing up to that time. Idaho only had about twenty-five thousand acres in potatoes. Dad only raised Rurals until about 1920. We started raising Russett Burbanks in 1921.

The potato market then was very, very poor. There was no market that you could depend on. Around 1921 and 1922 our potatoes didn't even sell. Wisconsin and other states in the Midwest were getting two or three times as much as we did in Idaho. Then from 1922 to 1924 things changed, and we got three times the prices those states got. The industry just kept growing from then on. Now we have up to 350,000 acres in potatoes, and we can sell them all.

Half of the potatoes in those days were left in the ground. The ones that did sell brought two bits. The potatoes were just no good, they were full of disease. The potato has more disease than any other vegetable. Isn't that peculiar? It has black leg, it has ring rot, it has curly leaf. There are just dozens of diseases that potato has.

So he went up in the high mountains—the Tetons—at Victor and Ashton. He tried to grow the seed at seven thousand feet and had some success. But he couldn't get a continual big crop because of the cold weather. Then he brought it down to six thousand. That was a little cold, so he brought it down to five thousand around Ashton. That is where they developed the seed. It finally paid off. He went to Oregon and all over to get seed—wherever they had good seed—and brought it in.

Dad's field rotation, before they had fertilizer, was five years in hay. He wouldn't take it out no matter what. Then he could have it four years out in spuds, then beans, then spuds and beans. Then it would go right back to alfalfa. I don't think he ever got less than two or three hundred sacks per acre. Other people tried to rape their soil; they got down to where they couldn't grow one hundred sacks.

Chicago was Dad's main market point, and Milwaukee. They wanted good Idaho potatoes. The Idaho potato was mealy, whereas the others were kind of soggy. They bake and they fry and they make the best french fries.

## How to Bake Potatoes ala Charlie Marshall

You can't bake a potato by putting it in the oven and covering it. The Idaho potato has the ability to expel moisture. That makes it mealy. If you cover it up, the moisture stays in the potato. So bake them without tin foil. It's okay to put it on after you bake them, but don't put it on before you bake them. Try to get as much moisture out as you can.

The potato was something you could control after you grew it. Farmers have no control over things like grain. When Dad had anything, he always controlled it. He built the cellars so he could store them, because otherwise he lost control of them. He got other farmers to build cellars so they could store theirs and keep the glut off the market. Control stayed with the people who grew the potatoes. If the market wasn't right, they wouldn't sell them. If a buyer had bought them, he would just keep moving them even if the market was glutted.

He walked the streets of Chicago because he was after the restaurant trade. His fancy potatoes all went to Chicago and the big cities for the restaurants. The other market was for the housewife. For that he had the consumer-sized bag: small bags made of cotton. He had a big market in Milwaukee for those. He used fifteen pound bags in the 1920s. The housewife wants to go in and buy a small bag, she doesn't want a hundred pounds. Maybe she did years ago, but she doesn't now. They even have them down to five pounds now. He used a strong cotton bag that kept the potatoes from greening.

He didn't believe in mesh bags, because potatoes would green in the stores. When we kept potatoes in the cellar, we didn't have any way to air it out, except to open the doors. So the first bins would be covered with sacks. They never left light bulbs on, because even they will green potatoes. He was very careful. Women willingly paid more for Blue Diamond potatoes because there was less waste. The goods inside the sack looked like the ones on the outside.

Not all growers shared the same ideas about quality at the time. Some growers used a sack, called a mugg bag,

*Courtesy of Charles Marshall*
**Joe Marshall, Potato King & his displays**

that would hold about ninety pounds. Then they would put ten pounds on top and weave and sew those ten pounds on top so it looked good. They would all be big potatoes. It was a mess because in handling them, one or two potatoes would get out through the twine. Then the sack would be half empty. That didn't go. They tried every scheme in the world. Stove-piping actually happened—where the center of the sack is nothing but culls. My dad wouldn't do that.

He started the industry shipping two inch potatoes. They used to ship an inch and a half or an inch and five-eighths. He said that by the time they were peeled there wasn't anything left. He figured if you put two-inch potatoes in the sack, people would pay more. Now that standard is statewide. Before that, they were shipping little stuff. Well, when the housewife got them, she would peel it and then she didn't have anything. He stopped that. He just fought for everything he believed in.

They had some big trade shows in Texas, Kansas City, or Chicago. He never missed one. I went with him once and met Mr. Tofanetti, who talked about what the Russet had meant to him. After a trade show maybe he would have eight or ten thousand pounds of potatoes (from the displays). He would always give them to the orphans or some charitable organization. It always made a big hit; the governors liked it, the states liked it. That was good advertising, too; it helped.

Joe is the one that helped start the Advertising Commission about 1937. He always promoted. It was hard to do anything until they got the advertising. I suppose Marilyn Monroe was my favorite advertising. They fixed a potato sack and dressed her up in it. I used to have it. But not our advertising. Dad didn't go for that stuff. She was a nice looking girl and it looked pretty good and got a lot of attention, but Dad liked the regular display of his potatoes. That was his advertising. And I think that was a good way, it was beautiful.

Every time Senator Borah came to Idaho, he came to see Dad. And every time Dad went to Washington, he went to see Borah. If Dad had anything that he wasn't getting fair play on, he'd get Borah to help him. Borah would do the job. That helped. You've got to have help from people with strength to help you out. Borah had the strength. They were the best of friends.

He just loved to help people, especially widows and people who had lost their farms. He helped a lot of people during the Depression save their farms. He never asked for interest. He just wanted the money back that he loaned to people.

We never use the Blue Diamond bag anymore because we couldn't do the job of keeping up with his standards. So we just retired it. It's like these football players do to their numbers: we retired his bag. I have my own, but I'm not doing very much in the fresh potato business.

They called him the King of Potatoes. He really earned it. All the states gave him a big plaque. They did that years ago because he worked for it. He never missed a meeting and he never asked for anything. He was aggressive. He just believed in what he did and kept pushing. He produced. He furnished the spuds most of the time for nothing if it would benefit Idaho. He was a good friend to Maine growers. He went to Oregon to help them. He wanted to promote the potato, not only in Idaho, but every place. He wasn't a selfish man at all. But they named him "Potato King." He loved it, too, don't kid yourself.

*Open lines of communication between farmers and scientists has always been a characteristic of the industry in Idaho. In 1910 and 1911 the farmers around Aberdeen asked the University of Idaho to help them solve some of the problems related to irrigated agriculture. Scientific experimentation began to unlock one secret after another of potato biology and culture: optimum size of the seed, optimum planting distances, how to prevent knobby potatoes, and how to eliminate ringrot. The Aberdeen station still operates, and the potato research building is now named after Joe Marshall.*

*The breakthroughs permitted significant expansion of the industry, giving Idaho farmers a competitive edge in the national market. Dr. Walter C. Sparks is research professor emeritus at the University of Idaho, who refers to himself as one of Idaho's "potato men." He entered the potato scene shortly after World War II, just as industrialists like J. R. Simplot were trying to develop a market for frozen french fries.*

I was born and raised on a seed potato farm in Colorado. I went to Colorado State University and got my bachelor's and master's degrees there. I worked in the summertime roguing potatoes. Then I started to work on my Ph.D. in Minnesota. When there was an opening for a potato research man at Aberdeen, I applied, came out, was interviewed and accepted. So I came to Idaho. That was 1947.

Potato growing then was on a much smaller scale than it is now. It was not totally involved with the Russet Burbank, but had a lot to do with the Russet Rural potato. The Russet Burbank was just beginning to be more important.

When I came along, potato processing was just being born. Processing plants were only operating eight or nine months at the maximum. At the end of the nine months, the potatoes were not suitable for high quality product. Therefore, the processors asked, "How can we maintain these potatoes in a high state of quality over a longer period of time so that we can run our processing industry, as well as our fresh market industry, over a period of twelve months?" So I started working on potato storage.

I solved the problem by determining the best temperature to store potatoes in order to maintain the highest quality. That happened to be at forty-five degrees Fahrenheit. But at that temperature the potatoes sprouted after a few months. This led to solving the problem of preventing potatoes from sprouting. For this we had to find some type of chemical inhibitor to prevent the potatoes from sprouting. We ran many, many trials on all types of chemicals

*Walter C. Sparks*

and inhibitors, even irradiation and came up with the best way. It was to use a chemical known as CIPC, which was introduced to the potato pile through the ventilation system under conditions of high humidity and good air distribution. We also found that we could use a chemical known as maleic hydrazide and spray it on the green growing plant in the field where it would be absorbed and translocated to the tubers.

After that we had to determine how high we could keep the humidity in storage in order to maintain the potatoes in their highest quality. It was thought that maybe 85 percent would do it, but due to my research I found that 95 percent or higher gave a much higher quality product. We had to remember one or two facts of physics—never blow warm air onto cold potatoes. If the ventilating air was always colder than the tubers, we never had condensation on the tubers themselves. This kept them in a state of very good quality all through an eleven- or twelve-month period.

If we keep the humidity high enough, we do not get the bottom potatoes flattened. Or, as many people say, "pressure bruised." We keep them full of water, so that we do not get flattened potatoes.

All of that took, I would say, at least ten or twelve years. We just increased our knowledge year by year by year, and improved and improved. At the present time, we can keep potatoes for almost the entire year in a very high state of quality.

Before all this, the farmers just had a cellar, usually a dugout. They put the potatoes in about eight feet deep, with no ventilation tubes underneath the potatoes at all. Then they would open up the doors to cool the potatoes off. The temperature would fluctuate very greatly, however. Due to the specifications required for high quality french fries, you had to maintain a temperature within very narrow limits. As soon as the temperature got below about forty-five degrees, you get a build-up of sugar in the potato. When you deep-fat fried them for french fries or potato chips, you got dark colored potato chips. These were not acceptable to the consumer. Therefore, you have to maintain the temperature above forty-five degrees in order to maintain a high quality product to the consumer.

At that time, you rogued potatoes to keep diseased ones out of the field. But one of the main things we do now is use elite seed. This means to grow a potato—maybe even in a test tube—and completely eliminate all diseases, bacteria, viruses, and fungi. We grow these in greenhouses and then in the fields in isolated areas. Then the potatoes that we use for seed are almost completely free of any disease.

Before, we used "one-year-out" or "two-year-out" seed. This meant that it was just one or two years out of the field, even though it was supposedly certified seed. The amount of disease we have now is minimal compared to what we used to have in our seed potatoes. In fact many of our processors now state in their contracts that the seed potatoes used by the farmer must be certified or better quality. Today we have even gone to the point of genetic engineering. I am very proud to say that I think the University of Idaho and the state of Idaho, have some of the highest quality seed potatoes of any place in the world.

The station at Aberdeen was donated to the university back about 1910. The Commercial Club of Aberdeen, which was like the chamber of commerce, donated the land. It was to be used for grains and potatoes. To begin with it was dry land with some irrigation. Very shortly thereafter it became almost completely irrigated. It grew from an original eighty acres to about three hundred or four hundred acres now. It also is the repository for germ plasm of small grains for the entire United States.

It has the leading potato breeding program for the United States, but it is not the repository for potato germ plasm, which is located in Sturgeon Bay, Wisconsin. We use all of their species of germ plasm in the breeding program here. Each year we grow approximately 100,000 individual seedlings, each of which is potentially a new variety. Only those parents which give us the best-looking product are maintained in the breeding program.

It used to be that potatoes were considered a cool weather crop only grown in areas where the potatoes could have a cool temperature. Because of research in the germ plasm of the potato, I personally have seen potatoes grown in very tropical lowlands along the seacoast, farther north than the Arctic Circle, at the end of Cape of Good Hope in Africa, the southern end of Chile, and New Zealand. I have seen them as high as thirteen thousand feet in the South American Andes. So it is one of the most universal crops. It is very high quality food; every amino acid necessary for human growth is contained to some extent in the potato.

Scientific research has done a tremendous amount to shape the industry in Idaho, even though we have been unable to change the variety, Russet Burbank. All of the technology in the processing industry—the making of dehydrated and french fried potatoes—is based upon the particular characteristics of the Russet Burbank potato. The prevention of disease and obtaining disease-free seed has done tremendous good for the potato industry.

The future in potato technology is going to carry on right from where we are now. You cannot immediately change the tastes of people who expect a given flavor and taste in french fries. So we are going to have to choose new potatoes to fit in with what we have now. Gradually we can go from there to new varieties which will give us higher yield, and more disease resistance. We are gradually incorporating insect and disease resistance into potatoes which look and taste like the Russet Burbank. In the future I think we may get some that are going to be very excellent.

*J. R. Simplot of Boise, founder and chairman of the board of the company which bears his name, is of the generation that followed Joe Marshall's. He was a progressive grower who absorbed Joe Marshall's lessons: growing potatoes only from certified seed, for example. He went on then to exploit the possibilities in economies of scale, new product development, vertical integration, and company research.*

*One of his first innovations was the use of chemical fertilizer as a substitute for crop rotation, something he discovered almost by accident. While he was experimenting with a product from Pacific Guano Fertilizer Company one day, his spreader machine did not operate properly, releasing more fertilizer over part of the field than the instructions called for. The results at harvest impressed him, for the part of the field which had received the "extra" fertilizer grew lush plants with a bounty of potatoes, and the part of the field where the fertilizer had not been applied "was where we ran out of potatoes."*

*He exploited the efficiency of the electric potato sorter. A farmer could dump the potatoes on a conveyor belt, allowing people on each side to sort, while others at the end could bag and load. Since the machine was portable, he could train a crew, take the whole package to each farmer's cellar, plug it into the light bulb socket, do the work, and move to the next cellar.*

*Simplot revisited his parents' homestead, the Declo Hotel, the site of his old pigfood cooker, and other sites that recalled the days when he got started.*

I left school at fourteen and got me a room in a rooming house in Declo. I built it all from there. Nobody ever put a penny in my company, not one red cent. I did it by taking care of business, I guess. That's what my job was. And it was tough, tough, tough.

When I moved to that hotel, I had a few dollars. I was just a kid, but times were tough. There were eight or ten school teachers living there and getting about forty dollars every two weeks, paid in warrants. They weren't checks, just an IOU. They didn't have any money because the school districts didn't have any money. Well, I bought those warrants for about fifty cents on the dollar from those teachers. I would take them to town, and the bank would give me face value for them and honor my note. I secured my note with these warrants. That's really how I got started in the potato business.

I had left home. I came back to look for a place to feed these pigs. So Dad helped me build a pig pen. We built a hell of a pig pen, I'm telling you. We built a great big cooker. It held about two or three tons of potatoes and two horses. I'd go out in the desert and shoot a wild horse or two, jerk the hide off of them, and bring them back in and cook them with the potatoes. I fattened those hogs on horse meat and cooked potatoes. In the spring, when I bought those hogs, you could get them

*J.R. Simplot and his sister Peg*

for nothing. I fed them all winter and I worked like hell.

The next spring we had a hot hog market. I sold those damn hogs for seven cents a pound. That was more that hogs had brought for years. The check was $7800 when I got it. That was a fortune. And that's what got me started. I bought me eight head of horses and a line of farm machinery and went to farming. I leased 120 acres from Lindsey Maggert, and planted potatoes, beans, hay and grain.

We bought our seed potatoes from a farmer in Ashton, Idaho. Maggert, who was one of the big farmers in Cassia County, and I were invited on an elk hunting trip near Ashton. Anyway, that's when I bought my potato sorter. Along the way I heard there was an electric potato sorter being built. We stopped in Shelley, Idaho. Lindsey and I bought this electric potato sorter on a joint account. They shipped it down to Declo in a box car. I unloaded it and went to sorting potatoes. A close friend of Maggert complained because I was sorting all the neighbors' potatoes around there. So Maggert came out one day, early in the spring, and said, "Jack, you have to put up that potato sorter." I said, "I made a promise to sort potatoes for these people. It's obligated." He said, "You don't need to worry about it, it's time to go to farming anyway." So, we got in a little argument. I said, "Well, there is only one way to settle this thing, Lindsey. Let's just flip a dollar and see who owns it." He pulled a dollar out of his pocket. He flips it up in the air and I call it. He turns around and walks off, grumbling. That put me in the potato sorting business, and I grew from there.

If I hadn't won that sorter, it could have changed my whole career because I would have gone back to farming, I guess. Or I may have gone and bought another one, I don't know. That was one of the turning points. I've had two or three like that in my life. I built that potato sorter business during the thirties, and accumulated about thirty warehouses—wasn't much but just cellars—and we worked out of those cellars. Then I got in the onion business and it was profitable. We made a little money in onions and a little money in potatoes.

I wasn't a detail man. I didn't have any education. I had a hell of a time billing and routing cars. I worked day and night on those things when I was doing them alone, and then I hired a fellow by the name of Burdell Curtis. He was a schoolteacher who could type and take shorthand. I got him and then I started to go. I could do the trading and he did the detail.

We built a company during the thirties. I imagine we were among the biggest potato and onion shippers in Idaho. Then the war came on. We got in the onion drying business. The real money, the first money I ever made that amounted to anything, was when I got into the onion dehydration business. The first month we ran that onion plant we made fifty thousand dollars clear. That was more money than we ever made in a year. We made a lot of money drying onions. It was what got me really started.

The Army sent a colonel by the name of Logan. He said, "Simplot, you are going to work for the Army. You're going to dry vegetables for the Army." I said, "Fine, give me the tickets and I'll do them the best I know how." That got me in the dehydration business in a big way. I built plants all over America—Maine, North Dakota, Colorado, California, Oregon. I really got things going on dehydration. I finally wound up supplying more potatoes to the Army than anyone else. That led into the fertilizer business. I had to have fertilizer to grow the potatoes, and I couldn't buy any. So I decided to make some. And I did.

# Potatoes

I didn't start out big. The future is not ours to see and it never has been. But looking back, how did I get big in the potato business? I guess I worked at it. I got more cellars. I got more good people working at the same job, and we made a success out of it. Who would have thought forty or fifty years ago we would be shipping five or six times the amount of potatoes out of Idaho? And 85 percent of them going out ready to eat? You couldn't see that coming, but here it is.

The tools we have to work with today are so fantastic—we are getting into genes and antibodies and enzymes and cloning. It is awesome what you're going to see happening in this world. You take those genes, and voila, we've got some tools there that are real and it's no hocus pocus. You'll advance the world, all species, from where they're at today and where they're going to be tomorrow. Let your imagination run. The same with cloning—you can take a piece of leaf from here and one from there, stick them together and come up with awesome results. I can see potatoes twice as big as they are today, with double the solids. We're working on it, but it won't come tomorrow.

Look how far we have come with computers in my life. Hell, I was fifty years old or more before I ever heard of a computer. Today we couldn't start to run our business without computers. We got everything computerized and we're doing awesome things with them, like sorting out the black spots on french fries. We take them out so fast you can't even see it happen, and they're gone. We do it with computers. And you know we're just unlocking the door to them.

I don't know how far this thing is going, but I can see us really getting big. I mean big. We're on our way, on the right track.

*The requirements for raising any crop remain what they have been for millennia: prepare the soil, apply water, and pay attention. However, the methods for doing each have changed drastically. Idaho potato farmers prosper not only because of the accumulated science, public relations, marketing, enterprise, innovation, and engineering passed down in eighty years of development, but because of their attention to detail. Walt Coiner, a Magic Valley potato producer, spends part of each day during the critical part of the growing season in his field, and was in his field to discuss his work.*

*Walt Coiner*

It takes years of planning to prepare a field for a potato crop. Potatoes take a lot of nutrients out of the soil. We have to build up the soil with nitrogen, potassium, phosphorus, and trace minerals. We do that with legumes like alfalfa and barley that add humus.

271

Those are primarily the crops that historically we've used in this area to bring the fertility of the soil up to an optimum level.

The year before, we put a barley crop in, thrashed it, then irrigated it again to allow all the volunteer barley to sprout and grow up. Then rather than plow like we used to, we try to use the ripper and a disk to leave the mulch on top of the ground. This is better than turning it over and creating a hard pan in the field. We just loosen it up as much as we can with large rippers.

We try to get as much work done in the fall because it allows the winter moisture to seep into it and soften the clods. As soon as the ground is dried to the point where we are not going to compact it with the large tractors that we use, we loosen it up one more time in the spring with our rippers.

From there, we plant. We use a little starter fertilizer and systemic to give us seasonal control of our Colorado potato beetles. Hopefully, that will be all the pesticides we'll need to apply during the year.

The blue grass that they're bringing into the valley now may prepare the ground adequately for a potato crop. We usually use barley as a crop to get that humus in the soil. My barley crop is an Anheuser Busch malt barley which is grown for Budweiser beer. New in the area, they have bought a lot of contracts because of the dependability of the growing season and water. They can get high quality barley from their growers. But this Kentucky Blue Grass may work out. I'm hedging on it. It will be five years before I get a potato crop on those grass fields. I think it'll be okay; I'll still be farming in five years. Hopefully the prices of my commodities will keep me in business.

A lot of organic material helps to keep the soil loose. This particular field had a crop of barley on it last year. That was to keep the soil loose and provide a lot of humus. The crop before that was an alfalfa crop. We plowed the third cutting down into the field. I've been working on this field for seven years in preparation of this particular potato crop.

When you're raising a spud crop, you can't just go by what it costs you that particular year. You have to take the year before, and perhaps the year before that. It's not a year-by-year type situation; it's more like a five- or seven-year cycle. That's basically what we have to farm by.

It's tough because you don't really know what's going to happen with the markets in five years. But a good potato will sell itself. You have to have faith in your ability to raise potatoes and do a decent job. Then they'll sell themselves. It's pretty hard to screw them up if you really watch them. But if you turn your back on them, they're really treacherous. They will turn around and give you a lot of problems.

This area would be a desert without the Twin Falls Canal Company and the canal system that they developed the first of the century. I order the water and twenty-four hours later I can take it. They control the gates and allow the water to flow into my settling pond, where we settle out all the weeds and silt. From the pond, the water is pressurized by large electric motors and pumps. In case the power goes off there is a valve to keep the water from flowing back into my settling pond. It takes over $250,000 to set up a pumping station.

These turbines are probably worth $100,000, and the valves about half of that. There are half a dozen valves, so with the welding and all the different check valves, this is quite expensive. We have to pay Idaho Power quite a bit of money every year

*Courtesy of Idaho Potato Commission*

**Potato Promotions**

to get hooked up. My power bill last month was twelve thousand dollars for these eight hundred acres. That will be one of the larger bills.

I use a high pressure system; the optimum operating pressure is about sixty-five pounds per square inch. High pressure irrigation systems give a pretty even water pattern across the field. If the pressure drops, the pattern tends to look like donuts. There are different sprinkling systems. This particular system is called Solid Set. We set the sprinklers out in the spring and pick them up in the fall.

On an average I water these potatoes eight hours a shift every five days throughout the summer. Earlier in the year you can probably get away with eight hours every seven or eight days. In the height of the season you probably come back every four days. Now that their demand is down, we probably water it every seven to ten days.

I'll irrigate this field around ten to fifteen times according to how dry the year is. This year particularly has been kind of dry and warm, so I'll probably irrigate fourteen or fifteen times in eight-hour shifts. My pumps put out three thousand gallons a minute on this set and I've got six of these sets in these two fields. So I put over eight million gallons of water on every time I irrigate. It's a tremendous amount of water that these potato plants require.

I want to keep the soil nice and cool with the water. Not too wet, or they start to decay; too dry, the potato stops growing. Then if water starts again, you get weird shapes. Too much fertilizer, they grow too fast. Not enough fertilizer, they stop growing and then start back up again.

You have to maintain a constant feeding program throughout the year. We put a starter fertilizer on in the spring, just to get them going when we plant them. Four, five or six times a year, I try to put fertilizer on through irrigation. We have an injecting station to inject the fertilizer into the sprinkler lines.

The nature of the potato is treacherous. We are trying to keep the potato at a certain moisture—ideally in a range between 65 and 85 percent. I've got to come out here every day and check it. We have tensiometers, radar guns, and infrared photography to tell us. But the best way is your shovel—just get out there and do it. I just have to take the time every day to go out there and dig.

Anytime a potato grows against a hard spot in this soil, the tuber will malform. If the moisture band is above 65 percent and below 85 percent, potatoes will grow at a consistent rate. If there is too much or not enough moisture, too much or not enough heat, then you start getting your Star Wars type potatoes, those malfunction kinds that go every which way. That's the real trick with these potatoes. You have to just watch them.

To cure the blight, they have different foliar sprays that you can spray on top of it. You can't really ever get rid of it, you just put it in check. A healthy plant will pretty much be able to ward it off. But as the season progresses, the plants lose their resistance, so different diseases move in and can take over. You just want to keep them healthy as long as you possibly can.

In this area we can keep them healthy till mid-October. Then we start worrying about frost. Up in Washington they have a longer growing season so they can get extra tonnage. We can't, but the potatoes aren't the same. Their's don't meal up as nicely. People can just tell the difference, you know.

I always like to count and see how many potatoes I get in a hill. You can determine what you're going to get at the end of the season. If they aren't the right size for the dinner table, they will go into french fries.

We still really have to demand a premium on our product. The Idaho potato is superior to any other potato grown in the United States. Hopefully, we can keep that good Idaho potato name.

# *Sun Valley*
## IS THAT IN IOWA?

*After 1870 when the East industrialized in earnest, a growing class of wealthy people could afford the costs of tourist travel in the West. Railroads made luxurious train cars available for sale or lease to wealthy families. Elegant travel led to elegant resorts, and railroad companies promoted tourist travel on their lines. They also invested in destination resorts, a practice that eventually gave Idaho Sun Valley. Averell Harriman, chairman of the Union Pacific Railroad board, opened the resort in 1936.*

*In the 1930s, highway construction began to expand significantly in Idaho, as it did elsewhere in the country. More people could afford to own and drive automobiles, and the middle class began to take up tourist travel. Entrepreneurs began making money selling gasoline and setting up auto camps, and then motels and restaurants.*

*By the 1990s travel opportunities have multiplied for all classes of people, conventions and conferences have made business travel common for large numbers of employees in addition to managers and owners, and second home ownership is not unusual for more and more people. Sun Valley reflects those changes. It is no longer only a resort for those looking for a prestigious way to demonstrate their success and relax, but part of a huge travel industry which uses vocabulary like "market penetration," "segmentation," "positioning," "packaging," and "value messaging." Sun Valley has emerged as a permanent Idaho community with its own unique mix of year-round and part-time residents, tourists, skiers, and conference vistors. It now shares the concerns about zoning, land use conflicts, revenue generation, and growth management that affect any other Idaho community.*

*Gretchen Fraser was the first American to win any medals in an Olympic ski event. In 1948 at St. Moritz, Switzerland, she won a gold medal for the special slalom and a silver for combined downhill and slalom. She trained at Sun Valley and, with her husband Don, is now one of its permanent residents.*

Don came to Sun Valley when they first opened in 1936, and I came the next year. We were on the racing circuit in the Northwest, and had come over for the Harriman Cup race. We always had a competitors' meeting the night before up at Trail Creek Cabin, where we received our numbers. Averell said that it would be nice if Don and I were married. That was a little premature, but Don did ask me six months later. Don was working for Mr. Harriman on publicity for Sun Valley. When we advised him that we were being married, Averell said he wanted us to live at Sun Valley. Don took over as sports director, and we lived here for two and a half years before World War II. Most of my racing has been under my married name, and the Sun Valley Ski Club.

In the early days, those of us who were racing sort of banded together. There was no lift on the Warm Springs (north) side of Bald Mountain, so we had to either walk up or go up the other side and ski down and have a bus or car waiting for us. We had raced two years before that by walking up Baldy. We used to figure between three hours or more to get up to the race course and wax our skis. We wore climbers. There was none of this snow packing equipment, none of these beautiful Piston Bullys on the mountain all night smoothing the slopes down. If you wanted to take a short cut on the course, you would go pack it when no one else was looking and then just hope you could find it when you were coming down. It now takes nine minutes on the new Quad Lift to get from the bottom to the top.

At the 1948 Olympics, no one expected us to do well and no one ever took pictures of us or interviewed us. It was a thrill to win the first medal for the United States, which was a silver. Most of the writeups were "pigtailed housewife from America has won a silver medal." I was delighted two days later to win a gold

GRETCHEN FRASER
*Courtesy of Gretchen Fraser*

**Gretchen Fraser**

medal. At that point they said I was a complete unknown. None of us had ever raced in Europe. It is always a thrill to do something for your country and be recognized. It changes your life. You meet wonderful people through an experience like that. I still get some very interesting fan mail; about two-thirds of it comes from Europe. They ask for pictures.

My husband started the first ice show in 1939. We had no budget, our costumes were made by the housekeeping department in the Lodge out of paper. We had no suitable tights or winter underwear to wear. The night of the ice show it was seventeen below zero. We were out there in our paper costumes. Things are a lot different now.

Averell was very interested in seeing Sun Valley become a summer resort, too, not just a winter resort. So then came the golf course, the trapshooting, and the purchase of a ranch down on Silver Creek for hunting and fishing. The original Lodge structure was designed as a very exclusive, very expensive hotel. The next year, Averell had the Sun Valley Inn designed, structured more after an Austrian chalet, a little community. That was less expensive accommodations. Then he realized there were some of us who were in school and just didn't have the money, but who loved to come over to race. So they built little chalets with four bunks to a room that were very inexpensive.

This was just a small western town. Everyone was friendly, and people who came here originally felt that way. No one said, "Are you a movie star?" or "Are you a millionaire from somewhere?" Everyone was accepted on the same grounds and enjoyed it. I think that's why Norma Shearer spent so much time here.

Celebrities could get away and live the life they wanted to, away from cameras. But they were all usually very generous about giving interviews. Today they go around anonymously. We were at a party recently with Barbra Streisand. I think she'd been there an hour before I even noticed who it was. You don't go out seeking. Everyone just enjoys people who come. I think it is appealing for people to be able to come and be left alone.

Business executives like the relaxed life. Most of them believe in athletic activity, and they can partake of that in any form here. They enjoy the casualness of the country—they can go on a picnic up in the mountains or they can get a good golf game in the summer or go fishing. They get away from the hustle and the bustle of the city and hours of commuting time. Here it's really distant if you go fifteen minutes. If you see a friend in the street, you stop and talk. Seldom does anyone honk and tell you to get out of the way. You seldom see a person who's fat or obese.

Don and I try to help with the sports we enjoy, and that civic work carries on to the community, too, such as the Special Olympics, the Art Center, and the Ski Education Foundation.

I don't object to progress. It's nice to get on that lift now and be at the top in nine minutes. They do very careful impact studies on facilities before they are put in. They have careful control of housing and where various buildings can be put. Ketchum has committees to determine those kinds of things also.

Now we have hundreds of races—cross-country races, ski races, running, triathlons, bicycle races. They are developing a very good bicycle path system, so you can go down and up the valley. There is much more to do today. We have such beautiful golf courses, championship courses, and I couldn't tell you how many tennis courts are in the valley.

The challenge of tourism is trying to separate activities so that you're not infringing on someone else's fun. You can't run a bicycle path and a footpath and put horses on it, too. Then you upset riders and horses by rolling by on a bicycle. Motorcycles have to be controlled as to where they go. If they can go up into the mountains, they tend to dig furrows in the trails which then become water troughs in the rainy season. They have been designating certain areas for cross-country skiing, and other areas for snowmobiling. Snowmobiles are not allowed here in the valley, so their noise does not disturb people.

I think it is possible to have too many tourists, but I think that Sun Valley has grown with dignity. We have forbidden high-rise buildings. Builders are restricted to three stories. There are a lot of people coming here for the same reason we have—we love it. In the summertime you just go out your door and you can walk up little ravines on some of the smaller mountains. Or you can get in a car and not have to go very far for good fishing.

Fortunately, the amenities have grown with the lower valley. No one thinks of this as being a polo area. While we probably have some three hundred families living in the valley, we also have three polo fields. There is a very active summer group that plays polo. We have three private barns that would stand up to anything in the country. There are some wonderful show horses here, so riding complexes have developed. The company has a good rental barn. People can go out on a dude string and see more natural country than you can with cars.

I suppose we all, at times, tend to want to see it stay as it is. But none of us can stop progress. They have been careful enough to have planning and zoning. We have a very fine small hospital here; some of our tax monies help for that, and we have ambulance service, and a helicopter that stands by. All those things come with a larger number of people.

*Skiing was the original attraction of Sun Valley as a resort, and the superior snow and mountain trails still draw thousands of skiers to the area. Don Rhinehart manages the Sun Valley Ski School where hundreds of beginners get their start in the sport every year.*

I came to Sun Valley in August of 1947. I was affiliated with Otto Lang's ski school. I've been here quite a while. The big changes happened in skiing after the war. Skiing became more popular and very rapidly expanded. Then with new lifts and technology there has been a really rapid advance. The economy has improved. We've set new records in

**Don Rhinehart**

ski school attendance this winter at Sun Valley.

Since it opened, Sun Valley has been known as the Queen Mother of destination resorts. People have always come—and come back. The charisma here is why it has always remained family oriented. People like the atmosphere. People in Idaho and the Wood River Valley are very friendly. The word gets around. People who come here feel that they are warmly, genuinely welcomed. For forty years I've been told that. They say it's just wonderful.

The snow is one of the reasons. If we don't have mother nature helping us, the Sun Valley Company spends million of dollars on snow-making equipment. When we advertise for a season opening date, we make it.

The thing that's helped skiers change is the advancement in the equipment. Their desires are the same, but the equipment has changed more than the skier. Advancement in the sport comes more rapidly.

In teaching we went to the "graduated length method." This means that when you're a beginner, you start with a fairly short ski. With this there is less resistance. As you start skiing faster, you need more of a platform to stand on. In 1948 everyone started with a ski that was approximately seven feet three inches long. Today they start on a four and a half foot ski. You used to have to work like a horse. Now it's a lot easier.

A person who is very adapted to sport doesn't have to worry about small things, like what type of gloves to wear. But beginners do. Every instructor in the ski school goes through a clinic every year. We are trained to notice small things. So we ask, "How are your feet, do they hurt? Do you have a pressure point in this boot?" Maybe they are developing a blister. An instructor can stop that immediately. You may have saved the person's whole vacation.

To handle tourism, you have to be a professional. You have to care more than anything about what you're doing and care about the people who are coming to you. Certainly they have different attitudes when they come to you—some are friendly, others are demanding. You have to accept all of them the same.

One time a student came to Dollar Mountain, a beginner. She kept stumbling and falling just walking over to where we were gathering. The instructor thought, "Maybe she has a physical handicap or something." When she got a little closer, he noticed that she had her boots on the wrong feet. The buckles kept snagging, and she kept falling down. That actually happened.

We've had people who brought their husband's or their child's skis by mistake. It's amazing what you can take in with one glance. You can tell a lot by the way people are dressed or the way they approach. You watch it all. I don't want to make fun of anybody, but some are pretty comical.

The instructors are a good bunch of people, clean living. They can be the best skiers, but if they don't fit in with their morals, their personalities, or they are more interested in their girlfriend during working hours, we don't want them in the school. We really screen them.

I've skied in Europe and most every place in the United States and Canada. I've taught here with many of the boys who have taught in Australia, South America, and Europe. All say this is the best ski mountain in the world. Dollar Mountain is the best beginning and intermediate teaching mountain. Professional hard-core skiers all say that Baldy Mountain is the best ski mountain in the world.

You have anything that you want. If you want fast steep runs, you don't have to pole very much to get going. But Seattle Ridge and the cat tracks coming down into Warm Springs or Lower College can still bring intermediate skiers down off of the mountain without subjecting them to rough, bumpy, or steep terrain. Overall, it's a great mountain. I don't know what else to say. I've been on all of them and it's the best there is.

Some of the people who live here have Ph.D.s, and might work in the ski shop just because they like to live here. Lots of people come from the big cities, and have to sacrifice to stay here. A lot of them do it. It's worth it. I've been here forty years and I don't have one regret.

*The mayor of Sun Valley is Ruth Leider, a resident for eighteen years, and mayor for nine. As Sun Valley has changed, so has the mayor's job.*

If I had to boil it down to one major change, it is that we've gone from a resort community to a residential community of which the resort is a part. That has been aided and abetted by a lot of cooperation with neighboring Ketchum. We have practically merged, what with the expansion of homes and condominiums.

Back in 1971, this was a company town. The government was company oriented, and 50 percent of the acreage of the city of Sun Valley was totally unused. It was just a virgin valley. Elkhorn is now our growth center and political base. That is where the year-round residential population and newcomers seem to be concentrating,

**Ruth Leider**

particularly the younger population. The Sun Valley side of the hill tends to be more of the older Sun Valley supporter.

Growth has to spread out. Infrastructure is dependent upon the spread of growth. Sun Valley as a community is not only a community of young retirees, but also a second-home community. It is definitely the tourist nucleus. Ketchum used to be the service community where Sun Valley's employees lived. That is no longer true. Ketchum is suddenly a factor in primary and second homes for people wanting to move to recreational communities. Hailey and Bellevue have become very important to us as providing housing for policemen, firemen, and hospital employees. We are the only city in Idaho that owns a hospital. It employs about a hundred people. They have to live within a response time of ten minutes. Spreading the growth, but not having to spread it too far away, is very important to us.

I hope people love this area enough to stay, but whether we love it to death or not is a concern I have. When we tackle such problems as affordable housing to accommodate the employees at the hospital, people who take care of homes around here, who wait on tables, and man the galleries, I just hope that we can solve them without "building a church just for Easter." I would hate to think that we go out and condemn land to build a lot of affordable housing and then have those people who have the money simply shift and go to another location. That could happen if they become disenchanted with the lack of services. It's a Catch 22 situation. You want to make sure that you're taking care of servicing the residents and the second home owners, but you also don't want go to too much of an expense. Should the second homeowners and guests go to another area, we would not want to be locked in with a very large expense and a lot of unfilled housing.

The money we have put into marketing has paid off. That's a logical outcome of our contributing $150,000 to the Ketchum/Sun Valley Chamber of Commerce, which Ketchum also matches. There is a selfish interest. We have a resort city local option tax. Two percent is charged on all purchases. That stays in the city; it does not go to the state government. It is about a third of our budget, so it is very important to us. It is very logical to contribute to marketing.

We can qualify which seasons we need to market. In general there is a lot of emphasis being put on summer. Our local option tax revenues prove that summer is practically equal in business to winter. We would be stupid not to try bring that up to winter par. There are more peaks and valleys in the winter season than there are in summer, so it's good business to promote summer. You get more consistent income.

I love being mayor. Mayors don't have to, but they can perform marriage ceremonies. I like to welcome the convention people. That is often requested. If you are going to be a mayor, you might as well be mayor of Sun Valley. It's a fun city to be mayor of. Did you see my license plate? "Mayher." Everyone says I'll never give up being mayor because I don't want to give up my license plate. I like meeting the people I get to meet as mayor.

The issues are very interesting. They are traumatic, and I must admit I'm a stress-oriented person. When you talk about affordable housing, density, growth, the hospital, Medicare, legislative problems at the federal level, it's not a play job. When I first started I thought it was a kindergarten birthday party, but it has turned into a real job. It was not full-time, but I've made it that. I think the requirements of the job have made it that. It's my gardener. That's why I don't garden.

I came out here to do a story for *Sports Illustrated* and was anxious to get away from New York again, which I've done many, many times in my career. I picked up a job at Sun Valley Company and handled publicity for them, then moved on and handled marketing for Elkhorn. I got my real estate license, but I was running out of ideas and reasons to get up in the morning, to tell you the truth. So I looked into politics. I became a member of the city council and then was appointed mayor when our previous mayor had to resign. Then I ran three times.

I love it, it's great. It is the way I want to live in Sun Valley. It gives me reasons to get back to Washington. We're getting into the mainstream of state and federal legislation. We have to be there. We've grown up and we have to keep growing, there is no getting around it. We've got have our finger on the pulse of the county, neighboring cities, state and the federal government.

Sun Valley and Idaho are going to play a very, very large part in the federal tourist picture. The United States is marketing tourism. One of the most attractive elements in marketing to Asian and European countries is the wide open spaces. Fishing, camping, hiking, river trips—that is what people are coming to the United States for. Sure, they want to see Washington, D.C., and New York and Los Angeles, but they want to see Yellowstone and the likes of Sun Valley. They want to get into the hills. In Japan, for the sake of argument, they don't know what it's like to be able to take a walk to the top of a mountain.

Sun Valley will always be considered a unique piece of the jigsaw puzzle of Idaho. I must admit, in the 1970s we were probably floating around and didn't fit into the total picture. But lobbying over in Boise and getting legislation through has been beneficial to resort areas. The establishment of the Department of Commerce at the state level and the Idaho Travel Councils have pulled us into the mainstream of Idaho. I think we're considered a part of it now.

# *Fire*

# IDAHO ON THE FRONT LINE

The first fire lookout tower in the United States was probably the one erected in 1900 at Bertha Hill in the Clearwater country of Idaho. The Clearwater Timber Company paid the lookout's first occupant, Mabel Gray, to stand the watch. When she sighted smoke she fired her rifle, saddled up, and rode off to round up the work crew to put it out.

The idea of "cooperative forestry" was born a few years later, when three men stood together one night watching the Packer John Fire about forty miles north of Boise. They talked about how better cooperation among themselves could combat fires like this one. One was a timber landowner, another was the supervisor of the newly formed Payette National Forest, and the third was soon to become Idaho's first land commissioner.

Private Idaho timber interests took the national lead in forming protective associations as a means of dealing with wildfire. They formed four in the northern part of the state and one in the south. They were so successful that other states referred to the "Idaho Idea" when they formed similar associations all over the United States. The principle was simple: Timber owners assessed themselves and assigned timber patrols, advocated laws, and otherwise cooperated in the face of danger. It was not long before public forest lands were part of the cooperative network.

In 1909 the representatives of several associations from the Northwestern states formed a regional association—the Western Forestry and Conservation Association (WFCA)—to share their experiences. They began one of the first systematic programs in the United States aimed at preventing fires. WFCA's director began a "Keep them Green" program, a massive media effort at the time, that included distributing thousands of pamphlets and erecting sequenced posters along the highways. The organization promoted ideas such as piling brush, disposing of slash, and removing combustibles from road right-of-ways. The next year, the WFCA helped persuade President Taft to send federal troops to help fight the 1910 Fire in North Idaho.

The 1910 Fire, called the Big Blowup because of its massive size and intensity, inspired even greater cooperation and harmony among landowners—private, state, and federal. At the fledgling United States Forest Service, which had only been formed in 1905, the chief quickly nationalized a fire protection program. The Forest Service thereafter fought the practice of "light burning," the periodic burning of brush and understory, which Indians and pioneer settlers in Idaho and elsewhere had used to manage their forest lands.

Idaho forests and foresters continued to be at the vanguard of innovation in fire fighting. Around 1939 the Forest Service was ahead of the U.S. Army in understanding the role that parachutes might play in the delivery of people and equipment to backcountry areas. One of the three Forest Service parachute training areas was located in McCall, Idaho. After World War II, Idaho's roadless areas were part of an "air control" experiment in which detection and fire suppression would be handled entirely by air. Meanwhile, on the ground, the Forest Service began to organize interregional "hot shot" crews as rapid deployment forces around 1961.

After 1964 and the passage of the Wilderness Act, the idea that all wildfire should be suppressed began to lose its power. Fire suppression was prohibited under most circumstances in Wilderness areas. The jargon of ecology began to intrude on the jargon of warfare used to describe fire control strategies. The ancient role of fire in the preservation and evolution of wild lands won acceptance in national fire policy. Each forest now has its own fire management plan.

Cooperative fire fighting continued among the different land owners. Even municipal fire departments joined in establishing cooperative fire fighting arrangements as cities and towns began to grow closer to the margins of forests. However, the logic of cooperation had not yet reached its natural conclusion—and would not until after a certain 1964 fire near Elko, Nevada, triggered another innovation in fire emergency management—the Boise Interagency Fire Center (BIFC).

By 1989, nearly 90 years after Mabel Gray shot off her first rifle warning, fire suppression activity in Idaho was being influenced by three major events—the Yellowstone Fire of 1988, increasing settlement of people and homes within the forests of the state, and a persistent drought. The Yellowstone Fire brought into renewed doubt the policy of permitting wildfires to burn unhindered. The presence of people and buildings in Idaho forests influenced how and where fires would be fought. The drought intensified fire damage—and the expense of fighting it.

The fire season of 1989 was one of intense activity for the directors of BIFC, fire crews, and residents of the Lowman area, some of whom lost all or part of their homes or businesses. The "Lowman Complex" of fires was still burning as people talked about BIFC, fire policy, and personal experience with the fires.

Each agency participating in BIFC has a director. Jack Wilson is the director for the Bureau of Land Management.

BIFC was first formed about 1965, after a very severe fire storm in Elko County, Nevada. It took all the fire crews from most of the Intermountain West to fight those fires. About the time the crews were totally involved, a bunch of fires blew up on the Wasatch Front in Utah. That was a higher priority, and the Wasatch districts wanted their crews back, but couldn't get them.

That fall we formed the Western Wild Fire Coordinating Council. That very quickly evolved into the Great Basin Fire Center. A year later it became the Boise Interagency Fire Center (BIFC). The title says Boise, but it is a national center. Sometimes this gives us problems, because people think we are the Boise Fire Department.

The day-to-day operations are under the jurisdiction of the Bureau of Land Management. Most of the people that make things happen around here are people from the BLM. When we start allocating priorities and working in a multi-agency context, then we convene a multi-agency coordinating group comprised of the five member agency directors. They make determinations on an interagency basis.

There is a long list of things that make a fire a priority. The threat to life and property is the most critical one. Then there are extremely valuable resources like major city watersheds or a seed orchard, or other vital resources that have a second priority. The third priorities are timber stands, critical game ranges, watersheds, and so on.

I'm biased, but I think BIFC is run extremely well. I don't know of many other organizations that can mobilize thirty thousand people in four days, completely equipped, have them in the field, move them, sustain them there, and do it in a cost-effective manner.

*Jack Wilson*

Six million dollars a day is the ballpark estimate for what that costs. Since all of the orders for everything are centralized through one point, we don't duplicate, we don't compete for the same transportation, we don't compete for vendors. Centralizing all orders through one point is a better alternative.

A fire camp can vary in size from five or six people to five thousand or six thousand people. The more complex they get, the more like a city they become. You have all the problems of a city—sanitation, enforcement, security, shelter, food, transportation. The main function of a camp is to handle your troops, to feed and rest them.

A fire camp today invariably has a caterer, an excellent food source. They almost always have showers. If they are close enough they have entertainment and telephones. In the good old days, you had none of that and slept on the ground.

In most normal times the fire center is composed of seven different agencies, each with its own particular program. They work in their own areas, but as activity increases, it becomes an inter-agency affair. We go through briefings, and catch up on what happened during the night. We hear what plans are afoot for the day shift. We look at the potential for lightning. Then we go back and clean up all the messes that need addressing: Are we going to order more crews? Are we going to order buses? Are we going to bring in different aircraft, or move aircraft around? That takes up a good share of the early morning.

The afternoon is our quietest time. We've done all we can do until an order starts coming in from the fires in the evening. Then we spend most of the night filling the orders. That's the routine. We brief again at eight o'clock at night to assess what has happened during the day. Most fires don't do their damage till late in the day, usually after six o'clock. So ten o'clock at night is one of our critical times.

Yellowstone wasn't any different than most other fires. That year the fires in

Yellowstone were concentrated in one area. This year (1989) fires are scattered all over. That makes it much tougher logistically.

Last year we could go into one area on good oiled roads and deposit the whole load right there. Now we have to go into remote areas with little sites for four to ten people. These are scattered all over the country. We have to air drop some, helicopter them in. Some of them have to come out on pack mules. We're lucky to bring in a few in pickups. Lines are longer, access is more difficult.

The seasons have been severe for a couple of reasons. One is the build-up of fuels—we probably have a fuel crisis. Secondly I think we're looking at global warming. The drought is more extended. We're having lightning in diverse places that we didn't have before. Storm tracks are different, the weather patterns are different. Most of our fires are coming later and lasting longer into the season. We're having very dry springs. This is not what we've been used to.

My philosophy is that fighting fires is a direct function of population and development. I don't think that here in the United States, with 250 million people, there are very many fires that we can afford to let burn. It threatens the lives of people and their developments.

The "urban/wild land interface" is where people move into wild lands. I hope that local governments, which develop zoning ordinances, will tighten things up and at least require that people adopt safe practices if they move into wild land.

People go out and build shake-shingled roofs. They don't clear brush and vegetation away from their houses. They stack firewood underneath their porch. All it takes is a spark, and you lose the whole structure.

*Dick Stauber*

*Dick Stauber is the Forest Service Director at BIFC*

The cooperation among agencies has been building over the last several years. It gets better and better every year. BIFC was the first major effort. Recently the incident command system, developed for use first in Southern California, has spread throughout the nation. It has become the basis for cooperation in emergency situations.

BIFC's role is to help people find resources. We're sort of a broker. If a particular area of the country runs out of fire fighters, they come to us. We have geographic areas we deal with, the Southeast, the Northeast, Southern California, Northern California, etc. When a geographic area runs out of firefighters or resources, they ask us. We find them. At this moment we're bringing fire fighters from Alaska and Florida. Forty-three states are helping with people and/or equipment.

This year there are many small and medium fires burning. We have California,

Oregon, and Idaho involved all at the same time. We have about the same number of people deployed as we had last year during the "Yellowstone" episodes. There are over twenty-three thousand fire fighters in the field right now.

Human intervention can make good progress putting out fires. However, the day so many fires started, we had eight percent humidity with ninety degree temperatures at elevations over five thousand feet. Those conditions are deadly. Fires burn very aggressively. When the humidity goes up to thirty percent, that's a very great break in the weather for us. Even so, we made great progress on those fires without any major changes in the weather.

The general technique is to flank the fire from its base and cut it off. Sometimes we pick good strategic points like ridge lines for that, depending on how aggressively the fire is burning. If it's a small fire you just walk up and dig a trench around it, throw dirt on it with a shovel or shoot it from a fire engine. In most of this country, fire trucks aren't helpful because the country is too steep. Most fire fighting here is done the way it was many years ago—with a shovel, a pulaski, and hard work. Those are the main tools.

I do not have a personal opinion on global warming. A Russian forester visited recently who has been studying it. He was firmly convinced that global warming is a fact. Nature has a tendency to have highs and lows which average out. It is hard to tell which direction trends are going. But the two years before this were very tough. This is the third tough year in a row. That in itself is unusual.

All agencies have a fire policy. "Let burn" is not a correct term. We have prescribed fires that are naturally set by lightning, and prescribed fires that firefighters set themselves. It is a good policy. It needs to be carefully monitored with good planning done in advance. We all need to be careful, because fire can be an unpredictable commodity. In a wilderness setting, where we are allowing nature to take its course, fire was a natural part of the environment and should continue to be.

Now that more people have moved their homes into the woods they are actually becoming part of the fuel for the fire. This is a real pressing problem for fire fighters for two reasons. One is the possible loss of life. Second, and more difficult, is that it takes more resources to protect each house. If a big wildfire is burning in a place where houses are scattered through the woods, you spend your time protecting the houses instead of putting out the fire. You actually get more devastating fires from that. Homes built in brush land should be fire-protected themselves. We have a program called Wildfire Strikes Home that helps people do that.

Most fire people, like myself, believe that a person's home is important to them. There is no way to judge the comparative value of a stand of timber or someone's house and life and property. It would be nice to be able to put all the resources on the fire, but we consider life and property as top priority.

The difference between last year and this year is the speed at which everything occurred. Last year the fires grew over a period of time. This year we had several hundred fires start last Thursday. We built up the fire fighters in this area very rapidly. Within a few days we had about twenty thousand people in the field fighting fires in the United States.

We moved very rapidly and quite smoothly. We had to activate some Army units. We now have three Army battalions in place and a fourth arriving today. There are a thousand telephone calls that make that work well. Logistics and military people have been working very well together. Since we did it last year it is easier.

BIFC grows in importance every day. We not only do fire coordination for the nation as a whole, but we do emergency coordination both locally and overseas. We've recently helped in Russia with satellite communication. The system was sent there to assist doctors treating burn victims from a train wreck. Fire fighters have been to Mexico to advise on major fires in the Yucatan. Overseas work is coordinated through the State Department. When we get a request, we find people with the abilities to provide the service. We arrange to transport them anywhere they want them to go.

The future will see expanded interagency cooperation. We have limited resources in the United States. The more we use the total resources, the better off we are. Cooperation between agencies is our only solution.

*Steve Brown of the National Weather Service is the staff meteorologist at BIFC.*

Weather is the element which starts half the wildfires in the West. There is a lot of territory not settled by people. Thunderstorms produce lightning, so we have a lot of lightning starts in the summer months. We track lightning strikes on a day-to-day basis.

The Fire Weather Program issues a forecast for the various national forests, BLM districts, the Fish and Wildlife Service, and all of the land-management agencies. We pinpoint the weather that has the potential to cause or contribute to the spread of fire—temperature, relative humidity, wind speed and direction. Agencies can then predict where the problems are going to be weather-wise, and plan for deploying their fire-fighting forces.

*Steve Brown (standing) at the weather monitoring center, BIFC*

We have a lightning detection system. Detectors are in a grid all across the United States now. Lightning strike information is recorded at each site and transmitted to a satellite, and then to BIFC. Position analyzers plot the lightning strikes and map their locations. Computers do all the work very rapidly, so the strikes are plotted almost as soon as they happen.

Sometimes lightning-caused "sleeper" fires don't show up for a couple of days after the strikes. We send out warnings so that people in land-management agencies can patrol those areas by land and air.

The weather this year is not particularly bad. We have had several bad fire seasons. This year's problems are directly related to the drought problems we've been having in the West for the past three or four years. We had fairly decent precipitation over the Pacific Northwest and northern Rockies this last winter, but further south, the drought was still in effect. During the spring the Pacific Northwest and northern Rockies did not receive a tremendous amount of precipitation, and the forest fuels dried out rapidly once again. We are having normal summer thunderstorm activity, but with dry fuels, lightning starts are all the more probable.

We will continue to see bad fire seasons until we get a good year of precipitation—normal or above—which extends well into the spring. Precipitation and drought are cyclic. We happen to be in a dry period now.

We feel weather forcasters are very important in fire fighting. We can identify situations so others will have a chance to do some good work around the line and get things accomplished. Short-term trends and forecasts are the most important to the land agencies, and we provide an excellent service. Long-term trends are more difficult to predict, but we make improvements in those all the time. In the last couple of days, I've been telling them that things are going to flare up again.

*Dale Holcomb lost the Haven Lodge in the Lowman fire.*

When the flames started coming up, I was inside cooking fire fighter dinners, along with everybody else. We had fifty to do that night, I think. I walked outside and the flames were already over the top of us. Pretty soon the Forest Service came through and said, "You have to evacuate." At that time we all left.

The flames came up over the ridge right behind us. They blew over the top, ignited the backside of the mountain, and then everything converged in the center. That's what they call a true fire storm.

At that point, nothing could have been done. When they give you five minutes' notice, there is nothing you can do. We hauled fire hoses on the roof and turned them on and left. It's been a pretty trying thing.

You have intense heat. Clouds look like they're on fire. Everything in the world seems to blow down. The pine cones are ignited and going through the air. It looks like a tornado. Since we were right in the center of it we could actually see a hole clear up through and see blue sky. But when it gets to that point you're pretty close to being burnt down yourself.

I imagine everything at the lodge probably ignited about the same

*Dale Holcomb in front of the burned Haven Lodge*

time. We had already left, so I have no idea. As far as I know, there was nobody there when everything started to burn. There may have been a Forest Service person hanging around the corner or something. Normally they leave about the same time.

These fires started on Tuesday, I believe. We watched a lightning storm come through. It set off three smokes back on Banner Ridge. There were some other smokes elsewhere. Those three were close together. They finally converged and came through here. If they'd had helicopters with buckets, they could have been up there and put them out that day.

They did not do us justice, I do know that. Had we had four hours' warning, we could have saved this building and probably a few others. But that we didn't get. Somebody fell down on the job someplace.

I think things have been handled very poorly. Without getting into it at this point, very poorly. We'd been in contact with the Forest Service for three days in a row and they indicated, "No problem whatsoever. You're in no danger here." Five minutes before we're burnt out, they come and tell us, "Well, you're burnt out." The burning of these parts could have been prevented. That's the sad part of it.

Unless we get a lot of help from someplace, there will be no rebuilding. This was not insured, none of the structures down through here were insured. My private residence was insured and that was about it.

The valley is not going to do as well as it did. The recreation, the scenery—all that is burnt away. The Forest Service has a hundred-year plan, they tell me. Maybe in a hundred years my grandkids can come up here. I don't know. If things continue the way it's going, they won't have anyplace to come either.

We're going to stay here as long as we can. I figure within thirty days it will be pretty well laid out whether we will be here or not. If there's no money come available to rebuild, we won't be here. That's guaranteed. Not much else I can say about this mess.

Hell of a wasted life. I bought this three and a half years ago. I put my life savings into it. My other partner put his life savings into it. We're financially broke at this point. I imagine this will wipe out my retirement. So all I can do is start over. Maybe try for something.

Before I came here, I was living in Boise. I grew up in Boise. I grew up in this area. In the sixties, my dad was up here logging in this area. I had been in Alaska off and on for the last ten years. That's where I wanted out of. This was my retreat.

*Tom Riley has a home in the Payette Plateau Subdivision near Lowman.*

I've lived here for the last three years building my cabin. I'm glad that my place didn't burn, but I'm sorry that the others did. I really hated it.

It didn't burn here because they backfired. Initially the fire came through six hundred feet above the road. The holocaust went through. Then they backfired because they had doubts about it. I put a sprinkler on top of my trailer and I had one down at the barn so it was pretty well protected.

I left Saturday around one o'clock. But I came in that night around ten to get some pans and stuff for camping out. I walked up here and saw the fire getting close to the cabin. I went down the road to where there was a big fire truck pulled in. I took him up there and he foamed down the cabin with one of those big trucks. That's sure nice equipment.

I could see the fire up the draw here. The trees were burning. They would light up the hillside. I stayed all that night. My daughter and grandson were here with me. I talked to one of the fire fighters, and he said that they were going to be here all night. They had two units and some fire fighters coming in. So I slept here part of the night.

Then the next day the county sheriff, Chuck Richards, came in and told me I'd better get out and I left. And after that I've been a yo-yo back and forth. I came in once and saw a friend's cabin had burned and I decided I was going to stay. I've done a little good. I've put several fires out that were threatening. I feel a lot better because this is my home.

I didn't have insurance. I have had a lot of help protecting it. It wasn't just me. I appreciate the Forest Service protecting it. I kind of feel like I can't compliment the Forest Service because I do know the fire got away from them.

It really hurt me when I came in that morning and saw that cabin gone. But I had to leave. I felt I let it burn; I felt the Forest Service made me leave. But anyway, that's just my feelings, I ought to keep it to myself.

**Tom Riley**

**Muriel Farber**

*Muriel Farber, a year-round resident at Lowman with her husband Les, also recalls the unusual wind storm that destroyed many standing trees in its path a few years before the fires.*

You can see the devastation. We were fortunate that it went around us. We feel so sorry for the ones who lost everything. The fire came in from the northeast. We did have our winter supply of wood in the garage. It charred. The freezer was over there, right under where it began. We did have a lot more lumber in here than we needed to have, but Les used it for a lot of things. His shop was over on that side and didn't get quite as much damage as this side. There was nothing to damage the cellar, it just smells of smoke. The fire just went around, and came in from the north. They did save the power pole because fire fighters happened to be here when it started to burn.

The guest cabin that was about two hundred yards down the path is gone completely. The reason the satellite dish is intact, is that we had two Rainbirds sprinkling. You can tell where the spray of water went.

The refrigerator and the stove were propane, but the tank did not burn. It was seventy percent full, but did not heat up. The fire went so quickly, that it didn't heat up enough to blow. It's devastation. I hope we have some heavy equipment to come in and help us clean. That's about all we can do. We can't do it ourselves. We have no way of loading it. We'll have to depend on heavy equipment.

Three years ago we had the windstorm go through. It took thirty trees down, you can see the stumps. Perhaps that saved us damage to the house. We had lots of trees around the house. You can see how the ground is, just like it's been sandblasted. It's so terribly charred. The smoke has been so bad that it's hard to breathe.

We didn't have insurance. We had insurance until three years ago. After the windstorm, we had real trouble getting more insurance. It was terribly high. One insurance company cancelled. We tried to get another, but they wouldn't insure for fire. Then the premium on the insurance we still had was too high, so we let it lapse.

The fire fighters have been terrific. They do such a good job. This was the first area struck. It was a fire storm, not a forest fire. The heat was so intense, nothing could have stopped it. Nothing man could do could have stopped it, it was so intense. Just fireballs; fireballs came.

They worked a tremendous amount of long hours. They just have done great with all the fire equipment they had. Not a soul was hurt. We're just fortunate that no lives were lost.

*Robert Baker, at the time of the Lowman fires, was a fire information officer working for the Boise National Forest.*

*Robert "Spike" Baker*

Two or three years of drought affects the large fuels, even when there was a good snow pack. We had very cold temperatures in southern Idaho last winter. The wood freezes and is not able, then, to absorb moisture. There is a chemical process where snow moisture can go directly from a frozen state to evaporation. We can get this effect on wood. So it stays dry and burns in a fire, even if it looks green.

The live fuels—the brush and huckleberry bushes and willows—have been consumed just like they were dead fuel. The "live fuel moisture" was so low, that instead of being a heat sink, the green fuels were actually providing a fuel source for the fire.

If you can keep a fire on the ground, it moves so you can control and suppress. We talk about ladder fuel. If there is a continuous avenue for the fire to move up into the crowns of the trees, then we get erratic fire behavior. Fire will carry across the road or the fire line. We can limb the trees to try and keep the fire on the ground.

The duff and litter on the forest floor carries the flame. Normally this time of year you would expect some moisture a few inches below the surface. But it is still bone dry at five or six inches. This contributes to the spread of the fire.

In a controlled burn, which we do at certain times of the year in the right conditions, the fires just move around on the ground. We burn out some of the underbrush in those cases, but don't harm the larger mature trees.

Different types of timber contribute to the problem of ladder fuels. If you have a mature ponderosa pine or Douglas fir stand, it will be pretty clean underneath. There aren't the ladder fuels. There's a separation between the ground fuels and the tree canopy. The fire can often just burn through on the ground. It burns slower and safer and is easier to control. But where you have the types of timber that have dead limbs and moss hanging down closer to the ground, the fire can catch it and go right up into the tree. That is much more dangerous and difficult to control.

The mature ponderosas are going to survive because of the thickness of the bark. It provides an insulating layer that protects the living cambium layer. If there were more fuel here and the bark gets burned away, then it burns into a "catface." The tree may still survive, but it will allow heart rot to get into the tree. It will reduce the value of the tree as timber, perhaps a great deal. If the rot only goes so far up the tree, they may only lose the first log. But, naturally, that first log is the most valuable one in the tree, when you look at from a commercial point of view—it is the largest part, clean of limbs, and better lumber.

The objectives of on-the-ground fire control technique haven't changed much in recent years. The objective is to build a fire line and remove all the fuels down to mineral soil. We try to isolate an unburnable area to retard the spread of the fire. What has changed dramatically are the tools we use: aircraft, air tankers, and helicopters. The helicopters drop water and transport personnel. We used to have to hike tremendous distances back to spike camps. We used to use pack strings to supply food to them. People now get fed better, get more rest, and do more productive work. If we do have to have a spike camp, we can support it with a large helicopter. Our ability to get tools and firefighters out to fires has increased.

But once you get out to the dirty, arduous work of putting out the fire, it's the same shovels and axes and firefighters. It's a lot like warfare. It's almost hand-to-hand with the fire in places.

Strip burning preheats the fuels. If the fire wants to come up the hill, you start at the top and burn it in strips. This is a common technique aimed at keeping the intensity of the fire down. You can burn just a little area and then go down another six to ten feet and burn another strip out.

One of the things we have to be careful of is dead stumps, particularly close to the fire line. Fire can actually be carried down through the roots. It's not unusual that they burn clear under a line and into another area. If it's in a really hazardous area we just have to be dug clear out to make sure all the roots are out. It's a tremendous, dirty, nasty, job—one of the most disagreeable parts of fire fighting. Water can be a tremendous tool in fire suppression efforts, but it takes training and experience to use it effectively.

There is a lot of grubbing on a slope like this when we are building a roll trench. One of the problems is that once the fire has burned the brush, the logs, which normally are held back by vegetation, just roll down the hill. If all you do is dig a fire line in plane with the hill, logs will roll right over it. So we dig a trench—just like a gutter—and it catches the logs. It's quite dramatic to see a burning ember roll down the hill and be caught. Then it doesn't burn on down the hill.

The real threat to fire-crew safety is in working in steep terrain like this. If a fire starts below them, unknown to them, and roars up out of the canyon and traps them, they may not have time to escape. The crew posts a lookout, someone to make sure they have a safe avenue of escape. We don't want anybody hurt or killed.

*Ron Mitchell, Boise, is executive director of the Sportsmen's Coalition, a citizen group interested in influencing U.S. Forest Service management practices.*

This year man is going to be doing most of the damage to the land rather than the fire due to a "total suppression policy" passed down to the Forest Service from the administration in Washington, D.C. All fires will be extinguished this year rather than allowed to burn under the "let burn" policy of

***Ron Mitchell***

the past. Under that policy, all fires which threatened man-made structures were put out, and the fires in roadless and wilderness areas—where there was no danger to human life—were allowed to burn.

This year all fires will be extinguished. We believe it is an over-reaction to the Yellowstone Fire and is occurring despite the overwhelming scientific evidence that the Yellowstone fire did far more good than harm. Fires are an integral component of the natural ecosystem, and the Yellowstone ecosystem is going to be much more varied as a result of the fire.

Bureaucrats in Washington, D.C., and congressmen have suddenly opposed the "let burn" policy; its opposite—the total suppression policy—is going to have damaging effects in several respects. There is tremendous environmental damage when you build a fire line with bulldozers. They push up huge barricades six or seven feet high that will be there for sixty or seventy years as ugly scars through our wilderness and roadless areas. Fire suppression prevents fires from burning the fuels which release nitrogen, phosphorus, and calcium to enrich the streams. The fires also create nutrient-rich forage for big game.

Fires have sustained this process for eons. The "total suppression" policy eliminates it. Furthermore, the money spent to unnecessarily eliminate this natural cycle is almost obscene. In fighting Idaho fires that harm no one, three hundred thousand to five hundred thousand dollars a day is being spent. We've got approximately thirty-eight fires being fought and only four of those pose any threat to mankind. The millions of dollars spent far exceeds the value of any resources "saved."

The total suppression of fire today ensures that we're going to have the same kind of huge, hot wildfires in the future. The reason that we're having big conflagrations instead of many small fires is because of fifty years of fire suppression in which the Forest Service has put out every fire that they possibly could. The fuels have built up in the forest. By putting these fires out instead of letting most of them burn, we're simply ensuring that we're going to have the same problem next year, and it's going to be even worse. It's a totally ridiculous policy. We should go back to the "let burn" policy that the Forest Service recently adopted to counteract fifty years of fire suppression. That's the policy that really makes sense.

Whether or not we'll get back to the let "burn policy" is open to question. So far, the public hasn't expressed very much outrage at the expense of the fires. The media presents the fires to the public as the enemy of man, as a war, and fire fighters are even referred to as "troops." The public doesn't realize that the issue is not that fire is good or bad, but that fire is necessary to create the biological diversity of plants and animals that we have in the Rocky Mountain West.

Until that concept changes I don't think that the public is going to protest having our tax dollars wasted needlessly. Ultimately only such public pressure on elected representatives will change this insane policy.

*Dave Rittersbacher is supervisor of the Boise National Forest.*

**Dave Rittersbacher**

It is no mystery why some cabins and some residences burn faster than others in wild land fires. Many of the houses I saw the other day that survived the Lowman fire had metal roofs. People can do things to help protect their structures. The way they design and maintain houses makes a difference. Counties and fire protection agencies are going to have to work a lot closer together to help fireproof the subdivisions proliferating on the range and forest lands in the west.

We've had about a hundred and fifty fires so far this year just in the Boise National Forest. The number of fires seems to be similar to recent years, but the acreage in the last four or five years has been increasing. In 1986, 36,000 acres burned, in 1987 about 60,000; last year 80,000. So far we are up to 70,000 acres this year.

I believe there may be something to global warming. I also know that our drought conditions are just the opposite of trends in other parts of the country. The west does seem to be getting drier. Long-term global warming would mean that our vegetation would change to that of a more arid climate. Vegetative types that we normally find in the middle latitudes would probably shift north.

The benefits of wild land fires are numerous. One is the reduction of fuels. For years we have kept fire out of some our ecosystems. Fuels have built up in a lot of places to a catastrophically high hazard level. Fires reduce these fuels and create some breaks in our continuous forests. Opening up a forest canopy is often beneficial to wildlife, depending on the type of wildlife. Deer and elk benefit from openings. Fire is a natural part of the ecosystem. We try to control fire so that our losses are acceptable and not excessive.

On the other hand, fire causes the expenditure of public resources and money. The fires in the Boise National Forest have cost about ten million dollars in the past eight days. That's pretty high. I expect that figure to triple before we control the fires currently going. That does not count anything that hasn't started yet. Another cost is the loss of resource values. We have lost about seventy million dollars of timber. Many of our people were doing other types of work on trails, recreation, timber management, and watershed management. Now just about the entire work force is diverted toward the fire effort.

The Yellowstone experience would show that there are people very much interested in coming and seeing what happens after some of these disasters, and watching the recovery that takes place. These forests are not destroyed forever. In a few years it's amazing to see what recovery there is. There is a vegetative response that naturally comes after fires.

The Forest Service takes action on all wild fires. We make decisions as to what the strategy should be. Sometimes we directly attack the fire line, sometimes we have indirect attack methods. Indirect methods have nothing to do with wilderness, backcountry, or park areas. Sometimes it is sound strategy to back up and hold your ground and let what is in front burn. In most cases our plans have proved to be sound.

I don't think we should just let forests burn for the sake of letting them burn. That is not appropriate at all. The fire can take a path that is completely unacceptable to society or local people. When any natural disaster occurs, humankind is smart enough to figure out a way to minimize the loss.

We can't stomp out every single spark. Somehow fire has to be a part of the natural ecosystem. But we can help control it. For example, we use prescribed fires at times of the year when conditions are not extreme. We do spring burning to enhance deer and elk ranges quite frequently. But we are in control. We clean up logging operations, generally in the fall, sometimes in the early spring, depending upon what we want the burning operation to accomplish.

If we choose our times, we can restore fire to the ecosystem in a way that is acceptable. We should not let fire run wild in the middle of the summer in the middle of a drought year.

# Wake Island

## IDAHOANS AT WAR

When the Japanese formulated their war plan in 1938, one of its components was "Capture Wake." They estimated that the project would require about 450 men. They needed to capture Wake Island because American bombers based there could reach their own airbase installations at Kwajalein Atoll and elsewhere. The Japanese wanted control of the Pacific as far east as Hawaii.

Meanwhile, the United States' war plan, "Rainbow 5," called for a line of bases on the five Pacific islands of Johnston, Palmyra, Samoa, Midway, and Wake. From these islands, bombers and fighters could take off and move west. The effect would be like that of having a moving wall of fire power that would prevent the Japanese from getting close to Hawaii, the center of U.S. Pacific operations.

To that end, the Navy contracted for the construction of an air and submarine base at Wake Island. The Morrison-Knudsen Company of Idaho and several other contractors formed a consortium called Pacific Naval Air Bases and in January of 1941 began to transform the delicate little bead of an island into a military fortress.

The United States implemented its war plan too late and it failed. The five-island wall was not in place in time, and the Japanese bombed Pearl Harbor and Wake as part of one coordinated move. There were about 1,200 civilian construction workers, 388 Marines, 12 Army soldiers, and 60 Navy sailors on the island at the time. The majority of the construction workers were from Idaho because Morrison-Knudsen's headquarters was in Boise.

The Japanese, however, had severely underestimated the tenacious men on Wake, and therefore, the requirements to capture the island. A seige began that lasted sixteen days. The Japanese took the island, but lost more than a thousand men, sixteen bomber aircraft, one seaplane, four carrier-based aircraft, one submarine, and one other ship. Additional ships and aircraft were damaged. Hearing the news of the heroic Wake Island defense gave much-needed encouragement to the American public, since all the other news from the Pacific was of one defeat after another.

Clint Haakonstad of Boise was one of the civilians on the island when the Japanese struck.

I was over there because I wanted employment and a chance to see some of the world. I was a truck driver, having driven for several years in the Civilian Conservation Corps and for road construction.

The overall job was building an airport so they could get planes in. The other part of it was for a submarine refueling base. That was not yet under construction when I arrived, nor was the runway. By the time the war started it was pretty well to the point where they could bring in the bigger planes.

That's the way it was when I arrived there on Easter Sunday in 1941. I started work immediately that day, driving truck and hauling cargo. At that time we lived in tents, because they didn't have the barracks built yet. The ship that I came in on was loaded to the point where you wondered how much freeboard there was. They hauled all the equipment, lumber, and supplies to build our main camp, which was probably one and a half or two miles from the subcamp that we were in.

*Clint Haakonstad*

Oh, we had some concerns, because we would hear a certain amount of news around the island. My mother wrote me in October and said, "Clint, I think there is going to be war. I think you ought to think about coming home. Things don't look good." I wrote back and told her, "Mother, don't worry. Uncle Sam will take care of us. I don't see any problem."

In November, ambassadors from Japan on their way to Washington, D. C., to talk "peace" stayed overnight at Wake. We had questions about that. Then some ship was taking American women and kids from the Philippines and the Shanghai area back to the States. We wondered about that, too.

But I felt that somehow or other, we'd be protected by our armed forces or the government or taken off the island. In November my mother insisted that I ought to come home. I said, "No, I have just a short time to go on my contract. I don't want to go back in the winter." My contract was for nine months, but you could stay as long as you wanted, just renew it again.

I was making good money. I got $145 per month base pay, and room and board. There wasn't anything that I had to buy in particular except light clothing. The food was good, you couldn't beat it. We had so much variety on the table, you didn't have to be finicky about what you ate. I liked it.

Well, the idea of an attack crossed my mind all right. My mother had reminded me that these were the Marshall Islands, and the Japanese were pretty close by. But I felt that our government would protect us. So I didn't really worry too much about it. I just figured, "What will be, will be." That's the way it went until the day it broke.

The day that it happened, I had taken a crew of men to the waterfront. The camp where we had the tents was about two miles from the main camp. The Marines were stationed there now. When I came to where they were stationed, here they were out on the road and they didn't move off the road. There seemed to be some excitement among the men. I had to drive off the road around them to get to the waterfront with the crew that I had. On the way back, it was the same thing. Then when I got into camp to see what my next assignment would be, it was coming in on the radio that Honolulu had been bombed. Pearl Harbor. We didn't know to what extent because it was difficult to get much news. This was about eight o'clock in the morning there.

That made us wonder what was happening, too. But there was no stoppage of work. Everything went on just as usual. Just before noon, I started picking up the men for lunch. I got past the airport and stopped to pick up some men there. I looked back up in the sky. They were coming with what I thought was twenty-seven airplanes. They just dropped down on the airport, and Bam! the black smoke flew. They came right on over the top, where we were, machine guns popping. We could see the pilot in the plane, they were that low.

I told the men on the truck to jump out and hit the ground because we were under attack. In the excitement I hadn't taken the truck out of gear while I waited for the men to get on; I jumped out and left the truck running. The truck started moving on slowly. I jumped back in and cut it off, and then got behind some small brush.

The planes went on over and then came around to the main camp, machine-gunning. When they got to Pan American Airways they bombed that. Then they hit the waterfront and blew up something down there, fuel tanks I think, that threw up a lot of black smoke. They came right back over the top of us again.

Well, we were lucky. None of the men in the group I had were killed. But believe me, two feet can run damned fast.

When they finally left, we drove into camp. Things were in a turmoil there. Several had been killed. They had riddled buildings with machine gun fire. Dan Teeters, the camp superintendent, and (Major James) Devereux from the Marines got up on a truck. They didn't spell out what we were going to do. They just said it would be "every man for himself."

We didn't know what to do then. After the meeting broke up, I went to the truck boss, my leader. He said, "We have an assignment for you. Go over to the Marines and pick up a Marine sergeant. They're going to distribute water." All our fresh water was distilled at a big plant. It was used only for cooking and washing. We bathed in saltwater. He said to distribute the barrels of water around over the island. So the sergeant went with me and a crew to take the barrels.

When I got through with that, I said to the sergeant, "Being in this truck alone, I have no defense whatsoever. Is there a rifle or a pistol or something?" He said, "I don't know. Let's check when I get into the warehouse and see if they have any." He came out and all he had was a steel helmet, one from World War I. He said all the guns were gone. So that was it.

When I came back into the main camp, the truck foreman said, "Well, how is your stomach?" I said there was nothing wrong with my stomach. He said, "I got a job for you. The man that's been working at the hospital got sick and couldn't take it. I want you to go down there. We are taking the dead from there and putting them in refer (refrigerator) boxes."

The refer boxes were large, probably fifteen feet high and six to eight feet on the interior. It was muggy, hot, about eighty-five degrees. We had to take the dead men who had been killed. They were lying covered on the floor. Picking them up was kind of sickening because the smell was already starting. When you tried to pick up one of them, you didn't know whether he had his head was intact or not.

We put them on the truck and loaded them into the refer boxes. We finished clearing out that evening. I washed out the bed of my truck because there was blood from those we had transported. About that time there was nothing left to do, because it was dusk.

I got together with a friend of mine, another who was driving truck. We said, "What are we going to do? We don't dare stay in the barracks." So he and I, with our trucks, drove off from where the airport was. There was a pretty good-sized brush, tall enough to camouflage the trucks, sort of. We laid there and watched the moon come up over the ocean, a beautiful full moon. The sea was calm. We talked about what would happen next.

When the attack began, several of us realized that we were in a possible case of guerrilla warfare which carried no protection for us under any law. We asked if we could join the military service so that we would be protected from that standpoint. The officers said they couldn't conscript us. We worried about it.

The next morning we went back to see what line of work we'd be involved in. We were assigned different work, and I never did see my friend again until after the capture and he'd been wounded, shot in the heel.

The Japanese came in the next day again. There was more loss because they were doing a more thorough job of bombing. Our machine shop and the garage were destroyed. Other buildings were damaged.

They came in nearly every day, then every other day, usually in the afternoon. They were taking reconnaissance photos, to see where we had our artillery. We didn't have much artillery. I think there were about three anti-aircraft guns, two five-inch guns, one without a range finder. Every night we moved the anti-aircraft guns and placed them in another area and re-sandbagged them. That fooled the Japanese. They never did hit them. We'd leave a dummy behind when we moved them, and they would get the dummy every time. That went on up until the time that they decided they were going to come in and take us—invade.

They came in with a cruiser and some destroyers. They thought they had taken care of whatever was on the island. There were no signs that there was any activity. A cruiser was coming in close to where the five-inch gun was. Our gunners had to use the bore for sighting the ship. The order was that they would not fire until the ship got within close range. Then we blasted that ship. The other ships left. We didn't have any more trouble, except for planes and bombs, until the twenty-second of December, when we noticed something going on.

Before midnight, I'd taken a crew of men out to store ammunition near the five-inch gun. The lieutenant in charge came over and said, "There's an unknown ship out at sea." We could see the lights of one of them to the north of us. He said to take the men back to wherever they were staying.

There was an aggregate plant on the island. We used corral rock to make cement. There were different grades stacked in piles thirty feet high. Underneath these pyramids, there was a tunnel with a large belt. They could drop a proper amount from each pile onto that belt, and it would go to the cement mixer. After the second night, when I had not been able to find my friend, another friend from Boise had asked me where I was going to stay. I had been planning to sleep on the bed of my truck, since there were too many rats to sleep on the ground. He suggested I come and stay in the tunnel, on the belt. He said it was a safer place than being outside. I decided that sounded pretty good, so that's where I stayed.

So that night, after seeing this ship out at sea, I decided to climb on top of the aggregate to see if I could spot anything. You could see it out there, and hear the noise, and see the men there. But it was a camouflage for where they were really going to make the landing. This was north, and they were going to land on the south. It must have been twelve or one o'clock, the time escapes me, and flares started going up on the south where the Japanese were making the landing.

We could hear the gunfire. It put fear in us; we didn't know what was going to happen next. Here we were, not armed; we had nothing. It kept up until the next day. When things did quiet down, we came out of the tunnel to look around. There were a number of little Japanese fighter planes just flying low over the top of the trees, looking for anyone that might be moving around. They didn't bother us as long as we were out there by the tunnel. They didn't fire at us.

This kept on during the day. You could hear gunfire from time to time. Then around four o'clock in the afternoon, up the road came a truck with one of the marine officers—I don't remember whether it was Devereux or who it was—and two Japanese on each side of him. There were some guards on the back of the truck, and the Japanese flag was flying.

That was a sick time, I tell you. They had a bullhorn and ordered everyone out into the road. So we went out in the road and they dropped off one of the soldiers. He had a machine gun. They ordered us to strip down to our shorts. They threw our clothes off on the side of the road. They marched us up the road about fifty to a hundred feet from where the clothes were and told us to sit down. He sat in front of us with a machine gun. I thought, "This is going to be my last day."

On Christmas Day, they brought some water and some old stale bread and distributed it. But the water was from gasoline drums. If you drank it, you felt like you'd been drinking gasoline. That wasn't much help. It was probably about four o'clock when one of the Japanese officers in a white uniform got up on the truck with the bull horn. He told us that his imperial highness of Japan had spared our lives. If we cooperated with the greater East Asia Co-prosperity Sphere, maybe someday we would be able to go home to our families. Some Christmas present!

I thought maybe there was a little hope and that I wasn't going to be killed right away. We were marched back to the barracks that night. That was the first time they let our cooks fix the food. We had a tuna fish casserole, with some kind of gravy. Oh that was good, after not eating for about three days.

The next day they put us to work putting up barbed wire along the beaches and cleaning up. They wanted to know where the big guns were. Well, there were no big guns. They said we could not have done so much with what they had seen. They thought we had buried them. Of course, by the time we surrendered, we had no ammunition left. It was gone. So they didn't find the ammunition.

We just kept on working. On January tenth or eleventh, they pulled us onto the parade ground in front of the barracks and told us to be prepared to move, and to gather cold weather clothing. They named off those who were going to go. They left about four hundred people there. We went with our baggage down to the waterfront. They took us out on barges to get on their ship. When we boarded the ship, they took us past a hole along the side and said to toss our clothing there. That was the last time we saw our clothes.

Then there was an open hole where we had to go down a ladder about twenty feet down to the next deck. They put us on three of the lower decks. I was in the middle one. There was a little straw on the steel deck. There was a five-gallon can in each of the four corners for elimination. We had one blanket apiece. We had to huddle up as close as we could get, because they packed us in there.

We first docked in Yokohama. They took off some of the men there for interviews and publicity to show off these prisoners they had. Then they sent the ship into Woo Sung, China, just out of Shanghai. As we came up out of the hole, there were two lines of sailors, each with a billy club. We had to run the gauntlet to get off of the ship. Then we stood there looking kind of funny because we'd been twelve days in the hole with no water to wash, nothing.

They started marching us toward the camp that we were to be in. I was at the tail end of the group. And in front of us were some Merchant Marines that they had picked up in Shanghai. It was around five miles that we had to march. Most of that time I spent running. Those Merchant Marines were well fed and healthy and picking up a pretty good pace. But they would start lagging; then the Japanese soldiers would start nudging them with their bayonets to hurry up.

When we walked in the gate of the camp, I knew I could not have walked another quarter of a mile, I had such a pain in the groin. They stood us there while their interpreter came out and gave a speech. He said the fence was electric. "You touch, you die."

They gave one of my friends a cigarette. I was used to smoking. Here we'd been twelve days without. He took a couple of drags and I'd take a couple of drags. I got so dizzy I almost had to hang onto the guy next to me. After that, we were distributed to different barracks.

When we were taken prisoner, a number of us had a light chain around our necks with what we called a dog tag, it had our work number on it. When the Japanese saw these, they thought that the United States had sent prisoners to work on Wake. They were afraid of what kind of men we might be. It finally soaked into their heads that we were not prisoners, that we were civilian workers.

They fed us three times a day, usually about a teacup of rice each time and a watery bowl of vegetable tops and trimmings. There was no seasoning in anything. Of course we had come out of a tropical climate. There was an old water tank about thirty feet off the ground that had icicles clear down to the ground. The barracks had no insulation, no sidewall, and no heat. They issued us Japanese soldiers' uniforms, made of cotton. That first winter, we would go up and down the aisle with our blankets on, trying to keep warm.

After the winter they decided that we would go to work building a gunnery range, so they moved us to a camp at Kai-Wong, Japan. We could see the hotels in Shanghai from our camp. Then they put us to cleaning canals.

*The Japanese transferred Haakonstad and the other prisoners to several other camps in Japan and China to work in shipyards and carbide steel factories. For the duration of the war, he suffered pheumonia, an appendectomy, lack of medicine, malnutrition, beatings, indifference, brutality, and lice. There was no communication with families waiting at home.*

*As Japanese military fortunes declined and food became scarce even for the Japanese, the care and treatment of prisoners declined as well. The Japanese surrendered in August, and by September, Haakonstad was on his way to Guam.*

They took us into Guam, where we stayed about a week. They examined us for communicable diseases that we could carry back to the United States. Those that had them were held over. We got a chance to send a telegram to our families and we each got five dollars from the Red Cross. The cooks in that camp outdid themselves as far as food goes. Nobody told us not to eat too much. Well, after you've been hungry for almost four years, you can't stop eating. It's no different than a man on a desert who finds water—he'll drink himself to death. The same thing applied to us. I got so doggone bloated up with food, because I couldn't stop eating. It hurt to bend over and tie my shoelaces.

Well they took us off after about a week. We came in to San Francisco. When we came underneath the bridge, they met us with a boat that had a band on it, playing. You get so choked up coming back into home, that you can't even yell. You can't. You just feel like you can't say anything. The only welcome we got was from the Red Cross volunteers who transported us to our hotel.

My family informed me that my kid sister had passed away in 1944 while I was in prison camp. I knew nothing about it because I didn't receive mail. It came as a shock to me. Later I was in Cascade and found out one of the foremen, Ray Quinn, from Wake was there. He said, "Well, Clint, why don't you come out here and show these guys how to drive a truck?" I said, "No, Ray, I'm through. I will not drive another truck on construction. I've had enough of it." My health would not permit it.

The experience changed my life to where I value life and freedom far more. When I saw that Japanese flag and we surrendered, it was the hardest thing to accept. We saw the American flag going under Japanese rule. To live through and come out of it, I thank God for that. I prayed the whole time I was in there. And let me tell you, at the time we surrendered, I didn't find any heathens or unbelievers. They were all praying that somehow they were going to survive that ordeal over there.

It brought back to me more the value of living in a country where we had freedom, where we could choose our work and do and live without having somebody telling us how to do it. I tried to make the most of it during the period. But I believe in the Golden Rule: Do unto others as you would have them do unto you.

# Appaloosa

The image of a spotted horse appears on the cave paintings at Lascaux in France, on Greek vases from the first century, and on old Italian tomb walls. The Spanish brought horses with them when they came to conquer the New World. Spotted horses are thought to have been sent from Spain to Vera Cruz, Mexico in 1621. As the Spanish moved north, so did their cattle ranches. The only way to manage cattle was upon horseback, so horses moved as well.

Although Spanish law forbade Indians to ride horses, they nevertheless managed to acquire horses of their own. By around 1700, it is probable that the Indian people of Idaho had acquired them by trade. The Indians found the horse to be an excellent labor-saving device, and they rapidly adapted their cultures and customs to the animal, which gave them much improved access to buffalo grounds, speed, and pleasure.

The cultivation of the spotted horse or Appaloosa continues to thrive, although the horse nearly disappeared from the earth when the Nez Perce lost their roaming way of life and the U.S. Army destroyed or dispersed their stock.

But William Cody wanted spotted horses for his Wild West shows, and circuses kept up a demand for them, so they did not entirely disappear. Historian Francis Haines published an article about the Appaloosa in Western Horseman in 1937 which attracted a great deal of interest, and the following year the Appaloosa Horse Club was formed. The club started an Appaloosa registry in 1938. Ten years later the club headquarters moved to Moscow, Idaho.

Edith Stanger of Idaho Falls, an Appaloosa breeder, and George Hatley of Moscow, an early participant in the establishment of the Appaloosa Horse Club at Moscow, and now a consultant with the Appaloosa Horse Club, talked about the Appaloosa breed and how it was saved.

STANGER: When Chief Joseph and his band were captured at the Bearpaws, just this side of the Canadian border, the United States Army sold a lot of their horses for slaughter. Many of them were deliberately bred with heavy draft animals. The army realized that they were a potent weapon of war.

HATLEY: The breed was almost lost because of the nature of the country where it was raised. The Palouse country happened to be an unusually fertile area. It was very quickly homesteaded and plowed up. Farmers brought horses to mate with the native horses to produce farm horses for farm power. That is how the breed was nearly lost.

The reason we still have Appaloosas is because there were some canyons of the Snake and Clearwater that were not farmable. Land there was used for grazing, and there was a lot of cattle ranching. Ranchers kept Appaloosas for ranch horses. The draft horses replaced the Appaloosa in the Palouse country.

As I was growing up as a boy, I would quite often see horses in a thirty-three horse combine hitch. There might be four or five part-Appaloosa draft horses in the hitch. The results of mating draft horses to the native mares was still evident when I was growing up as a boy. The Indians had used them for buffalo hunting and travel in rough country. The horse was, therefore, very adaptable for cattle ranching. For the Palouse wheat farmers, the horse was at least readily available. By crossing the native mares with draft horses, they did produce a usable farm horse.

The Appaloosa did what the Nez Perce wanted a horse to do. They needed a

*George Hatley*

horse to help them move from where they lived in the winter, which was along the water courses along the Snake and Clearwater and Salmon, to the prairies or the edge of the mountains for summer. They wanted a horse that would carry them over to Montana, to hunt buffalo, visit the Crows and Flatheads, and cover rough country. This horse would do a good job of that.

Racing was the chief sport of the Nez Perce and Palouse men. They wanted a horse that was fast because there was a lot of prestige to having a fast horse. So, for these reasons they wanted sure-footed fast horses with good endurance. That is why they liked the Appaloosa. Some Appaloosas are colorful, eye-catching. That might have been a factor with some people, although not the big factor. They wouldn't have sacrificed anything for a colorful horse.

STANGER: The Nez Perce Indians, unlike all of the other Indian tribes in the entire country, practiced selective breeding with their animals. That is, they gelded the colts that perhaps didn't have as desirable a conformation as other animals. They based a lot of their breeding practices on the horses' ability to perform. For example, they used different kinds of tests—like the length of time it took to break a horse to lead or to learn to do a particular task. Lots of the old horses had real fine manes and tails, which was a characteristic that the Nez Perce bred for because they didn't leave a track when they were going through brushy country. There were no horsehair tails hanging up on the brush.

They were also interested in sheer speed and endurance. The Nez Perce were formidable warriors. Being well mounted was an advantage in war. A superior war horse was highly prized. So selective breeding made for performance rather than color. Of course, color was very desirable for Indian people. As it is for all of us today, a brightly colored horse is still highly prized. By any Appaloosa breeder.

HATLEY: Sam Fisher, a Palouse Indian breeder of Appaloosas I used to know, was quite interested in horses having spots on the hips. He had a paint mixture, a sort of magic formula. He would dip his fingers in it two or three times during the mare's pregnancy, and then put it on the hip of the pregnant mare. He felt that this would help assure that the foal would have those spots on its hips. So some Indians did place importance on the spots.

STANGER: An Appaloosa horse is a unique animal. There are no two Appaloosas that are exactly alike, which is one of the things that makes them so appealing to people. An Appaloosa horse has stamina, it has endurance, it has a world of common sense. It is a tremendous all-around "using" horse that, as the old timers say, we could use for anyone from grandmother to the baby. Yet, if you have a job to be done on a ranch, or in a show ring, or a cutting arena, an Appaloosa horse is the one to use.

For our ranch in the high country in southeastern Idaho, there are a lot of badger holes and downed timber. You need a horse with a lot of balance. You don't want a horse carrying a lot of heavy muscle that gives you a jolty ride, but something that you can ride eight to twelve hours and come home without being totally worn out. Appaloosa horses can do that. They don't hesitate to cross streams. They have lots of "bottom," or staying power. We find them just the best kind of horse for all-around work in rough country.

The Appaloosa generally stands about 15.2 hands high, weighing around eleven hundred pounds. They have a fine head and a real clean throatlatch, a good short back, and are straight on their legs. They are well balanced.

They come in three major color patterns. The first is leopard, which is a solid background color with spots usually black or sorrel over the entire body, like a leopard. They also come blanketed. Sometimes it is a clear white blanket over the hips that can go almost to the shoulders. Sometimes it's a blanket with spots, often referred to as halo spots, with a shadow ring around or a peacock spot. Then there is the mottled, which frequently is not a real pretty color. It looks sort of like a rusty horse all over.

HATLEY: An Appaloosa has parti-colored skin. The hooves are an extension of the skin around the coronary band. Therefore, the hooves are also parti-colored. It is the nature for black hooves to be rather hard and brittle. And it is the nature of white hooves to be rather tough, but also a little soft, so they don't chip and break like the black hooves. So the parti-colored hoof has the effect of lamination. You get the toughness from the white and the brittleness from the black. Appaloosa hooves are a little tougher than others.

During the Nez Perce War, this fact was confirmed by the fact that the cavalry had shod horses, whereas the Nez Perce had unshod horses, but still managed to keep ahead of the cavalry. Of course, not all of the Nez Perce horses were Appaloosas.

The parti-colored skin is very noticeable about the horse's nose and eyes. It is a mixture of pigmented and white skin. Another characteristic of the Appaloosa is a white sclera around the eye, like the human eye. It gives it a rather distinctive appearance.

STANGER: It is hard to predict what color you will get when you breed a stallion to a mare. There doesn't seem to be any way that we've discovered yet, of "cracking" that genetic color code. They say that Appaloosa breeders never die in the spring because they are waiting to see how much color they get in a colt crop. You can breed the same stallion and mare to produce a foal every year for ten years. You may get two or three of the same color patterns in those ten foals or ones that come with no color or characteristic or marginally colored ones.

There are some ways to breed where you're more apt to get color. Using a mare that has a lot of real strong characteristics, like a lot of pink or parti-colored skin and a real prominent Appaloosa eye, will frequently produce a lot more color than a brightly colored animal. I don't think that there is a knowledgeable Appaloosa breeder who will ever say, "We have a 100 percent stallion"—a stallion that has produced 100 percent color. If they do say that and can prove it, it probably means the stallion only produced one or two foals that both came colored. I've never known of one yet that really has been totally dependable.

It wasn't until the early 1930s that Claude Thompson, who had found Appaloosa mares still in the Palouse area, deliberately started buying them and concentrating a gene pool of Appaloosa mares. He crossed them with an Arabian stallion. Claude worked a long time on this endeavor.

After World War II George Hatley volunteered to take over the secretarial duties of this fledgling association. George lived in Moscow, Idaho. That is where the center of the Appaloosa industry was located, there in the Palouse River area in Washington and Idaho.

HATLEY: My family owned Appaloosas since the time of the Nez Perce War. I was very interested in the breed, so I offered to put out a little newsletter for the president of the Appaloosa Horse Club in 1946. He gave me the title of assistant secretary and said to go ahead. I started publishing the newsletter every other month. At that time it was a mimeographed sheet called *Appaloosa News*, but eventually it grew into a full-scale magazine. Today the *Appaloosa Journal* is a big slick magazine.

Then I felt that there should be a national show where everybody could bring their horses to compete in different classes. I thought there should be a stud book published of existing Appaloosas. The president and the directors decided that if I was willing to do that, I probably ought to be made executive secretary. So all the records moved to my home in Moscow. That is how I became involved with the Appaloosa Horse Club.

We got the club going mostly by advertising the fact that there was a breed association. The first stud book was published in 1947. Then we had the first national show in 1948. Getting the publication widely circulated helped bring back the breed.

In the early fifties regional interest in Appaloosas began to grow. Regional Appaloosa clubs were started. People promoting Appaloosas on this regional basis were very helpful in reestablishing the horse.

*Edith Stanger*

STANGER: We have shipped a planeload of horses to Venezuela for the Venezuelan government to use for military color guards and parades. We helped ship two planeloads to Japan for use on guest ranches and riding academies. Two truckloads went down to Guatemala City in Central America. We've shipped individual loads of two or three to Australia and Europe. Presently I'm working on a ten head load to go to Taiwan for a guest ranch. It is a very exacting thing. Every country's requirements vary—to some you cannot ship geldings, to others you can only send geldings. They always want brightly colored horses.

Appaloosas are becoming tremendously popular in Europe. Italy has been one of the leaders in breeding. They have huge expositions in which Appaloosas are very prominently featured. Breeding horses will bring real good prices. The people purchasing them from overseas are always knowledgeable horsemen. You shouldn't assume because a person doesn't live in the United States that they don't know much about horses. Because they do. A lot.

HATLEY: The reason I have Appaloosas is because I was born and raised in the Palouse country. My family had them since they arrived in the Palouse country by wagon train in 1876, a year before the Nez Perce War. I was very interested in history and since Appaloosas were a part of it, I thought they were something that I should own. I owned cattle ever since I had a high school agriculture project. Since Appaloosas were good cow horses, I had a good reason to own them, because I needed horses for cattle.

STANGER: The Appaloosa is a very unique part of Idaho. It is something no other state has. They stand for something—like our state's people generally do—sort of a rugged individualism. We can be proud that it is truly a part of our state.

# Appendix

## Interview Data

| Name | Date | Location | Interviewer |
|------|------|----------|-------------|
| Abraham, Raymond | November 12, 1988 | Bonners Ferry | Royce Williams |
| Albertson, Joe | March 22, 1990 | Boise | Royce Williams |
| Anderson, Andy | August 17, 1989 | Salmon | Barbara Pulling |
| Anderson, Ted | July 26, 1989 | Middle Fork of the Salmon River | Barbara Pulling |
| Andrus, Cecil | November 1, 1989 | Boise River | Joan Cartan |
| Aripa, Lawrence | May 31, 1989 | Plummer | Barbara Pulling |
| Arnold, Ramona | June 28, 1989 | Wallace | Barbara Pulling |
| Bahe, Velma | November 11, 1988 | Bonners Ferry | Royce Williams |
| Baker, Robert | August 4, 1989 | Lowman | Peter Morrill |
| Bennett, Earl | May 12, 1989 | Moscow | Barbara Pulling |
| Bethke, Dave | November 1, 1988 | American Falls | Royce Williams |
| Bolton, Roscoe | July 28, 1988 | Soda Springs | Royce Williams |
| Bourne, Peter | November 26, 1989 | Leadore | Peter Morrill |
| Bowman, Florence | April 12, 1989 | Rexburg | Barbara Pulling |
| Breckenridge, Roy | January 30, 1989 | Moscow | Roy Breckenridge |
| Brown, Steve | August 7, 1989 | Boise | Joan Cartan |
| Bryan, Alan | June 17, 1988 | Wilson Butte Cave | Royce Williams |
| Bryant, Jr., Roy | April 11, 1989 | Lowman | Barbara Pulling |
| Burke, Carl | August 29, 1989 | Boise | Joan Cartan |
| Butler, Richard | December 5, 1989 | Hayden Lake | Barbara Pulling |
| Cada, Joe | January 28, 1989 | Potlatch | Royce Williams |
| Cardwell, Floyd | August 14, 1989 | Coeur d'Alene River | Barbara Pulling |
| Church, Bethine | September 4, 1989 | Payette Lake | Barbara Pulling |
| Church, F. Forrester | September 4, 1989 | McCall | Barbara Pulling |
| Clagett, Fred | June 2, 1989 | King City, Oregon | Barbara Pulling |
| Cobb, Jerry | May 30, 1989 | Wallace and Kellogg | Barbara Pulling |
| Coiner, Walt | April 28, 1989 | Twin Falls | Jeff Tucker |
| Colson, Dennis | September 12, 1989 | Moscow | Barbara Pulling |
| Connolly, Thomas | August 15, 1989 | Cataldo Mission | Barbara Pulling |
| Cooper, Dixie | November 12, 1988 | Kootenai Natl. Wildlife Preserve | Royce Williams |
| Cope, John and Ted | October 24, 1989 | Lochsa | Peter Morrill |
| Corlett, John | February 20, 1990 | Boise | Joan Cartan |
| Dann, Emma | November 3, 1988 | Fort Hall | Royce Williams |
| Day, Earnest | October 10, 1989 | Stanley Basin | Barbara Pulling |
| Dellwo, Robert | June 2, 1989 | Spokane | Barbara Pulling |
| Dinoto, Michael | December 7, 1989 | Moscow | Barbara Pulling |
| Dutton, Howard | March 30, 1989 | Pocatello | Royce Williams |
| Ensunsa, John | December 20, 1988 | Buhl | Royce Williams |
| Farber, Muriel | August 7, 1989 | Lowman | Peter Morrill |
| Fisher, Vardis | March 20, 1967 | Vermillion, South Dakota | John Milton |
| Fraser, Gretchen | January 5, 1989 | Sun Valley | Royce Williams |
| Fuentes, Jr., Alberto | July 7, 1989 | Weiser | Barbara Pulling |
| George, Emmaline | Apr. 12 and Sept. 20, 1989 | Fort Hall | Barbara Pulling Peter Morrill |
| Givens, Jeanne | May 31, 1989 | Plummer | Barbara Pulling |
| Glimp, Hudson | May 30, 1989 | Dubois | Royce Williams |
| Grover, Dean | November 5, 1989 | Idaho Falls | Joan Cartan |
| Gruhn, Ruth | June 17, 1988 | Wilson Butte Cave | Royce Williams |

| | | | |
|---|---|---|---|
| Haakonstad, Clint | June 22, 1989 | Boise | Barbara Pulling |
| Hagadone, Duane | December 5, 1989 | Coeur d'Alene | Barbara Pulling |
| Haight, Stella | May 23, 1989 | Boise | Barbara Pulling |
| Harding, Ralph | February 28, 1990 | Pocatello | Joan Cartan |
| Hatley, George | October 2, 1989 | Moscow | Jeff Tucker |
| Hawley, Jr., Jess | November 14, 1989 | Boise | Barbara Pulling |
| Hayashida, Seichi and Chiyeko | September 29, 1989 | Jerome | Royce Williams |
| Heckman, Don and Pam | July 17, 1989 | Whitebird Ranch | Royce Williams |
| Heimgartner, Gertrude | January 30, 1989 | Juliaetta | Royce Williams |
| Hill, Barney | August 10, 1988 | Emmett | RoyceWilliams Eric Korte |
| Holcomb, Dale | August 7, 1989 | Lowman | Peter Morrill |
| Hugues, Cap | March 30, 1989 | Pocatello | Royce Williams |
| Hulet, Reed | May 11, 1990 | Wendell | Royce Williams |
| Jensen, Quincy | November 6, 1989 | Rexburg | Joan Cartan |
| Johnson, Bob | August 13, 1988 | Challis | Royce Williams |
| Jones, Grace | March 7, 1989 | Boise | Jerry Jones |
| Laird, Phyllis | May 17, 1989 | Dubois | Royce Williams |
| Leonhardy, Frank | July 17 and July 27, 1989 | Hells Canyon | Barbara Pulling, Jeff Tucker |
| Lesser, Rob | August 8, 1989 | N. Fork of the Payette River | Bruce Reichert |
| Lewis, Roger | August 11, 1988 | Twin Falls | Royce Williams |
| Lieder, Ruth | October 11, 1989 | Sun Valley | Barbara Pulling |
| Lombard, Ernest | March 5, 1990 | Boise | Peter Morrill |
| Lopez, Camilo | December 15, 1989 | Caldwell | Barbara Pulling |
| Luther, Jerry | January 27, 1989 | Garfield Bay, Lake Pend Oreille | Royce Williams |
| Macken, Barry | October 24, 1989 | Lochsa country | Peter Morrill |
| Magnuson, Harry | August 16, 1989 | Wallace | Barbara Pulling |
| Malde, Harold | October 2, 1988 | Shoshone Falls | Royce Williams |
| Marshall, Charles | March 1, 1990 | Twin Falls | Barbara Pulling |
| Miller, Susanne | May 13, 1988 | Owl Cave | Royce Williams |
| Mitchell, Ron | August 8, 1989 | Lowman | Jeff Beaman |
| Moosman, Kerry | August 30, 1989 and February 19, 1990 | Atlanta | Peter Morrill |
| Morey, Clifton | January 30, 1989 | Juliaetta | Royce Williams |
| Morris, Tom | August 16, 1989 | St. Maries | Barbara Pulling |
| Moulton, Chet | April 26, 1990 | Boise | Joan Cartan |
| Nettleton, Tim | May 26, 1988 | Owyhee County | Royce Williams |
| Norlen, Art | September 14, 1989 | Cataldo | Barbara Pulling |
| Ogle, James | February 5, 1990 | Boise | Joan Cartan |
| Oliver, Dean | July 23, 1988 | Nampa | Royce Williams |
| Pavesic, Max | October 20, 1988 | Wees Bar | Royce Williams |
| Peterson, Helen | June 2, 1989 | Portland, Oregon | Barbara Pulling |
| Piekarski, Pete | September 14, 1989 | Cataldo | Barbara Pulling |
| Reed, Scott | December 4, 1989 | Coeur d'Alene | Barbara Pulling |
| Reedy, Penelope | July 11, 1989 | Twin Falls | Royce Williams |
| Rhinehart, Don | January 3, 1989 | Sun Valley | Royce Williams |
| Ricks, Mark | April 13, 1989 | Rexburg | Barbara Pulling |
| Riley, Tom | August 7, 1989 | Lowman | Peter Morrill |
| Rittersbacher, Dave | August 7, 1989 | Boise | Joan Cartan |
| Romrell, Marjorie Ricks | November 3, 1989 | Sugar City | Joan Cartan |
| Russell, Bert | September 13, 1989 | Harrison | Barbara Pulling |
| Sappington, Lee | July 17, 1988 | Lochsa River | Royce Williams |
| Shultz, Elvin | September 14, 1989 | Cataldo | Barbara Pulling |
| Simon, William | May 28, 1988 | Fairfield | Royce Williams |
| Simplot, J. R. | June 26, 1989 and October 20, 1989 | Boise Declo | Barbara Pulling |
| Slickpoo, Sr., Allen | September 19, 1988 | Spalding | RoyceWilliams |

| | | | |
|---|---|---|---|
| Smiley, Charles | May 11, 1989 | St. Maries | Barbara Pulling |
| Smylie, Robert | November 13, 1989 | Boise | Barbara Pulling |
| Sorrels, Rosalie | August 22, 1989 | Grimes Creek | Barbara Pulling |
| Sparks, Walter | February 27, 1990 | Aberdeen | Joan Cartan |
| Stanger, Edith | September 20, 1989 | Idaho Falls | Peter Morrill |
| Stauberg, Dick | August 7, 1989 | Boise | Joan Cartan |
| Stensgar, Ernest | August 15, 1989 | Coeur d'Alene | Barbara Pulling |
| Stevens, Marjorie | January 30, 1989 | Juliaetta | Royce Williams |
| Stewart, Tony | December 6, 1989 | Coeur d'Alene | Barbara Pulling |
| Studebaker, William | November 27, 1989 | Twin Falls | Barbara Pulling |
| Swisher, Perry | June 13, 1989 | Boise | Barbara Pulling |
| | | | |
| Tinno, Keith | March 31, 1989 | Fort Hall | Royce Williams |
| Titmus, Gene | May 2, 1988 | North of Snake River | Royce Williams |
| Trejo, Judy | June 19, 1988 | Owyhee County | Royce Williams |
| Trice, Amy | November 12, 1988 | Bonners Ferry | Royce Williams |
| Trienen, Sylvester | November 28, 1989 | Arco | Barbara Pulling |
| Troutner, Art | September 30, 1988 | Hagerman Valley | Royce Williams |
| Tuttle, Armoral | May 26, 1989 | New Plymouth | Barbara Pulling |
| | | | |
| Weasma, Ted | July 7, 1988 | Hagerman Horse Quarry | Royce Williams |
| Weathers, Jim | May 25, 1989 | Emmett | Barbara Pulling |
| Weston, Hazel | June 13, 1989 | Boise | Barbara Pulling |
| Wilson, Jack | August 7, 1989 | Boise | Joan Cartan |
| Woods, James | June 9, 1988 | Blue Lakes | Royce Williams |
| | | | |
| Yost, Willis | November 7, 1989 | Idaho Falls | Joan Cartan |
| Young, Barbara and Richard | June 6, 1988 | Salmon | Royce Williams |
| | | | |
| Zabala, Thomas | November 14, 1989 | Boise | Peter Morrill |
| Zinser, Elisabeth | October 11 and 27, 1989 | Moscow | Barbara Pulling |

# Bibliography

The following bibliography represents a scratch on the surface of Idaho historical materials. It is intended only to suggest a few directions for further inquiry, and to provide citations for works mentioned by participants in the book.

## CONSTITUTION

*Constitutional Convention: Convention Proceedings and Debates of the Constitutional Convention of Idaho, 1889.*

## PREHISTORIC PEOPLE

Butler, Robert. *A Guide to Understanding Idaho Archaeology* (Third edition). Pocatello: Idaho State University Museum Special Publication, 1968.

Kurten, Bjorn. *How to Deep Freeze a Mammoth.* New York: Columbia University Press, 1986.

Tobias, Nell. *The Wees Bar Petroglyph Field, Southwestern Idaho.* Boise: Boise State University and Idaho State Historic Preservation Office, 1981.

Plew, Mark; James Woods; Max Pavesic. *Stone Tool Analysis, Essays in Honor of Don E. Crabtree.* Albuquerque: University of New Mexico Press, 1985.

Plew, Mark. *Archaeology in Southern Idaho.* Twin Falls: College of Southern Idaho, 1979.

Woods, James. "Don E. Crabtree." *Idaho Archaeology* 4 (Spring 1981): p. 1.

## INDIANS

Josephy, Jr., Alvin M. *The Nez Perce Indians and the Opening of the Northwest.* University of Nebraska Press, 1979.

_____. *Red Power, The American Indians' Fight for Freedom.* University of Nebraska, 1985.

_____. *Now That the Buffalo's Gone.* New York: Alfred A. Knopf, 1982.

McKinney, Whitney. *A History of the Shoshone-Paiutes of the Duck Valley Indian Reservation.* Institute of the American West and Howe Brothers, 1983.

Madsen, Brigham D. *The Shoshoni Frontier and the Bear River Massacre.* Salt Lake City: University of Utah Press, 1985.

Sturtevant, William C., ed. *Handbook of North American Indians, Volume 11: Great Basin.* Washington, D.C.: Smithsonian, 1986.

## SETTLEMENT, ETHNIC GROUPS

Bieter, Pat. "Reluctant Shepherds: The Basques in Idaho." *Idaho Yesterdays* 1 (Summer 1957): p. 10-15.

Crowder, David. *Rexburg, Idaho: The First One Hundred Years, 1883-1983.* Rexburg: Crowder, 1983.

Gentry, James R. "Czechoslovakian Culture in the Buhl-Castleford Area." *Idaho Yesterdays* 30 (Winter 1987): p. 2-14.

Holmes, Alvin C. *Swedish Homesteaders in Idaho on the Minidoka Irrigation Project.* Twin Falls: Holmes, 1976.

Lane, Richard H., William A. Douglas. *Basque Sheepherders of the American West.* Reno: University of Nevada Press, 1985.

Petersen, Keith. *Company Town: Potlatch, Idaho and the Potlatch Lumber Company.* Seattle: Washington State University Press and Latah (Idaho) County Historical Society, 1997.

Riedesel, Gerhard. *Arid Acres, A History of the Kimama-Minidoka Homesteaders 1920-1932 By People Who Were There.* Pullman: Riedesel, 1969.

Scheuerman, Richard D., and Clifford E. Trafzer. *The Volga Germans, Pioneers of the Northwest.* Moscow: University Press of Idaho, 1980.

Sims, Robert. *Japanese-American Contributions to Idaho's Economic Development.* Boise: Boise State University, 1978.

Tsai, Henry Shih-shan. *China and the Overseas Chinese in the United States, 1868-1911.* Fayetteville, Ark: University of Arkansas Press, 1983.

## RELIGION

Sappington, Roger. *The Brethren Along the Snake River.* Elgin, Ill.: Brethren Press, 1966.

Schoenberg, S. J., Wilfred. *A History of the Catholic Church in the Pacific Northwest, 1743-1983.* Washington, D.C.: Pastoral Press, 1987.

## GEOLOGY

Malde, Harold. "The Catastrophic Late Pleistocene Bonneville Flood in the Snake River Plain, Idaho."USGS Professional Paper 596, 1968. (52 pages.)

Stanley, George D. "Travels of an Ancient Reef." *Natural History* 96 (November 1987): p. 37.

"The Borah Peak, Idaho, Earthquake of October 28, 1983." *Spectra* 2 (November 1985).

Van Andel, Tjeerd H. *New Views on an Old Planet, Continental Drift and the History of the Earth.* Cambridge: Cambridge University Press, 1985.

## WATER

Reed, Scott. "Should Rivers Have Running? Toward Extension of the Reserved Rights Doctrine to Include Minimum Stream Flows." *Idaho Law Review,* 12 (1976): 158-160.

_____. "The Scenic St. Joe: A Study of Resistance to Federal River Protection." *Northwest Environmental Journal,* Vol 1:1, p. 171-185.

## COMMERCE, INDUSTRY, ECONOMICS

Arrington, Leonard. *Beet Sugar in the West: A History of the Utah-Idaho Sugar Company, 1891-1966.* Seattle: University of Washington Press, 1966.

Arrington, Leonard. "From Panning Gold to Nuclear Fission, Idaho's Economic Development 1860-1960." *Idaho Yesterdays* 6 (Summer 1962): p. 2-10.

Hidy, Ralph; Frank Ernest Hill, Allan Nevins. *Timber and Men: The Weyerhaeuser Story.* New York: MacMillan Co., 1963.

Idaho Mining Association. *Mining Salutes Idaho's Fifty Years of Statehood* Boise: Idaho Mining Association, 1940.

Lee, Lawrence. "William Ellsworth Smythe and the Irrigation Movement: A Reconsideration." *Pacific Historical Review* 41 (August 1972): p. 289-311.

McCarthy, Max R. *The Last Chance Canal Company.* Provo: Brigham Young University, Charles Redd Center for Western Studies, 1987.

Paul, Rodman Wilson. *Mining Frontiers of the Far West, 1848-1880.* Albuquerque: University of New Mexico Press, 1974.

Pomeroy, Earl. *In Search of the Golden West: The Tourist in Western America.* New York: Alfred A. Knopf, 1957.

Rabe, Fred W., David C. Flaherty. *The River of Green and Gold.* Moscow: Idaho Research Foundation Natural Resource Series #4, 1974.

Vlasich, James A. "Bayhorse: A Sketch of Mining Camp History." *Idaho Yesterdays* 27 (Summer 1983): p. 25-32.

Walker, Eugene. "Oneida Salt." *Idaho Yesterdays* 6 (Fall 1962): p. 8-11.

Yost, George; Dick d'Easum. *Idaho: The Fruitful Land.* Boise: Syms-York, 1980.

## BIOGRAPHIES

Ashby, Leroy. *The Spearless Leader: Senator Borah and the Progressive Movement in the 1920s.* University of Illinois Press, 1972.

Church, F. Forrester. *Father and Son.* New York: Harper and Row, 1985.

Johnson, Claudius O. *Borah of Idaho.* Seattle: University of Washington Press, 1967.

McKenna, Marian. *Borah.* Ann Arbor, Mich.: University of Michigan Press, 1961.

Woodward, Tim. *Tiger on the Road.* Caldwell: Caxton, 1989.

Wyler, Wanda Ricks. *Thomas E. Ricks: Colonizer, Founder.* Provo: M.C. Printing, 1988.

## SPIRIT

McFarland, Ronald, and William Studebaker. *Idaho's Poetry: A Centennial Anthology.* Moscow: University of Idaho Press, 1988.

Milton, John. *Three West*. Vermillion: Dakota Press, 1970.

Reedy, Penelope. *The Redneck Review*. Editor, Published two times a year, spring and fall. Address: P.O. Box 730, Twin Falls, Idaho 83303. Phone: 208-734-6653.

Russell, Bert. *Calked Boots*. Harrison, Idaho: Lacon, 1967.

_____. *North Fork of the Coeur d'Alene River*. Harrison, Idaho: Lacon, 1984.

_____. *Swiftwater People*. Harrison, Idaho: Lacon, 1979.

_____. *Hardships and Happy Times*. Harrison, Idaho: Lacon, 1978.

Sorrels, Rosalie. *What, Woman and Who, Myself I Am, Songs and Poems by Women, an Anthology of Songs and Poetry of Women's Experience*. Sonoma, California: Wooden Shoe Publishing, 1974.

_____. *Way Out in Idaho, Folk Songs and Stories of Idaho*. Boise: Idaho Arts Commission and Idaho Centennial Commission, 1990. publication anticipated 1991.

_____. Recordings: "Folksongs of Utah and Idaho," Folkways Records; "Rosalie's Songbag," Prestige Records; "If I Could Be the Rain," Folk Legacy; "Traveling Lady," Sire/Polydor; "Whatever Happened to the Girl That Was?" Sire/Paramount; "Traveling Lady Rides Again," Philo; "Always a Lady," Philo; "Moments of Happiness," Philo; "Lonesome Roving Wolves," Green Linnet; "Miscellaneous Abstract Record #1," Green Linnet; "Then Came the Children, Aural Tradition," Vancouver Folk Festival Label (Canada).

Studebaker, William. *The Cleaving: Poems*. Confluence Press, 1985.

_____. *Everything Goes Without Saying*. Confluence Press, 1988.

## SUN VALLEY

Oppenheimer, Doug, and Jim Poore. *Sun Valley, A Biography*. Boise: Beatty, 1976.

Taylor, Dorice. *Sun Valley*. Sun Valley, 1980.

## POTATO

Davis, James W. and Nikki Balch. *Aristocrat in Burlap: A History of the Idaho Potato*. Boise: Idaho Potato Commission, 1975.

## WILDFIRE

Curtis, Albert B. *White Pines and Fires, Cooperative Forestry in Idaho*. Moscow: University of Idaho Press, 1983.

Pyne, Stephen J. Pyne. *Fire in America, A Cultural History of Wildland and Rural Fire*. Princeton: Princeton University Press, 1982.

Spencer, Betty. *The Big Blowup*. Caldwell: Caxton, 1958.

Western Forestry And Conservation Assn. *Forty Years of Western Forestry: A History of the Movement to Conserve Forest Resources by Cooperative Effort 1909-1949*.

## THE DEFENSE OF WAKE ISLAND

Cunningham, Winfield Scott. *Wake Island Command*. Boston: Little, Brown, and Co., 1961.

Kephart, Rodney. *Wake, War, and Waiting...* New York: Exposition Press, 1950.

## APPALOOSA

Haines, Francis. *Appaloosa, The Spotted Horse in Art and History*. Fort Worth: Amon Carter Museum of Western Art, 1963.

*The Appaloosa Journal*. Published monthly by Appaloosa Journal, P.O. Box 8403, Moscow, Idaho, 83843.

## GENERAL

Etulain, Richard W., ed. *The Idaho Heritage, A Collection of Historical Essays*. Pocatello: Idaho State University Press, 1974.

Ericson, Stacy. *The Idaho Small Town Experience: 1900-1925*. Boise: Idaho State Historical Society

Reps, John. *Cities of the American West, A History of Frontier Urban Planning*. Princeton: Princeton University Press, 1979.